Having Visions

HAVING VISIONS

The Book of Mormon
Translated and Exposed in
Plain English

by

Susan Stansfield Wolverton

Algora Publishing
New York

ISBN: 0-87586-308-6 (softcover)
ISBN: 0-87586-309-4 (hardcover)
ISBN: 0-87586-310-8 (ebook)

Library of Congress Cataloging-in-Publication Data

Wolverton, Susan Stansfield.
 Having visions : the Book of Mormon Translated and Exposed in Plain English
/ by Susan Stansfield Wolverton.
     p. cm.
  Includes bibliographical references.
  ISBN 0-87586-308-6 (pbk. : alk. paper) — ISBN 0-87586-309-4 (hard cover :
alk. paper) — ISBN 0-87586-310-8 (ebook)
  1. Book of Mormon—Paraphrases, English. 2. Book of Mormon—Controversial literature. I. Title.

  BX8627.A2W65 2004
  289.3'22—dc22
                        2004006348

Front Cover: A professor researching Mormon history reads an old document.
Brigham Young University, Provo, Utah.

© Phil Schermeister/CORBIS
Photographer: Phil Schermeister
Date Photographed: ca. 1988

"Behold, I have dreamed a dream; or, in other words, I have seen a vision."

— The prophet Lehi, in The First Book of Nephi, *The Book of Mormon*,
as translated from ancient golden plates by Joseph Smith

TIMELINES OF THE EVENTS DISCUSSED IN THE BOOK

150,000 BC to AD 2000

3.8 Billion BC - The point when life first begins on Earth

150,000 BC - Homo erectus evolves into homo sapiens. The significant difference between modern man and these ancestral humans is acquired knowledge - behaviorally, physiologically and intellectually they are the equivalent of modern man.

115,000 BC - Homo sapiens begin migration out of Africa

40,000 BC - Oldest known cave paintings

23,000 BC - Bering land bridge opens

18,000 BC - Asians cross land bridge to North America

9,000 BC - End of the Pleistocene Epoch; glaciers retreat and Bering land bridge is flooded

8,000 BC - Humans reach tip of South America

October 23, 4004 BC, 9:00 AM - God creates the Earth and heavens (Archbishop Ussher)

2200 BC-AD 420 - The events covered by The Book of Mormon take place

1492-AD 2000 - Modern times

2200 BC to Joseph Smith's Prophecies

Events Described in The Book of Mormon

2200 BC - Jaredite migration to America

600 BC - Lehite and Mulekite migration to America

AD 1-35 - Jesus Christ lives, dies, and is resurrected

AD 420 - Moroni buries the golden plates

AD 1492 - Columbus discovers the New World

AD 1805-1844 - Joseph Smith's lifetime

AD 1492 to Present

1492 - Columbus arrives in the New World

1492-1776 - Spain explores, conquers, and colonizes the Americas

1540 - DeSoto encounters the Mississippian Culture

1620 - Mayflower Puritans settle Massachusetts

1620-1776 - English, Dutch, French, and German settlers establish colonies in northeastern America

1776-1882 American Revolutionary War

1786 - U.S. Constitution ratified

1788 - Washington elected as first U.S. president

1805 - Birth of Joseph Smith

1820 - Joseph Smith's first vision

1823 - Joseph Smith discovers golden plates

1826 - Joseph Smith convicted of fraud for treasure-seeking

1830 - The Book of Mormon is published and Mormon Church founded

1844 - Joseph Smith is killed, Brigham Young succeeds him as Mormon Church prophet

1847 - Brigham Young leads Mormon emigration to Utah

1861-1865 - U.S. Civil War

1890 - Mormon Church declares an end to polygamy

1890 - Mormon Church splinters into hundreds of new sects, many of which favor polygamy

A Map of Human Time
From Our Origins to the Present

150,000 BC—Homo erectus evolves into Homo sapiens—the most significant difference between modern man and these ancestral humans is acquired knowledge; behaviorally, physiologically and intellectually they are the effective equivalent of modern man.

115,000 BC—Homo sapiens begins migration out of Africa

150,000 BC | 100,000 BC

← **3.8 Billion BC**—The point at which life on Earth begins is approximately 4.2 miles off of this page

Timeline One—150,000 BC–AD 2000 / 1" = 14,000 years

2200 BC—Jaredite migration to America

600 BC—Lehite & Mulekite migrations to America

2000 BC | 1000 BC

Timeline Two—2200 BC–AD 2000 / 1" = 380 years

1492—Christopher Columbus arrives in the New World

Spain explores, conquers and colonizes the Americas

1500 | 1600 | 1700

1540—DeSoto Expedition encounters Native American Mississippian Culture

1620—Mayflower Puritans settle Massachusetts

English, Dutch, French and German settlers establish colonies in the Americ

Timeline Three—1492 AD–AD 2000 / 1" = 46 years

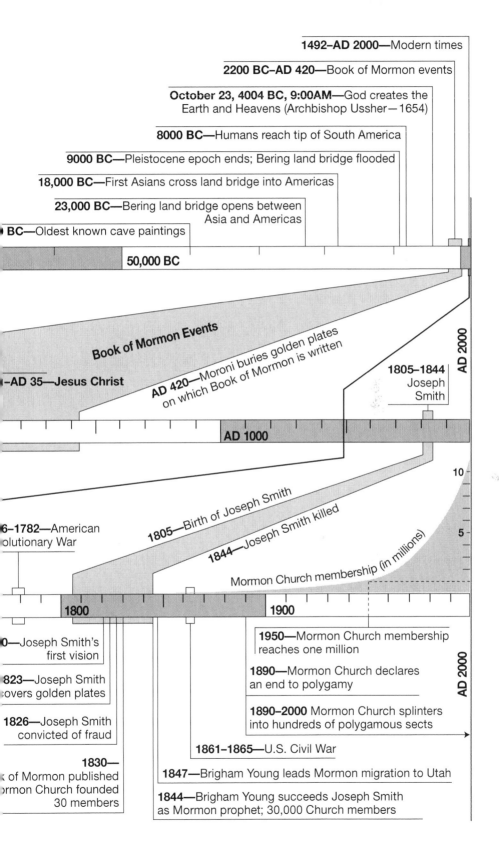

1492–AD 2000—Modern times

2200 BC–AD 420—Book of Mormon events

October 23, 4004 BC, 9:00AM—God creates the Earth and Heavens (Archbishop Ussher—1654)

8000 BC—Humans reach tip of South America

9000 BC—Pleistocene epoch ends; Bering land bridge flooded

18,000 BC—First Asians cross land bridge into Americas

23,000 BC—Bering land bridge opens between Asia and Americas

● BC—Oldest known cave paintings

50,000 BC

Book of Mormon Events

AD 420—Moroni buries golden plates on which Book of Mormon is written

–AD 35—Jesus Christ

1805–1844 Joseph Smith

AD 2000

AD 1000

1805—Birth of Joseph Smith

1844—Joseph Smith killed

6–1782—American olutionary War

Mormon Church membership (in millions)

10

5

1800

1900

AD 2000

0—Joseph Smith's first vision

823—Joseph Smith covers golden plates

1826—Joseph Smith convicted of fraud

1830— of Mormon published rmon Church founded 30 members

1950—Mormon Church membership reaches one million

1890—Mormon Church declares an end to polygamy

1890–2000 Mormon Church splinters into hundreds of polygamous sects

1861–1865—U.S. Civil War

1847—Brigham Young leads Mormon migration to Utah

1844—Brigham Young succeeds Joseph Smith as Mormon prophet; 30,000 Church members

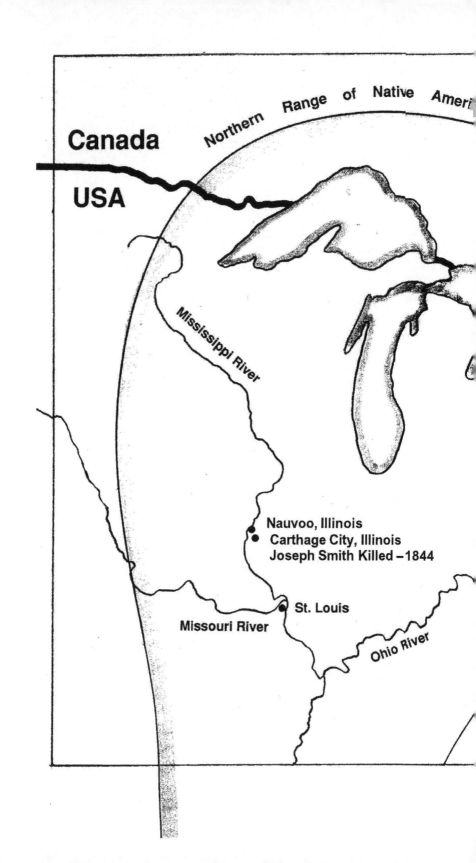

Canada

USA

Northern Range of Native Ameri

Mississippi River

Nauvoo, Illinois
Carthage City, Illinois
Joseph Smith Killed –1844

St. Louis

Missouri River

Ohio River

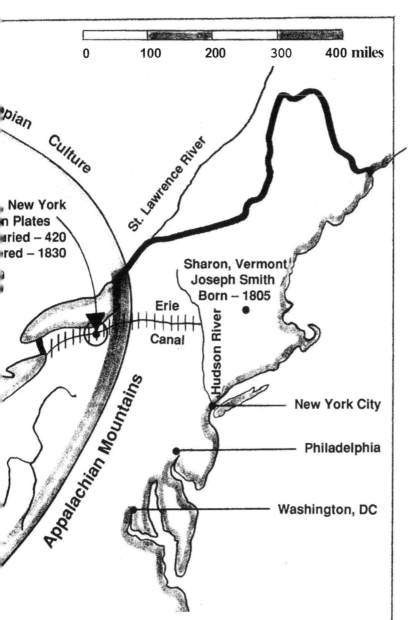

Joseph Smith's America
1805 – 1844

Scale: 0 100 200 300 400 miles

pian Culture

St. Lawrence River

New York
n Plates
ried – 420
red – 1830

Sharon, Vermont
Joseph Smith
Born – 1805

Erie
Canal

Hudson River

Appalachian Mountains

New York City

Philadelphia

Washington, DC

TABLE OF CONTENTS

Preface

Faith, dictionaries inform us, is an unquestioning belief in something: in a person, a religious doctrine, or an ideal. Faith asks the believer to accept an absence of proof, and to overlook contradictory evidence. There are countless religious sects, past and present, that ask their members to believe, on faith, that their religion is exclusively the correct one, and that all others are incorrect. In this respect the Mormon religion is no different from many others.

Before 1991, I had virtually no knowledge of the Mormon faith, or *The Book of Mormon* from which that faith is derived. It was in that year that my husband accepted a company transfer to an office in southern Idaho, and our young family moved west. Having grown up in the East, my vision of the West was one of mountains, broad open spaces, and clean air. The idea that we would be moving to a predominantly Mormon community never even occurred to me. Since then, I have become a student of the Mormon faith and its doctrine. I did this to understand the community I live among.

As we settled into our new home that summer, we were very soon approached by our neighbors. Most of them were Mormons and they wanted to share their faith with us. Our children were invited to attend church social functions and we were all welcomed to Sunday services. Before I'd been there a week, I was given my first copy of *The Book of Mormon* and was earnestly told that it was the true gospel of Jesus Christ. I opened it with great curiosity but was blocked from reading very much of it by language such as this: "Yea, verily, verily I say unto you, if all men had been, and were, and ever would be, like unto Moroni, behold, the very powers of hell would have been shaken forever; yea, the Devil would never have power over the hearts of the children of men."[1] When I asked if there was a modern language version of *The Book of Mormon*, I was told that there was not. "You can't edit or summarize the word of God without corrupting the Gospel." Then I learned that the Mormon Church itself had made thousands of editing changes to the original version.

I grew up attending a Methodist Church and my husband grew up within the Roman Catholic tradition. While my husband and I loosely considered ourselves Christians, we were not particularly devoted to church attendance or to any particular denomination. We had faith in a conceptual God and readily accepted the faiths of others.

In Idaho, our children made friends with Mormon children and became increasingly interested in the social events sponsored by the Mormon Church. As much as anything, it was my children who inadvertently propelled me to learn about and understand *The Book of Mormon*.

After attending my first Sunday service, I became a recipient of regular visits from the cleanly scrubbed and conservatively dressed young missionary "Elders" whose goal was to convert me, and my family, to the "one true faith." I remember being puzzled at the time that adolescent boys, who were not married, had never raised children, had never had to fully support themselves, and who presumably had never engaged in sex, could pose as elders or spiritual authorities. Nonetheless, I listened, asked questions, and learned.

I learned that according to Mormon doctrine, all of the Christian traditions that are derivative from Jesus Christ's teachings in the Old World had been profoundly perverted by corrupt priests intent on leading people astray. The Mormon faith, I was told, was a true restoration of Jesus Christ's actual doctrine. All other Christian doctrines were considered abominations in the eyes of God. The Bible was considered the true word of God only as it was "correctly interpreted" by the Mormon prophet Joseph Smith, through divine revelation.

As I read and tried to understand *The Book of Mormon*, troublesome questions of world history arose. When I asked my neighbors about their understanding of its content, I discovered that I was not the only one who had difficulty reading and clearly understanding it. Surprisingly, most of the Mormon women that I knew had found it as impenetrable as I had, and had put it aside, devoting themselves instead to the social and cultural aspects of the broad Mormon community. The more I learned, the more curious I became.

The Book of Mormon is the story of three pre-Columbian transoceanic migrations of people from the Middle East to the Western Hemisphere. It is a tale of magical objects, multiple sets of records inscribed on metal plates, divine

---

1. Joseph Smith, Jr., *The Book of Mormon* (Palmyra: Grandin, New York, 1830), pages 358-359; compare to *BOM* (Salt Lake City: Church of Jesus Christ of Latter-day Saints, 1981), Alma 48:17, page 329.

prophecies, and visions. According to the story, these migrations resulted in the populating of the American continents and accounted for the Native Americans that Christopher Columbus met when he arrived in the New World in 1492. *The Book of Mormon* is the history of these peoples, their prophecies, their relationship to Jesus Christ, and their sacred relationship with God.

I do not presume to judge the truthfulness or untruthfulness of *The Book of Mormon*. What I want to do is to present an objective, respectful, and faithful translation of its content, accompanied with an historical and scientific context for understanding its insertion into the body of human affairs. In *The Book of Mormon*, the ancient American prophet Mormon presents the history of his people, the Nephites. My intent is to present "his story as told," and its relationship to "history as known," without altering its essence.

Early readers of this translation have commented on the cardboard characters, the superficial story line and the repetitious narrative. "The battle scenes lack drama and suspense," they've said. "Your writing drones on like a grade-school text book." My answer is simple. That's the way *The Book of Mormon* presents the material. I have sought to trace the narrative through a bewildering stream of verbiage (without straying from a function of translation into analysis), but many sections remain confused; to add drama and elegance of language would be to introduce elements that just are not there. Other readers have been mystified by the inconsistencies in tense, style and narration; Mormon authorities explain them by noting that *The Book of Mormon* compiles the writings of 27 different authors, later abridged by two different editors before Joseph Smith.

Like Joseph Smith and the prophets in *The Book of Mormon*, I too have had visions. While working in my 21st-century study, translating this ancient text using my computer and Internet resources as my divining tools, I have envisioned 19th-century Joseph Smith sitting in a room divided by a blanket hanging from a rope. He puts the magic "seer stones" to his eyes and reads from the ancient golden plates, dictating his translation to a scribe sitting on the other side of the room, behind the blanket. In my own modern way, I am carrying on his tradition.

I have written this book so that Mormons and non-Mormons alike can easily understand *The Book of Mormon*. Because I so wished for such a book myself, and found it missing, I have made it my task to bring it to others.

Susan Stansfield Wolverton
May, 2004

The Church of Jesus Christ of Latter Day Saints? or The Mormon Church?

When reference is made to "Mormons" or the "Mormon Church," most people think of the prominent Utah-based church and its members, and most of the time, that's right. However, while the great majority of practicing Mormons officially belong to the Utah-based organization, The Church of Jesus Christ of Latter Day Saints, it is important to know that there have been hundreds of Mormon sects based on *The Book of Mormon* and the prophecies of Joseph Smith. Many of these factions are now extinct, but many more are continuously being formed. Most of the people belonging to these groups consider themselves to be the true Mormons, and also call themselves "Latter Day Saints."

Since Mormonism was founded in 1830, the large Utah branch has used five different official names. At this time, this sect of Mormons wishes to be officially called The Church of Jesus Christ of Latter Day Saints. According to The Church's official style guide, they request that, when reference is made to their church, the full name be used as an initial reference, and after that, the names "The Church of Jesus Christ" or "The Church" are encouraged. Calling it the "Mormon Church" is to be discouraged, the guide says, as is the use of the names "LDS" or "LDS Church."

Without intending disrespect to The Church of Jesus Christ of Latter Day Saints or its members, this book does use the convention of calling their church the Mormon Church. It is not practical to use the full name at every reference; calling it The Church of Jesus Christ is unnecessarily provoking to other Christian religions; and calling it The Church seems a little too sweeping. Because most people know The Church of Jesus Christ of Latter Day Saints as the Mormon Church, this book follows that familiar convention. Likewise, the term "Mormons" or "Mormon people" will be used to identify members of the Mormon Church. I apologize if this is uncomfortable to members of The Church of Jesus Christ of Latter Day Saints. When references to other Mormon sects are made, they will be differentiated.

PART I. THE BROAD VISION

The broad vision and aim of this book is to address three questions raised by the existence of *The Book of Mormon*.

- What does *The Book of Mormon* really say?
- What is the historic and contemporary scientific context associated with *The Book of Mormon*?
- What is the relevance of *The Book of Mormon* to the present and to the future?

The Book of Mormon is a record of three transoceanic migrations from the Holy Land of the Old Testament to the Western Hemisphere, and a record of God's dealings with these emigrant peoples. According to *The Book of Mormon*, one of these migrations occurred in 2200 BC, and two separate migrations followed in 600 BC.

In the first migration, God commanded the Jaredite people to leave Babylon at the time when he halted the construction of the great tower of Babel. The Jaredites arrived in America, prospered, and built a huge civilization which numbered many millions. They eventually lost God's blessing because of their refusal to abide by his laws. Afterwards, the Jaredites destroyed themselves down to the very last person.

In the second migration, God commanded the Lehite people to leave Jerusalem just prior to its destruction by conquering Babylonian armies in 600 BC. The Lehite people were an internally contentious group. After arriving in America, they divided into two separate nations: the Nephites and the

Lamanites. When the Lamanites refused to follow his laws, God punished them by transforming their skin color and appearance from "white and delightsome people" into "dark" and "loathsome" people, as a mark of his curse. The story of the conflict between the Nephites and the Lamanites comprises a large portion of *The Book of Mormon*. The hatred, battles, slaughters, and 1,000 years of warfare between these two opposing groups forms the backdrop against which the Mormon religious doctrine is composed and defined. By AD 420, the white Nephites were completely exterminated by the dark Lamanites, whose descendants were the Native American people discovered by Christopher Columbus in 1492.

God guided the third migration of people, the Mulekites, to the Americas at about the same time that the Lehites made their journey. Around 140 BC, 460 years after their arrival, they encountered and were merged into the Nephite culture.

The Book of Mormon story line is primarily a history of the rise and cataclysmic fall of the Nephite civilization. For a thousand years the Nephites built cities, practiced intensive agriculture on a large scale, and spread out across the American continent from their original landing point in Central America. They raised cows and sheep, rode in horse-drawn chariots, and manufactured steel long before it was invented anywhere else on earth. Prophet-scribes kept detailed, written records of their rulers and political events upon metal plates.

The Book of Mormon records a 2,620 year succession of prophets and prophecies. Its prophesies include: the Babylonian conquest of Jerusalem in 599 BC; the life and death of Jesus Christ; the great apostasy of Jesus Christ's true doctrine in the Old World following his death; the rise of the "great and abominable" Christian Church in the Old World led by the devil himself; the discovery of America by Christopher Columbus; the mass European emigration to America; the conquest of the Native Americans by Europeans; the creation of the United States of America as an independent nation; the discovery of the golden plates upon which *The Book of Mormon* was inscribed and their translation by a man named Joseph; and the restoration of the true gospel and true church of Jesus Christ by latter day saints once *The Book of Mormon* was known to the world.

Some argue that the startling accuracy of many of the prophecies is akin to forecasting yesterday's weather from the vantage point of historical knowledge available in 1830. Others argue that the accuracy of these prophecies proves that *The Book of Mormon* is true.

The Book of Mormon prophesies the life and death of Jesus Christ in great detail. The Nephite prophets were told precisely when and where he would be born to a virgin named Mary, how he would be baptized, what he would teach, how he would be disbelieved, how he would be tormented by the Jews, how he would die by crucifixion, how he would be resurrected, how he would visit the Nephite people in America after his resurrection, how he would fulfill God's plan for the salvation of mankind, and how he would redeem men's sins. God revealed these details to one *Book of Mormon* prophet after another, starting in 2,200 BC. For centuries before he was even born, the Nephites worshipped Jesus Christ, baptized people in his name, and devoted their lives to him. According to *The Book of Mormon* these ancient Americans were the first people on earth who were formally known as Christians.

Throughout *The Book of Mormon* there is a recurrent theme, repeated over and over, page after page, chapter after chapter, by each major narrator. This theme is: Jesus Christ is coming (or in the period after his Nephite visitation, has come, and will come again); repent your sins, believe in Jesus Christ, and be baptized in his name. People who do these things are promised a reward of everlasting peaceful life in the kingdom of heaven in the presence of God. People who fail to do these things will be punished with eternal torment in hell in the service of the devil. There is no middle ground. *The Book of Mormon* text refers to Jesus Christ more than 650 times, repentance for sins 360 times, and baptism 145 times.

The Nephite authors of *The Book of Mormon* were told by God that a man named Joseph would find their golden plates in the latter days, bring the gospel to the world, restore the church of Jesus Christ, and redeem mankind. It was for this destiny that God commanded the Nephite authors to keep their records.

The Book of Mormon story is littered with examples of people who did not believe in Jesus Christ, disobeyed his laws and were punished. It is also filled with examples of those who believed in Jesus Christ, followed his laws, and were rewarded. *The Book of Mormon* is a parade of events against which people's obedience and goodness are played out against a backdrop of other people's disobedience and evil.

The Nephite story climaxes with the death of Jesus Christ in Jerusalem and his subsequent appearance to the Nephite people in the Western Hemisphere. Upon Jesus' death catastrophic fires, storms, earthquakes, flooding, and landslides destroy the Nephite cities and kill everyone who is unholy. Immediately following this wholesale destruction, the land falls into total darkness for three days, from the time of Jesus Christ's death until the time of his resurrection. When the light returns, Jesus Christ appears to the Nephites in person. He gives the surviving Nephites his doctrine, and outlines a plan for saving mankind. He selects twelve Nephite disciples, advises people how to find peace in life and eternal salvation after death, and establishes the true church of Jesus Christ. He stays and teaches for several days and then returns to heaven.

The Christian nation of Nephites prospered in peace for several generations after Jesus Christ's visit, then declined into mass apostasy and sin. Deprived of God's favor and protection, the Nephites were destroyed by the Lamanites in a succession of wars and battles. In a climactic battle near Palmyra, New York, hundreds of thousands of Nephites were killed. Mormon's son Moroni escaped death at this battle, survived for another 21 years as the last living Nephite, completed *The Book of Mormon*, and then buried it for the benefit of future generations.

HOW DID *THE BOOK OF MORMON* COME INTO THE WORLD?

Mormon is the name of a person who, according to the book that bears his name, lived in ancient America from AD 320–400. He was a prophet, a great military general, an historian, and a scribe. He consolidated, abridged, and recorded the writings of earlier prophet scribes onto a set of golden plates, as commanded by God. Before he was hunted down and killed by an opposing army, Mormon concealed the golden plates in a secret place, told his son Moroni where they were hidden, and asked him to add his record to the golden plates if he survived. Moroni continued his father's work with an abridgement of another ancient text and made further additions of his own. Upon Moroni's completion of the book in the year 421, the golden plates of *The Book of Mormon* were deposited in a stone box and buried on a hill in present-day New York State, along with magical tools for their interpretation and translation.

Fourteen-hundred years later, on the evening of September 21, 1823, the same Moroni who buried the plates appeared as a vision in the bedroom of 17-year-old Joseph Smith, Jr. The angel Moroni arrived bathed in blazing glory, and announced to Joseph that God had great work for him to do. During this visitation the angel Moroni told Joseph about the golden plates and their location. The angel explained that the golden plates were a record of former American inhabitants, and an account of how these people came to be here.

The following day, on September 22, Joseph made his way to the hill described by the angel Moroni and found the plates along with the magical translation devices. While attempting to remove the plates, Joseph was again visited by the angel Moroni, and was advised that the plates needed to stay in the stone box on the hill for another four years while he matured spiritually. Only when Joseph was ready might they be removed. The angel Moroni directed

Joseph to return annually to the same spot to meet him and receive God's instructions. For three years, Joseph Smith did this.

In the fourth year, on September 22, 1827, the angel Moroni allowed Joseph to take temporary possession of the golden plates until translation and publication of them were completed. Afterward, Joseph Smith returned the original plates to the angel Moroni and they were carried away to heaven.

In his introduction to *The Book of Mormon,* Joseph Smith tells us that this is an abridged record of ancient American peoples (the Nephites, Lamanites, and Jaredites) written for modern day Lamanites (the Native Americans) so that they might be saved through knowledge of their ancestry as a remnant of Israel's descendants. It is also written, we are told, for "the convincing of the Jew and Gentile that JESUS is the CHRIST, the ETERNAL GOD."[2]

The official Mormon Church introduction to *The Book of Mormon* states that it is a "volume of holy scripture comparable to the Bible,"[3] and is the foundation of the Mormon religion. The Mormon Church requires its members to subscribe to 13 Articles of Faith that were articulated by Joseph Smith. One of these articles states, "We believe the Bible to be the word of God, as far as it is translated correctly; we also believe *The Book of Mormon* to be the word of God."[4] *The Book of Mormon* clearly states that the Bible, as most people know it, is a corrupted document that was deliberately altered to lead men astray. During his lifetime Joseph Smith "correctly" re-translated the Bible through inspired revelation by God, and restored the true gospel of Jesus Christ. These corruptive changes were allegedly made by a "great and abominable church," also referred to as "whore of all the Earth," which is led by the devil himself. Without directly naming it, *The Book of Mormon* clearly suggests, through description, that the church referred to as "the great and abominable church" is the Roman Catholic Church and infers the condemnation of all other traditional Christian religions that have descended from it. In a vision, an angel of God shows the prophet Nephi this future church:

> Look, and behold that great and abominable church, which is the mother of abominations, whose foundation is the devil. Behold, there is, save it be, two churches: the one is the church of the Lamb of God, and the other is the church of the Devil; wherefore, whoso belongeth not to the church of the Lamb of God,

---

2. Joseph Smith, Jr., *The Book of Mormon* (Palmyra: Grandin, New York, 1830), Title Page, compare to BOM (Salt Lake City: Church of Jesus Christ of Latter-day Saints, 1981), Title Page.

3. The Church of Jesus Christ of Latter Day Saints, Introduction to *The Book of Mormon* (Salt Lake City: Church of Jesus Christ of Latter-day Saints, 1981).

4. Joseph Smith, Jr., *The Pearl of Great Price,* (Salt Lake City: Church of Jesus Christ of Latter-day Saints, 1967), page 59.

belongeth to that great church, which is the mother of abominations; and she is the whore of all the earth.[5]

In a foundational and celebrated vision central to the Mormon religion, God and Jesus Christ appeared in person to Joseph Smith, Jr. at a young age. When Joseph asked them which religion was true, and which one to join, he says God told him that "I must join none of them, for they were all wrong, and the Personage who addressed me said that all their creeds were an abomination in his sight."[6]

WHY IS THERE A NEED FOR A MODERN LANGUAGE TRANSLATION OF *THE BOOK OF MORMON*?

The published *Book of Mormon* is a translation by Joseph Smith of the golden plates he discovered in 1827. The golden plates that Joseph Smith found were inscribed in an ancient language that ancient inhabitants of America called "reformed Egyptian." Magical interpreting tools, called the Urim and Thumim, were buried in a stone box alongside the golden plates. These devices permitted the user to translate the golden plates into his own language through the gift of God.

Using the Urim and Thumim, and later, his own personal "seer stones," Joseph Smith dictated the content of the golden plates to a scribe. But instead of translating the golden plates into American English as it was spoken in New York in 1827, they were translated into an antiquated form of the English language from two hundred years before Joseph Smith's time.

The 19th-century American dialect spoken and written at the time of Joseph Smith is faithfully exemplified and easily recalled from Mark Twain's books, such as *The Adventures of Tom Sawyer*. Even a casual glance at *The Book of Mormon* will reveal that the language use and style does not compare with the English language used in other 19th-century American writings.

The language in *The Book of Mormon* does compare to, and does resemble, the Elizabethan dialect of 16th- and 17th-century England. This dialect and style are most commonly known to us from the writings of William Shakespeare. The first translation of the Bible from Latin into English, the familiar King James Version, was also written in Elizabethan dialect.

---

5. Joseph Smith, Jr., *The Book of Mormon* (Palmyra: Grandin, New York, 1830), page 33, compare to (Salt Lake City: Church of Jesus Christ of Latter-day Saints, 1981), BOM 1Nephi 14:9-10, page 28

6. Joseph Smith, Jr., *The Pearl of Great Price*, (Salt Lake City: Church of Jesus Christ of Latter-day Saints, 1967), page 48.

While people in 19th-century America didn't speak this Elizabethan dialect, most of them were familiar with its style because it still remained the only available English translation of the Bible. Because the Bible was presented in this dialect, this style of presentation was, and perhaps still is, associated with religious expression and God's way of speaking to men. The Bible as we know it was not written originally in an Elizabethan dialect, of course, but is a derivative of several translations through Aramaic, Greek, and Latin.

The current version of *The Book of Mormon* is presented in a form much like that of the Bible. It is comprised of 14 Books. Each book is divided into numbered chapters, and then subdivided into numbered verses.[7]

Nowhere is the similarity to Elizabethan language more striking than in the chapters of *The Book of Mormon* which correlate identically to chapters from the *King James Version of the Holy Bible*. About 9% of *The Book of Mormon's* content is also found in the Old Testament, and about 1% is found in the New Testament. Most of this common content is nearly identical, word for word and verse for verse. In addition, enormous amounts of the Bible have been excerpted, combined, blended, and re-assembled into *The Book of Mormon,* coming from the mouths and writings of ancient American prophets.

The congruent chapters between *The Book of Mormon* and the Bible are explained by the assertion that authors of *The Book of Mormon* represent themselves to be descendants of Abraham, through Isaac, Jacob, and Joseph of Egypt, who left Jerusalem around 600 BC and carried with them to America the records of their ancestors, written on brass plates. These Nephite records are known to us as those parts of the Old Testament written prior to 600 BC. Even so, it is quite surprising that the King James translations of these records, flowing on the one hand through Jewish and European cultures, identically matches the translations flowing through ancient American and 19th-century American cultures on the other hand.

The archaic Elizabethan dialect and vocabulary in which *The Book of Mormon* was originally translated is cumbersome to read and difficult to understand for 21st-century readers, making the language itself a barrier to knowing its content. While both the Bible and *The Book of Mormon* are written in a similar dialect, one reads like poetry and the other reads like a repetitive textbook. Let's look at a representative example.

The following passage from *The Book of Mormon* is presented as having been written by the prophet Nephi around 550 BC and concerns the baptism of Jesus

---

7. In the original 1830 version (one of thirteen different published versions), *The Book of Mormon* was not divided into chapters and verses. These chapter and verse divisions were a subsequent improvisation.

Christ by John the Baptist some 580 years into the future (from Nephi's time). In this passage, Nephi tells his people of the importance of baptism by water, following the example of this prophesied future event:

> And now, I, Nephi, make an end of my prophesying unto you, my beloved brethren. And I cannot write but a few things, which I know must surely come to pass; neither can I write but a few words of my brother Jacob. Wherefore, the things which I have written, sufficeth me, save it be a few words which I must speak, concerning the doctrine of Christ; wherefore, I shall speak unto you plainly, according to the plainness of my prophesying. For my soul delighteth in plainness: for after this manner doth the Lord God work among the children of men. For the Lord God giveth light unto the understanding: for he speaketh unto men according to their language, unto their understanding. Wherefore, I would that ye remember that I have spoken unto you, concerning that Prophet which the Lord showed unto me, that should baptize the Lamb of God, which should take away the sins of the world.
>
> And now, if the Lamb of God, he being holy, should have need to be baptized by water, to fulfil righteousness, O then, how much more need have we, being unholy, to be baptized, yea, even by water. And now, I would ask of you, my beloved brethren, wherein the Lamb of God did fulfil all righteousness in being baptized by water?
>
> Know ye not that he was holy? But notwithstanding he being holy, he showeth unto the children of men, that according to the flesh, he humbleth himself before the Father, and witnesseth unto the Father that he would be obedient unto him in keeping his commandments; wherefore, after that he was baptized with water, the Holy Ghost descended upon him in the form of a dove. And again: it sheweth unto the children of men the straightness of the path, and the narrowness of the gate, by which they should enter, he having set the example before them. And he saith unto the children of men, Follow thou me. Wherefore, my beloved brethren, can we follow Jesus, save we shall be willing to keep the commandments of the Father? And the Father saith, Repent ye, repent ye, and be baptized in the name of my beloved Son. And also, the voice of the Son came unto me saying, He that is baptized in my name, to him will the Father give the Holy Ghost, like unto me; wherefore, follow me, and do the things which ye have seen me do.[8]

The following is an excerpted translation of this same passage from Part III of this book:

> God has shown me that Jesus Christ, who will remove the sins of the world, will first be baptized by a prophet. If Jesus Christ in his holiness needs to be

---

8. Joseph Smith, Jr., *The Book of Mormon* (Palmyra: Grandin, New York,1830), pages 118-119, compare to *BOM* (Salt Lake City: Church of Jesus Christ of Latter-day Saints, 1981), 2 Nephi 31:1-12, page 113.

baptized by water in the name of God, then surely those of us who are unholy have even greater need of baptism, ourselves. By humbling himself before God, Jesus Christ bears witness that he will keep God's commandments, and the Holy Ghost descends upon him in the form of a dove. By doing this act, Jesus Christ shows us the example which we should follow. The voice of God came to me saying, "Repent and be baptized in the name of my Beloved Son." And the voice of the Son, Jesus Christ, came to me saying, "He who is baptized in my name will receive the Holy Ghost. Follow me, and do the same things that you've seen me do."

WHAT DOES *THE BOOK OF MORMON* REALLY SAY?

Following this broad introductory vision, this book is divided into Part II, Context, and Part III, Content. Part III is a modern language translation of *The Book of Mormon's* content, with general summaries preceding each of *The Book of Mormon's* 15 sections. If the reader wants a quick overview of the whole *Book of Mormon*, it is possible to scan these summaries in rapid succession and come away with a working knowledge of *The Book of Mormon's* content in very little time. The translation uses a little less than half the number of words found in the original 1830 version of *The Book of Mormon* from which it is derived. The combined section summaries represent approximately 4% of the size of *The Book of Mormon*.

While it is possible that some meaning may have been lost, or confused, in some places from this book's translation of *The Book of Mormon*, every possible attempt and review has been made to keep the translated summary faithful to the original story line, doctrine, and general picture. Embellishments, exaggerations, and omissions of general meaning have been studiously avoided.

WHAT IS THE HISTORIC AND CONTEMPORARY SCIENTIFIC CONTEXT ASSOCIATED WITH *THE BOOK OF MORMON*?

Part II of this book addresses the question of the context, history, and contemporary scientific understanding that is associated with *The Book of Mormon*. It examines the life and times of Joseph Smith, the discovery and translation of the golden plates on which *The Book of Mormon* was written, analyzes *The Book of Mormon's* content and context, and assesses the contemporary relationship between *The Book of Mormon* and the Mormon religion. It places *The Book of Mormon* story within a contemporary historical and scientific framework with regard to the origins of the Native Americans, and the possibility that an ancient Nephite civilization ever existed in America.

Exhaustive archeological, genetic, and linguistic research has been undertaken by both proponents for, and detractors of, the existence of the Nephites. So far, no evidence supporting this claim has ever been found for any place, person, or event mentioned in *The Book of Mormon*, while abundant contradictory evidence has been discovered and independently verified.

WHAT IS THE RELEVANCE OF *THE BOOK OF MORMON* TO THE PRESENT AND TO THE FUTURE?

The Mormon religion is fast becoming the first new worldwide religion to emerge in over a thousand years. At present, it has over 12 million members worldwide, making it larger than the Jewish religion. It is the fastest growing religion on both of the American continents. If it sustains its current growth rate, it could grow to over 250 million members in the next 75 years.

The Mormon Church currently fields an army of 56,000 missionaries in the United States and abroad. They hand out *The Book of Mormon* and tell the world that theirs is the only true gospel of Jesus Christ — believe it and be saved, or dismiss it and be condemned.

In the United States there are already more Mormons than Episcopalians or Presbyterians. The Mormon Church has mounted massive political campaigns to promote its conservative social agendas, and is instrumental in changing public policy nationwide. If the current growth rate of the Mormon Church in the United States is sustained, they may well dominate American politics within the next 50 years. Given this potential for domestic and international influence, it only makes sense to know the foundations of the Mormon religion.

The Book of Mormon is based on the prophecies and records of an ancient Nephite civilization in America, and Jesus Christ's visitation with them. Its complete publication title is *The Book of Mormon, Another Testament of Jesus Christ*. But what if this horse-and-chariot Nephite civilization never existed? If the Nephites didn't exist, how could Jesus Christ have visited them? If Jesus Christ didn't visit the Nephites in America, how can the gospel of his visit possibly be the one true gospel of Jesus Christ?

Whether you believe or disbelieve in the Mormon faith, these are questions that need to be raised, considered, and answered. For believers and prospective believers alike, it is important to know the basis of the faith they are expected to adopt. For non-believers, the Mormon Church's growing influence in national and international affairs is becoming too significant to ignore. The purpose of this book is to make the content and the context of *The Book of Mormon* easily available to anyone who wants to pursue answers to these questions for themselves.

PART II. CONTEXT: *THE BOOK OF MORMON'S* HISTORY AND ASSOCIATED SCIENTIFIC PERSPECTIVE

JOSEPH SMITH, JUNIOR, 1805–1844

The Mormon religion was born in myth and legend through the discovery and translation of a set of golden plates on which *The Book of Mormon* was inscribed. This myth is inseparable from its founder and first prophet, Joseph Smith, Jr.[9], who was born on December 23, 1805 in Sharon, Vermont and was murdered by an enraged mob on June 27, 1844 at the age of 38 in Carthage, Illinois.

When Joseph was born, Thomas Jefferson presided as the third President of the United States and the Lewis and Clark Expedition was encamped on the Pacific Coast near the mouth of the Columbia River. Just two years earlier the United States had purchased from French Emperor Napoleon Bonaparte 530 million acres for $15 million, or 4 cents an acre, a spread covering the entire western basin of the Mississippi River from the Gulf of Mexico to Canada, from Louisiana to Texas, Minnesota, and Montana. It was the biggest real estate deal in history, and today includes all or part of 13 states. The Louisiana Purchase represents a third of the landmass of the United States between the Atlantic and Pacific Oceans.

When Joseph entered the world, Lewis and Clark were inventorying the nation's newly acquired assets and liabilities: the gold, timber, land, and Native

---

9. For convenience and brevity, the person "Joseph Smith, Jr." hereafter will be referred to as "Joseph." Other people who share his first name (Joseph's father, Joseph Smith, Sr., Joseph of Egypt, etc.) will be identified by their full names.

American people.[10] They were the first European descendants to cross the North American continent and see its scope. Their glowing reports would fuel the American westward expansion that began when the 13 original states transcended their initial perceptions of national boundary.

In 1805, the fledgling United States of America was only 29 years old (since its Declaration of Independence from Great Britain) and only 23 years had passed since the American Revolution had been successfully concluded. The United States' Constitution had been adopted 19 years earlier, and only 17 years had passed since George Washington was elected as the country's first President. Washington died just 6 years before Joseph was born. In 1805, many of the founding fathers of America were still alive.

Concurrent with Joseph's life was an American cultural phenomenon that historians would later name the Second Great Awakening. The First Great Awakening occurred in the American colonies during the 40 years preceding the American Revolution and involved contagious enthusiasm for reviving unquestioning faith in fundamental biblical scriptures. It was a pendulum swing's backlash of conservatism against the period's Age of Scientific Enlightenment and reasoning. The passionate embrace of evangelism was divisive and polarizing, driving a wedge between those who did and those who did not agree with it. Part of its affect was a widening chasm between the different Protestant Christian sects.

As the Second Great Awakening evolved, it set the stage for Joseph and the Mormon Religion. Fiery preachers traveled the country overseeing religious revivals involving tens of thousands of people. The differentiated Christian sects competed fiercely with each other for members, each claiming to be the "one true church." Western New York State played host to so many revivals that it was known as "the Burned-Over District." The Second Coming of Jesus Christ was considered imminent, between 1800 to 1840, and this era of emotionally-charged religious fervor that spanned the entire country included most of Joseph's lifetime.

On July 4, 1823, exactly 50 years to the day after signing the Declaration of Independence, two of the most prominent Founding Fathers died, within hours of each other. With the passing of John Adams, the second President, and Thomas Jefferson, the third President and principal author of the Declaration of Independence, the Second Great Awakening offered guidance to many in a time when the old leaders were being ushered off stage.

---

10. While Joseph Smith and his peers certainly thought of America's indigenous peoples as "Indians," the term "Native Americans" is more accurate; and for the current discussion it is meant to include all the pre-Columbian, indigenous peoples of North America, Central America, and South America.

When Joseph Smith was killed on June 27, 1844, the pendulum was starting to swing back towards reason, and away from unbending religious faith. John Tyler was the tenth President of the United States and the passions that would create the Civil War were brewing.

During his brief 38 years of life, Joseph began a new religion that, some 200 years later, continues to grow. Mormon Church President and Prophet Joseph Fielding Smith said of Joseph, in the 1970s:

> Mormonism must stand or fall on the story of Joseph Smith. He was either a Prophet of God, divinely called, properly appointed and commissioned or he was one of the biggest frauds this world has ever seen. There is no middle ground. If Joseph was a deceiver, who willfully attempted to mislead people, then he should be exposed, his claims should be refuted, and his doctrines shown to be false, for the doctrines of an imposter cannot be made to harmonize in all particulars with divine truth. If his claims and declarations were built upon fraud and deceit, there would appear many errors and contradictions, which would be easy to detect.[11]

The following historical selections from Joseph's life are not meant to be a complete biography. Others have done that job very well. The brief summary is included for the purpose of shedding more light on the 19th-century origins of *The Book of Mormon*.

JOSEPH SMITH'S CHILDHOOD, 1805–1818

Joseph was the third-eldest of the eight children born to Joseph Smith, Sr. and Lucy Mack Smith. Joseph Smith, Sr. was a poor New England farmer, odd job laborer, schoolteacher, speculator, and treasure finder who moved from one tenuous circumstance to another.

During Joseph's first five years of life, the Smith family lived in four different communities in Vermont and New Hampshire. At the age of ten, the Smith family was driven from Vermont by crop failures and abject poverty. Joseph stood witness as voracious creditors seized the Smith's possessions. By 1816, the Smiths had moved twice more before finally settling in the town of Palmyra, in western New York, south of Lake Ontario and east of present-day Rochester.

When the Smith family arrived in Palmyra, they found a bustling town of several thousand people. There were schools, a lending library, churches,

---

11. Joseph Fielding Smith, *Doctrines of Salvation*, (Salt Lake City: Bookcraft, 1954) Vol. 1, page 188.

commercial businesses, newspapers, and printing presses. Palmyra lay on the surveyed path of the Erie Canal which would soon connect Buffalo on Lake Erie to Albany on the Hudson River. Construction of the Erie Canal began in 1817, a year after the Smiths' arrival. Armies of immigrants descended on the area to dig the 363-mile-long waterway through thick forests and swamps, using little more than shovels and horses. It was a monumental undertaking that promised to connect the isolated Great Lake region with the Hudson River Valley and the ocean port of New York City. It would make travel and the shipment of goods within the region quick, inexpensive, and easy. Real estate speculation was intense. The Smith family bought a farm in nearby Manchester at the peak of the real estate boom and lived in Palmyra for two years before moving onto their land.

When the Erie Canal was completed in 1825, it created a ribbon of navigable water forty feet wide with 77 locks. It allowed a barge, towed by horses along its banks, to carry a shipment of 30 tons along its length in just eight days. This was a phenomenal achievement of inland transportation for its time. It led New York City to triumph over Philadelphia as the economic center of America and transformed Buffalo, Syracuse, and Rochester into major cities. The Erie Canal literally opened up the American West before the age of railroads. Joseph was 11 years old when the canal construction began and 19 years old when it was completed. He was able to watch firsthand its creation and the effects it had on the area where he lived.

The Smiths, as a poor family, couldn't afford private tuition and educated their children largely at home. The children learned to read and write from their mother Lucy, and their father Joseph Smith, Sr., who was an occasional schoolteacher himself. One only needs to read *Biographical Sketches of Joseph Smith the Prophet and His Progenitors for Many Generations by Lucy Smith — Mother of the Prophet* to recognize that Lucy Smith was quite literate and undoubtedly capable of teaching some degree of English composition to her children. Lucy Smith wrote, "As our children had, in a great measure, been debarred from the privilege of schools, we began to make every arrangement to attend to this important duty. We established our second son Hyrum in an academy at Hanover; and the rest, that were of sufficient age, we were sending to a common school that was quite convenient. Meanwhile, myself and companion were doing all that our abilities would admit of for the future welfare and advantage of the family."[12]

For most home-taught families, religious education and bible study were critical components, and the Smith family was no exception. Both of Joseph's

---

12. Lucy Mack Smith, *Biographical Sketches of Joseph Smith the Prophet and His Progenitors for Many Generations by Lucy Smith — Mother of the Prophet*, (Liverpool: Orson Pratt, 1853), page 60.

parents were deeply religious Protestant Christians but not specifically connected with any particular sect.

One enduring myth within Mormon culture presents Joseph as an ignorant farm boy who was chosen by God to be his vessel. By extension, it is argued that Joseph couldn't possibly have known enough to have composed and created *The Book of Mormon's* text from his own reservoir of knowledge. While Joseph may have been uneducated in a formal sense, he was a very capable reader. Early samples of his handwriting clearly demonstrate that he was capable of composing thoughts in handsome penmanship. When this capacity for reading is coupled with the easy availability of reading material and a highly inquisitive mind, an image quite different from that of an ignorant farm boy emerges. While Joseph's early spelling was not good in relation to 21st-century standards, it wasn't until 1828 that the first American dictionaries were published and the spelling of words became standardized. Joseph was very much a product of his era, deeply schooled in the Bible, and very familiar with a knowledge of the world that was contemporary with his time and place. He was not the illiterate young man that Mormon myth often ascribes to him.

Prior to 1819, little recorded notice was made of Joseph. Anecdotal tales from his childhood showed him to be an imaginative, intelligent, and charismatic young boy. But Joseph's anonymous and innocent childhood was on the cusp of dramatic change.

JOSEPH SMITH, ADOLESCENT TREASURE HUNTER, 1819–1826

Dreams of buried treasure or veins of gold lying beneath the poor flinty soil were commonplace amongst 19th-century New England farmers. In Vermont and New Hampshire, where Joseph's family lived until 1816, settlers eagerly looked for gold among the rocks that their plows unearthed. Hopeful treasure seekers also deliberately dug in special places where they believed legendary treasure might be found.

Western New York settlers, like Joseph's family, found a landscape littered with another kind of potential treasure. The vanished Mississipian Indian culture, the Mound Builders, had left behind hundreds of archeological sites scattered with human skeletons, silver, copper, and stone artifacts. The Smith farm in Manchester was located within easy walking distance of many of these sites, and people were drawn to these mysterious places. Young Joseph was not immune to the allure exerted by the potential treasure to be found.

When an itinerant treasure seeker named Luman Walters, or "Walters the Magician," entered the Palmyra area, he inspired enough confidence that locals paid him to search for buried treasure on their land. While Walters used traditional divining techniques, he also read from an ancient book of what he claimed were old "Indian" records, written in an incomprehensible language. These ancient records allegedly revealed the location of the buried "Indian" treasures. When Walters moved on to greener pastures, having milked the Palmyra locals long enough, he was succeeded in the treasure-seeking profession by Joseph and his father. Together they achieved local notoriety for oracular treasure finding. The earliest accounts of this father-and-son treasure-finding team date from around 1819, when Joseph was thirteen years old.

From 1819 to 1826, Joseph was actively engaged in part-time treasure seeking, using his native charisma and performance theatrics along with seer stones, folk magic, and occult rituals. But there are no accounts of any treasure ever actually having being found. During this period, Joseph surpassed his father in popular reputation as a practitioner of this suspect activity. There was a problem however; it was against New York state law at the time to engage in treasure-seeking for hire.

In his 1939 autobiography, Joseph indirectly addressed and excused his treasure seeking period, saying, "I was left to all kind of temptations; and, mingling with all kinds of society, I frequently fell into many foolish errors, and displayed the weakness of youth, and the foibles of human nature; which, I am sorry to say, led me into divers temptations, offensive in the sight of God. In making this confession, no one need suppose me guilty of any great or malignant sins. A disposition to commit such was never in my nature. But I was guilty of levity, and sometimes associated with jovial company, etc., not consistent with that character which ought to be maintained by who was called of God as I had been."[13]

In 1825, Joseph was hired by farmer Josiah Stowel of Bainbridge, New York (100 miles southeast of Palmyra), to look for a lost Spanish silver mine. Joseph was paid fourteen dollars a month, plus room and board. In March 1826, a complaint and arrest warrant were filed against Joseph by Peter Bridgman, a neighbor of Stowel's. Joseph was charged with being an impostor and for disturbing the peace. On March 20, 1826, at the age of twenty, Joseph stood trial in the Chenango County Courthouse in the case of "People of State of New York vs. Joseph Smith." This is the earliest known public record of Joseph.

---

13. Joseph Smith, Jr., *The Pearl of Great Price*, (Salt Lake City: Church of Jesus Christ of Latter-day Saints, 1967), page 50.

The record of the trial is sparse but conveys a straightforward narrative of the proceedings, and offers a birds-eye view into the world of 1826. In addition to the Court records there are two Bainbridge newspaper articles that corroborate the proceedings.

During the course of the trial Joseph was questioned, and answered that he had "part of time been employed looking for mines," and "that he had a certain stone, which he had occasionally looked at to determine where hidden treasures in the bowels of the earth were; that he professed to tell in this manner where gold mines were."[14]

Testifying on Joseph's behalf, Stowel said that Joseph had indeed been employed by him to look for buried money with a certain stone, "and that he positively knew that the prisoner could tell, and professed the art of seeing those valuable treasures through the medium of said stone."[15] Stowel went on to say that they "did not exactly find it, but got a piece of ore, which resembled gold."[16] Stowel testified that Joseph had said of the treasure, "that it was in a certain root of a stump five feet from surface of the earth and with it would be a tail-feather; that said Stowel and prisoner thereupon commenced digging, found a tail-feather, but money was gone; that he supposed that money moved down."[17]

Several witnesses, including Josiah Stowel's brothers, Horace and Arad, testified against Joseph. Horace Stowel testified that "he see prisoner look into hat through stone, pretending to tell where chest of dollars were buried."[18] Jonathan Thompson testified that he witnessed Joseph searching for a chest of money one night, saying:

> ...that Smith looked in hat while there, and when very dark, and told how the chest was situated. After digging several feet, struck upon something like a board or plank. Prisoner would not look again, pretending that he was alarmed the last that he looked, on account of the circumstances relating to the trunk being buried came all fresh to his mind; that the last time that he looked, he discovered distinctly the two Indians who buried the trunk; that a quarrel ensued between them, and that one of said Indians was killed by the other, and thrown into the hole beside of the trunk, to

---

14. Fawn M. Brodie, *No Man Knows My History.* (New York: Vintage Books, 1995), Appendix A, Court Record — State of New York vs. Joseph Smith, page 427.

15. *Ibid.*, page 428.

16. *Ibid.*, page 428.

17. *Ibid.*, page 428.

18. *Ibid.*, page 428.

guard it as he supposed. Thompson says he believes in the prisoner's professed skill; that the board which he struck his spade upon was probably the chest, but, on account of an enchantment, the trunk kept about the same distance from them.[19]

The trial record concluded, "And thereupon the Court finds the defendant guilty."[20]

Following the publication of *The Book of Mormon* in 1830 over a hundred of Joseph's Palmyra and Manchester neighbors made sworn affidavits regarding his treasure seeking activities between 1819 and 1826. The following are excerpts from some of those affidavits.

Peter Ingersoll testified that he'd known the Smiths as neighbors since 1822, and that, "The general employment of the family, was digging for money. I had frequent invitations to join the company, but always declined...the said Joseph, Sen. told me that the best time for digging money, was, in the heat of summer, when the heat of the sun caused the chests of money to rise near the top of the ground."[21]

William Stafford testified that he'd known the Smith family since 1820, because they lived a mile and a half from him. He said:

> A great part of their time was devoted to digging for money: especially in the night time, when they said the money could be most easily obtained. I have heard them tell marvellous tales, respecting the discoveries they had made in their peculiar occupation of money digging. They would say, for instance, that in such a place, in such a hill, on a certain man's farm, there were deposited keys, barrels and hogsheads of coined silver and gold — bars of gold, golden images, brass kettles filled with gold and silver — gold candlesticks, swords, &c, &c...Joseph Jr. had discovered some very remarkable and valuable treasures, which could be procured in one way. That way, was as follows: — That a black sheep should be taken on to the ground where the treasures were concealed — that after cutting its throat, it should be led around a circle while bleeding. This being done, the wrath of the evil spirit would be appeased: the treasures could then be obtained, and my share of them was to be four fold. To gratify my curiosity, I let them have a large fat sheep. They afterwards informed me, that the sheep was killed pursuant to commandment; but there was some mistake in the process, it did not have the desired effect.[22]

---

19. *Ibid.*, pages 428-429.

20. *Ibid.*, page 429.

21. *Ibid.*, Sworn Statement of Peter Ingersoll, page 432.

22. *Ibid.*, Sworn Statement of William Stafford, page 434.

Willard Chase testified that he had known the Smith family since 1820. "At that time, they were engaged in the money digging business, which they followed until the latter part of the season of 1827."[23]

Isaac Hale, Joseph's father-in-law, testified that he had known Joseph since November of 1825. "He was at that time in the employ of a set of men who were called "money diggers"; and his occupation was that of seeing, or pretending to see by means of a stone placed in his hat, and his hat closed over his face. In this way he pretended to discover minerals and hidden treasure."[24]

Joseph Capron testified that, "The family of Smiths held Joseph Jr. in high estimation on account of some supernatural power, which he was supposed to possess. This power he pretended to have received through the medium of a stone of a peculiar quality. The stone was placed in a hat, in such a manner as to exclude all light, except that which emanated from the stone itself. The light of the stone, he pretended, enabled him to see anything he wished. Accordingly he discovered ghosts, infernal spirits, mountains of gold and silver, and many other invaluable treasures deposited in the earth."[25]

Following his conviction in 1826, Joseph abandoned the practice of treasure seeking but kept his seer stone and all that he'd learned about alluring people with convincing presentations. Joseph's period of treasure seeking spanned seven years, from age 13 through age 20. During this time, there is no record of Joseph ever having found any gold or buried treasure. Eighteen months later, in 1827, when Joseph first reported the discovery of the golden plates, his neighbors were understandably skeptical. Who could have foreseen that this adolescent treasure finder would receive revelations from angels, find golden tablets, establish himself as a prophet, and emerge as the leader of a new religion?

While working for Stowel in 1825, Joseph had met Isaac Hale, an associate of Stowel's, and his beautiful daughter Emma. The Hale home was located in Harmony (now Oakland), Pennsylvania, about 25 miles south of Bainbridge, New York. Joseph and Emma were deeply attracted to each other but her father disliked and distrusted Joseph because of his treasure seeking activities, and vigorously opposed any relationship between the two. During the winter and spring of 1826, Joseph clandestinely continued seeing Emma, with whom he fell increasingly into reciprocal love. Following his trial and conviction, he asked permission to marry Emma and was unconditionally refused by her father. On January 18, 1827, Joseph and Emma defied Isaac Hale and eloped. With Stowel's

---

23. *Ibid.*, Sworn Statement of Willard Chase, page 434–435.
24. *Ibid.*, Sworn Statement of Isaac Hale, page 438–439.
25. *Ibid.*, Sworn Statement of Joseph Capron, page 437.

help they were married in Bainbridge. The newlyweds then returned to live on the Smith family farm in Manchester, New York.

Eight months after their marriage, Joseph and Emma returned to Harmony to retrieve some of Emma's possessions, and hired Peter Ingersoll to help with the move. Ingersoll later wrote:

> In the month of August, 1827, I was hired by Joseph Smith, Jr. to go to Pennsylvania, to move his wife's household furniture up to Manchester, where his wife then was. When we arrived at Mr. Hale's in Harmony, Pa. from which place he had taken his wife, a scene presented itself, truly affecting. His father-in-law (Mr. Hale) addressed Joseph, in a flood of tears: "You have stolen my daughter and married her. I had much rather have followed her to her grave. You spend your time in digging for money — pretend to see in a stone, and thus try do deceive people." Joseph wept, and acknowledged he could not see in a stone now, nor never could; and that his former pretensions in that respect, were false. He then promised to give up his old habits of digging for money and looking into stones.[26]

Joseph was now 21 years old and married, with his adolescence behind him. Nine months after marrying Emma, he announced the discovery of the golden plates, and began the substitution of religion and prophecy for his former practice of folk magic.

JOSEPH SMITH'S FIRST VISION, 1820–1822

Joseph's pivotal first and second visions are often confused with one another, or are sometimes combined into one composite vision. The second vision is briefly discussed in Part I of this book, and involves the appearance of the angel Moroni in Joseph's bedroom on the night of September 21, 1823 advising him of the existence, nature, and location of the buried golden plates upon which *The Book of Mormon* is inscribed.

The first vision occurred in either 1820 or 1822, depending on which of three versions of this vision is used as a reference. This vision occurred when Joseph (then 14 to 16 years old) retreated to the forest to pray to God for guidance. Joseph wanted to know which of the many competing Christian sects was the one which truly spoke in God's name. Which one should he join? In the place now called "the Sacred Grove," God answered these prayers. Regardless of

---

26. *Ibid.*, Sworn Statement of Peter Ingersoll, page 433.

which version is considered, this event falls in the heart of Joseph's treasure-seeking period.

The background against which the first vision arose is critical to its understanding. As mentioned earlier, the Palmyra area during the early 19th century was a magnet for new people, ideas, itinerant workers, and settlers. New sects and religious excitement grew like weeds among the uprooted emigrants to the area. People felt that they were living in the shadow of the "end times," just before the second coming of Jesus Christ.

This particular place and period were unique in American history for the intensity, variety, and frequency of religious excitement. The western New York area was called "the Burned Over District" in reference to the sweeping frequency and scope of revivals, emergence of new religions, fragmentation of existing sects, frontier blends of evangelism, Christian-based spiritual experimentation, folk religion, magic, occult practices, visions, and speaking in tongues. Much of this was a populist rebellion against the stale, traditional worship in an exciting new place and time.

Some historians who study the Second Great Awakening attribute the upheaval of religious values and interpretations to the passing of the generation of political leaders who'd brought America to independence and formed the world's first democratically elected government. In 1820, America was led by its fifth President James Monroe, who was 18 years old when America had declared independence from Great Britain.

The passing of the revolutionary leaders left a vacuum of moral authority in which Americans searched for a new, emerging identity. In western New York State, as the Erie Canal was being built, this search focused on envisioning new forms of religious expression. The American nation was in the hands of a new generation for whom the Revolutionary War was mostly myth and legend. The vision of this generation was one of westward expansion, Manifest Destiny, and religious fulfillment.

Visions are a common theme in *The Book of Mormon*, within Joseph's family and within their culture. Joseph Smith, Sr. received multiple mystical visions which were described and recorded in detail by his wife, Lucy Smith. She, as well as her father and her sister, all reported seeing visions. Lucy's brother, Jason, was a paid faith healer.

Joseph Smith, Sr.'s first vision included "an attendant spirit" who guided him to find "on a certain log a box, the contents of which, if you eat thereof, will make you wise, and give you wisdom and understanding."[27] However, because

---

27. Lucy Mack Smith, *Biographical Sketches of Joseph Smith the Prophet and His Progenitors for Many Generations by Lucy Smith — Mother of the Prophet*, (Liverpool: Orson Pratt, 1853), page 57.

the box was guarded by "all manner of beasts, horned cattle, and roaring animals,"[28] he'd had to leave it behind. Joseph's father's visions were a substantial component of the Smith family lore. Dreams, fantasies, visions, and reality blended together like smoke rising from incense.

Joseph Smith, Sr.'s second vision came in 1811. One of seven visions recorded by his wife, it is virtually interchangeable with a major vision of Lehi from the First Book of Nephi found in *The Book of Mormon*:

> So I asked myself, "What motive can I have in travelling here, and what place can this be?" My guide, who was by my side, as before, said, "This is the desolate world; but travel on."...I came to a narrow path. This path I entered, and, when I had travelled a little way in it, I beheld a beautiful stream of water...as far as my eyes could extend I could see a rope, running along the bank of it, about as high as a man could reach, and beyond me was a low, but very pleasant valley, in which stood a tree, such as I had never seen before. It was exceedingly handsome, inasmuch that I looked upon it with wonder and admiration...it bore a kind of fruit...as white as snow, or, if possible, whiter...I drew near, and began to eat of it, and I found it delicious beyond description. As I was eating, I said in my heart, "I cannot eat this alone, I must bring my wife and children, that they may partake with me." Accordingly, I went and brought my family...and we all commenced eating...While thus engaged, I beheld a spacious building standing opposite the valley which we were in, and it appeared to reach to the very heavens. It was full of doors and windows, and they were all filled with people, who were very finely dressed. When these people observed us in the low valley, under the tree, they pointed the finger of scorn at us, and treated us with all manner of disrespect and contempt...I asked my guide what was the meaning of the spacious building that I saw. He replied, "It is Babylon, and it must fall. The people in the doors and windows are the inhabitants thereof, who scorn and despise the Saints of God, because of their humility."[29]

The following are extracts from Lehi's vision in *The Book of Mormon*, from Part III of this book:

> A man in a white robe appeared and asked me to follow him. For many hours we traveled through a dark, dreary wasteland. Eventually we arrived in a broad field that held a beautiful tree with white fruit. When I tasted the white fruit I was instantly filled with joy and wanted to share it with my family. It was truly the best fruit imaginable. Beside the tree ran a river...When I called to them, they came and also tasted the fruit...Also

---

28. *Ibid.*
29. *Ibid.*, page 58-59.

along the river's bank was an iron handrail leading directly to the tree, and a straight and narrow path beside the handrail... Across the river there was a great building so tall that it seemed to float high in the air above the earth. It was filled with people of all ages who were finely dressed, pointing their fingers and mocking those who were sampling the fruit...The multitudes who entered the great building all pointed their fingers of scorn at those who tried the fruit. Lehi saw that those who followed the words of scorn were lost and fell away, while those who ignored the scorn and ate the fruit were saved.

Even though the Smith family was deeply religious, with regular bible reading and study, they chose not to align themselves with any particular church or denomination. During Joseph's childhood and adolescence Palmyra had well-established Methodist, Quaker, Baptist, and Presbyterian congregations. He was confronted with a broad array of religious choices, traveling evangelical preachers, and exposure to religious variety.

Shortly after publication of *The Book of Mormon* in 1830, Joseph began talking about a soul shattering vision he'd had eight years earlier, when he was 16 years old. In 1832, he dictated an autobiography and a history of the beginnings of the Mormon Church to his secretary. This rough, unfinished, and unpublished text was transcribed and then set aside. It contains the earliest known written mention of Joseph's first vision.

Joseph Smith's First Vision, Version One, written in 1832[30]

I cried unto the Lord for mercy for there was none else to whom I could go and obtain mercy — and the Lord heard my cry in the wilderness — and while in the attitude of calling upon the Lord in the 16th year of my age — a piller of light above the brightness of the sun at noon day come down from above and rested upon me — and I was filled with the spirit of God — and the Lord opened the heavens upon me and I saw the Lord — and he spake unto me saying — Joseph my son thy Sins are forgiven thee — go thy way walk in my statutes and keep my commandments — behold I am the Lord of glory — I was crucified for the world that all those who believe on my name may have Eternal life — behold the world lieth in sin at this time and none doeth good — no not one — they have turned asside from the gospel and keep not my commandments — they draw near to me with their lips while their hearts are far from me — and mine anger is kindling against the inhabitants of the earth to visit them according to their ungodliness — and to bring to pass that which hath been spoken by the mouth of the Apostles

---

30. Dashes added, as there is no punctuation at all in the original manuscript.

— behold and lo I come quickly as it is written of me in the cloud clothed in the glory of my Father — and my soul was filled with love and for many days — I could rejoice with great joy and the Lord was with me — but could find none that would believe the hevenly vision — nevertheless I pondered these things in my heart...[31]

Four years after the publication of *The Book of Mormon*, Joseph wrote a history of the Mormon Church's beginning for the church newspaper in 1834. In this history Joseph explained, and made amends for, his history as a youthful treasure hunter which had recently been brought to light by his critics. But he made no reference at all to the pivotal occurrence of the first vision. He wrote, "At the age of ten my father's family removed to Palmyra, New York, where, and in the vicinity of which, I lived, or, made it my place of residence, until I was twenty-one; the latter part, in the town of Manchester. During this time, as is common to most or all youths, I fell into many vices and follies."[32]

On November 9, 1835, the second written account of the first vision was recorded by his secretary in a daily journal. During a visit with a mysterious Jewish minister named Robert Mathias, Joseph again related the story of his first vision.

Joseph Smith's First Vision, Version Two, written in 1835

Being wrought up in the mind respecting the subject of Religion, and looking at the different systems taught the children of men, I knew not who was right or who was wrong, but considered it of the first importance to me that I should be right, in matters of so much moment, matter involving eternal consequences. Being thus perplexed in mind I retired to the silent grove and there bowed down before the Lord, under a realizing sense (if the bible be true) ask and you shall find, and again, if any man lack wisdom, let of God who giveth to all men liberally & upbraideth not. Information was what I most desired at this time, and with a fixed determination to obtain it, I called on the Lord for the first time in the place above stated, or in other words, I made a fruitless attempt to pray. My tongue seemed to be swoolen in my mouth, so that I could not utter, I heard a noise behind me like some one walking towards me. I strove again to pray, but could not; the noise of walking seemed to draw nearer, I sprang upon my feet and looked round, but saw no person, or thing that was calculated to produce the noise of walking. I kneeled again, my mouth was opened and my tongue loosed; I called on the Lord in mighty prayer. A pillar of fire appeared above

31. Joseph Smith, Jr., *The Papers of Joseph Smith, Autobiographical and Historical Writings*, Edited by Dean C. Jessee (Salt Lake City: Deseret Book Company, 1989), vol. 1, pages 6-7.

32. Joseph Smith, Jr., *Latter-Day Saints Messenger and Advocate*, Vol. 1, (Kirtland, Ohio, November 6, 1834), page 40.

my head; which presently rested down upon me, and filled me with unspeakable joy. A personage appeared in the midst of this pillar of flame, which was spread all around and yet nothing consumed. Another person-age soon appeared like unto the first: he said unto me thy sins are forgiven thee. He testified also unto me that Jesus Christ is the son of God. I saw many angels in this vision. I was about 14 years old when I received this first communication.[33]

In this second version the one personage mentioned in the first version became two personages, and Joseph's age at the time of the vision had changed from 16 to 14. The following version, written five years later as part of Joseph's 1939 autobiography, is the official historical version now enshrined as holy scripture by the Mormon Church.

Confused by competing religious agendas, the 14-year-old Joseph retreated to the forest for guidance from God and received a vision from God and Jesus Christ.

Joseph Smith's First Vision, Version Three, written in 1839

There was in the place where we lived an unusual excitement on the subject of religion. It commenced with the Methodists, but soon became general among all the sects in that region of country. Indeed, the whole dis-trict of country seemed affected by it, and great multitudes united them-selves to the different religious parties, which created no small stir and division amongst the people, some crying "Lo, here!" and others. "Lo, there!" Some were contending for the Methodist faith, some for the Presbyterian, and some for the Baptist... a scene of great confusion and bad feeling ensued — priest contending against priest, and convert against convert; so that all their good feelings one for another, if they ever had any, were entirely lost in a strife of words and a contest about opinions...

In process of time my mind became somewhat partial to the Methodist sect, and I felt some desire to be united with them; but so great were the confusion and strife among the different denominations, that it was impos-sible for a person young as I was, and so unacquainted with men and things, to come to any certain conclusion who was right and who was wrong.

---

33. Joseph Smith, Jr., *The Papers of Joseph Smith, Autobiographical and Historical Writings*, Edited by Dean C. Jessee (Salt Lake City: Deseret Book Company, 1989), vol. 1, pages 125-127.

My mind at times was greatly excited, the cry and tumult were so great and incessant. The Presbyterians were most decided against the Baptists and Methodists, and used all the powers of both reason and sophistry to prove their errors, or, at least, to make the people think they were in error. On the other hand, the Baptists and Methodists in their turn were equally zealous in endeavoring to establish their own tenets and disprove all others.

In the midst of this war of words and tumult of opinions, I often said to myself: What is to be done? Who of all these parties are right; or, are they all wrong together? If any one of them be right, which is it, and how shall I know it?

While I was laboring under the extreme difficulties caused by the contests of these parties of religionists, I was one day reading the Epistle of James, first chapter and fifth verse, which reads: *If any of you lack wisdom, let him ask of God, that giveth to all men liberally, and upbraideth not; and it shall be given him.*

Never did any passage of scripture come with more power to the heart of man than this did at this time to mine. It seemed to enter with great force into every feeling of my heart. I reflected on it again and again, knowing that if any person needed wisdom from God I did; for how to act I did not know; for the teachers of religion of the different sects understood the same passages of scripture so differently as to destroy all confidence in settling the question by an appeal to the Bible.

At length I came to the conclusion that I must either remain in darkness and confusion, or else I must do as James directs, that is, ask of God. I at length came to the determination to "ask of God," concluding that if he gave wisdom to them that lacked wisdom, and would give liberally and not upbraid, I might venture.

So, in accordance with this, my determination to ask of God, I retired to the woods to make the attempt. It was on the morning of a beautiful, clear day, early in the spring of eighteen hundred and twenty. It was the first time in my life that I had made such an attempt, for amidst all my anxieties I had never as yet made the attempt to pray vocally.

After I had retired to the place where I had previously designed to go, having looked around me, and finding myself alone, I kneeled down and began to offer up the desires of my heart to God. I had scarcely done so, when immediately I was seized upon by some power which entirely overcame me, and had such an astonishing influence over me as to bind my tongue so that I could not speak. Thick darkness gathered around me, and it seemed to me for a time as if I were doomed to sudden destruction.

But, exerting all my powers to call upon God to deliver me out of the power of this enemy which had seized upon me, and at the very moment when I was ready to sink into despair and abandon myself to destruction — not to an imaginary ruin, but to the power of some actual being from the unseen world, who had such marvelous power as I had never before felt in any being — just at this moment of great alarm, I saw a pillar of light exactly over my head, above the brightness of the sun, which descended gradually until it fell upon me.

It no sooner appeared than I found myself delivered from the enemy which held me bound. When the light rested upon me I saw two person-ages, whose brightness and glory defy all description, standing above me in the air. One of them spake unto me, calling me by name, and said, pointing to the other — *This is My Beloved Son, Hear Him!*

My object in going to inquire of the Lord was to know which of all the sects was right, that I might know which to join. No sooner, therefore, did I get possession of myself, so as to be able to speak, than I asked the person-ages who stood above me in the light, which of all the sects was right — and which I should join.

I was answered that I must join none of them, for they were all wrong, and the personage who addressed me said that all their creeds were an abomination in His sight: that those professors were all corrupt; that "they draw near to me with their lips, but their hearts are far from me; they teach for doctrines the commandments of men: having a form of godliness, but they deny the power thereof."

He again forbade me to join with any of them: and many other things did he say unto me, which I cannot write at this time. When I came to myself again, I found myself lying on my back, looking up into heaven.[34]

In this third version Joseph was thirty-three years old, writing about an incident that had taken place nineteen years earlier. While this version lacks the many angels mentioned in the second version, the most critical new detail in the third version is God's rejection and invalidation of all the religious sects present at the time, and his admonishment that Joseph should join none of them. Today, 180 years later, Joseph's first vision is a central and defining moment for the Mormon religion, retroactively setting the contextual stage for the coming second vision and the presentation of *The Book of Mormon*. In the chronology that proceeds through Joseph's life, the angel Moroni appeared to him three (or five) years later, in 1823, and showed him the golden plates on which the true word of God was written.

In his 1839 autobiography Joseph mentioned, as he does in the first version, that upon describing his first vision he is met with disbelief:

---

34. Joseph Smith, Jr., *The Pearl of Great Price*, (Salt Lake City: Church of Jesus Christ of Latter-day Saints, 1967), pages 46-48.

Some few days after I had this vision, I happened to be in the company with one of the Methodist preachers, who was very active in the before mentioned religious excitement; and, conversing with him on the subject of religion, I took occasion to give him an account of the vision which I had had. I was greatly surprised at his behavior; he treated my communication not only lightly, but with great contempt, saying it was all of the devil, that there were no such things as visions or revelations in these days; that all such things had ceased with the apostles, and that there would never be any more of them.

I soon found, however, that my telling the story had excited a great deal of prejudice against me among professors of religion, and was the cause of great persecution, which continued to increase; and though I was an obscure boy, only between fourteen and fifteen years of age, and my circumstances in life such as to make a boy of no consequence in the world, yet men of high standing would take notice sufficient to excite the public mind against me, and create a bitter persecution; and this was common to all the sects — all united to persecute me.

It caused me serious reflection then, and often has since, how very strange it was that an obscure boy, of a little over fourteen years of age, and one, too, who was doomed to the necessity of obtaining a scanty maintenance by his daily labor, should be thought a character of sufficient importance to attract the attention of the great ones of the most popular sects of the day, and in a manner to create in them a spirit of the most bitter persecution and reviling. But strange or not, so it was, and it was often the cause of great sorrow to myself.

However, it was nevertheless a fact that I had beheld a vision. I thought since, that I felt much like Paul, when he made his defense before King Agrippa, and related the account of the vision he had when he saw a light, and heard a voice; but still there were but few who believed him; some said he was dishonest, others said he was mad; and he was ridiculed and reviled. But all this did not destroy the reality of his vision. He had seen a vision, he knew he had, and all the persecution under heaven could not make it otherwise; and though they should persecute him unto death, yet he knew, and would know to his latest breath, that he had both seen a light and heard a voice speaking unto him, and all the world could not make him think or believe otherwise.

So it was with me. I had actually seen a light, and in the midst of that light I saw two Personages, and they did in reality to speak to me; and though I was hated and persecuted for saying that I had seen a vision, yet it was true; and while they were persecuting me, reviling me, and speaking all manner of evil against me falsely for so saying, I was led to say in my heart: Why persecute me for telling the truth? I have actually seen a vision; and who am I that I can withstand God, or why does the world think to make me deny what I had actually seen? For I had seen a vision; I knew it, and I knew that God knew it, and I could not deny it, neither dared I do it; at least I knew that by so doing I would offend God, and come under condemnation.

I had now got my mind satisfied so far as the sectarian world was concerned — that it was not my duty to join with any of them, but to continue
as I was until further directed.[35]

If this public disbelief and broad persecution truly happened, there is no
record made of it until well after the publication of *The Book of Mormon.* There are
no newspaper records from this period that mention the vision or any
persecution. Joseph's mother Lucy Smith acted as the family scribe by writing
letters and keeping records of events like this vision in the lives of her husband
and children. In all of her writings from 1820 to 1830 there is no mention of
Joseph's first vision or any persecution of him for it. As with Joseph, it was only
later that accounts of the first vision showed up in her writings. Records also
show that Lucy Smith continued to attend a local Presbyterian church until
1828. Even in 1831, when his mother did write about the beginnings of the
church, no mention of the first vision was made.

Like *The Book of Mormon* itself, the all important first vision is clouded in
controversy and general skepticism outside of the Mormon religion. Within the
Mormon religion, the third version of the first vision is accepted as historical
fact. On Sunday, October 6, 2002, at the semi-annual Mormon Church
conference held in Salt Lake City, the Mormon Church Prophet and President
Gordon B. Hinckley spoke of Joseph's first vision in the Sacred Grove. Before a
gathering of 20,000 in the Mormon Church Conference Center, and a live
audience of millions by worldwide satellite, he said, "Our whole strength rests
on the validity of that vision. It either occurred or it did not occur. If it did not,
then this work is a fraud. If it did, then it is the most wonderful and important
work under the heavens." Hinckley concluded by saying that this "unique,
singular and remarkable event is the pivotal substance of our faith." [36]

THE ANGEL MORONI AND JOSEPH SMITH'S SECOND, THIRD, FOURTH, FIFTH,
SIXTH, SEVENTH, EIGHT, NINTH, AND TENTH VISIONS, 1823 – 1827

Joseph's second through tenth visions all involved the Angel Moroni and
the golden plates on which *The Book of Mormon* was inscribed. In his second vision
the nature and location of the golden plates were revealed to the 17-year-old
Joseph. Like the first vision the following nine visions' origins are obscure, but
became increasingly well defined as the years following the publication of *The*

35. *Ibid.,* pages 49-50.
36. Gordon B. Hinckley, "Hinckley Wraps Up Conference With Vigorous Defense of Faith," by
Peggy Fletcher Stack, *The Salt Lake Tribune,* Monday (October 07, 2002), Page A-6.

Book of Mormon passed. Also, like the first vision, no record or account of these visions exists from the time period during which they occurred, which was again concurrent with the height of Joseph's treasure-seeking period. Lucy Smith, the family scribe, made no record of these momentous visions or discoveries during the four-year period in which they occurred. At an important Mormon Church Conference held on October 25-26, 1831 the official minutes reflected Joseph's hesitancy to clearly spell out the details about the origins of *The Book of Mormon* at that time:

> "Brother Hyrum Smith said that he thought best that the information of the coming forth of the Book of Mormon be related by Joseph himself to the Elders present, that all might know for themselves."
> "Brother Joseph Smith, Jun., said that it was not intended to tell the world all the particulars of the coming forth of the Book of Mormon; and also said that it was not expedient for him to relate these things." This will account for the Prophet confining himself to the merest generalities in all his statements concerning the coming forth of the Book of Mormon[37]

By the time that Joseph wrote his autobiography in 1839, however, the particulars of his second vision and the subsequent discovery of the golden plates, was revealed in brilliant and breathtaking clarity:

> I continued to pursue my common vocations in life until the twenty-first of September, one thousand eight hundred and twenty-three, all the time suffering severe persecution at the hands of all classes of men, both religious and irreligious, because I continued to affirm that I had seen a vision....on the evening of the above-mentioned twenty-first of September, after I had retired to my bed for the night, I betook myself to prayer and supplication to Almighty God for forgiveness of all my sins and follies, and also for a manifestation to me, that I might know of my state and standing before him; for I had full confidence in obtaining a divine manifestation, as I previously had one...
> While I was thus in the act of calling upon God, I discovered a light appearing in my room, which continued to increase until the room was lighter than at noonday, when immediately a personage appeared at my bedside, standing in the air, for his feet did not touch the floor.

---

37. Joseph Smith, Jr., *History of the Church of Jesus Christ of Latter Day Saints*, (Salt Lake City: Deseret Book Co., 1980) vol. I, page 220.

He had on a loose robe of most exquisite whiteness. It was a whiteness beyond anything earthly I had ever seen; nor do I believe that any earthly thing could be made to appear so exceedingly white and brilliant. His hands were naked, and his arms also, a little above the wrist; so, also, were his feet naked, as were his legs, a little above the ankles. His head and neck were also bare. I could discover that he had no other clothing on but this robe, as it was open, so that I could see his bosom.

Not only was his robe exceedingly white, but his whole person was glorious beyond description, and his countenance truly like lightning. The room was exceedingly light, but not so very bright as immediately around his person. When I first looked upon him, I was afraid; but the fear soon left me.

He called me by name, and said unto me that he was a messenger sent from the presence of God to me and that his name was Moroni; that God had a work for me to do; and that my name should be had for good and evil among all nations, kindreds, and tongues, or that it should be both good and evil spoken of among all people.

He said there was a book deposited, written upon gold plates, giving an account of the former inhabitants of this continent, and the sources from whence they sprang. He also said that the fullness of the everlasting Gospel was contained in it, as delivered by the Savior to the ancient inhabitants; also that there were two stones in silver bows — and these stones, fastened to a breastplate, constituted what is called the Urim and Thummim — deposited with the plates; and the possession and use of these stones were what constituted "Seers" in ancient or former times; and that God had prepared them for the purpose of translating the book... he told me, that when I got those plates of which he had spoken — for the time that they should be obtained was not yet fulfilled — I should not show them to any person; neither the breastplate with the Urim and Thummim; only to those to whom I should be commanded to show them; if I did I should be destroyed. While he was conversing with me about the plates, the vision was opened to my mind that I could see the place where the plates were deposited, and that so clearly and distinctly that I knew the place again when I visited it.[38]

The angel Moroni departed and returned two more times that night (the auspicious evening of the fall equinox) and conveyed the same message each time. These three nocturnal visitations are counted as Joseph's second, third and fourth visions. On the third and last visit before morning the angel Moroni added to his previous messages, "telling me that Satan would try to tempt me (in consequence of the indigent circumstances of my father's family), to get the plates for the purpose of getting rich. This he forbade me, saying that I must have no other object in view in getting the plates but to glorify God, and must not be

---

38. Joseph Smith, Jr., *The Pearl of Great Price*, (Salt Lake City: Church of Jesus Christ of Latter-day Saints, 1967), pages 50-52.

influenced by any other motive than that of building his kingdom; otherwise I could not get them."[39]

The following day, September 22nd, 1823, Joseph reported such physical weariness out in the field that his father told him to go home and rest. On his way back, he fell to the ground and was visited by the angel Moroni for a fourth time, and received his fifth vision. The angel Moroni repeated everything said the previous night, and commanded him to go tell his father of his visions, and then to go seek the plates in the revealed location. This he did. After finding the plates the Angel Moroni visited Joseph for a fifth time, in Joseph's sixth vision:

> I left the field, and went to the place where the messenger had told me the plates were deposited; and owing to the distinctness of the vision which I had had concerning it, I knew the place the instant that I arrived there.
>
> Convenient to the village of Manchester, Ontario county, New York, stands a hill of considerable size, and the most elevated of any in the neighborhood. On the west side of this hill, not far from the top, under a stone of considerable size, lay the plates, deposited in a stone box. This stone was thick and rounding in the middle on the upper side, and thinner towards the edges, so that the middle part of it was visible above the ground, but the edge all around was covered with earth.
>
> Having removed the earth, I obtained a lever, which I got fixed under the edge of the stone, and with a little exertion raised it up. I looked in, and there indeed did I behold the plates, the Urim and Thummim, and the breastplate, as stated by the messenger. The box in which they lay was formed by laying stones together in some kind of cement. In the bottom of the box were laid two stones crossways of the box, and on these stones lay the plates and the other things with them.
>
> I made an attempt to take them out, but was forbidden by the messenger, and was again informed that the time for bringing them forth had not yet arrived, neither would it, until four years from that time; but he told me that I should come to that place precisely in one year from that time, and that he would there meet with me, and that I should continue to do so until the time should come for obtaining the plates.
>
> Accordingly, as I had been commanded, I went at the end of each year, and at each time I found the same messenger there, and received instruction and intelligence from him at each of our interviews, respecting what the Lord was going to do, and how and in what manner his kingdom was to be conducted in the last days.[40]

If these annual, fall equinox visitations from the angel Moroni in 1824, 1825, 1826 and 1827 are counted individually they are Joseph's seventh, eighth, ninth,

---

39. *Ibid.*, page 52.
40. *Ibid.*, page 53.

and tenth visions. During those four years Joseph continued his busy career as a treasure-seeker until his arrest and conviction on March 20, 1826.

Barely eighteen months later, on September 22, 1827, Joseph returned to the Hill Cumorah in the company of his new wife Emma. Legend has it that on the previous year's visit Moroni had told Joseph that he would be given the plates only if he returned with a wife. Jon Krakauer, in *Under the Banner of Heaven*, describes how,

> After being denied the plates on his previous four visits, this time he left nothing to chance. Carefully adhering to the time-honored rituals of necromancy, the young couple were dressed entirely in black, and had traveled the three miles from the Smith farm to the hill in a black carriage drawn by a black horse. High on the steep west slope of the hill, Joseph again dug beneath the rock in the dark of night, while Emma stood nearby with her back turned to him. He soon unearthed the stone box that he had been prevented from removing four years earlier. This time, however, Moroni allowed him to take temporary possession of its contents.[41]

When he and Emma returned home at dawn the next morning, Joseph carried with him news of his gold discovery like a 19th-century Moses coming down from the mountain. These were not stone tablets inscribed by God that he carried but golden tablets inscribed by an ancient American prophet named Mormon and his son Moroni. He showed them to no one, not even his wife, mother or father. To see them, other than by divine command, was certain death and destruction for any curious observer. Joseph had been given temporary possession of these plates, he said, for their translation, publication, and dissemination. He was twenty-one years old.

THE TRANSLATION OF THE GOLDEN PLATES, 1828-1830

The golden plates themselves were described as being six inches wide by eight inches high, bound with three rings, and inscribed with characters in a unique language that Joseph Smith called "reformed Egyptian". The individual plates were as thick as heavy paper. They stacked up five or six inches high, and weighed forty or fifty pounds. The plates were left in Joseph's hands subject to the condition that he safeguard them from harm or theft. In his 1839 description of his second vision Joseph described the terms that the angel Moroni placed on his custodianship of the golden plates:

---

41. Jon Krakauer, *Under the Banner of Heaven*, (New York: Doubleday, 2003) page 59.

The same heavenly messenger[42] delivered them up to me with this charge; that I should be responsible for them; that if I should let them go carelessly or through any neglect of mine, I should be cut off; but that if I would use all my endeavors to preserve them, until he, the messenger, should call for them, they should be protected.

I soon found out the reason why I had received such strict charges to keep them safe, and why it was that the messenger had said that when I had done what was required at my hand he would call for them. For no sooner was it known that I had them, than the most strenuous exertions were used to get them from me. Every stratagem that could be invented was resorted to for that purpose. The persecution became more bitter and severe than before, and multitudes were on the alert continually to get them from me if possible. But by the wisdom of God they remained safe in my hands, until I had accomplished by them what was required at my hand. When, according to arrangements, the messenger called for them, I delivered them up to him; and he has them in his charge until this day.[43]

After several unsuccessful attempts were made by his Palmyra neighbors to find and steal the golden plates from him, Joseph and his wife Emma returned to the relative quiet of Harmony, Pennsylvania. During the winter of 1828 they began the translation, using the magic spectacles that had been provided with the plates. Joseph dictated and Emma transcribed. Progress was slow and cumbersome. In April of 1828 Martin Harris, a prosperous Palmyra farmer and early believer in Joseph's golden plates, came to relieve Emma of the transcription.

Joseph worked with Harris for two months. The accumulated transcription from both Emma and Harris amounted to 116 handwritten pages. Because Harris had pledged to help finance the publication he convinced Joseph to allow him to take these pages back to Palmyra to show his wife who was not very enthusiastic about this venture. Mrs. Harris, outraged at her husband's willingness to squander their wealth on what she saw as a foolish undertaking, stole and presumably destroyed the pages. She regaled her husband afterwards, and declared that if the pages were truly translated by revelation, they shouldn't be so difficult to replace.

This put Joseph in an awkward position. If he made another translation and the first one was recovered but didn't match, he'd be declared a fraud. In July he received a revelation from God in which he was commanded not to attempt a

---

42. The angel Moroni.

43. Joseph Smith, Jr., *The Pearl of Great Price*, (Salt Lake City: Church of Jesus Christ of Latter-day Saints, 1967), page 54.

re-translation of the lost pages, but rather to continue forward from the place where he'd left the translation in June. The missing pages, he was told by God, were part of The Book of Lehi, a political record that was somewhat duplicated in another portion of religious-oriented text written by Lehi's son, Nephi.

Throughout the summer and fall of 1828 Joseph did no translating at all. He began again in the winter of 1828 when Harris returned to Harmony to continue the transcription. In April of 1829 a young schoolteacher named Oliver Cowdery came to visit with one of Joseph's brothers. Cowdery had already been exposed to the stories of the golden plates during a stay with the Smith family in Manchester, and was eager to meet Joseph. Joseph quickly recognized Cowdery as a more suitable scribe than Harris and conscripted him on the spot. Cowdery, at age twenty-two, was one year younger than Joseph. Between April and July of 1829 they translated and transcribed the remainder of *The Book of Mormon*.

A variety of translation techniques was used during Joseph's dictation to his three scribes: Emma, Harris, and Cowdery. In the beginning Joseph strung a rope across the translating room, and hung a blanket from the rope to divide the room in half. Using the magic spectacles he read aloud from the golden plates on one side of the blanket, and dictated to the scribe who was seated at a table on the opposite side of the blanket. God would be angry, he said, if anyone saw the plates without divine authorization. A casual, unauthorized viewer could be immediately struck dead by God if they saw the golden plates without his specific command to do so. Mostly, the golden plates were not present at all. Witnesses including his scribes Emma, Cowdery, and Harris reported that Joseph would place a magical seer stone in his hat, bury his face in the hat, and then dictate *The Book of Mormon* to them. The notion that Joseph was looking directly at, studying, and referring to the golden plates during his "translation" of them is not consistent with the recorded accounts at all. For the most part, the translation was accomplished without any guise of direct reference to the plates.

Emma later described the translation to her son, Joseph Smith III, "In writing for your father I frequently wrote day after day, often sitting at the table close by him, he sitting with his face buried in his hat, with the stone in it, and dictating hour after hour with nothing between us."[44]

A friend of Martin Harris' and a Mormon church authority named Edward Stevenson wrote about the translation method, "Martin explained the translation as follows: By aid of the seer stone, sentences would appear and were read by the Prophet and written by Martin and when finished he would say 'Written,' and if correctly written that sentence would disappear and another

---

44. Emma Smith, *History of the Reorganized Church of Jesus Christ of Latter-day Saints*, (Independence, Missouri: Herald House, 1951), "Last Testimony of Sister Emma," Volume 3, page 356.

appear in its place, but if not written correctly it remained until corrected, so that the translation was just as it was engraven on the plates, precisely in the language then used."[45]

In 1834 Oliver Cowdery told how he "had seasons of skepticism, in which I did seriously wonder whether the prophet and I were men in our sober senses when we would be translating from plates through 'the Urim and Thummim'; and the plates not be in sight at all."[46]

David Whitmer was one of the witnesses who later testified that he actually saw the golden plates. It was in Whitmer's Harmony, Pennsylvania home that most of *The Book of Mormon* was translated. In 1887, he said:

> I will now give you a description of the manner in which *The Book of Mormon* was translated. Joseph Smith would put the seer stone into a hat, and put his face in the hat, drawing it closely around his face to exclude the light; and in the darkness the spiritual light would shine. A piece of something resembling parchment would appear, and on that appeared the writing. One character at a time would appear, and under it was the interpretation in English. Brother Joseph would read off the English to Oliver Cowdery, who was his principal scribe, and when it was written down and repeated to Brother Joseph to see if it was correct, then it would disappear, and another character with the interpretation would appear. Thus *The Book of Mormon* was translated by the gift and power of God, and not by any power of man."[47]

In an interview in 1881, Whitmer recounted, "I, as well as all of my father's family, Smith's wife, Oliver Cowdery and Martin Harris, were present during the translation. . . . He did not use the plates in translation."[48]

Emma Smith's father Isaac Hale stated in an 1834 affidavit: "The manner in which he pretended to read and interpret, was the same as when he looked for the money-diggers, with a stone in his hat, and his hat over his face, while The Book of Plates were at the same time hid in the woods."[49]

It is interesting to observe the similarities between Joseph's hat and magic seer stone translation techniques, with the hat and magic seer stone treasure finding techniques he employed prior to his treasure seeking conviction in 1826.

---

45. Edward Stevenson, 'One of the Three Witnesses,' reprinted from *Deseret News*, November 30, 1881 in Millennial Star, 44 (6 Feb. 1882): 86-87.

46. Oliver Cowdery, *Latter Day Saints Messenger and Advocate*, October 1834.

47. David Whitmer, *An Address to All Believers in Christ*, Richmond, Missouri: n.p., 1887, p. 12.

48. David Whitmer, Interview given to *Kansas City Journal*, June 5, 1881, reprinted in the *Reorganized Church of Jesus Christ of Latter Day Saints Journal of History*, vol. 8, (1910), pp. 299-300.

49. Affidavit of Isaac Hale dated March 20, 1834, cited in Rodger I. Anderson, *Joseph Smith's New York Reputation Reexamined*, (Salt Lake City: Signature Books, 1990), pp. 126-128.

The sworn testimonies of Horace Stowell and Jonathan Thompson in the 1826 trial, and the later sworn testimonies of Joseph Capron and Isaac Hale, all mention the hat and magic seer stones; and bear a striking resemblance to the translation reports of Emma Smith, Martin Harris, Oliver Cowdery, and David Whitmer.

THE ELEVEN WITNESSES AND THE THIRTEENTH VISION, 1830

Fearing that the public would disbelieve him, Joseph arranged for witnesses to testify that they had actually seen the golden plates. Joseph had these witnesses sign one of two documents that he'd prepared to verify this. The first document was signed by Oliver Cowdery, David Whitmer, and Martin Harris. The second document was signed by Whitmer family members Christian, Jacob, Peter Jr., and John; Hiram Page (David Whitmer's son in law); Joseph's father and two of his brothers, Hyrum Smith and Samuel Smith.

The first three witnesses testified that an angel of God had actually come down from heaven, appeared to them in person, and showed them the golden plates. Joseph was present with these three witnesses during the course of this, his thirteenth vision[50] in which God himself also spoke to the four men. Joseph Smith's prepared statement said:

> ...that we, through the grace of God the Father, and our Lord Jesus Christ, have seen the plates which contain this record, which is a record of the people of Nephi, and also of the Lamanites, his brethren, and also of the people of Jared, which came from the tower of which hath been spoken, and we also know that they have been translated by the gift and power of God, for his voice hath declared it unto us; wherefore we know of a surety that the work is true. And also we testify that we have seen the engravings which are upon the plates; and they have been shewn unto us by the power of God, and not of man. And we declare with words of soberness, that an angel of God came down from heaven, and he brought and laid before our eyes, that we beheld and saw the plates, and the engravings thereon; and we know that it is by the grace of God the Father, and our Lord Jesus Christ, that we beheld and bear record that these things are true, and it is marvellous in our eyes: Nevertheless, the voice of the Lord commanded us that we should bear record of it; wherefore, to be obedient unto the commandments of God, we bear testimony of these things.[51]

---

50. The 11th and 12th visions had taken place in the preceding month, May of 1829.

51. Joseph Smith, Jr., *The Book of Mormon* (Palmyra: Grandin, New York, 1830), Witness Page, compare to BOM (Salt Lake City: Church of Jesus Christ of Latter-day Saints, 1981), Witness Page.

When Martin Harris was questioned later by a Palmyra attorney about what he'd actually seen, his answer was not terribly convincing. "Did you see the plates and the engravings upon them with your bodily eyes?" the attorney asked. "I did not see them as I do that pencil-case, yet I saw them with the eye of faith; I saw them just as distinctly as I see anything around me — though at the time they were covered with a cloth,"[52] Harris replied. Letters and reports from the times indicate that none of the three witnesses actually saw the plates with their eyes, but rather saw visions of them. David Whitmer also reported seeing not only Mormon's golden plates, but also the sword that *The Book of Mormon* character Nephi used to cut off the head of Laban, multiple other plates and records, and Lehi's magic brass compass, the Liahona.

Several of the eight witnesses later reported being led into a room as a group which contained a box said to contain the plates. Following lengthy prayer and other spiritual exercises they were commanded to see the plates when the box was opened. If they found the box empty, more prayer was prescribed until they were eventually able to see the plates. According to the report this supplication to God lasted for over two hours. These witnesses signed Smith's second prepared statement saying, "that Joseph Smith, Jr., the Author and Proprietor of this work, has shewn unto us the plates of which hath been spoken, which have the appearance of gold; and as many of the leaves as the said Smith has translated we did handle with our hands; and we also saw the engravings thereon, all of which has the appearance of ancient work, and of curious workmanship."[53]

Mormon educator Grant H. Palmer, who spent his career working for the Mormon Church explains the testimony of the 11 witnesses like this:

> The witnesses to the Book of Mormon reportedly saw both secular and spiritual treasure guardians by "second sight" or through "the eyes of our understanding." Their testimony of the Book of Mormon was not of a secular event. Their emphasis was on seeing an angel and handling plates of gold, which was impressive for its metaphysical aspects. Today we see the witnesses as empirical, rational, twenty-first-century men instead of the nineteenth-century men they were. We have ignored the peculiarities of their world view, and by so doing, we misunderstand their experiences. Over time, we have reinterpreted their testimony so that, like with the other foundation stones, it appears to be a rational, impressive, and unique story in the history of religion.[54]

---

52. John Alonzo Clark, *Gleanings in the Way*, (Philadelphia, 1842), pages 256-257.

53. Joseph Smith, Jr., *The Book of Mormon* (Palmyra: Grandin, New York, 1830), Witness Page, compare to BOM (Salt Lake City: Church of Jesus Christ of Latter-day Saints, 1981), Witness Page.

"The Testimony of Three Witnesses" and "The Testimony of Eight Witnesses," along with the names of the witnesses, appears in each published copy of *The Book of Mormon*. Shortly after the completion of the translation Joseph again met the angel Moroni, and returned the plates to him.

Ultimately there either was or was not a set of golden plates that Joseph Smith translated into *The Book of Mormon*. Eleven witnesses signed sworn statements, written by Joseph Smith, saying that they had seen the golden plates. Either they truly saw and handled the golden plates as represented, or they were sufficiently persuaded by Joseph Smith's charisma and charmed by his guided imagery to say that they'd seen them. If the angel Moroni hadn't retrieved the plates from Joseph and taken them away, perhaps we could see them for ourselves in a museum setting, allow our scientists and linguists to examine them, and be convinced of the genuineness of their antiquity. Maybe then, there would be less controversy about *The Book of Mormon's* origin.

THE BOOK OF MORMON PUBLISHED, 1830

During the translation of *The Book of Mormon* Martin Harris had offered to help finance its printing. In the summer of 1829 a Palmyra printer, Egbert Grandin, agreed to produce 5,000 copies of the already controversial book but wanted to be paid $3,000 up front for this unusually large order. When Joseph asked Harris to honor his promises of financial help, he balked. Joseph then received a revelation from God ordering Harris to capitulate and pay up:

> I am Alpha and Omega, Christ the Lord; yea even I am he, the beginning and the end, the Redeemer of the world...For, behold, I am endless, and the punishment which is given from my hand is endless punishment, for Endless is my name. Wherefore – Eternal punishment is God's punishment. Endless punishmet is God's punishment. Wherefore, I command you to repent, and keep the commandments which you have received by the hand of my servant Joseph Smith, Jun., in my name... I command thee that thou shalt not covet thine own property, but impart it freely to the printing of the Book of Mormon, which contains the truth and the word of God...Behold, this is a great and the last commandment which I shall give unto you concerning this matter; for this shall suffice for thy daily walk,

---

54. Grant Palmer, *An Insider's View of Mormon Origins*, (Salt Lake City: Signature Books, 2002), page 260.

even unto the end of thy life. And misery thou shalt receive if thou wilt slight these counsels, yea, even the destruction of thyself and property...Pay the debt thou hast contracted with the printer. Release thyself from bondage."[55]

Terrified at the possibility of incurring God's anger and punishment, Martin Harris sold his farm to cover the first printing of *The Book of Mormon*. Typesetting from the finished manuscript began in August 1829, and on March 26, 1830 the first copies were finished and on for sale in the Palmyra bookstore. On April 2, 1830, *The Book of Mormon* was reviewed for the first time, in the *Rochester Daily Advertiser*:

> Blasphemy: *The Book of Mormon*, Alias the Golden Bible
>
> The *Book of Mormon* has been placed in our hands. A viler imposition was never practiced. It is an evidence of fraud, blasphemy, and credulity, shocking both to Christians and moralists. The author and proprietor is Joseph Smith, Jr., a fellow who by some hocus pocus acquired such influence over a wealthy farmer of Wayne county that the latter mortgaged his farm for $3,000, which he paid for printing and binding five thousand copies of the blasphemous work.

The Mormon Church clearly states and perpetuates its position that *The Book of Mormon* is an historical fact, and not an allegory or myth. Either Joseph Smith was a divine prophet to whom a new scripture of God and Jesus Christ was revealed, or *The Book of Mormon* was an elaborate hoax.

Mormon Apostle Orson Pratt wrote in 1851,"*The Book of Mormon* claims to be a divinely inspired record...This book must be either true or false...If false, it is one of the most cunning, wicked, bold, deep-laid impositions ever palmed upon the world, calculated to deceive and ruin millions who will sincerely receive it as the word of God...If true, no one can possibly be saved and reject it; if false, no one can possibly be saved and receive it."[56]

---

55. Joseph Smith, Jr., *Doctrine and Covenants*, Section 19 (Salt Lake City: Church of Jesus Christ of Latter-day Saints, 1968), pages 27-29.

56. S. Orson Pratt, *Divine Authenticity of The Book of Mormon*, Orson Pratt's Works (Liverpool, 1851) page 1.

JOSEPH SMITH, PROPHET, SEER, AND REVELATOR; THE ELEVENTH, TWELFTH, FOURTEENTH, AND FIFTEENTH VISIONS, 1829–1843

Even before Joseph Smith and Oliver Cowdery finished translating *The Book of Mormon*, a religion based on it was very much on Joseph's mind. Cowdery, his scribe and chief confidant, questioned whether Joseph could found a religion, given that he was not an ordained minister. On May 15, 1829, two months before Joseph and Cowdery completed the translation from the golden plates, the two went into the woods to pray. In answer to their prayers they received Joseph's 11th vision, when John the Baptist came down from heaven to meet them in the form of an angel. The angel John granted them the power to baptize and to ordain each other as priests, in what he called the true Hebraic Priesthood of Aaron. After completing the angel's instructions and baptizing each other in Pennsylvania's Susquehanna River, both Joseph and Cowdery became ordained priests in a new religion. Joseph was just twenty-three years old. Ten years later he described his vision like this:

We on a certain day went into the woods to pray and inquire of the Lord respecting baptism for the remission of sins, that we found mentioned in the translation of the plates. While we were thus employed, praying and calling upon the Lord, a messenger from heaven descended in a cloud of light, and having laid his hands upon us, he ordained us, saying:

Upon you my fellow servants, in the name of Messiah, I confer the Priesthood of Aaron, which holds the keys of the ministering of angels, and of the gospel of repentance, and of baptism by immersion for the remission of sins; and this shall never be taken again from the earth until the sons of Levi do offer again an offering unto the Lord in righteousness.

He said this Aaronic Priesthood had not the power of laying on hands for the gift of the Holy Ghost, but that this should be conferred on us hereafter; and he commanded us to go and be baptized, and gave us directions that I should baptize Oliver Cowdery, and that afterward he should baptize me.

Accordingly we went and were baptized. I baptized him first, and afterwards he baptized me — after which I laid my hands upon his head and ordained him to the Aaronic Priesthood, and afterwards he laid his hands on me and ordained me to the same Priesthood – for so we were commanded.

The messenger who visited us on this occasion and conferred this Priesthood upon us, said that his name was John, the same that is called John the Baptist in the New Testament, and that he acted under the direction of Peter, James and John . . .

Our minds being now enlightened, we began to have the scriptures laid open to our understandings, and the true meaning and intention of their more mysterious passages revealed unto us in a manner which we never could attain to previously, nor ever before had thought of. In the meantime we were forced to keep secret the circumstances of having received the Priesthood and our having been baptized, owing to a spirit of persecution which had already manifested itself in the neighborhood.[57]

Soon after the baptism they received Joseph's 12th vision, in which they reported seeing the Apostles Peter, James, and John, who ordained them both into another, higher layer of priesthood. This Melchizedek Priesthood was also known as the Holy Order of the Son of God. It conveyed, to initiates, the ability to heal by the laying on of hands, the ability to give the blessings of Jesus Christ, and the ability to ordain new members into the priesthood.

Just ten days after the publication of *The Book of Mormon,* Joseph formally incorporated his new church, The Church of Christ, on April 6, 1830, at David Whitmer's log home in Fayette, New York. Joseph announced his official position as "seer, a translator, a prophet, an apostle of Jesus Christ, and elder of the church through the will of God the Father, and the grace of your Lord Jesus Christ."[58] The thirty believers who were present were told that they were now missionaries for the propagation of the new faith. Joseph's church would eventually proceed through four more name changes until becoming the institution now known as The Church of Jesus Christ of Latter Day Saints. Joseph was now twenty-four years old.

In addition to receiving visions and revelations for himself, Joseph had also learned that he was capable of inducing visions in others. Since his first revelation in 1828 (regarding the 116 stolen pages of the first transcription) through the founding of his church in 1830, he began having revelations with great regularity about all manner of things, from the divine to the petty. In a critical biography of Joseph Smith that challenged the truth of *The Book of Mormon,* entitled *No Man Knows My History,* Mormon historian Fawn Brodie wrote:

Within two years of his first revelation, which had sprung out of the of the mundane crisis of the lost manuscript, he had established the true "Church of Christ," bulwarked by the ancient priesthood of Israel and claiming to be, not another fragment of Protestantism, but the restored religion of Jesus himself. But since the history of this period is based on docu-

---

57. Joseph Smith, Jr., *The Pearl of Great Price,* (Salt Lake City: Church of Jesus Christ of Latter-day Saints, 1967), pages 56-57.

58. Joseph Smith, Jr., *Doctrine and Covenants,* Section 21 (Salt Lake City: Church of Jesus Christ of Latter-day Saints, 1968), page 35.

ments written many years later, one cannot see the stumblings and hesitations that must have attended Joseph's transformation...Joseph's great dramatic talent found its first outlet in the cabalistic ritual of rural wizardry, then in the hocus-pocus of the Gold Bible mystery, and finally in the exacting and apparently immensely satisfying role of prophet of God.[59]

When other church members began claiming revelations of their own, Joseph countered with yet another revelation, proclaiming that God gave only him the authority to direct the new church. It said, "Behold, I say unto thee...no one shall be appointed to receive commandments and revelations in this Church, excepting my servant Joseph Smith, Jun., for he receiveth them even as Moses."[60] This revelation became part of a collection of revelations called *Doctrine and Covenants*, a continuing documentation and record of Joseph's divine commandments which still guide the Mormon Church.

About his power of revelation Joseph said, "A person may profit by noticing the first intimation of the spirit of revelation; for instance, when you feel pure intelligence flowing into you, it may give you sudden strokes of ideas, so that by noticing it, you may find it fulfilled the same day or soon; (i.e.,) those things that were presented unto your minds by the Spirit of God, will come to pass."[61]

Like *The Book of Mormon's* text, the revelations in *Doctrine and Covenants* are expressed in Elizabethan dialect in numbered verses. During his lifetime as a prophet Joseph recorded 120 revelations in the book *Doctrine and Covenants*. The revelations all establish that the presenter is God or Jesus Christ, speaking through Joseph. They instruct, advise, warn, command, admonish, threaten, and praise their designated recipients. Multiple revelations identified specific individuals who were commanded to repent or be punished.

One revelation ordered Joseph's follower, Martin Harris, to pay the printer or be punished by God. Multiple revelations affirm Joseph as the only living prophet of God. One revelation directed Joseph's wife Emma to quit complaining about being denied the sight of the golden plates, to accept the opportunity to select hymns instead, and to take delight in the glory of her husband. Multiple revelations affirmed that *The Book of Mormon* was true. In multiple revelations God advised the church to buy real estate. In one revelation, God directed the church to subdivide church property into building lots. Multiple revelations directed specific individuals to go out on missions and make converts. In 1842, God

---

59. Fawn M. Brodie, *No Man Knows My History.* (New York: Vintage Books, 1995), pages 84-85.

60. Joseph Smith, Jr., *Doctrine and Covenants*, Section 28 (Salt Lake City: Church of Jesus Christ of Latter-day Saints, 1968), page 42.

61. Joseph Smith, Jr., *Teachings of the Prophet Joseph Smith*, Compiled by Joseph Fielding Smith, (Salt Lake City: Deseret Book Co., 1959), page.151.

revealed that it was not adulterous for Joseph to have multiple wives, and ordered Joseph's wife Emma to abide by Joseph's direction or be destroyed.

The inheritance of this established authority as prophet, seer, and revelator would continue after Joseph's death. A continuous succession of Mormon Church leaders have since been held by its members to assume the same status of living prophet, seer, and revelator of God once held by Joseph; but hundreds of Mormon splinter sects also claim that their leader is the true prophet of God and the rightful successor to Joseph's legacy.

Doctrine and Covenants also contains details of Joseph's 11th, 12th, 14th, and 15th visions. The 11th and 12th visions in 1829 involved angelic instruction in the ordination of the priesthood mentioned earlier. In February, 1832, Joseph and his associate Sidney Rigdon received Joseph's 14th vision. While in prayer, God, Jesus Christ, and a company of angels appeared to them. In this vision people were promised redemption if they obeyed God's rules and were threatened with punishment if they disobeyed, and the geography of heaven was explained to them. Joseph received his 15th and final vision in the company of Oliver Cowdery in April 1936, when Jesus Christ, Moses, Elias, and Elijah all appeared to them giving affirmations and confirmation of fulfilled prophecies.

The church grew quickly under Joseph's magnetic personality and the enticing stories told in *The Book of Mormon*. To its converts, the 19th-century Mormon Church seemed to be more exciting and forward-looking than its stricter Protestant cousins. They were in the last days, Joseph assured his members with his enormous charisma, and the Mormons were truly Latter Day Saints. If anyone had doubts, *The Book of Mormon* proved it to be true. But for every new convert, there were dozens who recalled Joseph's treasure-seeking period and his conviction as an impostor. Those who did not join Joseph's new church saw his doctrine as blasphemy against Christianity. Angry mobs began to threaten the new church and Joseph was repeatedly arrested. These charges resulted in acquittals based on laws protecting freedom of religious expression.

But the seeds for the Mormons' *mythos* of persecution were planted. This perception of themselves as a persecuted people grew from that time on, through Joseph's murder and into the present. Using martyrdom and persecution as a theme, Joseph and his church linked themselves to early Christian martyrs nearly two thousand years earlier, and gathered internal confirmation of their truth from the harsh treatment they received at the hands of others. Between 1830 and 1832, Joseph's church left inhospitable New York behind and spread into Ohio and Missouri. By 1832, Joseph had gathered over a thousand people to his flock of believers.

In 1831, Joseph began his "correct" translation of the *Holy Bible*. In *The Book of Mormon*, an angel showed the prophet Nephi a vision about the future formation of a:

> ...great and abominable church, which is the mother of abominations, whose foundation is the devil. And he saith unto me, Behold, there is, save it be, two churches: the one is the church of the Lamb of God, and the other is the church of the Devil; wherefore, whoso belongeth not to the church of the Lamb of God, belongeth to that great church, which is the mother of abominations; and she is the whore of all the earth. And it came to pass that I looked and beheld the whore of all the earth, and she sat upon many waters; and she had dominion over all the earth, among all nations, kindreds, tongues, and people.[62]

According to *The Book of Mormon*, the Bible had been corrupted by this "abominable church," which had removed and changed text in order to purposefully lead people astray. The prophet Nephi tells of a vision in which God shows him how this would happen:

> ...thou seest the foundation of a great and abominable church, which is the most abominable above all other churches; for behold, they have taken away from the Gospel of the Lamb, many parts which are plain and most precious; and also, many Covenants of the Lord have they taken away; and all this have they done, that they might pervert the right ways of the Lord; that they might blind the eyes and harden the hearts of the children of men; wherefore, thou seest that after The Book hath gone forth through the hands of the great and abominable church, that there are many plain and precious things taken away from The Book, which is The Book of the Lamb of God; and after that these plain and precious things were taken away, it goeth forth unto all the nations of the Gentiles; and after it goeth forth unto all the nations of the Gentiles, yea, even across the many waters which thou hast seen with the Gentiles which have gone forth out of captivity; and thou seest because of the many plain and precious things which have been taken out of The Book, which were plain unto the understanding of the children of men, according to the plainness which is in the Lamb of God; and because of these things which were taken away out of the Gospel of the Lamb, an exceeding great many do stumble, yea, insomuch that Satan hath great power over them;[63]

---

62. Joseph Smith, Jr., *The Book of Mormon* (Palmyra: Grandin, New York, 1830), page 33, compare to *The Book of Mormon* (Salt Lake City: Church of Jesus Christ of Latter-day Saints, 1981), 1 Nephi 14:9-11, pages 28-29.

63. *Ibid.*, page 30, compare to *The Book of Mormon* (Salt Lake City: Church of Jesus Christ of Latter-day Saints, 1981), 1Nephi 13:26-29, page 25.

Like a jazz musician riffing on a musical theme, Joseph took the Bible and began to adapt and change it to fit a doctrine consistent with the emerging and evolving Mormon religion. To *The Book of Genesis* he added a verse in which Joseph of Egypt prophesizes the future Joseph Smith, "Thus saith the Lord God of my fathers unto me. A choice seer will I raise up out of the fruit of thy loins...and his name shall be called Joseph, and it shall be after the name of his father."[64]

Without any physical text as a reference he dictated changes, and restored lost books and parts of the Bible. As a prophet of God, Joseph could receive, by revelation, the exact text as it had been prior to corruption. Upon completion, Joseph's correct translation included 3,410 verse changes, or verse additions, to *The King James Version of the Bible.*

Since its publication after Joseph's death in 1844, this translation has become known as *"The Inspired Version of the Bible"* and also as *"The Joseph Smith Translation of the Bible."* According to Mormon doctrine, the corrected Bible itself stands witness to its previous corruption and Joseph's revelations prove this to be true. According to Joseph, "I believe the Bible as read when it came from the pen of the original writers. Ignorant translators, careless transcribers, or designing and corrupt priests have committed many errors."[65]

In addition to his restoration of the corrupted text of the Bible, Joseph added two entire "lost" books. In 1830, Joseph received *The Book of Moses* by direct revelation, without benefit of plates, parchment, or any physical reference. In 1835, Joseph procured possession of several Egyptian papyri from a traveling showman. Joseph had determined, by revelation, that the papyrus texts contained the writing of Abraham, in ancient Egyptian hieroglyphics, by Abraham's own hand. Using his inspired translating powers again, Joseph wrote *The Book of Abraham.* At the time, hieroglyphics were considered indecipherable. Since then, scholars have learned to read hieroglyphics, and modern Egyptologists protest that the papyrus are standard Egyptian funeral documents for a deceased priest. Like *The Book of Mormon, The Book of Abraham* was, and still is, highly controversial for its establishment of new theology derived from questionable sources. Both *The Book of Moses* and *The Book of Abraham* expand on material from the Bible's Genesis chapters, and both are contained in the standard volume of Mormon scripture, *The Pearl of Great Price.*

Biblical scholars outside of Mormon culture broadly reject the authenticity of *The Joseph Smith Translation of the Bible, The Book of Moses,* and *The Book of Abraham.*

---

64. Joseph Smith, Jr., *Joseph Smith's 'New Translation' of the Bible,* Genesis Chapter 50, (Independence, Missouri: Herald Publishing House. 1970), pages 114-115.

65. Joseph Smith, Jr., *Teachings of the Prophet Joseph Smith,* Compiled by Joseph Fielding Smith, (Salt Lake City: Deseret Book Co., 1959), page 327.

Within the Mormon Church these same additions and changes to the Bible are perceived as the "correct" word of God as translated and revealed through the prophet Joseph. Footnotes, references, and appendices in the official Mormon Church edition of *The King James Bible* incorporate and merge these documents as a cohesive whole. The Mormon Church's eighth article of faith says, "We believe the Bible to be the word of God as far as it is translated correctly,"[66] and the synthesis of Joseph's additions and changes are considered the "correct translation." From their point of view all other versions of the Bible and religions that use them are considered incorrect.

Between 1830 and 1844, no single thing has more profoundly affected Joseph's eventual demise, or the fracturing of his church, than his shifting positions on monogamy and polygamy. On February 9, 1831, four years after marrying Emma, Joseph received a revelation from God that insisted on monogamy. "Thou shalt love thy wife with all they heart, and shalt cleave unto her and none else...Thou shalt not commit adultery; and he that committeth adultery, and repenteth not shall be cast out." [67]

By 1835, however, the charismatic prophet found that he both attracted the attention of beautiful women and was in turn attracted to them. Not wanting to be an adulterer, he reflected on the ancient practices of plural marriages witnessed in the Old Testament, and according to correspondences from the period began to discuss it with members of his inner circle. Between 1835 and 1843, Joseph married dozens of women in secret ceremonies reenacting in his own life the marital practices of the ancient patriarchs Abraham, Isaac, and Jacob. On July 12, 1843, God formalized this practice for Joseph in the form of a revelation that opened the doors for polygamy:

> Verily, thus saith the Lord unto you my servant Joseph, that inasmuch as you have inquired of my hand to know and understand wherein I, the Lord, justified my servants Abraham, Isaac, and Jacob, as also Moses, David and Solomon, my servants, as touching the principle and doctrine of their having many wives and concubines...Therefore, prepare thy heart to receive and obey the instructions which I am about to give unto you...For behold, I reveal unto you a new and everlasting covenant... if any man espouse a virgin, and desire to espouse another, and the first give her consent, and if he espouse the second, and they are virgins, and have vowed to no other man, then he is justified; he cannot commit adultery for they are given unto him;

---

66. Joseph Smith, Jr., *The Pearl of Great Price*, (Salt Lake City: Church of Jesus Christ of Latter-day Saints, 1967), page 59.

67. Joseph Smith, Jr., *Doctrine and Covenants*, Section 42 (Salt Lake City: Church of Jesus Christ of Latter-day Saints, 1968), page 61-62.

for he cannot commit adultery with that that belongeth unto him and to no one else. And if he have ten virgins given unto him by this law, he cannot commit adultery for they belong to him, and they are given unto him; therefore he is justified.[68]

Unlike most of Joseph's revelations, this one was not publicly revealed to the members of the Mormon Church. Instead it sat smoldering beneath the covers, always threatening to set the bedroom on fire. Whenever smoke appeared Joseph and the trusted advisors with whom he shared the secret managed to keep the flames from being seen. But as the fire grew ever hotter ever larger, it became only a matter of time before this sex scandal would erupt.

DEATH OF THE PROPHET, 1844

By 1844, Joseph's church had moved from New York to Ohio to Missouri to Nauvoo, Illinois. From 30 members it grew to an estimated 30,000. An aggressive missionary program in England, started in 1837, brought thousands of converts each year from the working class poor who had been displaced by Europe's burgeoning Industrial Revolution. The opportunity to leave the misery and destitution behind for a promised Kingdom of God on Earth was very attractive. From these people Joseph organized the Nauvoo Legion, a standing army of 5,000 soldiers of which he was the commander in chief as Lieutenant-General.

Between 1830 and 1844, in addition to being a prophet of God, Joseph wore, sometimes simultaneously, the mantles of: candidate for President of the United States, secret husband of nearly fifty wives (aged 14 to 54), real estate speculator, faith healer, political schemer, merchant of the leading Nauvoo store, lieutenant general of his own army, mayor of Nauvoo, jailed prisoner accused of crimes, defendant in criminal trials, banker, failed banker of a collapsed bank, judge of the Nauvoo municipal court, building contractor, temple architect, hotel keeper, real estate developer, deed recorder, translator of ancient languages, steamboat owner, trustee of all his church's finances, and spiritual leader of tens of thousands. Joseph even went as far as to assign himself the officious title of King, Priest, and Ruler of Israel on Earth. At the time of his death, efforts were being made by the state of Missouri to extradite Joseph for trial as an accessory to an attempted murder of one of his political adversaries, Governor Lilburn Boggs.

The end of Joseph's life came suddenly and violently. The trouble began the year before, when a Mormon Church insider of high standing, William Law,

---

68. *Ibid.*, pages 239-245.

watched disapprovingly as Joseph married one woman after another and took them as multiple wives while publicly denying it. At least 11 of Joseph's wives were teenage girls, as young as 14 years of age. Many of these consummated marriages would have been grounds for the criminal charge of statutory rape if such laws had been applicable at the time.

When Joseph attempted to include Law's wife Jane in his circle of wives, Law threatened public exposure unless Joseph confessed and repented. Law took his time to act, following Joseph's unconditional refusal of his demands, preferring to find a way of reforming the church rather than destroying it. On June 7, 1844 Law followed through on his threats in the first and only issue of a newspaper he founded called the *Nauvoo Expositor*. In a straightforward and unsensational style Law told the story of a young English convert being seduced into marrying Joseph. He included signed affidavits attesting to the practice of Joseph's polygamy and widespread polygamy within the upper levels of the church hierarchy.

He went on to describe questionable church finances, real estate speculation, and the abuse of authority. "We do not believe that God ever raised up a Prophet to christianize a world by political schemes and intrigue...We will not acknowledge any man as king and law-giver,"[69] the *Expositor* said. Until this point, only Joseph's inner circle knew that he was privately doing exactly what he was publicly denying. Most of his followers graciously believed that the rumors of his multiple wives were lies spread by his enemies, but now the dam had burst wide open and Joseph was in a real crisis. His response was to burn and destroy the *Expositor's* press, and that was the flame that set the tinder ablaze. In her biography of Joseph, Fawn Brodie wrote:

> When Joseph Smith read the expose of his polygamy in the pages of the *Nauvoo Expositor*, published by a man whom he had respected and revered, he must have felt a shattering of his own grandiose and wholly unrealistic image of himself and his role in history. He reacted with rage and destroyed the press, though he was not normally a destructive man. He was a builder of temples and cities and kingdoms — most of all, a constructor of continuing fantasy. William Law attacked this fantasy with his simple, almost gentle exposition of reality. A man called Law had called him to account, as his parents never had, and he reacted with lawlessness. It was all extraordinarily symbolic.[70]

---

69. *Nauvoo Expositor*, (June 7, 1844).
70. Fawn M. Brodie, *No Man Knows My History*. (New York: Vintage Books, 1995), page 421.

As if they had been waiting for the opportunity, Joseph's enemies charged. Warrants for his arrest were issued, which Joseph eluded by crossing the flood-swollen Mississippi under the cover of darkness. He soon changed his mind, and returned. On June 24, 1844, Joseph and his brother Hiram turned themselves in, and were jailed in Carthage, Illinois, where guns were smuggled in to them by friends. After dark, on June 27, a hundred angry men with blackened faces stormed the Carthage jail and, in a two-sided gunfight with the Smith brothers, shot both Joseph and Hiram to death. Joseph died at the age of 38.

While the act that ignited the end was the destruction of Law's printing press, the underlying cause that fed the mob was something different. Rather than spreading out across the land and fitting into communities, as other sects did, the Mormons gathered. Wherever they congregated, their numbers were so great that they threatened the existing political and power structure by acting as an overwhelming group under the divine guidance of a prophet with a huge army. As converts flooded in and Joseph's power grew, so too did the local resentment, fear, and anger. In addition, the Mormon Church's presumptuous position as being the only true church of Jesus Christ was a grave affront and great insult to other Christians. The early Mormons were abused, terribly and unfairly, but theirs was not a simple case of one-sided antagonism.

The history of the early Mormon Church and of Joseph is a rich, ambiguous history, polarized and divergent, with many shades of gray. It ranges the full spectrum between the sanitized, official Mormon Church version, and other versions supported by actual historical archives and verifiable facts.

The broadly respected religious scholar Jan Shipps expressed it like this:

> In the sacred history, the divine is an actor in the drama, a direct partic-ipant, not a supernatural presence. Because the divine is a *natural* part of the process, sacred history inevitably takes on a mythic character, which makes it "truer than true," if by truth one means that which is established and verified according to the canons of historical scholarship. Sacred his-tory has other characteristics as well. It is stripped down — in artistic terms, stylized — so that the story is told in blacks and whites, with no grays. The persecuted and persecutors, the people of God and the people of Satan, good and evil are locked in mortal combat in which compromise is out of the question. All the ambiguity and complexity of human experience is shorn away. Moreover, the context is left ambiguous enough to keep the narrative from being either time bound or culture bound; it functions as scripture...Mormonism's sacred history, like all sacred history, is a part of the mythological dimension of this religion. By its very nature it can only be *retold* and defended; not reinvestigated, researched.[71]

In a cautionary speech to Mormon Church educators, the Mormon authority and Apostle Boyd K. Packer expressed the same subject like this:

> There is a temptation for the writer or the teacher of Church history to want to tell everything, whether it is worthy or faith promoting or not. Some things that are true are not very useful...
>
> In an effort to be objective, impartial, and scholarly a writer or a teacher may unwittingly be giving equal time to the adversary. In the Church we are not neutral. We are one-sided. There is a war going on and we are engaged in it. It is the war between good and evil, and we are belligerents defending the good. . .
>
> There is much in the scriptures and in our Church literature to convince us that we are at war with the adversary. We are not obliged as a church, nor are we as members obliged, to accommodate the enemy in this battle.[72]

The Mormon Church constantly revises its past so that its officially designated origins conform more comfortably to its current presentation of itself. It struggles to answer, defend, and address fundamental questions such as, "Who was the rightful successor to Joseph, given all that he built? Which portions of Mormon history should be told? Which portions should not be told? Which portions should be denied? And which portions should be hidden?"

After Joseph's murder the church splintered, as competing presumptive heirs fought with each other to assume the role of living prophet, seer, and revelator of the Mormon Church. Joseph left no clear successor, and worse, he had suggested several conflicting possibilities. While the majority of his followers still did not know about the magnitude of the practice of polygamy among the church leadership, the aspirants for his position knew very well what was going on and what was at stake. The lines of battle were drawn between those who supported polygamy and those who sought to end it. When Joseph's younger brother Samuel Smith was on the verge of uniting the church behind him and putting an end to polygamy, he died suddenly under highly suspicious circumstances. Poison was suspected.

With Samuel Smith dead, the strongest proponent for polygamy, Brigham Young, rose to the occasion and persuaded most of the latter day saints to follow him. The church promptly split into four factions, each of which went their

---

71. Jan Shipps, "The Mormon Past: Revealed or Revisited?" *Sunstone* 6 (November- December 1981): 57.

72. Boyd K. Packer, from a talk given at the Fifth Annual Church Educational System Religious Educators' Symposium, 22 August, 1981, Brigham Young University, Provo, Utah, Brigham Young University Studies, Summer 1981.

different ways. Emma Smith and the surviving remnants of Joseph's family joined with one of the minority factions and went on to help found The Reorganized Church of Jesus Christ of Latter-day Saints some years later. This sect, now named the Community of Christ, is the second largest of the Mormon splinter factions with a membership of 250,000 today.

With the opposition out of the way Brigham Young gathered together the majority of the Mormons and immediately began developing plans to leave the United States and emigrate to Utah, which at that time was part of the Territory of Mexico. It was only after they'd left Illinois and begun their long journey out of the country that Brigham Young shared Joseph's sacred revelation of polygamy with all of his followers. The Mormon Church continued to regard polygamy as a sacred obligation to God until, in the face of massive arrests, prosecutions, and denial of statehood for Utah, the Mormon Prophet Wilford Woodruff declared an end to it on October 6, 1890. But it did not disappear, it merely went underground. For the next twenty years, many Mormon Church leaders continued actively practicing polygamy even while they advised their membership against it.

To this day polygamy continues to be a dividing line between the great majority of Mormons and all of the splinter sects. The majority of Mormons, represented by The Church of Jesus Christ of Latter Saints and The Reorganized Church of Jesus Christ of Latter-day Saints, have renounced polygamy, while the fundamental minority fringe embraces it. These numerous Mormon fundamentalist sects have members in the United States, Canada, and Mexico that are estimated at around 100,000. All of these sects consider themselves to be the true successors to Joseph, follow the doctrines laid out in *The Book of Mormon*, and believe their leaders to be the true living prophet. They consider the multi-million-member Mormon Church to be a horrendous fraud and a grievous betrayal of Joseph's and Brigham Young's legacy. The agenda of most Mormon splinter groups is to restore the true church of Jesus Christ, put Joseph's church back in order, and to bring fulfillment of one of his most famous revelations:

> And it shall come to pass that I, the Lord God, will send one mighty and strong, holding the sceptre of power in his hand, clothed with light for a covering, whose mouth shall utter words, eternal words; while his bowels shall be a fountain of truth, to set in order the house of God; and to arrange by lot the inheritance of the saints, whose names are found, and the names of their fathers, and of their children, enrolled in the book of the law of God.[73]

---

73. Joseph Smith, Jr., *Doctrine and Covenants*, Section 85 (Salt Lake City: Church of Jesus Christ of Latter-day Saints, 1968), page 143.

Many have stepped forward to claim their role as the "one mighty and strong," and undoubtedly many more will follow.

ANALYSIS OF *THE BOOK OF MORMON*

Ever since its publication, *The Book of Mormon's* authenticity as an ancient text has been challenged by non-Mormons and defended by Mormons. Few people outside of the Mormon faith, who undertake a serious analysis of its origins based on history and facts, conclude that it is what it represents itself to be. Conversely, few people inside the Mormon faith ever look at the history and facts objectively. They conclude, based on prayer and faith, that it is a truthful representation of an ancient people of America. The Mormon Church is complicit in this non-critical evaluation of the accuracy of *The Book of Mormon*. The Church obscures its past, intimidates and excommunicates members who talk openly about the book's problems, and promotes the use of prayer and faith rather than modern conventions of fact testing to determine the book's authenticity. Within the past sixty years, however, the biggest challenges to *The Book of Mormon* have come from within the Mormon Church.

In 1945, Fawn McKay Brodie, the niece of the church's then President and Prophet David O. McKay, wrote a biography of Joseph Smith titled, *No Man Knows My History.* With painstaking care and elegant prose she laid bare many of the buried details of *The Book of Mormon's* 19th-century origins. Brodie was promptly excommunicated from the Mormon Church in a charge led by her uncle, the Mormon prophet. Mormons were told not to touch the book or give Brodie's heresy a moment's thought, but with this single publication the dam began to crumble and the reservoir of faith behind it trembled. *No Man Knows My History* has never gone out of print and remains a popular book to this day. Brodie went on to become a world famous biographer. She wrote the groundbreaking biography of Thomas Jefferson that first exposed Jefferson's intimate relationship with Sally Hemmings, his slave. She also wrote biographies of Richard Nixon, the 19th-century explorer Sir Richard Francis Burton, and the southern politician Thaddeus Stevens.

In 1987, Mormon historian and Brigham Young University professor D. Michael Quinn wrote an exhaustive and authoritatively researched book entitled, *Early Mormonism and the Magic World View,* which detailed the occult origins of *The Book of Mormon* and Joseph Smith's fascination with magic. It wasn't what the church wanted said. Quinn's descriptions of Joseph didn't match the modern, sanitized, official version of the prophet. He lost his job, and in 1993 was excommunicated for heresy. Quinn's book emerged again in 1998 as a revised and enlarged edition that continues to represent well-documented proof about Mormonism's obscure past.

In 1992 Wallace B. Smith, a former president of the Reorganized Church of Latter-Day Saints and direct descendant of Joseph, wrote, "One thing is clear. The genie is out of the bottle and it cannot be put back. Facts uncovered and the questions raised by the new Mormon historians will not go away. They will have to be dealt with if we are to maintain a position of honesty and integrity in our dealings with our own members as well as our friends in the larger religious community."[74]

In 2002, Mormon anthropology professor Thomas W. Murphy startled the Mormon Church with a paper entitled *Lamanite Genesis, Genealogy, and Genetics*. In what has been called a "Galileo event," this paper brought forward to a broad public audience conclusive evidence that the genetic ancestry of the Native Americans is derivative from northeastern Asians, and not from Middle Eastern emigrants to the Americas as represented in *The Book of Mormon*. The information is discussed in detail in a subsequent chapter of this book. When proceedings for his excommunication were initiated, public outcry from within the Mormon Church was so strong that the effort was withdrawn.

Also in 2002, Grant H. Palmer, a fourth generation Mormon, 34-year Mormon Church career educator, and director of Mormon studies, published a book entitled, *An Insider's View of Mormon Origins*. With unflinching honesty he confronted and examined the problems with the Mormon Church's present representation of its past:

> The following is a plausible scenario for how the Book of Mormon came to be. After Joseph's marriage to Emma Hale in January 1827, he promised his father-in-law that he would give up treasure hunting. Influenced by the revival fervor and by his mother's piety, his mind began to fill with impressions that blended his familiarity with Indian lore and his conviction of biblical promises. Perhaps the outline of a book began to form sometime before Martin Harris became his scribe in 1828. He had already experimented with seer stones, and perhaps he thought that through greater faith and concentration, God would open to his mind a vision of the secrets of the artifacts being discovered in upstate New York. The dictation proceeded, and after Martin lost the first 116 pages of transcription in mid-1828, this may have been fortuitous. An apprenticeship had been served, and the vision that was unfolding in Joseph's mind may have become more

74. Wallace B. Smith, 'Exiles in Time,' *Saints Herald* 139 (April 1992): 8.

clear. The dictation probably progressed haltingly at first, perhaps as a kind of stream-of-consciousness narrative. Before Oliver Cowdery became his new scribe in April 1829, the prophet had had nine months to ponder the details of the plots and subplots and to flesh out the time line. Given his familiarity with the Bible and with American antiquities, it would have become progressively easier for him to put form to the vision. He dictated the final manuscript in about ninety days. Over the next eight months, before the book was published in March 1830, he had the opportunity to make textual refinements. He thus had three years to develop, write, and refine the book — six years from the time he told his family about the project...[75]

...There is a lingering distrust of anything [within the Mormon culture] that hasn't come directly from, or with an endorsement by, the church leadership. Some of this research has been conducted by critics of the church. Some of it contains distortions and is unreliable. But much of what even the critics have written is backed by solid investigation and sound reasoning and should not be dismissed. Your friends don't always tell you what you need to hear...Over the years, scholars of all stripes have made contributions and counterbalanced each other by critiquing each other's works. We now have a body of authentic, reliable documents and a near-consensus on many of the details. From this base, the overall picture of Mormon origins begins to unfold. This picture is much different from what we were taught in Sunday school. But de-mythologized — placed in its original time and place, amid all the twists and turns that exist in the real world — it rings true...

Faith has to do with the unknown, not about what can be proven or can be shown to be reasonably based on the evidence. I have always thought that an unwillingness to submit one's beliefs to rigorous scrutiny is a manifestation of weakness of faith. Otherwise, everything becomes a matter of orthodoxy rather than truth...

I, along with my colleagues, and drawing from years of research, find the evidence employed to support many traditional claims about the church to be either nonexistent or problematic. In other words, it didn't all happen the way we've been told. For the sake of accuracy and honesty, I think we need to address and ultimately correct this disparity between historical narratives and the inspirational stories that we are told in church.[76]

Palmer goes on to build a convincing case that *The Book of Mormon* is an amalgamation and mosaic composition, drawn from the Bible and from the Evangelical Protestantism that was sweeping America during the Second Great

---

75. Grant Palmer, *An Insider's View of Mormon Origins*, (Salt Lake City: Signature Books, 2002), pages 66-67.

76. *Ibid.*, page viii-xii.

Awakening. He cites instance after instance in which the themes, motifs, style, form, patterns, and textual language of *The Book of Mormon* characters are drawn directly from counterparts in the Bible, or from the fiery sermons of 19th-century evangelical circuit preachers. As an example he cites the striking similarity of the lives, messages, and language of the Old Testament Moses leading his people out of Egypt with that of Nephi leading his people to America, and of the New Testament Apostle Paul with that of Nephite prophet-preacher Alma. He draws attention to the fact that in *The Book of Mormon's* Third Book of Nephi, the portion which covers the life span of Jesus Christ, 246 of the 490 verses are recognizable quotations or phrases from the *King James Version of the Bible.* "Even more significantly," he says, "there are no original motifs in 3 Nephi that are not already found in the Gospels."[77] While weaving together a story from disparate verses of the Bible is not an easy thing to do, it seems more likely that such a composition came from more modern origins than from ancient Americans who recorded it for posterity.

"It is reasonable to conclude that Joseph knew the Bible text intimately and used it extensively. LDS members have been slow to recognize this, while critics have recognized it from the beginning."[78] When Palmer lays out passages of *The Book of Mormon* alongside their correlating passages from the Bible, it is difficult to distinguish much difference in them aside from the knowledge that they've both been derived from substantially different contexts and allegedly presented by entirely different people.

On June 7, 1826, a Methodist revival camp was held in Palmyra that attracted 10,000 people from within 100 miles of the site. In the tradition of these camps, families arrived and pitched their tents in a semicircular layout enclosing the consecrated ground of the "chapel field," and faced a raised platform on which the preachers spoke. The emphasis of these revivals was emotionally charged preaching, mass ecstatic conversion, forgiveness of sins, warnings against the power of the devil, and demonstrations of the power of God through crying out, falling down, weakness, trembling, and other physical signs.

It is unlikely that Joseph did not attend such a spectacle so close to home. It is also quite likely that revival camps such as this one were the source of his consternation about which church was the true church of God. This particular event occurred when Joseph was 20 years old, only a couple of months after his conviction for treasure seeking, and only 15 months before he announced his discovery of *The Book of Mormon's* golden plates. While later in his life Joseph

---

77. *Ibid.*, page 82.
78. *Ibid.*, pages 84-85.

placed the time of his first vision some four to six years earlier, the context in which his first vision occurs resembles this period.

On a case-by-case, comparative basis, Palmer also presents the similarities between *The Book of Mormon's* phrasing, language, and themes to the sermons of the well known evangelist preachers from the early 19th century. The best example is King Benjamin's speech to the Nephite people in *The Book of Mormon's* Book of Mosiah. The people of the land gather around, pitch their tents with doors opened to King Benjamin's platform, hear his evangelical sermon, and ultimately join together in a mass conversion. In other examples the Nephite preachers Abinadi, Alma, Ammon, and Amulek also demonstrate this unmistakable evangelical style. Palmer says:

> The modern reader is unaware that he or she is reading revival literature in the Book of Mormon because it recasts and gives it a different setting. The advantage is that it removes the stigma often attached to evangelical meetings but allows the religious message to work upon readers' minds and emotions, bringing them to repentance and Christ....The biblical and revival elements also help us understand how Joseph could dictate the Book of Mormon in such a short period of time.
>
> Along with the preaching style and impact of the early nineteenth-century circuit preachers, theology in *The Book of Mormon* is also reminiscent of evangelical teachings and doctrines of the day.[79]

Observational Details about The Book of Mormon

The first edition of *The Book of Mormon* was 588 pages long, containing 275,000 words.

The five words "and it came to pass" are repeated 1,353 times, comprising a total of 6,675 words, and represent about 2.5% of the content of *The Book of Mormon.*

Much of *The Book of Mormon* is drawn straight from the Bible. It contains 21 chapters of Isaiah and 2 chapters of Malachi from the Old Testament. It includes 3 chapters of Matthew from the New Testament in which Jesus Christ delivers the Sermon on the Mount — in America. These inclusions account for about 10% of its content. In addition to these wholesale inclusions, close to half of *The Book of Mormon* is identifiably based on motifs, composites, phrasings, language, and direct quotations from the Bible put into the context of its story and characters.

---

79. *Ibid.,* page 118.

There are 350 different names mentioned in *The Book of Mormon*. 100 of those names are found in the Bible, and 100 more are Bible names with minor spelling changes.

Only 5 of the 249 named people in *The Book of Mormon* are female. With only one exception, no wife, mother, sister, or daughter is identified by name.

There are magical stones to seal written records, magical stones to translate written records, magical stones to light the insides of fully enclosed transoceanic ships, and a magical compass to point the way and convey God's words.

Multiple sets of ancient records inscribed on metal plates are mentioned and described within *The Book of Mormon*.

Many anachronisms are mentioned in *The Book of Mormon* for which there is no evidence in pre-Columbian America. These include the wheel, sophisticated steel metallurgy, wheat, barley, horse-drawn chariots, and other domesticated animals such as pigs, cows, oxen, goats, sheep, chickens, and even elephants.

ORIGIN OF THE NATIVE AMERICANS: A 19TH-CENTURY WORLD VIEW

The current published version of *The Book of Mormon* (1981) is subtitled *Another Testament of Jesus Christ*. The basis of this subtitle is the premise that after his resurrection in Jerusalem, Jesus Christ visited ancient America to deliver his true gospel and establish his church. *The Book of Mormon* could alternately have been subtitled, *Another Version of the Origin of the Native Americans*, since it identifies them as descendants of Jewish emigrants from biblical Jerusalem and describes in lengthy detail how the descendants of these emigrants came to populate the Western Hemisphere. In fact, this explanation of the Native Americans' ancestry is the primary substance of *The Book of Mormon's* story line.

When Christopher Columbus arrived in America in 1492, he assumed that he'd circumnavigated the earth and arrived in India. He therefore called the native people he found, "Indians." Later, 15th-century Europeans realized that a previously unknown continent had been discovered. A mystery then arose that continued well into the 20th century: where had the Native Americans come from? Had God, in his wisdom, independently created another race of humans to populate the American continents? Had the Native Americans migrated to that hemisphere from somewhere else? If so, from where, and when? These were subjects of hot debate in 19th-century European and American intellectual circles during Joseph's lifetime. To some extent, that debate continues even today, into the 21st century.

Scientific evidence shows that Native Americans are descendants of ancient Mongolians, who migrated to the Americas via a land bridge during the most recent Ice Age (10,000 to 20,000 years ago). Mormons are a significant and growing group of people who disagree with this view. Their explanation of the origin of Native Americans is presented in *The Book of Mormon* as the literal word of God.

The foundation of the Mormon position is based on a 19th-century explanation of the world, and of the universe. To understand this position it is helpful to look at the world through the eyes of Joseph and his contemporaries in the 1820s, when the golden plates were discovered.

In 1654, a preeminent theologian and scholar, the Anglican Archbishop James Ussher, published a definitive book titled *Annals of the World*. In it he revealed the time, date and year of the beginning of the Universe as well as the dates of other famous biblical occurrences. Ussher, like virtually all Europeans of his time, believed the Bible was the literal word of God. Working with the oldest available manuscripts, and counting back generations, years, and days through Moses, Noah's Flood, Adam and Eve, Ussher determined that God had created the Universe at 9:00 AM on October 23, 4004 BC. For the next two hundred years this was largely unquestioned as fact in European and American Christian cultures.

Eighty years after Ussher's pronouncement, the Bible was translated into the English language for the first time. The translation was ordered and authorized by England's King James, which is why it is known as *The King James Version of the Bible*. A copy of Ussher's dating was printed just inside the cover of the newly published edition. This timeline continued to be included in all printed *King James Version Bibles* into the 1850s. Until then, the King James Version was the only English language translation of the Bible.

In the 1820s, there were no publicly funded schools in America. Wealthy Americans' children were tutored, but the majority of children were either educated at home by their parents or not educated at all. Parents who home-schooled their children passed along what they knew. When the subject of reading arose, the lessons typically centered around reading and studying the most common English language text: *The King James Version of the Bible*. This was the case in Joseph's home throughout his childhood. There were no world maps on the walls and globes of the earth on the shelf.

In the 1820s, people knew that the earth orbited around the sun but they did not comprehend the enormous size of the sun, or the great distance to it. They did not know that the sun was an enormous thermonuclear furnace that released its energy by fusing hydrogen atoms together, or that stars were distant versions of the sun within a vast galaxy, dwarfed within a vast, galaxy-filled, and ancient universe. Geologists in this period were just beginning the controversial argument that the earth was profoundly more than 6,000 years old.

Charles Darwin was born in 1809, just four years after Joseph. When *The Book of Mormon* was published, Darwin was 21 years old and was contemplating a career as a country parson. He had not yet been invited to join the team on "The Beagle," as a naturalist, on the now famous nautical surveying journey that awakened his curiosity in evolution. His revolutionary book *The Origin of Species* wasn't published until 1859, fifteen years after Joseph's death. The theory that all biologic life, including human life, had evolved from ancient, common ancestors over immense spans of time was unknown. It took another hundred years after Darwin to unravel the role of the DNA molecule in establishing the size, shape, and physiology of individual biologic life forms.

Americans in the 1820s believed that heaven and earth were about 6,000 years old, and created by God. They believed that God had designed and created all plants and animals, that people were direct descendants of Adam and Eve, and that man had been created by God in his own image. During this period, very nearly all Americans of European heritage were descended through the Protestant Christian tradition. There were no alternative religious beliefs except for the newly arriving, and much disliked, Irish Catholics who swarmed to New York to build the Erie Canal. But even the Catholics subscribed to the same dating of literal biblical events.

In contrast, most scientifically educated, 21st-century people believe the universe has its origins in an event called the Big Bang some 13 billion years ago. They believe the earth was formed some 4 billion years ago of coalesced matter from exploded stars. Scientists further believe that all life on Earth, including human life, has evolved from ancestral single cell organisms over the past 3.5 billion years, and that the basis for all biological life are the blueprint building plans contained in DNA molecules within all living cells.

Joseph was a product of commonly shared early 19th-century knowledge and ignorance, just as we are a product of commonly shared early 21st-century knowledge and ignorance. We know more about the world and the universe than cultures that have preceded us, but many mysteries still remain.

In 1823, the origin of the Native Americans was a compelling mystery. Within European and American intellectual circles, there were many popular and competing theories concerning the pre-Columbian population of the western hemisphere. Some argued that God had independently created human life in both of earth's hemispheres. Others argued that the ancestral Native Americans had migrated here from a broad spectrum of prior homelands, including: the mythical continent of Atlantis, the British Isles, Iceland, Rome, Israel, Egypt, Carthage, and China. These migrants were presumed to have arrived either by walking across the sunken continent of Atlantis, by sailing across the oceans to America, or by crossing over a theoretical land or ice bridge between Asia and Alaska. Ideas were abundant and strongly held, while hard evidence was scarce and was frequently dismissed or incorrectly interpreted.

Migration from Asia seemed farfetched to early 19th-century Americans, who had meager knowledge of, or familiarity with, Chinese culture and the geographical relationship of Asia to Alaska. Without easily accessible maps or globes, they weren't aware that North America was visible from Siberia across a narrow and shallow strait. The area west of the Mississippi River was largely an unknown wilderness frontier that Europeans were just beginning to explore. The American coastline of the Pacific Ocean, and China beyond that, lay far, far away. The threatening Native Americans they knew and feared didn't look at all like the stereotypical Chinese: small, yellow-skinned, civilized people wearing finely-tailored silks. Nineteenth-century Americans naturally looked to the known world of Europe, North Africa, and the Middle East for the ancestral homelands of the Native Americans.

The most popular of these Old World homeland theories, in America and Europe, described the Native Americans as descendants of the Lost Tribes of Israel. The 12 Tribes of Israel are the fabled familial descendants of the Old Testament patriarch Jacob's 12 sons. The descendants of the Twelve Tribes are also known as the House of Israel. The most well-known of the twelve brothers was the celebrated son Joseph, who was sold into bondage by his brothers, became an adviser to the Pharaoh of Egypt, and ultimately became the protector of all his family. The Jewish people, or Hebrews, are the descendants of two of the twelve brothers, Judah and Joseph of Egypt. The Nephites and the Lamanites from *The Book of Mormon* are also identified as descendants of Joseph of Egypt. The descendants of the other ten brothers are referred to as the Lost Tribes of Israel.

For thousands of years, myths and legends have been told of Israel's lost tribes who separated, forgot their origins, and became the ancestors of other peoples. Familiarity with these legends fed the dominant 19th-century theory that the Native Americans were a lost tribe of Israel who had somehow gotten to America. Fanciful correlations between the ancient Hebrews and the Native Americans were drawn from festivals and customs, similar words and ceremonies, as well as the obvious arrangement of the peoples into tribes. Observers also pointed to similarities between the Native Americans' Great Spirit and the Hebrew God Yahweh. A 19th-century Native American historian named Josiah Priest wrote in his 1833 book, *American Antiquities*, "The opinion that the American Indians are descendants of the Lost Ten Tribes is now a popular one and generally believed."[80]

A highly visible and popular proponent of this theory was a Vermont pastor named Ethan Smith (no known relation to Joseph Smith, Jr.). In 1823, four years before Joseph's discovery of the golden plates, Pastor Smith wrote a well received and broadly distributed book called *View of the Hebrews*, which purported to document and prove the ancestry of the Native Americans as a lost tribe of Israel. *View of the Hebrews* was successful enough that it went into several printings between 1823 and 1825, and would have been easily available in Palmyra, New York. In fact, in 1826 Pastor Smith was in Palmyra while traveling and promoting his book. Back in Vermont, Pastor Smith was also the family minister for Joseph's primary scribe, Oliver Cowdery.

Given Joseph's lifelong infatuation with American Indian lore, it seems quite likely that Joseph heard of Pastor Smith's theories, and probably even read the book. Oliver Cowdery would have certainly seen a similarity and mentioned Pastor Smith to Joseph. In *View of the Hebrews*, Pastor Smith said:

> Israel brought into this new continent a considerable degree of civiliza-tion; and the better part of them long laboured to maintain it. But others fell into the hunting and consequently savage state; whose barbarous hordes invaded their more civilized brethren, and eventually annihilated most of them, and all in the northern regions![81]

Pastor Smith and Joseph were among a small host of writers who speculated on the origin of the Native Americans, but no two others had so many similarities. Both Smiths mention the destruction of Jerusalem as an impetus to emigration. Both books are deeply infused with prophecies of the Old Testament prophet Isaiah. Both books projected the mission of gathering the Native Americans into the Christian flock in the latter days before the millennium. Pastor Smith saw and described copper breast plates with white horn buttons taken from Native American mounds that he specifically said resembled the "Urim and Thumim" of the ancient Hebrews. Almost as if he too were making prophecies, Pastor Smith seemed to predict the discovery of the golden plates when he wrote, "If the Indians are of the tribes of Israel, some decisive evidence of the fact will ere long be exhibited."[82]

---

80. Josiah Priest, *American Antiquities, 1833,* referenced in Fawn Brodie's *No Man Knows My History.* (New York: Vintage Books, 1995), page 45.

81. Ethan Smith, *View of the Hebrews; or the ten tribes of Israel in America* (Poultney, Vermont, 1825), page 184.

82. *Ibid.,* page 217.

Since moving to New York in 1816 at the age of ten, Joseph had been fascinated with the American Indian mystery. Enormous Native American burial mounds silently co-occupied the Palmyra landscape with settlers such as the Smiths. With bones and ornamental artifacts of copper and silver from the mounds to spur them on, nearly everyone had a theory and knew someone who'd found something significant. As mentioned earlier, many of these sites lay within walking distance from the Smith farm in Manchester.

In her book *Biographical Sketches of Joseph Smith the Prophet and His Progenitors for Many Generations,* Joseph's mother Lucy described his adolescent enthusiasm for the ancient Native American cultures. "During our evening conversations, Joseph would occasionally give us some of the most amusing recitals that could be imagined. He would describe the ancient inhabitants of this continent, their dress, mode of travelling, and the animals upon which they rode; their cities, their buildings, with every particular; their mode of warfare; and also their religious worship. This he would do with as much ease, seemingly, as if he had spent his whole life with them."[83]

Persistent legends grew among the western New York settlers that the mounds and piles of skeletons were the consequence of a monumental battle and massacre that had happened at this particular location in ancient times. According to a popular myth of the time, a civilized race of city builders and farmers had been vanquished by warrior ancestors of the Native Americans. *The Book of Mormon* largely agreed with what most people of that period believed about the origins of the Native Americans, anyhow. What made it distinctive, among other claims, was the tale of the golden plates and the story of Jesus Christ's ancient mission in America.

The Book of Mormon chronicles the transoceanic migration of three peoples from the Middle East to America: the Jaredites in 2200 BC, and the Lehites and Mulekites in 600 BC. The 11,000 mile Jaredite migration would have involved a 5,000 mile land journey across northern Africa followed by a 6,000 mile sea journey across the Atlantic Ocean. The 20,500 mile Lehite migration would have entailed a 1,500 mile land journey across the Arabian Peninsula followed by 19,000 mile sea journey across the Indian and Pacific Oceans. The Lehites would also have needed to thread their way through the archipelago of islands between southeast Asia and New Zealand without accidentally making landfall across this virtual curtain of land between the Indian and Pacific Oceans. No mention is ever made of the Lehites having seen any land during their journey to the

---

83. Lucy Mack Smith, *Biographical Sketches of Joseph Smith the Prophet and His Progenitors for Many Generations by Lucy Smith - Mother of the Prophet,* (Liverpool: Orson Pratt, 1853), page 85.

Western hemisphere. A casual glance at an atlas demonstrates the difficulty of this navigational feat. The exact route of the Mulekite migration is not given.

When the Jaredites arrived the Western hemisphere was unoccupied by humans. By the time the Lehites and Mulekites arrived the Jaredites had been destroyed to the last person, which left a vacant hemisphere for the new arrivals. Only the Jaredites ruins and artifacts remained for discovery by the Lehites.

After the Lehites arrived in America, they broke into two factions. The Nephites and the Lamanites were the followers of Lehi's sons, Nephi and Laman. In general, the followers of Laman were contentious and war-like people. In general, the followers of Nephi were farmers and builders of civilization. When the Nephite and Mulekite descendants discovered each other hundreds of years after their separate arrivals, they merged together as a unified Nephite people.

God became highly displeased with the Lamanites for their murderous and sinful behavior, and physically transformed them from "white, and exceedingly fair and delightsome" people into dark skinned people who would be repellant and "loathsome" to the white Nephites. In *The Second Book of Nephi*, the prophet-scribe Nephi describes this event:

> And behold, the words of the Lord had been fulfilled unto my brethren, which he spake concerning them, that I should be their ruler and their teacher; wherefore, I had been their ruler and their teacher, according to the commandments of the Lord, until the time that they sought to take away my life. Wherefore, the word of the Lord was fulfilled which he spake unto me, saying: That inasmuch as they will not hearken unto thy words, they shall be cut off from his presence. And he had caused the cursing to come upon them, yea, even a sore cursing, because of their iniquity. For behold, they had hardened their hearts against him, that they had become like unto a flint; wherefore, as they were white, and exceeding fair and delightsome, that they might not be enticing unto my people, therefore the Lord God did cause a skin of blackness to come upon them. And thus saith the Lord God, I will cause that they shall be loathsome unto thy people, save they shall repent of their iniquities. And cursed shall be the seed of him that mixeth with their seed: for they shall be cursed even with the same cursing. And the Lord spake it, and it was done.[84]

The Book of Mormon uses the following words to describe the Lamanite people: cursed, dark, loathsome, evil, bloodthirsty, filthy, a scourge, ferocious, abominable, idolatrous, idle, and wild. Here are two sample passages:

---

84. Joseph Smith, Jr., *The Book of Mormon* (Palmyra: Grandin, New York, 1830), page 72-73, compare to *The Book of Mormon* (Salt Lake City: 1981), BOM 2 Nephi 5:19-23, page 66.

I bare record that the people of Nephi did seek diligently to restore the Lamanites unto the true faith in God. But our labors were vain; their hatred was fixed, and they were led by their evil nature, that they became wild, and ferocious, and a blood-thirsty people; full of idolatry, and filthiness; feeding upon beasts of prey; dwelling in tents, and wandering about in the wilderness, with a short skin girded about their loins, and their heads shaven; and their skill was in the bow, and in the cimeter, and the ax.– And many of them did eat nothing save it was raw meat; and they were continu-ally seeking to destroy us.[85]

I beheld, after they had dwindled in unbelief, they became a dark, and loathsome, and a filthy people, full of idleness and all manner of abomina-tions.[86]

After a thousand years of battles and warfare, *The Book of Mormon* explains how the dark skinned Lamanite warriors annihilated all of the civilized white Nephites, and became the ancestors of the Native Americans.

In a passage from *The Book of Mormon*, Mormon described the future state of the Lamanites' descendants, the Native Americans, at the time they would receive the gospel of Jesus Christ from 19th-century Mormons:

...the seed of this people may more fully believe his gospel, which shall go forth unto them from the Gentiles: for this people shall be scattered, and shall become a dark, a filthy, and a loathsome people, beyond the descrip-tion of that which ever hath been amongst us; yea, even that which hath been among the Lamanites; and this because of their unbelief and idolatry.[87]

How Extensive Were the Jaredite and Nephite Civilizations and Where Were They Located?

Although no place, person, or event mentioned in *The Book of Mormon* has ever been verified through archeological evidence, or specifically identified as to location by the Mormon Church, there is information in the book that points to distinctive geographical areas. The Jaredites and the Nephites had similar locations of arrival, sequences of expansion, and demises. Both groups left the Middle East, sailed across the ocean, and landed near "a narrow neck of land"

---

85. *Ibid.*, pages 144-145, compare to *The Book of Mormon* (Salt Lake City: Church of Jesus Christ of Latter-day Saints, 1981), Enos:20, page 137.

86. *Ibid.*, page 28, compare to *The Book of Mormon* (Salt Lake City: Church of Jesus Christ of Latter-day Saints, 1981), 1 Nephi 12:23, page 23.

87. *Ibid.*, page 528, compare to *The Book of Mormon* (Salt Lake City: Church of Jesus Christ of Latter-day Saints, 1981), Mormon 5:15, page 477.

between the sea to the east and the sea to the west. Both groups arrived in a land unoccupied by other inhabitants and developed huge civilizations, and were both completely destroyed to the last person in final, climactic battles that took place on the Hill Cumorah, just outside of present-day Palmyra, New York. Neither group left any artifacts behind that have been verified by contemporary archeologists.

The Jaredites sailed across the Atlantic Ocean from the west coast of Africa and arrived on the east coast of America around 2200 BC. According to *The Book of Mormon*, "they built a great city by the narrow neck of land, by the place where the sea divides the land. And they did preserve the land southward for a wilderness, to get game. And the whole face of the land northward was covered with inhabitants."[88] In the last days of the Jaredite civilization, the prophet Ether wrote of the regrets of his king, "He saw that there had been slain by the sword already nearly two millions of his people, and he began to sorrow in his heart; yea, there had been slain two millions of mighty men, and also their wives and their children."[89] Moroni described the location of the final battle where the Jaredite civilization came to an end, around 550 BC: "And it came to pass that the army of Coriantumr did pitch their tents by the hill Ramah; and it was that same hill where my father Mormon did hide up the records unto the Lord."[90]

The group who would later split into the Nephites and Lamanites, sailed from the east coast of the Arabian Peninsula across the Indian and Pacific Oceans and arrived on the west coast of America around 589 BC. The Nephites' capital city of Zarahemla is described as being near a point where, "it was only the distance of a day and a half's journey for a Nephite...from the east to the west sea; and thus the land of Nephi and the land of Zarahemla were nearly surrounded by water, there being a small neck of land between the land northward and the land southward."[91] This narrow strip of land between the oceans, and near the heart of the Nephite civilization, is also mentioned in six other passages.[92] At one point in the Nephites' story, they discovered the ruins of the Jaredite civilization nearby, which establishes the same geographic proximity for both groups:

---

88. Joseph Smith, Jr., *The Book of Mormon* (Salt Lake City: Church of Jesus Christ of Latter-day Saints, 1981), Ether 10:20-21, page 506.

89. *Ibid.*, Ether 15:2, page 516.

90. *Ibid.*, Ether 15:11, page 516.

91. *Ibid.*, Alma 22:32, page 266.

92. *Ibid.*, Alma 22:27, page 265; Alma 50:34, page 335; Alma 52:9, page 339; Alma 63:5, page 367; Mormon 2:28-29, page 472; & Mormon 3:5, page 473.

...they were lost in the wilderness for the space of many days, yet they were diligent, and found not the land of Zarahemla but returned to this land, having traveled in a land among many waters, having discovered a land which was covered with bones of men, and of beasts, and was also covered with ruins of buildings of every kind, having discovered a land which had been peopled with a people who were as numerous as the hosts of Israel. And for a testimony that the things that they had said are true they have brought twenty-four plates which are filled with engravings, and they are of pure gold.[93]

...Now after Mosiah had finished translating these records, behold, it gave an account of the people who were destroyed, from the time that they were destroyed back to the building of the great tower, at the time the Lord confounded the language of the people and they were scattered abroad upon the face of all the earth, yea, and even from that time back until the creation of Adam.[94]

The only narrow necks of land in the Western Hemisphere that lie between two oceans are found in Central America. Geographers point to two possibilities: the 135-mile-wide Isthmus of Tehuantepec just west of the Yucatan Peninsula in southern Mexico, and the 35-mile-wide Isthmus of Panama about 1,900 miles to the southeast of Tehuantepec. While the Isthmus of Panama more closely satisfies *The Book of Mormon* criteria of being a day and half's journey from one coast to the other, Mormon geographers have unofficially preferred to place the Nephites' narrow neck of land near the Isthmus of Tehuantepec because this is also the location of the vanished Mayan civilization and its numerous ruins.

The existence of the Mayan ruins was common knowledge in the 1820s, through the writing and publication of at least six books that focused on them. One book that was particularly celebrated and received wide distribution was Antonio Del Rio's 1822 *Description of the Ruins of an Ancient City, Discovered near Palenque, in the Kingdom of Guatamala*. Del Rio described palaces and large buildings in ruin, included illustrations of the structures, and plates that showed Mayan writing. The book speculated that the Mayan and Aztec god Quetzalcoatl was actually St. Thomas preaching the gospel to the ancient Americans. In 1824, John Yates and Joseph Moulton cited del Rios in their book, *History of the State of New York*,[95] and connected the Mayan ruins to the mysterious mounds of western New York. Dan Vogel, in his book *Indian Origins and The Book of Mormon*, summarized this aspect of the Yates-Moulton book:

---

93. *Ibid.*, Mosiah 8:8-9, page 163.
94. *Ibid.*, Mosiah 28:17, page 203.
95. Yates, John Van Ness and Joseph White Moulton, *History of the State of New York*. (New York, 1924).

Yates and Moulton trace the ancient and colonial history of New York, discussing in detail the problems and various theories of Indian origins in America. They describe mounds and fortifications in their state and neighboring states, as well as the ruins of an ancient city near Palenque. According to them, these mounds, part of a great chain running down through Mexico and into South America, were built by a separate race of white-skinned people who were destroyed by the Indians. They mention the discovery of hieroglyphic writing and mammoth bones, and include reports that Indians in certain locales possessed the signs and tokens of Freemansonry.[96]

It seems highly unlikely that young Joseph, given his infatuation with Indian lore, would not have been aware of this information. In the early 19th century, Joseph and early Mormons pointed to the Mayan ruins as proof of the historical accuracy of *The Book of Mormon*.

From this narrow neck of land the Nephites spread outwards:

> and the people began to be very numerous, and began to scatter abroad upon the face of the earth, yea, on the north and on the south, on the east and on the west, building large cities and villages in all quarters of the land.[97]

> ...they did multiply and spread, and did go forth from the land southward to the land northward, and did spread insomuch that they began to cover the face of the whole earth, from the sea south to the sea north, from the sea west to the sea east.[98]

> ...there was a large company of men, even to the amount of five thousand and four hundred men, with their wives and their children, departed out of the land of Zarahemla into the land which was northward. And it came to pass that Hagoth, he being an exceedingly curious man, therefore he went forth and built him an exceedingly large ship...and launched it forth into the west sea, by the narrow neck which led into the land northward. And behold, there were many of the Nephites who did enter therein and did sail forth with much provisions, and also many women and children; and they took their course northward...this man built other ships. And the first ship did also return, and many more people did enter into it; and they also took

---

96. Vogel, Dan, *Indian Origins and The Book of Mormon* (Salt Lake City: Signature Books, 1986), page 132.

97. Joseph Smith, Jr., *The Book of Mormon* (Salt Lake City: Church of Jesus Christ of Latter-day Saints, 1981), Mosiah 27:6, page 199.

98. *Ibid.*, Helaman 3:8, page 372.

much provisions, and set out again to the land northward...And it came to pass that one other ship also did sail forth; and whither she did go we know not. And it came to pass that in this year there were many people who went forth into the land northward.[99]

In AD 322, near the end of the Nephite era, Mormon journeyed from the north country to the capital city and saw the extensive breadth of the Nephite civilization along the way. "I, being eleven years old, was carried by my father into the land southward, even to the land of Zarahemla. The whole face of the land had become covered with buildings, and the people were as numerous almost, as it were the sand of the sea."[100]

The South American continent, to the south of the narrow neck of land, is often referred to as the wilderness lands, and the lands of the Lamanites. "And it came to pass that the Nephites had inhabited the land Bountiful, even from the east unto the west sea, and thus the Nephites in their wisdom, with their guards and their armies, had hemmed in the Lamanites on the south, that thereby they should have no more possession on the north, that they might not overrun the land northward."[101] In AD 349, the Lamanites and Nephites made a treaty that divided the Western Hemisphere at the narrow neck of land: "We made a treaty with the Lamanites and the robbers of Gadianton, in which we did get the lands of our inheritance divided. And the Lamanites did give unto us the land northward, yea, even to the narrow passage which led into the land southward. And we did give unto the Lamanites all the land southward."[102] In AD 400, the Lamanites pushed northward to New York State and exterminated the last 230,000 Nephites on the same Hill Cumorah where the Jaredites had destroyed themselves down to the last person standing, 1,000 years earlier.[103] This is also the same hill on which Mormon and Moroni hid the golden plates, and on which Joseph found them 1,400 years later, in 1823, after the angel Moroni appeared to him in a series of visions.

In the 19th century, the origins of the numerous Midwestern archeological mounds and artifacts were a mystery. They did not seem to be connected at all to the local Native Americans that settlers encountered. *The Book of Mormon* suggests Nephite battlefield casualties and earthwork fortifications as possible explanations of these mounds:

---

99. *Ibid.*, Alma 63:4-9, page 367.
100. *Ibid.*, Mormon 1:6-7, page 469.
101. *Ibid.*, Alma 22:33, page 266.
102. *Ibid.*, Mormon 2:28-29, page 472.
103. *Ibid.*, Mormon 6:7-22, page 479.

...dead bodies were heaped up upon the face of the earth, and they were covered with a shallow covering...[104]

...and the bodies of many thousands are laid low in the earth, while the bodies of many thousands are moldering in heaps upon the face of the earth.[105]

...Moroni...caused that his armies should commence...in digging up heaps of earth round about all the cities, throughout all the land which was possessed by the Nephites. And upon the top of these ridges of earth he caused that there should be timbers, yea, works of timbers built up to the height of a man, round about the cities.[106]

And he caused that they should build a breastwork of timbers upon the inner bank of the ditch; and they cast up dirt out of the ditch against the breastwork of timbers; and thus they did cause the Lamanites to labor until they had encircled the city of Bountiful round about with a strong wall of timbers and earth, to an exceeding height.[107]

In the current version of *The Book of Mormon*, the official Mormon Church introduction states, "The record gives an account of two great civilizations. One came from Jerusalem in 600 BC, and afterward separated into two nations, known as the Nephites and the Lamanites. The other came much earlier when the Lord confounded the tongues at the Tower of Babel. This group is known as the Jaredites. After thousands of years, all were destroyed except the Lamanites, and they are the principal ancestors of the American Indians."[108]

Joseph introduced *The Book of Mormon* on its title page by saying, "Wherefore it is an abridgment of the Record of the People of Nephi; and also of the Lamanites; written to the Lamanites, which are a remnant of the House of Israel."[109]

The current version of *The Book of Mormon* includes a "Testimony of the Prophet Joseph Smith" which recounts his second vision, in which the angel Moroni appeared to him. "He said there was a book deposited, written upon gold plates, giving an account of the former inhabitants of this continent, and the source from which they sprang."[110] Joseph also wrote:

---

104. *Ibid.*, Alma 16:11, page 249.
105. *Ibid.*, Alma 28:11, page 278.
106. *Ibid.*, Alma 50:1-2, page 333.
107. *Ibid.*, Alma 53:4, page 342.
108. The Church of Jesus Christ of Latter Day Saints, *Introduction to The Book of Mormon* (Salt Lake City: Church of Jesus Christ of Latter-day Saints, 1981).
109. Joseph Smith, Jr., *The Book of Mormon* (Palmyra: Grandin, New York, 1830), Title Page, compare to (Salt Lake City: Church of Jesus Christ of Latter-day Saints, 1981), Title Page.

In this important and interesting book the history of ancient America is unfolded, from its first settlement by a colony that came from the tower of Babel, at the confusion of languages to the beginning of the fifth century of the Christian era. We are informed by these records that America in ancient times was inhabited by two distinct races of people. The first were called the Jaredites and came directly from the tower of Babel. The second race came directly from Jerusalem, about six hundred years before Christ. They were principally Israelites, of the descendants of Joseph. The Jaredites were destroyed about the time that the Israelites came from Jerusalem, who succeeded them in the inheritance of the country. The principal nation of the second race fell in battle towards the close of the fourth century. The remnant are the Indians that now inhabit this country.[111]

Modern archeologists, linguists, paleontologists, geneticists, and cultural historians tell a different story. To date, no archeological, linguistic, or genetic evidence has been found that supports the story told in *The Book of Mormon*. Today the huge mounds that captivated and inspired Joseph's imagination have another explanation.

ORIGIN OF THE NATIVE AMERICANS: A 21ST-CENTURY WORLD VIEW

The Mound Builder Civilization of the Mississippi Valley

The New World hosted three significant civilizations when Columbus arrived in 1492: the Aztecs, the Incas, and the Mississippians. Yet many people have never heard of the Mississippian Civilization. Centered around present-day Ohio, they occupied the best farmland on the North American continent: the Mississippi River Valley from the Great Lakes to the Gulf of Mexico, and up the Ohio River to the Appalachian mountains. They supported a dense population and rich culture by growing corn, beans, and squash, and by harvesting fish and fowl from the bountiful riparian habitat. While the Mississippians successfully developed agriculture and organized a civilization, there is no evidence that they had any domesticated animals, other than dogs, or crossed the threshold from spoken into written language. Because of the numerous, huge, earthen mounds that they left behind the Mississippians are also known as the Mound Builders.

---

110. Joseph Smith, Jr., *The Pearl of Great Price*, (Salt Lake City: Church of Jesus Christ of Latter-day Saints, 1967), page 51.

111. Joseph Smith, Jr., *The Personal Writings of Joseph Smith*, Edited by Dean C. Jessee, (Salt Lake City: Deseret Book Co., 1984), page 215.

Archeologists believe it was these people who built the huge mounds that so mystified Joseph and other settlers in western New York.

There are many reasons why the Mississippian civilization is unfamiliar to most of us. Unlike the Aztecs and Incas, the Mississippians did not leave large stone structures or abundant, durable artifacts. They were not the legendary subject of a dramatic military conquest as were the Aztecs and Incas. They built their civilization of wood and soil, the materials abundantly available to them. Already in decline by 1492, they were casualties not of famous conquistadors but of insidious European germs and diseases. Epidemics raged after the germs of European infectious diseases were introduced to the coastal Native Americans during decades of Spanish presence. These diseases moved invisibly ahead of the European explorers and settlers. They spread across the landscape like a tidal wave, devastating the population densities of the Mississippians. In his Pulitzer Prize winning book, *Gun, Germs, and Steel*, UCLA physiologist Jared Diamond described the microbial battlefield:

> The main killers were Old World germs to which Indians had never been exposed, and against which they therefore had neither immune nor genetic resistance. Smallpox, measles, influenza, and typhus competed for top rank among the killers. As if these had not been enough, diphtheria, malaria, mumps, pertussis, plague, tuberculosis, and yellow fever came close behind. In countless cases, whites were actually there to witness the destruction occurring when the germs arrived. For example, in 1837, the Mandan Indian tribe, with one of the most elaborate cultures in the Great Plains, contracted smallpox from a steamboat traveling up the Missouri River from St. Louis. The population of one Mandan village plummeted from 2,000 to fewer than 40 within a few weeks.[112]

It was not until 48 years after Columbus's arrival that the 1540 Spanish expedition led by explorer Hernando de Soto brought the first Europeans into the area. De Soto crossed the southeastern United States, ventured into the lower Mississippi River Valley, and visited many large towns that had been deserted within the previous few years as a result of these epidemics. Other large towns were still intact and culturally vibrant in their density. Diamond reported that::

---

112. Jared Diamond, *Guns, Germs, and Steel: The Fates of Human Societies* (New York: W.W. Norton, 1997) pages 211-212

De Soto was able to see some of the densely populated Indian towns lining the lower Mississippi. After the end of his expedition, it was a long time before Europeans again reached the Mississippi Valley, but Eurasian microbes were now established in North America and kept spreading. By the time of the next appearance of Europeans on the lower Mississippi, that of French settlers in the late 1600s, almost all of those big Indian towns had vanished. Their relics are the great mound sites of the Mississippi Valley. Only recently have we come to realize that many of the mound-building societies were still largely intact when Columbus reached the New World, and that they collapsed (probably as a result of disease) between 1492 and the systematic European exploration of the Mississippi.[113]

The Mississippians constructed well planned cities with broad plazas and wide avenues. Earthen mounds towered above the level landscape, and some were shaped in the forms of serpents, birds and other animals. The mounds were constructed by hand carrying and placing countless baskets of dirt over many generations and hundreds of years. Native American historian Alvin Josephy Jr., in his book *America in 1492: The World of the Indian Peoples Before the Arrival of Columbus*, described the town of Cahokia, across the Mississippi from present-day St. Louis:

> About three hundred years before Columbus' voyage, the central city of Cahokia reached the peak of its architectural development and political prestige. Rising above the five square miles that constituted "downtown" Cahokia was a gigantic pyramid now called Monks Mound. An artificial heap of shaped earth, its base was 1,040 feet long and 790 feet wide; it rose 100 feet high to support a wattle-and-daub-walled temple on its truncated structure. More than a half million cubic meters of mound fill had been piled in stages over the decades by a local population that probably numbered more than 10,000 at its height. Another 100 ceremonial mounds were erected in the immediate vicinity, geometrically arranged around plazas, ritual precincts, and ball fields.[114]

The Mississippians cultivated the deep, black soil, harvested the abundant aquatic life, and developed a significant pottery industry. In a 1605 description of the De Soto Expedition, Garcilaso de la Vega wrote:

---

113. *Ibid.*, page 211.

114. Alvin Josephy, Jr., *America in 1492: The World of the Indian Peoples Before the Arrival of Columbus* (New York: Knopf, 1991) pages 139-140.

Human Migrations to the Wester

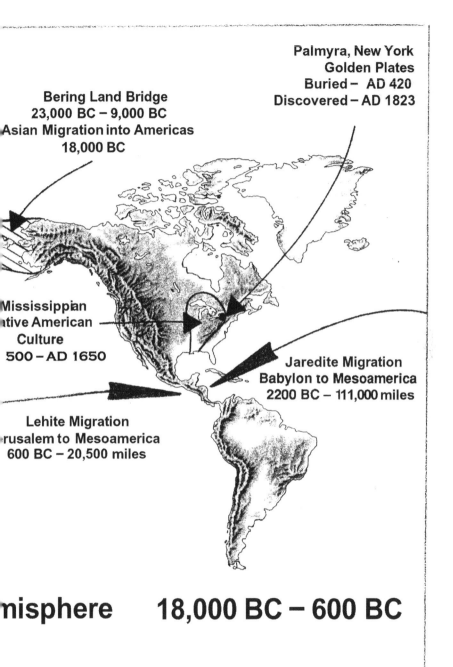

Palmyra, New York
Golden Plates
Buried — AD 420
Discovered — AD 1823

Bering Land Bridge
23,000 BC — 9,000 BC
Asian Migration into Americas
18,000 BC

Mississippian
tive American
Culture
500 — AD 1650

Jaredite Migration
Babylon to Mesoamerica
2200 BC — 111,000 miles

Lehite Migration
rusalem to Mesoamerica
600 BC — 20,500 miles

nisphere   18,000 BC — 600 BC

Because the whole country is very flat, and an elevated site is seldom found...they make it by their own labor. Amassing a very large quantity of earth, they pack it down by treading on it, raising it up in the form of a hill two or three pike-lengths in height. On top they make a level space large enough for ten, twelve, fifteen or twenty houses for the dwellings of the lord and his family and the people in his service...Then the rest of the common people build theirs, endeavoring not to be too far from the hill where the lord's house is; they try rather to surround his with their own.[115]

It was common for the Mississippians to dismantle structures on top of the mound, bury their dead there, and build again over a new layer of earth. The highest mounds were a hundred vertical feet above the surrounding grade. Although the area lacked exposed geology from which to derive metal ore or stones, these things came great distances to them as trade items. Copper from the Great Lakes was fashioned into bracelets, beads, rings, ear spools, and embossed effigies of birds. The deceased took their ornamentation to the grave and left behind the artifacts still found today.

By the time the fledgling American nation had reached the Great Lake region, the Mississippian civilization cities had been abandoned for only 200 years. Into the vacuum moved wilder and more migratory tribes. *The Book of Mormon's* time frame suggests dates for the New York mounds and artifacts at the end of the Jaredite civilization (2,550 years ago in 550 BC) and at the end of the Nephite civilization (1,600 years ago in AD 400). But according to archeologists, the mounds, artifacts, and relics that Joseph encountered around Palmyra, New York in the 1820s had been components of active, densely populated communities until about AD 1600.

The Ice Age Asian Migration

But who were the ancestors of the Mississippian Mound Builders?

Modern scientific researchers (outside of the Mormon culture) describe a lineage for all Native Americans that stretches across Alaska, the Bering Strait, and Siberia, to northeast Asia. Ancestors of the Native Americans left Asia around 20,000 to 11,000 years ago. They migrated north and east into an unbroken continental mass that included both Asia and North America. This land passage remained open, and connected North America with Asia, for 9,000 continuous years after the initial human arrival to the area.

---

115. United States National Park Service - Archeology and Ethnology Program, *Ancient Architects of the Mississippi* / http://www.cr.nps.gov/aad/feature/voices.htm

At present sea levels Asia and North America are just 53 miles apart at the Bering Strait. Each continent is visible from the other and the ocean depth of the Strait ranges from 98 feet to 164 feet. Climatic changes 25,000 years ago cooled the earth and created huge continental glaciers that locked away much of the earth's water. The sea level dropped 300 feet when seawater turned to continental ice, and revealed a thousand-mile wide, dry land bridge between Asia and North America. The Bering land bridge allowed humans to travel to North America until about 11,000 years ago. When the earth's climate warmed once again, the lowlands that connected the continents were flooded.

Paleontologists believe that the land bridge hosted a rich tundra ecosystem where caribou and other arctic animals flourished. The caribou would have followed the tundra vegetation between the continents, and the migratory humans would have followed their caribou food source. Some paleontologists have speculated that an equally rich coastal environment filled with fish, shellfish, sea mammals, and sea vegetation would have made an easy entry route into the American continents.

Whether the Asian emigrants were nomadic caribou hunters, coastal beachcombers, or some combination of both, they crept southward from Alaska into unoccupied, warmer lands. Archeological evidence confirms that the first humans reached the southern tip of South America around 10,000 years ago, and 12,700-year-old human bones have been discovered in central Mexico.

Contemporary archeologists, linguists, paleontologists, geneticists, and cultural historians support this Bering Land Bridge theory for a number of reasons. They agree with the geographic and geologic evidence of a physical land bridge between Asia and North America. By researching camp sites, tool use, and archeological relics, the dating and progression of humans into the Americas is shown to have started at the Bering Land Bridge and proceeded outward from there.

Linguists who analyze language patterns link the Native Americans back to Mongolia and, conversely, find no connection to Middle Eastern languages. A 1987 book titled *Language in the Americas*, by Stanford linguist Joseph Greenberg, divided American Indian languages into four groups derivative from Asian languages. This interpretation has since been adopted by most academic linguists. No remnant of any Middle Eastern language has ever been verified among any Native American population. There have been no discoveries of any evidence of Middle Eastern writing anywhere in the western hemisphere prior to 1492.

As genetic research into the origins of Native Americans has traced the divisions of human genetic populations, the results are found to correlate precisely with branching diagrams drawn from the analysis of languages. Leading population geneticist Luigi Luca Cavalli-Sforza developed this theme in his 1999 book, *Genes, Peoples, and Languages.* He notes that, "Genetic research can certainly help the understanding of linguistic evolution, and vice versa."[116] Research geneticists, using DNA comparisons, have found a positive correlation between Native Americans and Mongolians, and a negative correlation to people of Middle Eastern descent.

Lifelong efforts by many Mormon archeologists have failed to unearth a single definitive site or artifact that challenges the Bering land bridge theory or supports the Native American population explanations advanced in *The Book of Mormon.*

Molecular Anthropology

The strongest proof of the Asian ancestry of Native Americans comes from recent genetic link research. The DNA fingerprinting technology, utilized by courts of law and criminal investigations to prove paternity, guilt, or innocence, also allows scientists to look backwards into genetic ancestry. It has enabled us to trace the roots of our lineage, as well as the lineages of other peoples or species. Genetic research specialists who explore this arena of scientific inquiry are called molecular anthropologists. They map the variations of genetic codes between individuals, races of people, and species to show the genealogical history of evolution, and the geographic migration of groups.

Genetic markers are used to trace ethnic human population groups. These markers represent unique details of the human gene that have arisen in the past, and have been consistently propagated and perpetuated into the present through genetic inheritance. Common lineages share common markers, and lineages without common ancestry do not.

We now have access to the encyclopedia of earth's genetic record of biological organisms. We now know, for example, that 98.4% of our human genome is shared with the chimpanzee. These genetic markers show that chimps and humans shared a common ancestor in Africa about 6 million years ago, and that modern humans moved into Asia about 100,000 years ago. The ancestors of the Native Americans can be traced back to Asia by following the trail of these markers.

Over the past decade scientists have tested DNA from over 7,000 Native Americans, from 150 tribes spread broadly across the Western hemisphere from

---

116. Luigi Luca Cavalli-Sforza, *Genes, Peoples, and Languages* [New York: North Point Press, 2000] page 172.

the Arctic to Patagonia, from the Atlantic to the Pacific Ocean, from North America, Central America, and South America. These research scientists have also included Mormon biologists eagerly trying to verify the claims of *The Book of Mormon*. The results have indicated that over 99% of the DNA tested was derivative from northeast Asians and dated the separation at 12,000 years ago. The remaining fraction of 1% that was not of northeast Asian origin was derivative from European and African ancestry through intermarriage since 1492. No Middle Eastern DNA was found in any of the Native Americans genetic samples. Even the Mormon scientists involved in these research studies agreed with these conclusions.

In the year 2000, Brigham Young University microbiology professor Scott Woodward began an intensive research program, funded by Mormon philanthropists. By correlating DNA databases with the Mormon Church's extensive genealogical database, The Molecular Genealogy Research Group (MGRG) hoped to prove that the Lamanites (the principal ancestors of the Native Americans[117]) were descended from Middle Eastern Jewish ancestry. Such a discovery would have reinforced *The Book of Mormon's* legitimacy, but their efforts and conclusions were highly disappointing. In a 2002 paper entitled *Lamanite Genesis, Genealogy, and Genetics*, Mormon anthropologist Thomas W. Murphy wrote:

> Some optimism was expressed by (Mormon) church members that such research would vindicate the Book of Mormon as an ancient document. The hope was that DNA would link Native Americans to ancient Israelites, buttressing LDS beliefs in a way that has not been forthcoming from archeological, linguistic, historical, or morphological research. For those who held such an expectation, the data collected by MGRG and results of similar research projects have been disappointing. So far, the DNA has lent no support to the traditional Mormon beliefs about the origins of Native Americans. Instead, genetic data have confirmed that migrations from Asia are the primary source of American Indian origins. This research has substantiated already-existing archeological, cultural, linguistic, and biological evidence. While DNA shows that ultimately all human populations are closely related, to date no intimate genetic link has been found between ancient Israelites and indigenous Americans, much less within the time frame suggested by *The Book of Mormon*. Therefore, after considering the research in molecular anthropology summarized here, I have concluded that Latter-day Saints should not realistically expect to find validation for the ancient historicity of *The Book of Mormon* in genetics.[118]

---

117. The Church of Jesus Christ of Latter Day Saints, *Introduction to The Book of Mormon* (Salt Lake City: Church of Jesus Christ of Latter-day Saints,1981).

Luigi Luca Cavalli-Sforza and Thomas Murphy are not the only scientific voices who advocate an Asian ancestry for Native Americans, based on genetic evidence. They represent a virtually unanimous chorus of convergent opinion outside of Mormon culture. There are no genetic studies that refute their findings. Published supporters of this view include UCLA physiologist Jared Diamond, University of Kansas biological anthropologist Michael Crawford, Oxford geneticist Bryan Sykes, and Russian geneticist Miroslava Derenko, and many others. Not only do the genetic, archeological, and linguistic trails lead back to northeast Asia, but the Native American people of North, Central, and South America also visually resemble the peoples of northeast Asia.

Biological anthropologist Michael Crawford stated in his book, *The Origins of Native Americans: Evidence from Anthropological Genetics*, "This evidence indicates extremely strong biological and cultural affinities between New World and Asian populations and leaves no doubt that the first migrants into the Americas were Asians, possibly from Siberia."[119]

The Mormon Church's response to this was articulated by Mormon President and Prophet Gordon B. Hinckley, when he was asked during a 2002 German television interview, "What will be your position when DNA analysis will show that in the history [there] had never been an emigration from Israel to North America?" Hinckley answered, "That hasn't happened. That hasn't been determined yet. All I can say is that it is speculative. No one really knows that. Not at this point."[120] From the Mormon perspective, the spoken position of their living prophet overrules all scientific documentation to the contrary.

Time Frame, Anachronisms, and Belief

The time frame presented in *The Book of Mormon* is perhaps as large an issue as the ancestry of the Native Americans. Read literally, as interpreted by the Mormon Church, the Western Hemisphere was completely absent of human population before 2,200 BC when the first wave of Middle Eastern immigrants, the Jaredites, arrived. When the Lehites (Nephites and Lamanites prior to their division) and Mulekites arrived in 600 BC, the Jaredites were in the final, distant stages of destroying themselves near Palmyra, New York. Except for one

---

118. Thomas W. Murphy. 'Lamanite Genesis, Genealogy, and Genetics,' *American Apocrypha*, edited by Dan Vogel and Brent Lee Metcalfe (Salt Lake City: Signature Books, 2002) pages 47-48.

119. Michael Crawford, *The Origins of Native Americans: Evidence from Anthropological Genetics* (New York: Cambridge Free Press, 1998) pages 3-4.

120. Living Hope Ministries, *DNA vs. The Book of Mormon* (video cassette), (Brigham City, Utah: Living Hope Ministries, 2003).

encounter between the last living Jaredite and the Mulekites, no contact between the earlier and later emigrants is recorded in *The Book of Mormon*. Effectively, the American continents were emptied of human inhabitants for the Nephite, Lamanite, and Mulekite expansion. According to *The Book of Mormon*, the last of the civilized Nephites either died, in the case of Moroni, or were killed by the savage Lamanites by AD 420.

The time frame presented by molecular anthropology, archeology, and linguistics puts the first human populations inside a contiguous Asia/North America between 14,000–20,000 years ago. Archeologists and historians document well organized and populous civilizations along the Mississippi River valley at the time of Columbus' arrival in the New World in 1492. The people of this Mississippian civilization were the builders of the mysterious mounds that so influenced 19th-century legends of lost races in New York state. Rather than having been militarily destroyed 1,500 years earlier by Lamanite warriors, as *The Book of Mormon* suggests, these Mississippians had perished only 200 years earlier, the victims of European germs.

There is no evidence that the Mississippian culture possessed any form of written communication. No metal plates, stone engravings, or even clay tablets have been found. Even the sophisticated Incas lacked any form of written communication. Outside of the Mesoamerican cultures of the Aztecs and the Mayans, no evidence of New World writing has ever been found. None of the Mesoamerican writing samples discovered bears any resemblance to any known Old World writing system.

In addition, *The Book of Mormon* describes Old World plants, animals, and technology in the Americas in association with the Jaredites and Lehites. These introductions included sophisticated steel metallurgy, steel swords as weaponry, steel tools for agriculture, horse-drawn chariots, fine silk and linens, wheat and barley, cows, oxen, donkeys, goats, pigs, sheep, chickens, and domesticated elephants. There is no archeological evidence for any of these plants, animals, or technological innovations having been present in the Americas prior to the arrival of Columbus.

The Book of Mormon also describes the Nephites' use of barley and wheat as principle food plants. If these Old World food plants, derived from a dry Mediterranean climate, were introduced to tropical Central America it is highly improbable that they would have survived or yielded enough of a harvest to support a major civilization. Today, no wheat or barley are grown in Central America. Atlases show that Central America is principally tropical forest land. The agricultural products that are raised there include bananas, cocoa, coffee, sugarcane, corn, and rice.

Both the Jaredite and Nephite civilizations are described as utilizing steel technology to produce weapons and tools. While steel is primarily made of iron, the difference in the properties and production processes of cast iron and steel are significant. Weapons made of cast iron are heavy, rigid and brittle, while weapons made of steel containing about 1% to 2% carbon are stronger and more flexible. The higher temperatures and greater sophistication required to make true steel postponed its introduction in the Old World until after the migrations described in *The Book of Mormon*. The earliest known date of Roman steel is AD 17, while steel production in India dates back to 330 BC. If the Jaredites left Babylon in 2200 BC and the Nephites left Jerusalem in 600 BC, how did they learn about steel making? If the Jaredites possessed steel weapons, as represented in *The Book of Mormon*, they would have been the world's first people to do so, thousands of years before steel was first produced in the Old World. To date, no evidence of any pre-Columbian iron-based metallurgy has ever been found. The earliest known date of any copper-based metallurgy in the Western hemisphere was around AD 900, 480 years after the extinction of the Nephite people.

As for the chariots, there is no evidence that indigenous people anywhere in the American hemisphere ever invented or developed wheeled vehicles for transportation. This is probably due, in no small part, to their complete lack of any domesticated draft animals. *The Book of Mormon*'s claims notwithstanding, there is no archeological evidence whatsoever of horses, oxen, or donkeys in the Americas prior to their introduction by Europeans in the 16th century.

If *The Book of Mormon* view is adopted as literal truth, it is difficult to explain the complete absence of pre-Columbian steel artifacts, carbon-14 datable Old World livestock skeletons, or remnants of Old World food plants. The existence of millions of people with steel tools and weapons who raised Old World food plants and livestock is very questionable. Either evidence exists but has not yet been found, has inexplicably disappeared, or these items were never present. Given the scope and scale of the cities, the wars, and the human populations described, it seems hard to believe that a corroborating discovery would not have been made if *The Book of Mormon* were an accurate description of pre-Columbian America.

In an article for the Mormon journal *Dialogue*, titled "Mormons and Archeology: An Outside View," Yale archeologist Michael Coe wrote:

> There is an inherent improbability in specific items that are mentioned in *The Book of Mormon* as having been brought to the New World by Jaredites and/or Nephites. Among these are the horse (extinct in the New World since about 7000 BC), the chariot, wheat, barley, and metallurgy (true met-

allurgy based on smelting and casting being no earlier in Mesoamerica than about AD 800). The picture of this hemisphere between 2000 BC and AD 421 presented in the book has little to do with the early Indian cultures as we know them, in spite of much wishful thinking.[121]

Archeology and Carbon-14 Dating

Ever since *The Book of Mormon's* publication, members of the Mormon faith have eagerly looked forward to archeological proof of its historical truth. For a long time, the most likely prospect seemed to be the Mayan ruins in Central America. As archeological dating methods evolved, however, it was discovered that the Mayan civilization reached its climax 200 years after the complete destruction of the Nephites.

Not one place, person, or event connected with *The Book of Mormon* has yet been verified through archeological investigation, and it is not for lack of trying. Many Mormon archeologists and Mormon Church sponsored investigations have looked for the conclusive evidence to prove *The Book of Mormon's* historical accuracy. In 1979, the Mormon Church sponsored Foundation for Ancient Research and Mormon Studies (FARMS) was founded on the campus of the Mormon Church's Brigham Young University in Provo, Utah. Their purpose is to promote archeological research projects, and to publish books, reports, and periodicals, that validate *The Book of Mormon*. FARMS says of itself, "Work done in the name of FARMS rests on the conviction that *The Book of Mormon*, the Bible, and other ancient scripture such as *The Book of Abraham* and *The Book of Moses* are all the word of God, written by prophets of God, and that they are authentic, historical texts."[122] Critics of FARMS question the reliability of their science if their conclusion regarding the historical accuracy of *The Book of Mormon* precedes and excludes scientific evidence that contradicts their premise.

Archeologists today are able to calculate the age of biological samples (human remains, artifacts, organic garbage, campfire charcoal, etc.) up to 50,000 years old with a high degree of precision using the analytic process of "carbon-14 dating." Carbon-14 (C14) is an unstable, radioactive isotope of the element carbon that is constantly being generated in quantifiable amounts in the earth's upper atmosphere, when high powered cosmic radiation strikes common nitrogen-14 atoms. The energy absorbed by the nitrogen atom transforms one of its (positively charged) protons into an equally massive (but neutrally charged)

---

121. Michael Coe, "Mormons and Archeology: An Outside View," *Dialogue: A Journal of Mormon Thought* 8 (Summer 1973): 40-48.

122. The Foundation for Ancient Research and Mormon Studies (FARMS) website: http://farms.byu.edu/main.php?i=1

neutron. Since the chemical characteristics of an element are determined by the number of protons and electrons rather than by its atomic weight, these transformed atoms behave identically with any other common carbon atom. After this change the atom has one less proton than it did before, while still maintaining its atomic weight of 14.

The transformed and unstable C14 atoms have a predictable rate of atomic decay, in which their neutron eventually reverts to a proton. When this happens, the change releases energy, and the carbon-14 isotope reverts to a common nitrogen-14 atom. During the ongoing process of creation and decay, the atmospheric proportion of C14 atoms to common carbon-12 atoms (atomic weight 12) in the atmosphere remains constant, at approximately one C14 atom for every trillion C12 atoms.

Because all plant life takes in atmospheric carbon during photosynthesis, the same proportion of C14 atoms that is present in the atmosphere is also found in plants. Since animals either directly (as herbivores) or indirectly (as carnivores eating herbivores) derive their body carbon from plants, the same proportion is repeated in them. While a plant or animal is alive, it is continually renewing and maintaining this proportion through respiration and ingestion.

This process of renewal ends, however, when a plant or animal dies and the proportion of C14 begins to decline through a very predictable, clock-like radioactive decay sequence known as "half-life" decay. Every 5,568 years, one half of the C14 atoms present revert into N14 and half remains, in a constant, cumulative decay process.

Archeologists are able to accurately date sites by determining the age of bones, seeds, food remains, campfire charcoal, and wooden tools. Chemical analysts comparing this proportion of C14 to C12 can determine, with a high degree of accuracy, the year of death for plant and animal samples up to 50,000 years old. The decay process has run through so many half lives after 50,000 years that there isn't enough C14 left to make an accurate dating.

The carbon-14 dating process was developed in the 1940s by a team of scientists at the University of Chicago, led by Willard F. Libby. He was awarded the Nobel Prize for Chemistry in 1960 for this discovery. This method of dating biological artifacts has been refined and calibrated during the last 60 years, and the validity of the technique is widely accepted within the scientific community.

The "Limited Geography" Model

As the cumulative genetic, archeological, and linguistic evidence mounts, and the consensus among non-Mormon scientists becomes nearly unanimous that the Native Americans are not descendants of Middle Eastern people,

Mormon scholars have proposed an alternate model that doesn't violate the hard scientific facts they are confronted with. At this time, no Mormon scientists are contesting the genetic data but are instead proposing what they call a "limited geography" model to explain the existence of the Nephite civilization.

The chief proponent for the limited geography model is the Foundation for Apologetic Information and Research (FAIR). The foundation's mission is, in part, to "address the charges leveled at the doctrines, practices and leaders of The Church of Jesus Christ of Latter-day Saints (Mormons) with documented responses that are written in an easily understandable style. FAIR will use current scholarship, scripture, Church doctrine, historical literature and sound logic in constructing solid answers."[123]

The limited geography model is described in a FAIR editorial review and response written by Kevin L. Barney to an article by Thomas Murphy and Simon G. Southerton, titled "Genetic Research a 'Galileo Event' for Mormons," in the February 2003 edition of *Anthropology News*:

> When Lehi and his family arrived in the New World, was the land isolated and desolate, or were others already in the land? That is, in what fashion was the land peopled? And what was the sphere of their operations? Did they encompass the whole of the western hemisphere, or did they live in a more circumscribed area?
>
> The Church itself has resisted ever taking a formal position on these kinds of questions...There have been dozens of geographic theories regarding Book of Mormon events put forward over the years, but none has the official imprimatur of the Church, and none carries the authority of prophetic sanction.
>
> Probably the most common theory historically, and perhaps even yet today, was that no one else was in the land when Lehi and company arrived; Lehi and his wife then became the founders of all civilization and the forebears of all human inhabitants in North and South America; and their operations encompassed the whole of the western hemisphere. For simplicity, I shall refer to this as the "hemispheric" model. Under this theory, the lineage of all, or at least the vast majority of, Native Americans funnels through Lehi and his group.

---

123. The Foundation for Apologetic Information and Research (FAIR) website: http://www.fairlds.org/

For at least fifty years (and in some quarters substantially longer), serious students of the Book of Mormon have read that book in light of a different model. Under this model, Lehi and family represented a limited incursion into an extensive population that already existed in the Americas, and their sphere of operations was limited to Mesoamerica, ranging in the hundreds of miles, not thousands. For simplicity, I shall refer to this as the "limited geography" model.[124]

Proponents for the limited geography model propose a scenario that involves a smaller area in which the Nephites and Lamanites played out the events mentioned in *The Book of Mormon* in isolation from the indigenous population of the Western Hemisphere. They propose that all of the Nephite and Lamanites are extinct and that we have merely failed so far to find the cultural artifacts that verify their former existence. Their failure to interbreed or meet up with the Native Americans of Asian ancestry has resulted in the total loss of their DNA from the Western Hemisphere. The absence of human Middle Eastern DNA amid the abundance of human Asian DNA, they argue, does not prove that these people weren't there. It only shows that we have no evidence of it yet.

There are a number of problems with the limited geography model.

We now have the technological ability to run genetic tests on ancient skeletal remains. DNA tests on pre-Columbian human samples have not turned up any Middle Eastern human DNA. These samplings of ancient human DNA have included numerous tests from ancient Mayans and Central Americans.

Humans tend to fill up all available ecological niches in which they can survive. The likelihood that an isolated civilization of Lamanites and Nephites involving millions of people could have existed without ever running into and intermixing with a Native American population that co-occupied the Western hemisphere seems highly unlikely. The Nephites described in *The Book of Mormon* were prodigious record-keepers. It is unimaginable that they would have run into a population of different people and made no mention of it.

The geographic span from Mesoamerica, where the limited geography model places the homelands of the Nephites and Lamanites, to the Hill Cumorah in New York State where 230,000 Nephite soldiers lost their lives, and Mormon and Moroni hid the golden plates, is no small or limited distance. It is 2,400 miles from New York to the Isthmus of Tehuantepec, and 4,300 miles from New York to the Isthmus of Panama. If Native Americans had been present in North

---

124. *Ibid.*, website: http://www.fairlds.org/apol/bom/bom08.html

America during the period when the Lamanites pushed the Nephite army back to New York, surely some sort of meeting of the groups would have occurred.

Lastly, the limited geography model violates Joseph's prophecies, sworn testimonies, and the textual explanations of the Nephites and Lamanites described in *The Book of Mormon* and outlined in the previous chapter. Proponents of the limited geography model seem willing to deny Joseph's credibility and the historical truth of *The Book of Mormon* in order to demonstrate that it is a true record. Is this a good example of FAIR's "documented responses that are written in an easily understandable style...using current scholarship, scripture, Church doctrine, historical literature and sound logic in constructing solid answers"?[125] One of the principal prophecies in *The Book of Mormon* was that it was being written for the certain posterity of the remnant descendants of Lehi, who would be saved when they learned the truth of their history. *The Book of Mormon* does not describe a small group of people who fail to thrive or survive into modern times.

Did the Nephites and Lamanites Ever Exist?

Are the Native Americans descendants of biblical era Jewish emigrants to America? They either are, or they are not. Unless some strong scientific evidence arises in the future from the fields of genetics, molecular anthropology, or archeology to support *The Book of Mormon* perspective, people must either take the Mormon view on faith, or be led by the evidence on hand to conclude that the Native Americans are distant descendants of Asian peoples and none other.

In 1957, the future Mormon Church president and prophet Joseph Fielding Smith summed up the Mormon Church's position that the truth of *The Book of Mormon* should be tested by prayer rather than factual evidence when he wrote:

> It is the personal opinion of this writer that the Lord does not intend that the Book of Mormon, at least for the present time, shall be proved true by any archeological finding. The day may come when such will be the case, but not now. The Book of Mormon is itself a *witness* of the truth, and the promise has been given most solemnly that any person who will read it with a prayerful heart may receive the abiding testimony of its truth.[126]

While personal prayer may be a good way to determine ethical and personal choices in life, it is not a sound way to determine the reliability of scientific and historical facts. People who rely on prayer to answer these

---

125. *Ibid.*, website: http://www.fairlds.org/
126. Joseph Fielding Smith, *Answers to Gospel Questions* (Salt Lake City: Deseret Book Co., 1957-1966), volume 2, page 196.

questions will tend to live in a "magic world view" that does not conform well to observationally testable information.

The following thoughts were first presented in Part I of this book and need to be revisited again in light of the information presented in this chapter:

The Book of Mormon is based on the prophecies and records of an ancient Nephite civilization in America, and on Jesus Christ's visitation with them. Its complete publication title is *The Book of Mormon, Another Testament of Jesus Christ*. But what if this horse-and-chariot, Nephite civilization never existed? If it didn't exist, how could Jesus Christ have visited it? If Jesus Christ didn't visit the Nephites in America, how can the gospel of his visit possibly be the one true gospel of Jesus Christ?

WILL THE LAMANITES' SKIN COLOR TURN WHITE?

The Book of Mormon clearly states in the Second Book of Nephi that the Lamanites were physically transformed from "white, and exceedingly fair and delightsome" people into dark skinned people, who became the ancestors of the Native Americans. *The Book of Mormon* also tells that the Lamanites' skin color can be changed back to white, if they adopt the beliefs set forward in *The Book of Mormon*.

The prophet Nephi predicted (in 500 BC) that when the Native Americans ("remnant of our seed") received *The Book of Mormon*, in the latter days, they would again become "white[127] and delightsome people":

> And now, I would prophesy somewhat more concerning the Jews and the Gentiles. For after the book of which I have spoken shall come forth, and be written unto the Gentiles, and sealed up again unto the Lord, there shall be many which shall believe the words which are written; and they shall carry them forth unto the remnant of our seed. And then shall the remnant of our seed know concerning us, how that we came out from Jerusalem, and that they are a descendant of the Jews. And the Gospel of Jesus Christ shall be declared among them; wherefore, they shall be restored unto the knowledge of their fathers, and also to the knowledge of Jesus Christ, which was had among their fathers. And then shall they rejoice, for they shall know that it is a blessing unto them from the hand of God; and their scales of darkness shall begin to fall from their eyes; and many generations shall not pass away among them, save they shall be a white* and a delightsome people.[128]

---

127. In the 1981 version of *The Book of Mormon*, the word "white" was changed to "pure."

Much later in *The Book of Mormon* (in AD 13) another Nephite prophet reported that the skin color of the Lamanites who converted to Christianity was miraculously changed from dark to white:

> And it came to pass that those Lamanites which had united with the Nephites, were numbered among the Nephites; and their curse was taken from them, and their skin became white like unto the Nephites; and their young men and their daughters became exceeding fair, and they were numbered among the Nephites, and were called Nephites.[129]

At the semi-annual Mormon Church Conference in October 1960, the Mormon Apostle[130] Spencer W. Kimball gave an address highlighting Nephi's prophecy mentioned above, and described how some Native Americans were fast becoming a white and delightsome people:

> The day of the Lamanites is nigh. For years they have been growing delightsome, and they are now becoming white and delightsome, as they were promised. In this picture of the twenty Lamanite missionaries, fifteen of the twenty were as white as *Anglos*; five were darker but equally delightsome. The children in the home placement program in Utah are often lighter than their brothers and sisters in the hogans on the reservation.
> At one meeting a father and mother and their sixteen-year-old daughter were present, the little member girl — sixteen — sitting between the darker father and mother, and it was evident she was several shades lighter than her parents — on the same reservation, in the same hogan, subject to the same sun and wind and weather. There was the doctor in a Utah city who for two years had had an Indian boy in his home who stated that he was some shades lighter than the younger brother just coming into the program from the reservation. These young members of the Church are changing to whiteness and to delightsomeness. One white elder jokingly said that he and his companion were donating blood regularly to the hospital in the hope that the process might be accelerated.[131]

Thirteen years after this presentation, Mormon Apostle Spencer W. Kimball was ordained as the 12th President, Prophet, Seer, and Revelator of the Mormon Church. Kimball's remarks are just one example of many similar

---

128. Joseph Smith, Jr., *The Book of Mormon* (Palmyra: Grandin, New York, 1830), page 117, compare to *The Book of Mormon* (Salt Lake City: Church of Jesus Christ of Latter-day Saints, 1981), 2 Nephi 30:3-6, pages 111-112.

129. *Ibid.*, page 456, compare to *The Book of Mormon* (Salt Lake City: Church of Jesus Christ of Latter-day Saints, 1981), 3 Nephi 2:14-16, page 410.

130. Twelve Apostles reside one step below the First Presidency at the apex of the Mormon Church Hierarchy. Their public statements bear the stamp of full Church authority.

131. Spencer W. Kimball, 'The Day of the Lamanites,' *The Improvement Era*, Dec. 1960, p. 923

positions taken by Mormon Church officials since 1830 regarding Native Americans' skin color. Five passages in *The Book of Mormon* make reference to dark skin color as a sign of God's displeasure with his people.

Physiologists today believe that variation in human skin color is based on genetic instructions encoded in people's DNA, and is not a consequence of God's favor or disfavor with their ancestors. Evolutionary physiologists today say that dark skin among different human populations is an adaptive response to environmental circumstances over tens of thousands of generations. The idea that human skin color could change from light to dark, or vice versa, in a single person's lifetime is generally rejected.

Since 1981, the Mormon Church has downplayed the prophecies that the Native Americans' skin color can, and will, turn white. Prophet Kimball's testimony notwithstanding, there has been no reliable documentation or confirmation from unbiased, independent observers that such a change in skin color has ever taken place.

"THE LORD GOD DELIGHTS IN THE CHASTITY OF WOMEN"

References to Female and Male Gender Roles in The Book of Mormon

Gender sensitive readers of *The Book of Mormon* will find it difficult to ignore or disregard its portrayal and inclusion of female characters in comparison to its portrayal and inclusion of male characters. Only 6 of the 250 named people in *The Book of Mormon* are female. With only one exception, no wife, mother, sister, or daughter unique to *The Book of Mormon* is identified by name. Women are most frequently referred to as part of the more general grouping of "women and children" who need to run, hide, be protected, or be slaughtered. In fact, women are hardly ever mentioned. What these invisible women do is quietly bear children: millions and millions of them. When not being nurturing mothers, women are often portrayed as tempting seductresses who lead men into promiscuity. Typical references to women include:

> "Our women did bear children in the wilderness..."[132]
> "Our women did give plenty of suck for their children..."[133]
> "I, the Lord God, delight in the chastity of women..."[134]

---

132. Joseph Smith, Jr., *The Book of Mormon* (Salt Lake City: Church of Jesus Christ of Latter-day Saints, 1981), 1 Nephi 17:1, page 36.

133. *Ibid.*, 1 Nephi 17:2, page 36.

134. *Ibid.*, Jacob 2:28, page 121.

"I did cause that the women should spin, and toil, and work..."[135]
"Their women did toil and spin, and did make all manner of cloth..."[136]

In one particularly troubling passage, the prophet Alma referred to women as possessions in the same breath as livestock:

"May the peace of God rest upon you, and upon your houses and lands, and upon your flocks and herds, and all that you possess, your women and your children."[137]

In only four instances do women actively enter the narrative in the entire *Book of Mormon*; once as a seductive and murderous accomplice to attempted patricide[138], and the other three times as Lamanite queens.[139] None of these four women is identified by name; they are referenced only as the daughter and queens of their respective father or king. In all four of these instances the women are minor characters with miniscule parts who appear briefly (from three verses to fifteen verses) and then vanish from the story. If queens existed among the "white and delightsome" Nephite people, they are never mentioned. From inference it would appear that only the "dark and loathsome" Lamanite savages permitted their women to be designated as queens.

Rulers, judges, leaders, disciples, teachers, scribes, warriors, kings, priests, and God are all male. Except for a single prophetess, all the prophets are men. The Old World prophetess who is mentioned is merely included in part of a passage from a quote by the Old Testament prophet Isaiah.

Word searches of *The Book of Mormon* reveal the following counts —

6 — the number of different women who are identified by name

3 — the number of named women whose identity is derived from the Old Testament (Mary, birth mother of Jesus Christ; Eve, the mother of humanity; and Sarah, the wife of the patriarch Abraham)

11 — the total instances of occurrence of those 6 women's names

244 — the number of different men who are identified by name (includes 59 instances of repeated name use by different characters)

5,297 — total instances of occurrence of those men's names

---

135. *Ibid.*, Mosiah 10:5, page 166.
136. *Ibid.*, Helaman 6:13, page 382.
137. *Ibid.*, Alma 7:27, page 226.
138. *Ibid.*, Ether 8:8-12, pages 500-501.
139. *Ibid.*, Alma 19:2-17 pages 256-257; Alma 22:19-24 page 265; Alma 47:33-35, pages 327-328.

300 — occurrences of references to livestock animals (elephants, horses, cattle, pigs, oxen, sheep, goats, donkeys, chickens, herds, flocks, etc.)

412 — occurrences of female gender references (woman/women [60], she [56], her/hers/herself [79], sister/sisters [1], mother/mothers [21], daughter/daughters [90], wife/wives [56], mistress [1], concubine [9], harlots [8], maid/maiden [5], virgin [7], queen [25], priestess [0], prophetess [1], goddess [0])

15,477 — occurrences of male gender references using similar key words (man/men, he, his, him, brother, father, son, husband, servant, king, priest, prophet, god, etc.)

423 — occurrences of women's names and women's gender references combined

20,774 — occurrences of men's names and men's gender references combined

1 — occurrences of the words "sister or sisters"

725 — occurrences of words "brother, brothers, brethren"

32 — number of times in which the 52 occurrences of the word "women" is found in the phrase "women and children"

Sariah is the mother of Nephi, the most mentioned character in *The Book of Mormon*. Except for Sariah, the wife of the patriarch Lehi, no other non-biblical mother or wife is ever mentioned by name, nor do any of the major characters ever make specific reference to their wives. Of the 11 occurrences of 6 different women's names in *The Book of Mormon*, 5 of those instances involve Sariah, the mother of six sons and an unknown number of daughters who at one time are mentioned in plural. Other than complaining a little about their harsh journey in the wilderness, quietly obeying her husband, and pleading with Nephi's brothers not to harm him, Sariah also mourns and gives thanks to God. She is not a significant character.

Except for a single passage in which Nephi identifies his unnamed, unnumbered, and never again mentioned sisters, there is no mention of sisters in *The Book of Mormon*. "Wherefore, it came to pass that I, Nephi, did take my family, and also Zoram and his family, and Sam, mine elder brother and his family, and Jacob and Joseph, my younger brethren, and also my sisters, and all those who would go with me."[140]

After Sariah, the woman next most mentioned by name is Mary, the birth mother of Jesus Christ. The name Mary appears twice in *The Book of Mormon*. "And behold, he shall be born of Mary, at Jerusalem which is the land of our

---

140. *Ibid.*, 2 Nephi 5:6, page 65.

forefathers, she being a virgin, a precious and chosen vessel."[141] In 600 BC, Nephi had a vision in which he was shown Mary and the future birth of Jesus Christ. In the original 1830 version of *The Book of Mormon*, Mary was identified, controversially, as "the mother of God," "Behold, the virgin whom thou seest is the mother of God, after the manner of the flesh."[142] In subsequent versions this role was changed to the "the mother of the Son of God."

Abraham's wife Sarah, and Eve, the mother of all mankind, each receive a single, passing mention by name. The fifth named woman is Abish, a converted Lamanite maid to a Lamanite Queen.[143] The sixth is Isabel, a tempting prostitute who is mentioned in a sentence regarding a father's reprimand to his son. [144]

"When the Leaders Speak, the Thinking has Been Done" — Contemporary Mormon Gender Roles

To some degree, the role of contemporary Mormon women follows the lead presented in *The Book of Mormon*. Where Mormon men are encouraged to lead in spiritual, organizational, and business aspects of the Mormon Church, their women are encouraged to be become mothers and homemakers in complement to their men.

No positions of authority, power, or priesthood within the Mormon Church are open to women. It is a social order that largely relegates its female members to bearing and nurturing children, and supporting the men as spiritual leaders. A 12-year-old boy is given more power, authority, and relevance in the Mormon Church hierarchy than any woman will ever receive, regardless of her age, education, wisdom, experience, or vocation.

Women cannot achieve spiritual fulfillment on their own in the Mormon religion. Only through their husband's position of priesthood can they reach godliness. As a priest, the Mormon husband is recognized as the spiritual leader of his family — no questions asked.

An example of this gender bias can be as simple as a blessing given to an infant girl. In the Mormon religion it is considered an evil act to baptize young children before they have an opportunity to choose between good and bad, so they substitute "blessings" for infant baptism, and wait to baptize children until they reach the age of eight. At a Sunday service, a group of Mormon priests (all

141. *Ibid.*, Alma 7:10, pages 224-225.
142. Joseph Smith, Jr., *The Book of Mormon*, (Palmyra: Grandin, New York, 1830), page 25, compare to *The Book of Mormon* (Salt Lake City: Church of Jesus Christ of Latter-day Saints, 1981), 1 Nephi 11:18, page 20.
143. Joseph Smith, Jr., *The Book of Mormon* (Salt Lake City: Church of Jesus Christ of Latter-day Saints, 1981), Alma 19:16, page 257.
144. *Ibid.*, Alma 39:3, page 306.

adult Mormon men, and only men, are members of the Mormon priesthood) encircled a baby girl held in her father's arms. The priests put one arm around the shoulders of the fellow priest next to them and the laid their other hand on the baby girl, so that all the men were joined in a circle touching the girl. The blessing that was spoken was, "May she find a worthy man to take her to the temple." She wasn't wished happiness, success, or independence.

Boys join the Mormon priesthood at age 12 as *deacons* who can distribute sacrament, collect offerings, and help maintain their church building and grounds. At age 14, they become *teachers* who ordain *deacons*, prepare sacrament, speak at church meetings, and help with "home teaching," a monthly visit by male priesthood holders to each household in the Mormon Church system. At age 16, they become *priests*, who teach and counsel at home teaching visits, baptize, administer sacrament, and ordain *teachers* and *deacons* to the priesthood. At age 18 they become *elders*, qualified to give blessings and healings through the *laying on of hands*, ordain *priests*, hold positions of responsibility in the church, and *be called* for a mission. Mature, older men become *high priests*, with greater authority and responsibility. Volunteer lay *bishops* lead Mormon congregations. Several layers beyond *bishops* are the 12 *apostles* who help establish Mormon Church policy, and directly support the top position, the *president of the Church, prophet, seer, and revelator of God*.

Mormons consider the priesthood as a conveyance of the literal power of God to ordained men above the age of 12. The Mormon Church officially says that, "The priesthood is the authority to act in God's name. The same priesthood authority that existed in the original Church established by Jesus Christ exists in The Church of Jesus Christ of Latter-day Saints today. The Church is directed and led through this authority. All male members of the church who are prepared receive the priesthood in order to help lead the church and serve the Heavenly Father's children."[145]

On the official Mormon Church website, Mormon prophet and president Gordon B. Hinckley answers a frequently asked question, "Why don't women hold the priesthood?" He answers, "Women do not hold the priesthood because the Lord has put it that way. It is part of His program."[146]

To its credit, the Mormon Church has softened and modernized its position regarding the roles of men and women over the last hundred years; but

---

145. Official statement on the priesthood from the Mormon Church website: http://www.mormon.org/learn/0,8672,1083-1,00.html

146. The Mormon Church official website: http://www.mormon.org/question/faq/ category/answer/0,9777,1601-1-63-1,00.html

the way to modernization has been littered with the bodies of excommunicated women who spoke out or questioned the male church authorities. The Mormon Church is one of the most pyramidal, male dominated institutions on earth today. Yet, like all male dominated pyramids, it relies on women to provide sons.

The following chronology reflects church positions on male authority and the role of women:

1830 to the present — All Mormon Church prophets, apostles, priests, and leaders have been male.

1945 — "Any Latter-day Saint who denounces or opposes whether actively or otherwise, any plan or doctrine advocated by the prophets, seers, revelators of the church, is cultivating the spirit of apostasy...When our leaders speak, the thinking has been done. When they propose a plan — it is God's Plan. When they point the way, there is no other which is safe. When they give directions, it should mark the end of controversy. God works in no other way." — From a church-wide Ward Teachers Message.[147]

1960 — "Always keep your eye on the President of the church, and if he ever tells you to do anything, even if it is wrong, and you do it, the lord will bless you for it — but you don't need to worry. The lord will never let his mouthpiece lead the people astray." — Marion G. Romney, quoting Mormon Church Prophet and President Heber J. Grant[148]

1978 — "Young women should plan and prepare for marriage and the bearing and rearing of children. It is your divine right and the avenue to the greatest and most supreme happiness." — Mormon Church prophet and president Spencer W. Kimball, from an article entitled *Privileges and Responsibilities of Sisters* [149]

1979 — "When the Prophet speaks, the debate is over."[150]

---

147. Ward Teachers Message, *Deseret News*, Church Section p. 5, May 26, 1945 and in the Improvement Era, (June 1945).

148. Marion G. Romney, quoting LDS President (and prophet) Heber J. Grant. 'Conference Report', (Oct. 1960 page 78).

149. President Spencer W. Kimball, 'Privileges and Responsibilities of Sisters,' *Ensign*, (Nov. 1978, page 103).

150. N. Eldon Tanner, *Ensign* (August,1979, pages 2-3).

1980 — Mormon President and Prophet Ezra Taft Benson issued a formal written statement regarding the role of the Mormon prophet in the affairs of the Mormon believers: *Fourteen Fundamentals in Following the Prophets.* This statement includes the following section headings:

The prophet is the only man who speaks for the Lord in everything.

The living prophet is more vital to us than the standard works.

The living prophet is more important to us than a dead prophet.

The prophet will never lead the Church astray.

The prophet is not required to have any particular earthly training or credentials to speak on any subject or act on any matter at any time.

The prophet does not have to say "Thus saith the Lord" to give us scripture.

The prophet tells us what we need to know, not always what we want to know.

The prophet is not limited by men's reasoning. There will be times when you will have to choose between the revelations of God and the reasoning of men — between the prophet and the politician or professor.

The prophet can receive revelation on any matter, temporal or spiritual.

The prophet may be involved in civic matters.

The two groups who have the greatest difficulty in following the prophet are the proud who are learned and the proud who are rich.

The prophet will not necessarily be popular with the world or the worldly.

The prophet and his counselors make up the First Presidency — the highest quorum in the Church.

The prophet and the presidency — the living prophet and the First Presidency — follow them and be blessed; reject them and suffer.[151]

1995 to the present — Mormon Prophet and President Gordon B. Hinckley issued a formal written statement, titled *The Family: A Proclamation to the World,* which outlined the respective roles of Mormon men and women. This proclamation remains the official current position. "By divine design, fathers are to preside over their families in love and righteousness and are responsible to provide the necessities of life and protection for their

---

151. Ezra Taft Benson, *Fourteen Fundamentals in Following the Prophet,* BYU Devotional Assembly (February 26, 1980).

families. Mothers are primarily responsible for the nurture of their children."[152]

RE-VISIONS: 3,913 CHANGES TO THE ORIGINAL 1830 *BOOK OF MORMON*

Readers who open the current version of *The Book of Mormon* naturally assume that they are reading the same words that Joseph translated from the golden plates by the gift and power of God in 1828 and 1829. This is not the case. Between 1829 and 1981, there have been thirteen different English-language versions of *The Book of Mormon*, including the original handwritten manuscript, in which incremental revisions have been made by the Mormon Church.

Just as Joseph Smith's first vision went through a series of transformations and changes between his first recorded version in 1832 and his final version in 1839, *The Book of Mormon* has undergone a series of text changes since it was first published in 1830. Although the text has always been seen by Mormons as the divine word of God, it turns out that God's words are subject to revision. Although Joseph Smith declared that *The Book of Mormon* is "the most correct of any book on earth, and the keystone of our religion, and a man would get nearer to God by abiding by its precepts, than by any other book,"[153] subsequent administrations of the Mormon Church have made over 3,913 changes to the original.

In order to avoid copyright issues, *The Book of Mormon* translation contained in this book is based on the 1830 version. At the present time, two publishers keep the original 1830 version of *The Book of Mormon* in print. In addition, the complete text of the original version is free and easily available on the Internet.

In 1842, Joseph laid out the thirteen Articles of Faith that define the Mormon religion. The eighth article reads, "We believe the Bible to be the word of God as far as it is translated directly; we also believe the Book of Mormon to be the word of God."[154] Read literally, this places *The Book of Mormon* on a higher plane of accuracy than the Bible. Joseph blamed the abominable Catholic Church, corrupt priests, careless transcribers, and ignorant translators for the Bible's incorrectness. The prophets mentioned in *The Book of Mormon* text also repeatedly express indignation at the corruption of the gospel. Similarly, the

---

152. Gordon B. Hinckley, *The Family: A Proclamation to the World*, General Relief Society Meeting held September 23, 1995, in Salt Lake City, Utah.

153. Joseph Smith, Jr., *History of the Church of Jesus Christ of Latter Day Saints*, (Salt Lake City: Deseret Book Co., 1976) vol. 4, page 461.

154. Joseph Smith, Jr., *The Pearl of Great Price*, (Salt Lake City: Church of Jesus Christ of Latter-day Saints, 1967), page 59.

Mormon Church is held accountable by critics for corrupting and changing the original version of *The Book of Mormon.*

In its defense, the Mormon Church has said that it needed to correct minor typographical errors made by a hostile and perhaps incompetent original printer. However, close examination reveals that most of the changes are not typographical errors attributable to the printer. The infrequent spelling errors or archaicisms that do occur are largely consistent with the manuscript and were approved by Joseph's proofreaders. For example, every time the word "show" appears (in the current version), it was spelled "shew" (in the 1830 version), just as it was spelled in the manuscript. Most of the changes fall into two categories: doctrinal changes, and changes in syntax, wording, and continuity. Prior to the changes, critics pummeled *The Book of Mormon's* credibility because of God's apparent inability to express himself in correct grammar, or to keep proper chronological track of *The Book of Mormon* events and characters. After the changes were made, the criticism shifted to the changes themselves, especially the changes that reflected altered doctrinal positions.

Among the thousands of subjective doctrinal and grammatical changes, there are some significant changes to the objective details regarding Joseph Smith's relation to *The Book of Mormon.* In the original version, Joseph is identified as "Author and Proprietor" on both the title page and in "THE TESTIMONY OF EIGHT WITNESSES." In later versions, Joseph's identification is changed to "Translator." This, and other textual changes in "THE TESTIMONY OF THREE WITNESSES," makes the statements which Joseph prepared for the witnesses to sign different than what they actually did sign.

The changes to *The Book of Mormon* are a polarized and controversial subject. Entire books and websites are devoted to the subject. In Jerald and Sandra Tanner's book, *3,913 Changes in The Book of Mormon,* the authors have photocopied the entire text of the original 1830 version and overlaid the changes onto the copied pages, showing words added, words deleted, wording changes, and spelling corrections. Internet searches on the words "book of Mormon changes" show hundreds of entries expressing positions on both sides of the controversy.

It is also worth noting that similar changes have been made to Joseph's 120 recorded revelations in the book, *Doctrine and Covenants.* There are also changes in his book *The Pearl of Great Price,* which includes his controversial additions to biblical text, *The Book of Moses* and *The Book of Abraham.*

Within the Mormon Church, the leadership advises its members and teachers of doctrine to stick with the current interpretation. They are asked to avoid referring to past versions and to avoid books and magazines that are in any way critical of the Church. Independent scholarship is a touchy subject. Since most Mormon scholars work for the Church, they risk excommunication and loss of employment for critically examining or writing about anything that contradicts the current version.

It is not the intention or goal of this book to enter into either side of this voluminous debate, but rather to point out the historical fact of the changes and to pose the rhetorical question that this raises: Did God make mistakes in the translation from the golden plates; and if God did make mistakes, is it appropriate for the Mormon Church to correct him?

CONTEMPORARY RELEVANCE OF *THE BOOK OF MORMON* TO THE MODERN MORMON CHURCH

The Book of Mormon is to mainstream Christians what the New Testament is to Jews: a parting of the ways. While Mormons and mainstream Christians both acknowledge Jesus Christ as their savior, they also acknowledge the Bible as their Gospel. The figure that they each identify as Jesus Christ is, however, a somewhat different Jesus Christ, and their Gospel of the word of God is a different text. Mormons accept the Bible as the word of God only "as correctly translated" and restored by their prophet Joseph. Mormons also include as their holy scriptures *The Book of Mormon*, the revelations of Joseph known as *Doctrine and Covenants*, and *The Pearl of Great Price*, which they say includes the restored, lost *Books of Moses and Abraham*.

While Jews and mainstream Christians share the Old Testament, Jews reject Jesus as the Messiah and they reject the New Testament as part of their holy scripture. Similarly, mainstream Christians reject the notion of Joseph as a prophet and they reject *The Book of Mormon* as the word of God.

While Mormons and mainstream Christians both view themselves as Christians, neither views the other as fully Christian. As a sort of parallel case, mainstream Christians do not view themselves as Jews based on their observance of the Old Testament and Jesus Christ's heritage as a Jew. If such a claim were made, neither mainstream Jews nor the hypothetical Christian Jews would see themselves as fully Jewish. They would split over the addition of new scripture and the assertion of Jesus Christ's status as the Son of God.

Mormons take the position that a "Great Apostasy" occurred in the Old World shortly after the death of Jesus Christ's disciples. This Great Apostasy was invisible and unknown until God revealed it to Joseph 1,800 years later. The Mormon Church is seen by its members as a restoration of the true church of Jesus Christ in the latter days. Mormons believe that because of the Great

Apostasy and Joseph's subsequent restoration of Jesus Christ's church, only they are truly Christians. The Bible and Jesus Christ's ministry were corrupted, they believe, by "the great and abominable church, the whore of all the earth"[155] mentioned fifteen times in *The Book of Mormon*. According to Joseph Smith's first vision regarding the other sects of Christianity, "all their creeds were an abomination in his sight," and all of their claims of being truly Christian are false.

Throughout its history the Mormon Church has been headed by a succession of 15 presidents, each of whom is seen by Mormons as a prophet, seer, and revelator. The first of these prophet leaders was Joseph Smith. As a prophet of God, the Church's president is capable of changing old doctrine or making new doctrine as required, and may be instructed by God through revelation. This is seen in the multiple versions of Joseph's first vision, the multiple versions of *The Book of Mormon*, and the multiple versions of Joseph Smith's revelations and other church scriptures. The history of the church is under frequent revision and evolution. The Mormon religion is an institution devoted to fulfilling God's agenda on earth, as "translated correctly" by the current prophet through revelation.

In terms of doctrine, Mormons are divided from mainstream Christian by three critical points, identified by Mormon theologian B.H. Roberts:

> First, we believe that God is a being with a body in form like man's; that he possesses body, parts and passions, that in a word, God is an exalted, perfected man.
> Second, we believe in a plurality of Gods.
> Third, we believe that somewhere and some time in the ages to come, through development, through enlargement, through purification until perfection is attained, man at last may become like God — a God.[156]

Where Mormons see God as a physical being, mainstream Christians see God as a non-physical Spirit.

Where Mormons embrace a polytheistic view of multiple Gods, with new Gods emerging over time, mainstream Christians are resolute and unequivocal in their monotheistic view of a single God. In Mormonism, the Father, Son, and Holy Ghost are three separate personages, united in purpose. Traditional Christians view this Trinity as different aspects of one indivisible God.

---

155. Joseph Smith, Jr., *The Book of Mormon* (Salt Lake City: Church of Jesus Christ of Latter-day Saints, 1981), 1Nephi 22:13, page 51; 2 Nephi 28:18, page 108.

156. *The Mormon Doctrine of Deity: The Roberts-Van Der Donckt Discussion*, (Salt Lake City: Signature Books, 1988), page 11.

Where Mormons believe that they too may become Gods, mainstream Christians reject this notion as heresy. On April 7, 1844, just two months before his murder, Joseph Smith presented a discourse at the funeral ceremony of a man named King Follet, in which he first introduced the notion of man's transmigration towards Godhead.

> God himself was once as we are now, and is an exalted man, who sits enthroned in yonder heavens! That is the great secret. If the veil was rent today, and the great God who holds this world in its orbit, and who upholds all worlds and all things by His power, was to make himself visible, — I say, if you were to see him today, you would see him like a man in form — like yourselves in all the person, image, and very form as a man; for Adam was created in the very fashion, image and likeness of God, and received instruction from, and walked, talked and conversed with Him, as one man talks and communes with another....I am going to tell you how God came to be God.[157]

This doctrine is most famously paraphrased by the fifth Mormon Church president, Lorenzo Snow: "As man is, God once was. As God is, man may become." By promising eventual Godhead to devoted members, the Mormon Church has grown from its inception in 1830 to over twelve million members today.

The Book of Mormon is like an icon that can be held up and used to demonstrate that the Mormon religion is the "one true church." As a sales tool, *The Book of Mormon* is taken out into the world by Mormon missionaries who are able to introduce it as a new and improved form of Christianity that includes the Bible with which Christians worldwide are already familiar. By adding "Another Testament of Jesus Christ" onto the Bible, without asking people to surrender their present scriptures, missionaries are phenomenally successful in making new converts. The introduction to the current version of *The Book of Mormon* reads: "The Church of Jesus Christ of Latter Day Saints is the Lord's kingdom once again established on the earth, preparatory to the second coming of the Messiah."[158]

The Mormon Church's Articles of Faith are quite clear. "We believe the Bible to be the word of God as far as it is translated correctly; we also believe the Book of Mormon to be the word of God...We believe in the literal gathering of the Ten Tribes; that Zion will be built upon this [North American] continent;

---

157. Joseph Smith, Jr., *History of the Church of Jesus Christ of Latter Day Saints,* (Salt Lake City: Deseret Book Co., 1980) vol. 6, page 305.

158. *The Church of Jesus Christ of Latter Day Saints, Introduction to The Book of Mormon* (Salt Lake City: Church of Jesus Christ of Latter-day Saints, 1981).

that Christ will reign personally upon the earth; and, that the earth will be renewed and receive its paradisiacal glory."[159]

If we read *The Book of Mormon* literally, as the Mormon Church admonishes its members to do, the Mormon Church is the one and only true church on earth. People are expected to believe this because the prophet, Joseph Smith, has told them so. Joseph Smith knew this because God told him so. And now the Mormon Church sends a missionary army of 56,000 troops out into the world to proclaim that the Mormon religion is the one and only true religion of God.

In this age of inquiry, scientific knowledge, and reasoning, many Christians question the literal truth of the Bible; rather, they find it powerful as a metaphorical myth that continues to have profound relevance in their lives. Doing so makes room for also accepting the age of the universe, the age of earth, and the evolution of humans from ancestors shared with other species, as documented by demonstrated scientific evidence. The Mormon Church, on the other hand, continues to uphold the literal truth of *The Book of Mormon* regardless of what our scientific knowledge tells us about the origins of the Native Americans and the natural history of the human species. Ultimately, without any evidence to support the existence of the golden plates from which it was derived, or to support the story it tells, people are asked to accept *The Book of Mormon* on faith. You either believe it or you don't.

If you believe *The Book of Mormon* isn't the objective truth, then it also becomes difficult to believe in the truth of Joseph Smith's prophecies, his visions, and revelations, or in the Mormon religion itself. The Mormon religion is either the one and only true religion of God, or it isn't. At this point in time, the Mormon Church accommodates no middle ground from its members or prospective members. In order to belong, affirmation that *The Book of Mormon* is true is a rigid requirement.

---

159. Joseph Smith, Jr., *The Pearl of Great Price*, (Salt Lake City: Church of Jesus Christ of Latter-day Saints, 1967), page 59.

PART III. CONTENT: A MODERN LANGUAGE TRANSLATION OF *THE BOOK OF MORMON*

AN INTRODUCTION TO THIS TRANSLATION

This modern-language translation and summary is based on the 1830 version of *The Book of Mormon* printed in Palmyra, New York by Grandin Press, for Joseph Smith, Junior, Author and Proprietor. As of the year 2004, two publishers keep the original 1830 version of *The Book of Mormon* in print. In addition, the complete text of the original version is free and easily available on the Internet.

The translation of each of *The Book of Mormon*'s 14 "Books" is preceded by a summary of that particular book. In addition, each summary is preceded by a very brief, italicized synopsis of that book's general content.

Book, Chapter, and Verse

The original version reads more like a book with paragraphs, while the content of the 1981 version (still current) is divided into books, chapters, and numbered verses to resemble the book, chapter and verse system found in the Bible. Although there have been almost 4,000 textual changes introduced to *The Book of Mormon* throughout the history of its thirteen different English-language versions, the essence of it has not changed at all. In places where notable changes have taken place, these instances are footnoted in the modern-language translation presented in the following pages.

This translation utilizes a little less than half the number of words used in *The Book of Mormon* and the summaries that precede the translation of each "book" represent about 4% of the word count. What happened to the other half? Has any meaning been lost? *The Book of Mormon* is filled with repetitive phrasings and Elizabethan flourishes that add bulk but do not communicate any additional meaning. By eliminating 6,675 words (the 1,353 repetitions of "and it came to pass"), the word count is reduced by 2.5%. In Part I, an example was given of a particularly swollen passage: this modern-language translation uses just 156 words to convey the meaning of the original 414 words.

Twenty-six chapters in *The Book of Mormon* are nearly identical, word for word, to 26 chapters from *The King James Version of the Bible*. These chapters represent about 10% of the content of *The Book of Mormon*. Since there are numerous modern-language translations of the Bible, we have not included these chapters in the translation that follows; instead, they are briefly summarized. For readers who want good translations of these chapters, the equivalent chapters from the Bible are identified for external reference. To the degree that these chapters deviate from the Bible, these deviations are noted in the chapter summaries. The summarization of these 26 chapters considerably shortens the translation.

While it is possible that some meaning may have been lost, or confused, in some places, every possible attempt has been made to keep the translated summary faithful to the original *Book of Mormon's* story line, doctrine, and general picture. Embellishments, exaggerations, and omissions of general meaning have been studiously avoided.

The Book of Mormon is comprised of 15 "books." These books vary widely in size, from as little as 756 words (The Book of Jarom) to 115 times that size with 87,421 words (The Book of Alma). Regardless of the books' sizes, the same effort has been made to represent them faithfully in both the summary and the translation. Some of these books have single authors and some of them have multiple authors. Some books span relatively short periods of time (as little as 20 years), while others span much longer periods (as much as 1,650 years).

Since its original 1830 publication, *The Book of Mormon's* chapter numbering system has been changed, so that the chapters are about half as long and twice as numerous as the in the original version, while maintaining approximately the same word count in total. To help readers correlate this translation with either the original 1830 version or the current 1981 version, both chapter numbering systems have been indicated.

These chapters vary greatly in length. In the original 1830 version, the chapters range in size from as few as 91 words to 9,024 words for the largest chapter. In the current 1981 version, the disparity has been reduced from 100 times to 40 times as great, so that the chapters range in size from 92 words to 3,752 words.

Chronological Sequence of the Story

In order to present the material chronologically, one deviation of sequence from *The Book of Mormon's* presentation is made. *The Book of Mormon* is a story of three transoceanic emigrations from the Middle East to the Western Hemisphere, and the successive events of those peoples in the Americas. *The Book of Ether* tells of the first of these three emigrations, involving a group of people named the Jaredites, from the time of their departure from Babylon in 2200 BC until the time of their total destruction around 550 BC. While these records from The Book of Ether are chronologically the earliest accounts contained in *The Book of Mormon,* they appear sequentially near the end. In order to tell the story of *The Book of Mormon* from beginning to end, we have placed them at the beginning of this translation.

Book of Mormon Dating References

Embedded within *The Book of Mormon* are three separate reference points from which the passage of years are counted. These reference points begin after, and do not include, the time period covered in The Book of Ether. The first identified starting point is around 600 BC, the year when Lehi and his family leave Jerusalem. This reference point is used for counting the passage of years until 92 BC, when the retiring King Mosiah institutes a political system of democratically elected judges. From 92 BC through 1 BC, the years are referenced to the beginning point of these elected judges. In AD 1, Jesus Christ is born into the world and his birth becomes the reference point for all events after that.

Dates (years) for particular events in the translation are provided in brackets, where available. These dates have been extracted from footnotes in the 1981 edition of *The Book of Mormon.*

Gentiles, Jews, and the Family of Israel

The terms "gentile," "Jew," "Family of Israel," and "Lost Tribes of Israel" come up a great deal in *The Book of Mormon* and in the Mormon religion, and can engender a great deal of confusion for readers.

To modern Jews and historic Jews from *The Book of Mormon* (such as Nephi[1], Lehi[1], and the Lehites), the term "Gentile" means those who are not Jewish. From the Jewish point of view, Mormons are Gentiles. When reading *The Book of*

Mormon, the term Gentile is used from the point of view of the Nephites, and means those who are not Jewish or from the lineage of Lehi[1].

To Mormons, the term Gentile means those who have not been baptized into and accepted the Mormon faith. From the Mormon point of view, Jews are Gentiles. When Nephi[1] prophesied about future Gentiles receiving the true gospel of Christ, he is talking about the Mormons, who in their own time are not Gentiles.

The term "Family of Israel" or "House of Israel" refers to the descendants of the twelve sons of the patriarch Israel. Israel was the grandson of the patriarch Abraham through his son, Isaac. Israel started his life out under the name Jacob, and later changed it to Israel. The twelve sons of Israel are the heads of the Twelve Tribes of Israel. Only two of these tribes become the ancestors of the Jewish people. Accordingly, all Jewish people are members of the Family of Israel through Israel's sons Judah and Joseph, but not all the Family of Israel are Jewish.

The "Lost Tribes of Israel" refers to the descendants of the ten other sons of Israel (other than Judah and Joseph of Egypt) who have not been historically tracked to the present. These mythical lost tribes could, in theory, have migrated anywhere and become scattered among the Gentile nations.

Lamanites and Nephites

Who exactly are the Lamanites and the Nephites? In the beginning of *The Book of Mormon*, this question is clear and unambiguous. As the book progresses, however, it becomes confusing.

In *The Second Book of Nephi*, after the patriarch Lehi's death, his people divide into two groups led by his eldest son Laman and his third son Nephi. These two groups are called Lamanites and Nephites. When the Lamanites reject God they are cursed, and physically transformed from white-skinned people into dark skinned people.

In *The Book of Omni*, the migrating Nephites discover the Mulekites, another migratory, transoceanic band of people from Jerusalem, who promptly become Nephites also.

Later on, as Nephites become unrighteous, they are transformed into Lamanites with dark skin color. Reciprocally, as Lamanites become righteous, they are transformed into Nephites, first in name, and then into people with white skin color.

In The Third Book of Nephi, cataclysmic events occur at the time of Jesus Christ's crucifixion in Jerusalem, in which all the unrighteous people are destroyed. Within a year after Jesus Christ's resurrection, all the surviving

Lamanites are converted into Nephites. After 74 years pass without any Lamanites in *The Book of Mormon*, a small band of Nephites rebel, and become Lamanites.

From this second inception, the Lamanite population grows until they outnumber and overpower the Nephites. With Lamanites, Nephites, and Mulekites changing into one another from time to time, it is impossible to clearly establish the ancestry of the Lamanites who ultimately destroy all the Nephites, or the Nephites who are all destroyed.

Multiple Use of the Same Names

Throughout *The Book of Mormon*, the same names are used repeatedly by different characters. For example, there are four characters named Nephi, three characters named Lehi, three characters named Laman, and two characters named Moroni. When a new character is first introduced who has the same name as another mentioned character, the following translation attaches numbers to differentiate the new character (Nephi^1, Nephi^2, Nephi^3, etc.). These numbers are also placed in any location where there is a possibility of character confusion.

In the original 1830 version of *The Book of Mormon*, there is no indexing or dating footnotes to help separate the characters with common names. In the 1981 version of *The Book of Mormon*, an index at the end helps add clarity.

The following list identifies all characters in this translation of *The Book of Mormon* with multiple names, their approximate date of placement, and the "Books" in which they are living characters.

Aaron^1 90 BC, Book of Mosiah, Book of Alma, son of King Mosiah^2

Aaron^2 AD 330, Book of Mormon, a Lamanite king

Alma^1 100 BC, Book of Mosiah, founder of the Church of Christ

Alma^2 80 BC, Book of Alma, son of Alma^1

Amos^1 AD 180, Third Book of Nephi, Nephite record keeper, son of Nephi^4

Amos^2 AD 200, Third Book of Nephi, Nephite record keeper, son of Amos^1

Ammon^1 120 BC, Book of Mosiah, expedition leader

Ammon^2 100 BC, Book of Alma, son of King Mosiah^2

Coriantum^1 not dated, Book of Ether, Chapter 4 (1830 version)

Coriantum^2 not dated, Book of Ether, Chapter 4 (1830 version)

Coriantumr^1 550 BC, Book of Ether, the last living Jaredite

Coriantumr^2 50 BC, Book of Helaman, apostate Nephite and Lamanite commander

Helaman^1 130 BC, Book of Mosiah, son of King Benjamin

Helaman^2 70 BC, Book of Alma, son of Alma^2

Helaman^3 50 BC, Book of Alma, Book of Helaman, son of Helaman^2

Jacob^1 1800 BC, Book of Genesis, Old Testament, a.k.a. Israel, son of Abraham

Jacob^2 590 BC, Second Book of Nephi, Book of Jacob, son of Lehi^1 and brother of Nephi^1

Jacob^3 30 BC, Third Book of Nephi, apostate Nephite

Jared^1 2200 BC, Book of Ether, Chapters 1-6, founder of the Jaredite civilization

Jared^2 not dated, Book of Ether, Chapters 8-9, a Jaredite king

Joseph^1 1700 BC, Book of Genesis, Old Testament, son of Jacob^1

Joseph^2 590 BC, Second Book of Nephi, Book of Jacob, son of Lehi^1 and brother of Nephi^1

Laman^1 600 BC, Second Book of Nephi, Book of Jacob, son of Lehi^1 and brother of Nephi^1

Laman^2 200 BC, Book of Mosiah, Lamanite king

Laman^3 60 BC, Book of Alma, Nephite soldier

Lehi^1 600 BC, First Book of Nephi, Second Book of Nephi, father of Nephi^1

Lehi^2 80 BC, Book of Alma, Nephite military commander

Lehi^3 40 BC, Book of Helaman, son of Helaman^3

Morianton^1 not dated, Book of Ether, Jaredite king

Morianton^2 60 BC, Book of Alma, founder of Nephite city

Moroni^1 100 BC, Book of Alma, Nephite military commander

Moroni^2 AD 420, Book of Mormon, Book of Moroni, son of Mormon

Mosiah^1 200 BC, Book of Omni, Nephite king, father of King Benjamin

Mosiah^2 140 BC, Book of Mosiah, Nephite king, son of King Benjamin

Nephi^1 600 BC, First Book of Nephi, Second Book of Nephi, son of Lehi^1

Nephi^2 40 BC, Book of Helaman, son of Helaman^3

Nephi^3 AD 30, Third Book of Nephi, son of Nephi^2, apostle of Jesus Christ

Nephi^4 AD 40, Fourth Book of Nephi, son of Nephi^3

Pahoran^1 70 BC, Book of Alma, Nephite judge

Pahoran^2 50 BC, Book of Helaman, son of Pahoran^1, Nephite judge

THE BOOK OF ETHER — 2200 BC TO 550 BC

From Golden Plates Inscribed by Ether in 550 BC and later
Transcribed, Abridged, Annotated, and Added to the Book of
Mormon Plates by Mormon's son, Moroni[2], in AD 420

An account of the Jaredite people's transoceanic emigration from Babylon to the Western Hemisphere in 2200 BC, and the proliferation of their extensive civilization until the time of their total destruction in AD 550.

THE BOOK OF ETHER SUMMARY

The Book of Ether spans a sweeping 1,650-year time period. It covers the history of the Jaredite people between the time of their exodus from Babylon in 2,200 BC until their complete destruction in the New World around 550 BC. The Book of Ether is based on a set of 24 golden plates inscribed and then hidden away by the ancient prophet Ether, around 550 BC. Although Ether's plates were written in an unknown language, the Nephites were able to translate them into their language with the help of magical translation devices. The Book of Ether is a synopsis that was edited, transcribed, annotated, and then added to The Book of Mormon plates by Mormon's son Moroni[2] around AD 420. This is the same Moroni who appeared to Joseph Smith as an angel in a series of visions between 1823 and 1827, and revealed to him the golden plates on which The Book of Mormon was written. In 121 BC, 540 years before Moroni's time, Ether's 24 golden plates were discovered, translated, and kept thereafter by Moroni's ancestors.

Moroni made note that Ether's records were a hundred times more involved and lengthy than his transcription of them. Part of this omitted record included an account of the world's history from the time of its creation through the building of the tower of Babel (Old Testament, Genesis, Chapters 1 through 11). Moroni excused himself from including these stories in his transcription of The Book of Ether because God told him those stories had been faithfully kept by the Jews, and that the person (Joseph Smith) who would eventually find The Book of Mormon plates would already have this account of the world's beginning. Moroni tells his future readers that Ether's message is a warning and example of what will happen to people and nations who ignore or defy God's will.

Jared[1] (after whom the Jaredites are named) and his brother Mahonri lived with their families in the city of Babylon, in present-day Iraq. The Tower of Babel mentioned in the Old Testament's Book of Genesis was being constructed at that time and God was not at all happy with it. To disrupt this construction, he confused the languages of the workers so that no one could understand anyone else. Further construction of the tower then became impossible. Because of Mahonri's closeness to God, his family and group of friends were spared from the language confusion that God angrily inflicted upon the people of Babylon. God guided Mahonri's people, the Jaredites, westward across 5,000 miles of northern Africa to the Atlantic Ocean. There he instructed them to make eight shell-like boats in which to cross the sea to the vacant Western Hemisphere.

God appeared to Mahonri in a vision, upon completion of the boats, and identified himself as Jesus Christ. To illuminate the darkness inside the enclosed boats during their ocean crossing, Jesus Christ magically transformed 16 stones, provided by Mahonri, into sources of light. In this vision Jesus Christ also revealed the pageant of the human drama. Mahonri was shown the lives and events of all the people who had ever lived, or ever would live on earth, from its beginning to its end.

After the Jaredites loaded themselves, their livestock, and their luminous stones onto the boats, God drove them another 6,000 miles across the Atlantic Ocean with powerful, unrelenting winds while the people and animals huddled inside. After nearly a year at sea, they arrived on the east coast of the New World. Jared[1] and Mahonri grew old and died, but they left behind generations of descendants — who were sometimes good and sometimes not. A great civilization emerged where they had landed, near a narrow neck of land that separated oceans to the east and west, and lands to the north and south. The Jaredites built cities and made steel. They raised livestock including domesticated elephants, cows, horses, sheep, goats, oxen, asses, and pigs from the Old World. They farmed domesticated fruits and grains that they'd brought with them from Babylon. They produced fine linen and silk clothing. Eventually, their population grew to many millions of people.

For most of the Jaredite people's history, the details of their civilization are summarized very briefly and superficially. What historical detail is provided deals primarily with the beginning and end of the Jaredites' story line.

By Ether's time, the Jaredites were corrupt and had fallen from their lofty relationship with God. Earlier prophets had warned them to renew their faith in God or be destroyed and swept away from their lands. Unless they repented, the prophets said, God would usher in a new wave of favored people and replace them as heirs to this choicest of lands that they'd been given. When the prophets were ignored, the destruction that was foretold began to unfold.

Ether witnessed and recorded the total destruction of the Jaredite people as they fell into war and ruin. Eventually all of the Jaredite people, except for Ether, divided into two factions who fought and killed one another until only he and another combatant-king were left alive. In the end, God told Ether to go out and witness the fulfillment of his prophecies.

(The Book of Ether is filled with digressions, commentary, and explanations by Mormon's son Moroni. For the purpose of clarity, in the following translation, Moroni's editorial notations are presented in italics to distinguish his words from his abridgement of Ether's record.)

THE BOOK OF ETHER - TRANSLATION

Chapter 1. 1830 and 1981 Versions

*I am Moroni, the son of Mormon. The following account is the history of ancient inhabitants of this land, known as the Jaredites, who were destroyed by God. I make this account from a set of 24 golden plates called The Book of Ether which were discovered long ago by subjects of King Limhi.**

*Ether's plates were discovered in 121 BC, during the time of King Mosiah, 540 years before Moroni's time, and were preserved until Moroni's time by his ancestors.

The first part of this record tells of the creation of the world, the story of Adam, and the events of mankind up until the time when the great tower of Babel was being built. I know that the Jews have faithfully kept the creation story and the early stories of mankind intact and available. Therefore I will only inscribe that portion of Ether's words from the time of the tower, until the time when the Jaredites were destroyed.

The prophet and author Ether was a descendant of Jared, after whom the Jaredite people were named, through 29 ancestors who are individually named and recounted.

Jared and his brother Mahonri Moriancumer* lived in Babylon with their friends and families, at the time when the great tower of Babel was being constructed. God was displeased with the tower and expressed his anger by halting the construction. He did this by confusing the languages of the people so that no one could understand the words of anyone else. In dismay, the people fled, and were scattered across the earth. [2200 BC]

*Jared's brother is never mentioned by name in The Book of Mormon, but is always referred to as "the brother of Jared" — even though he is the most significant character in the Book of Ether. At a christening in 1841, Jared's brother's name was made known to Joseph Smith by revelation, as Mahonri Moriancumer; therefore, we refer to him by this name.

When Jared saw this happening, he turned to his big and mighty brother Mahonri, who was highly favored by God. "Please, ask God to spare our families and friends from mixing up our language," Jared said.

When God granted Mahonri's request, Jared again pleaded with Mahonri, saying, "Will you please go to God again, and ask him to preserve the language integrity of our friends?"

When God granted Mahonri's second request, Jared wanted him to ask for yet another favor. "Will you ask God whether he intends to drive us from this land? If so, please ask him where we should go. Maybe he will direct us to the choicest land on earth. If this is the case, let us be faithful to God so that we can receive this choice land for our inheritance."

God had compassion for Mahonri's group of family and friends. "Gather your families, your livestock, and seeds," he said. "When you have done that, lead them into the valley to the north, where I will meet you. I will lead you from there to the choicest land on earth, where I will bless you and your descendants. I will support your people there in building the greatest nation on earth. I do this because you have faithfully prayed to me for a long time, and have now cried out to me for help."

Chapter 2. 1981 Version

After traveling north, Mahonri's party arrived in a valley they named Nimrod. From there, God spoke with Mahonri from the clouds. He could be heard but not seen. He guided Mahonri's party westward through a wilderness that men had never previously entered. As they journeyed, God talked to them and gave them direction from the clouds. They crossed bodies of water on boats that God directed them to build, and then leave behind. They continued ever westward, towards the promised land. God swore to Mahonri that those who inherited this promised land would forever devote themselves to him, the one and only God, or suffer his anger and be swept away.

You can see from Ether's words, wrote Moroni, that whatever nation possesses this promised land must serve God or be swept aside by his anger. I say this to you, Gentiles, so that you will know what has been decreed. You have the opportunity to repent for you sinfulness and reform your ways before it is too late. Do not bring on God's anger, as the former inhabitants of this land did. God will keep it free from slavery or bondage to other nations as long as the people serve Jesus Christ, as is shown in these records.

Eventually, the Jaredites reached the coastline and lived on the seashore in tents for four years in a place they named Moriancumer. After the four years, God again came to Mahonri and spoke to him from the clouds. He chastened Mahonri for failing to call upon him. Mahonri apologized for his sins and begged for forgiveness.

"I will forgive you and your party for their sins," God said, "but do not sin anymore. If you do, you will be cut off. The land I am sending you to is the choicest land on earth. In order to reach it you will you need to build boats to cross the ocean."

God instructed Mahonri how to build eight small boats. The decks were designed almost like a mirror image of the boats' bottoms, so that the finished boats had the appearance of elongated, hollow nut shells. Designed to withstand the intensity of the ocean waves, the boats were the length of a tree and had watertight doors.

When the boats were finished, Mahonri prayed. "Oh God, I have built the boats according to your instruction. But how will be able to see inside their darkness, or be able to steer them?" he asked. "Once they are sealed up, how will we be able to breathe?"

"Cut small holes in the tops and bottoms of the boats, with fitted plugs," God replied. "When you need air, unplug the holes. When the waves are so great that they threaten to flood the boat, plug them up again so that you aren't drowned inside."

When Mahonri had done this, he cried out again, saying, "I have made the holes as you commanded, but they are still dark inside. How will we navigate them without being able to see?"

"What would you have me do to give you light inside the boats?" God asked. "You cannot have windows because the waves will break them to pieces. Neither can you build fires inside and go by their light. You will be like a whale in the sea. Mountains of waves will fall upon you, and I will bring you up from the depths. I will send forth winds and storms from my mouth to drive your boats across the ocean. Unless you are fully prepared for the intensity of the waves, the ocean cannot be crossed. What would you like me to prepare for you to light your boats when you are swallowed up by the depths of the sea?"

Chapter 3. 1981 Version

In order to provide light, Mahonri smelted 16 transparent white stones, two for each boat, and climbed a mountain to pray to God.

"Oh, God!" Mahonri prayed, "You say we will be embraced by floods as we cross the ocean. Please don't be angry with me for my weakness before you. I know that you are holy and that you live in heaven. We are unworthy because of our inclination to sin, but you have commanded us to call on you to receive your instructions and blessings. Even though you have punished us because of our sinfulness, and driven us forward for many years through the wilderness, you have also shown us great mercy. Please look upon me with pity and don't be angry when I ask that you not send us across the raging ocean in total darkness. I have prepared these stones you see before me from molten rock. Because of who you are, and your great power, you can do anything for the benefit of men. Would you touch each of these stones with your finger and make them luminous for us, so that they will light the vessels during our ocean crossing?"

According to Mahonri's wish, God appeared and laid out his hand to touch each stone individually with his finger while Mahonri prostrated himself before God in fear.

"Why have you fallen down, Mahonri?" asked God. "Arise."

"Seeing the finger of God become flesh, I was afraid that I would be killed for the insolence of my request," replied Mahonri.

"No man before you has ever held greater faith in me. It is your faith which allows you to see my finger, where no other man might have seen it. Did you see anything more than my finger?" asked God.

"No," replied Mahonri. "Will you show yourself to me?"

"Will you believe in me always, and in my word?" asked God.

"Yes," replied Mahonri, "for I know that you are a God of truth and cannot lie."

Upon hearing these words, God showed himself to Mahonri, saying, "Because you know these things, you will be redeemed from the fall, and brought back into my presence. I have prepared the redemption of my people since the foundation of the world was laid. I am Jesus Christ, I am the Father, and I am the Son. All of those who believe in me will be my sons and daughters, and have life everlasting. Before this, I have never shown myself to any man, because no man before you has ever believed in me as you have. I have created all men in my own image. The body you see before you now is my spirit body, in whose likeness all men are made. As I appear to you now, I will also appear some day to my people in flesh."

While I do not make a full account of Jesus Christ's appearance to Mahonri, wrote Moroni, it is enough to say that Jesus Christ appeared to him in the same manner and appearance in which he later showed himself to the Nephites [2234 years later in AD 34]. Jesus Christ ministered to Mahonri just as he did later, to the Nephites. Because Mahonri's faith was so great, he saw beyond the veil. He knew beyond doubt that it was Jesus Christ himself that he was talking with, and by whom he was being ministered to.

"But it is not yet time for men to know of me and my word," Jesus Christ said, as he continued talking to Mahonri, "so you will not permit others to hear what you have seen and heard. I command you to engrave on metal plates what has transpired, in an unknown language that cannot be interpreted by others." God then gave Mahonri two more magical stones with which to seal up the engraved plates of his record, telling him that in due time the stones would permit the translation of Mahonri's engravings.

After this, God showed Mahonri a vision of all the people who had ever lived and who would ever live on earth. God withheld nothing that would ever happen from Mahonri's sight, saying, "Because you believe in me, I show you everything. Engrave what I have shown you on the plates and seal them with the two stones I have given you. At the appropriate time, I will show them to all people, but until then show them to no one."

Chapter 4. 1981 Version

God then commanded Mahonri to return from the mountaintop.

Part of what Mahonri wrote was forbidden to men until after Jesus Christ was crucified, wrote Moroni. That is why King Benjamin* and his successors kept this knowledge so carefully guarded until after Jesus Christ showed himself to the Nephite people, and commanded that these things should be known.

*In subsequent versions of *The Book of Mormon,* the identified custodian and translator of Ether's golden plates has been changed from King Benjamin to King Mosiah. At the time the Nephites discovered and translated Ether's golden plates, King Benjamin was dead and his son Mosiah was the king and translator. King Benjamin never knew of the existence or the content of Ether's plates.

I have written part of what Mahonri saw because God has commanded me to do so. Never have greater things been revealed to men than were shown to him. God has also commanded me to seal up these records with the magical stones so that the rest of this record will not be known before its appropriate time.

"The content of these visions will be sealed and not given to the Gentiles until they repent and come clean before me," God said to Moroni. "When that day comes, and they show the same faith in me that Mahonri did, I will show them the same visions and revelations I have shown to him. Those who work against the word of God, on the other hand, will be cursed. At my command, the heavens can be opened and closed, the earth made to shake, and the people of earth destroyed. People who encourage others to do good in my name are with me, because only in my name can good be accomplished. I am the Father. I am the light, the life, and the truth of the world."

"If the Gentiles and descendants of Israel will come to me," God continued, "I will show them great things which are hidden because of their disbelief. When this record is received, the people will know that the time of revelation is near, and the final work of God has begun. So, repent and come to me. Believe in my gospel and be baptized in my name. Those who don't believe will be damned. On the last day of judgment, those who are faithful will be lifted up to live in the kingdom I have prepared for them. Behold, I have spoken."

Chapter 2. 1830 Version

Chapter 5. 1981 Version

I have transcribed these records as commanded, wrote Moroni. The part that is sealed up is forbidden until God allows it to be translated and revealed. When these records are eventually found, the golden plates themselves will be shown to three witnesses, by the power of God, so they can testify as to their existence. If you doubt my authority, you will see me on the last day and know then that what I say is true.

Chapter 3. 1830 Version

Chapter 6. 1981 Version

As Mahonri descended from the mountain, he brought with him the 16 stones that now shown brilliantly. When they were placed at both ends of each boat, they fully illuminated them. Mahonri's party then loaded the boats with their livestock, seeds for planting, food for the journey, fresh drinking water, and the rest of their belongings. They cast off from shore and trusted God to carry them safely across the broad ocean.

As promised, God caused a great wind to blow steadily across the ocean towards the promised land. The boats bounced on the waves and were sometimes buried underneath them, arising safely again like bobbing corks. Throughout the duration of the crossing, the wind never relented. The party prayed, sang, and gave praise to God for 344 days, until their boats all beached themselves together on the shores of the promised land.

Upon their arrival, they gathered together, bowed down, and gave thanks to God for delivering them safely. They offered their tears of joy before breaking the earth with their plows, and spreading their seeds across the new land.

From the original dozens who had traveled from Babylon, the young sons and daughters married, and had children themselves. As the Jaredites multiplied, they blessed God, and were blessed by God in return. Mahonri came to have twenty-two children, and his brother Jared had twelve. When Mahonri approached the end of his life, he gathered the people together and asked what he might do for them before he died.

The people, it turned out, wanted one of Mahonri's, or Jared's, sons to be declared king. To Mahonri, this was abhorrent. "Surely this will lead to tyranny and slavery," he said.

But Jared disagreed with his brother, saying, "Let them have a king."

Mahonri reluctantly went along. "Choose a king for yourselves from among our sons," he said.

When the people chose Pagog, Mahonri's first-born son, as their king, he declined. He didn't want to rule over them. When the people asked Mahonri to declare him king anyway, he refused to do so. One by one, all of Mahonri's sons were selected as king and each declined. Afterwards, each of Jared's sons was selected and each of them also declined, except for Orihah who accepted the call. Not long afterwards, Mahonri and Jared died. With their passing, Babylon and the journey to the promised land receded from the people's memory.

Orihah led his people well, throughout his long lifetime. He guided them according to the orders that God had given to Mahonri. By following God's instructions, the kingdom grew rich and flourished.

Chapter 7. 1981 Version

King Orihah passed the crown to his son Kib, who had many children, including a son named Corihor who conquered and imprisoned his own father. While he was imprisoned, Kib fathered another son, named Shule, who grew exceptionally strong and mighty in his judgment. He and his followers smelted ore and made steel swords for themselves. Shule organized a successful rebellion against his brother Corihor. After Corihor was defeated, Kib was restored as king, and designated Shule as his successor.

It was a time of convoluted royal family quarrels and intrigues. Corihor's son Noah rebelled and captured Shule, who was rescued by his sons. A son of Noah's, named Cohor, split the kingdom in two. A son of Cohor's, named Nimrod, restored the kingdom by conceding his father's kingdom to Shule.

During Shule's rule, God sent forth prophets who declared that the land was cursed because of the people's idolatry and wickedness. The prophets said that unless the people repented, they would be destroyed. Instead of listening to them, the people mocked and harassed the prophets. In his wisdom, King Shule punished these harassers and passed a law that encouraged the prophets to go everywhere and speak of God's word. Because of this, the people repented and peace and prosperity reigned during the days of King Shule.

Chapter 8. 1981 Version

King Shule passed the crown to his son Omer and the royal intrigues continued. Omer's son Jared[2] raised an army and conquered Omer, forcing his father to live in captivity and servitude. Then two of Omer's other sons defeated Jared and restored Omer as king. Jared would have been killed, along with his army, except for the compassion of his brothers, who granted him his life.

Afterwards, Jared was deeply depressed about having lost the kingdom and the glory it entailed. "Why are you so sad?" Jared's beautiful daughter asked. "Our ancient records tell of secret plans that can be used to obtain kingdoms and glory."

Jared conspired with his daughter, who proposed to regain the throne for him through trickery and seduction. According to his daughter's plan, they invited Akish, a close friend of King Omer's, for dinner. "Look at how beautiful I am," she said. "I will dance for him, and he will want me for his wife. When he asks for my hand in marriage, you can give your approval — on the condition that they deliver to us your father's head."

When Jared's daughter danced for Akish, he was smitten; and he agreed to murder his friend the king, just as Jared and his daughter had planned. Akish then formed a diabolical alliance of fellow conspirators and swore them to secret oaths. They swore to Akish, in the name of God in heaven, by the heavens, and by their lives, that they would not divulge any of the secrets that they swore to.

I will not divulge the details of their oaths and conspiracies because these exist among all men, wrote Moroni. They caused the destruction of the Jaredite people, and also my own people. Any people or nation who upholds secret conspiracies for power and gain will be destroyed in vengeance by God. This certain destruction is shown to you so that you will repent beforehand, and not commit this heinous act. Secret conspiracies are like poison to freedom in all lands and result in destruction to those who use them. They are tools of the devil. I write these words so that this evil will end, and the devil will lose his power over the hearts of men who have been persuaded to do good.

Chapter 4. 1830 Version

Chapter 9. 1981 Version

When God warned King Omer of the plot to kill him, in a dream, he and his family escaped to safety. Because of their evil conspiracy, Akish and his friends overthrew Omer's kingdom, and Jared was again made king. After marrying Jared's daughter Akish desired to be king himself, so he used his evil alliances to kill his father-in-law, and then crowned himself king. But corruption took hold of the kingdom like a disease. Suspicious jealousy caused Akish to kill one of his sons, and another son fled to unite with the exiled former King Omer. The remaining sons of Akish devised strategies to acquire wealth and power. Wars between Akish and his sons erupted and lasted for years. All of the people ended up killing each other except for the thirty who had fled with Omer, who returned afterwards and again regained his kingdom.

Omer passed the kingdom onto his son, Emer. During Emer's reign, peace and prosperity again prevailed. Their wealth included an abundance of fruit, grains, fine linen, silks, cattle, oxen, sheep, pigs, goats, horses, asses, and domesticated elephants. They also kept some large domesticated animals of unknown species (which were called cureloms and cumoms) that were especially useful to them. God poured forth his blessings with the understanding that if the people should falter in their righteousness, his wrath and destruction would fall upon them.

Omer passed the kingdom on to his son Coriantum[1], who continued the legacy of peace and prosperity throughout his 142-year life. Coriantum passed the kingdom on to his son Com.

Heth, the son of Com, embraced the old and evil ways by personally killing his father, and reigning as king afterwards. Again, the prophets arose and declared that unless the people repented, the land would be cursed and famine and destruction would prevail; but the people and King Heth paid no attention to them. They even went so far as to throw the prophets into pits to die. When the rains didn't come, the crops failed and the people died. Poisonous snakes arose that killed many people and drove their livestock away. When the

people saw that they were doomed to starvation, they repented and cried out to God. After they had humbled themselves sufficiently, God relented and sent rain. After the power of God was shown for all to see, the people revived and the harvests returned.

Chapter 10. 1981 Version

All of Heth's family died in the famine, except for a son named Shez. Remembering the destruction, Shez formed a righteous kingdom and restored peace and prosperity to the land. When he died, the kingdom passed to his son Riplakish.

Under Riplakish, the kingdom again strayed from God's good will. Riplakish had many wives and mistresses, and taxed the people heavily to pay for his luxurious palaces. Those who objected to the taxation, or were unable to pay, were thrown into jail. In jail, the prisoners were forced to work endlessly on the king's projects or be subject to execution. This example of promiscuity, greed, and abuse set the tone for the kingdom. After 42 years, the people rebelled, killed Riplakish, and drove his family out.

Many years later, a descendant of Riplakish, named Morianton[1], gathered an army of outcasts and made war on the cities. This bitter war lasted many years, but eventually Morianton gained power over all of the land and established himself as king. His reign was easier on the people than the war had been, so the people were relieved and openly acknowledged Morianton as king. He ruled the people with justice but practiced personal depravity, and was cut off from God.

Morianton was succeeded by his son Kim, who also ignored the will of God. Kim was overthrown by his brother and kept prisoner for the remainder of his life. As an aged prisoner, he fathered a son named Levi, and then died. Levi was imprisoned for 42 years before he overthrew the king and crowned himself.

Levi followed God's will and the people prospered. Levi passed the kingdom on to his son Corom, who also was favored by God.

Corom passed the kingdom on to his son Kish, who passed it on to Lib. Under Lib's guidance, God's laws were observed and the poisonous snakes were eliminated. Without the snakes to interfere with their passage, the people moved southward to hunt the abundant wild game. When the people came to a narrow neck of land, they stopped their migration and built a great city. The south land was left as a hunting preserve and the north lands became covered with people and their fine cities. They mined gold, silver, copper, and iron ore to make tools, weapons and ornaments. The people made fine cloth from silk and linen. Utilizing their excellent workmanship, they made highly specialized weapons, tools for agriculture, and tools for working with their animals. They were blessed by God and prospered in peace.

Lib passed the kingdom on to his son, Hearthom, who ruled until he was overthrown and spent the rest of his life as a prisoner. For four generations, the descendants of Hearthom lived their entire lives in captivity: Hearthom to Heth, to Aaron, to Amnigaddah, to Coriantum[2]. Coriantum's son Com rose up against his captivity and became ruler of the kingdom after many years of fighting. During Com's rule, robbers arose throughout the land and sought to destroy the kingdom with their secret oaths and alliances. King Com's efforts to overcome them were insufficient and the kingdom faltered.

Chapter 11. 1981 Version

During the time of Com's rule, many prophets foretold of the destruction of the great kingdom unless the people repented and returned to God. Instead of listening, the people turned on the prophets and tried to destroy them. Because he protected the prophets, King Com was blessed for the remainder of his life. Com passed the kingdom on to his son Shiblom.

Shiblom's brother Seth rebelled against him and brought war to the land, and death to the prophets. The prophets had made it clear that if the people misbehaved, then destruction on a horrendous scale would be assured. And this is what happened. War, famine, and disease stalked the land and killed the people. When the destruction became too great to bear, the people repented and God showed mercy on them.

Shiblom was killed, Seth was imprisoned, and Seth's son Aha became king. Aha paid no attention to God's laws and ruled briefly until

his death. Aha's son Etham followed him as king and continued the legacy of wicked rulers. Many prophets arose during Etham's reign, saying that unless things changed, God would utterly destroy everyone who did not repent. The people didn't listen.

Etham's son Moron reigned next. He was also disrespectful and defiant towards God. Moron put down one rebellion but was overthrown later by another challenger. Moron lived the rest of his life in captivity and fathered Coriantor, who lived his entire life in captivity. Coriantor fathered the prophet Ether, who was born into captivity.

The prophets continued to forecast doom, saying that God would cause the utter destruction of the Jaredites. They said that God would bring another group of people to possess this land that had once been given to their ancestors. Because of their wickedness, the descendants of Jared chose to ignore these warnings.

Chapter 5. 1830 Version

Chapter 12. 1981 Version

The prophet Ether lived at the end of the Jaredite people's time when a man named Coriantumr[1] was king. As he grew older, Ether spent all of his hours of all his days warning the people that unless they repented, and came again to align themselves with God, they would be destroyed. Ether prophesied amazing things; but the people didn't believe him, because they couldn't see for themselves what he was talking about.

Faith centers around things that are hoped for, but cannot be seen, wrote Moroni. Faith often determines what we see. It was by faith that Jesus Christ showed himself after his resurrection. It is by faith that we can hope to partake of Jesus Christ's gift. It was by faith that Mahonri was able to see the finger of God.

It is by faith that I know that this record, which God has commanded me to make, will come to the people of the earth in the last days. I have talked with God about the records and asked if it weren't the case that, "the Gentiles who will find these records will mock them because of the weak quality of our writing abilities."

"Fools who mock your records," God replied to me, "will be sorry. My grace will be sufficient for anyone who humbles himself before me and has faith in me. Your weak efforts will become strong for those who believe."

I prayed that God's words were true and that the future readers of my record would treat it charitably, and God replied, "If they don't receive your words generously, it will be through no fault of your own. You have been faithful to me. Because you see your weakness, you will be made strong, and a place will be made for you in my kingdom."

When we meet at the time of Jesus Christ's judgment, you will know that I have seen him and that he talked with me directly. Therefore, I advise you to seek out this Jesus Christ, about whom the prophets and apostles have written, so that his grace may rest on you.

Chapter 6. 1830 Version

Chapter 13. 1981 Version

None of Ether's warnings or teachings was heeded. He reviewed the history of the world from the time of God's creation. He foretold of Jesus Christ's coming, of the destruction of Old Jerusalem in Israel, of the descendants of Israel's son Joseph[1] of Egypt journeying to America as the Jaredites had done, and of the building of a New Jerusalem on the American continent by these descendants of Joseph. Ether's prophecies were thought to be ridiculous and he was banished from the people he sought to inform. He hid in a cave during the day and wrote his record. At night he went out and witnessed the judgments that were brought down upon the people.

Great wars engulfed all of the land and all of the people. God commanded Ether to seek out the king, Coriantumr, and bring his prophecy to him. God promised to restore peace, and the kingdom, and to spare the people if only Coriantumr would repent. Coriantumr was told that if he failed to repent, another people would receive this promised land, and all of Coriantumr's people would die, except for him. His life would be preserved long enough for him to see the truth of Ether's prophecy, and watch as another people received all the land that he now claimed as his. Ether's prophecy was rejected by Coriantumr's household. The wars and killings continued. Many people now wished Ether dead, and tried to kill him; but he eluded them by living apart from the people, in caves, watching as control of the land shifted back and forth between the warring factions.

A warrior named Shared arose, who overcame Coriantumr in battle and took him prisoner. Coriantumr's sons defeated Shared and reclaimed the kingdom for their father; but Shared continued his warfare against the kingdom. Coriantumr destroyed Shared's army during a series of battles, and killed Shared himself, but during the battle Shared wounded Corantumr badly. The king spent two years recovering while renegade warriors pillaged and killed across the land without any restraint.

Chapter 14. 1981 Version

The years passed. Wars spread their destruction everywhere. No one was safe and all property was subject to theft. Cities were overthrown, burnt, and ruined by warring armies. Women and children were left dead in the armies' wake.

In the interest of preserving their own security, the remaining people all gathered into two great, opposing armies. One army was lead by the warrior Shiz and the other by King Coriantumr. The land was littered everywhere with dead bodies, which were left to rot because there weren't enough people left to bury them. The armies only had time to march forward and make more war against each other. This left the stench of the dead behind them. As the armies of Shiz and Coriantumr moved across the land, they killed anyone they found who would not join them.

Again and again the armies clashed, with ever increasing casualties. In one battle, Coriantumr was badly injured. He fell unconscious and was carried away as if dead. Because the deaths of men, women, and children on both sides were so great, Shiz ordered his army to stop their hostilities against Coriantumr's army, and return to their camp.

Chapter 15. 1981 Version

Coriantumr recovered from his wounds and was reminded of Ether's prophecy. He thought of the evil that he had caused during his lifetime. Nearly two million of his soldiers had been killed in battle, and even greater numbers of women and children had died. When he realized that each, and all, of the prophecies were coming true, he repented — but to no avail. Coriantumr ultimately offered to surrender his kingdom to Shiz if his people would be spared. Shiz responded that if Coriantumr would surrender himself to Shiz, he would personally kill him with his own sword, and the lives of his people would be spared.

But the unrepentant people of Coriantumr would have none of that. They were too angry against the people of Shiz, who were in turn angry against Coriantumr's people. It was too late now for repentance to take root. The divisions and hatred between the two opposing peoples could not be recalled and brought to peace. Again, the army of Shiz brought war to the people of Coriantumr. In the ensuing battle, Coriantumr was again wounded and fell unconscious while his army turned the tide against the army of Shiz. The fleeing army of Shiz retreated to a hill named Ramah.

*This is the same hill, wrote Moroni, on which my father Mormon hid the sacred records.**

*This is also the place where Joseph Smith later discovered the golden plates on September 22, 1823 — 2,369 years after the events described by Ether, and 1,438 years after they were placed there by Moroni's father Mormon.

Over the next four years, all of the remaining Jaredite people gathered and joined one or the other of the opposing armies. Ether watched as the two armies prepared for the final battle of the war. Women and children armed themselves to fight alongside the men.

When all of those still alive had joined one army or the other, they prepared to fight. They fought a whole day long and many people were killed on both sides. Neither side was winning. They battled again the next day with similar results and mounting dead. The third and fourth days went the same, with ever growing anger, grief, and loss of life. At the conclusion of the fifth day's battle, only 52 of Coriantumr's army and 69 of Shiz's army remained alive. On the sixth day, these remaining few continued to fight with all their effort, until at the end of the day Coriantumr's people were reduced to 27, with Shiz still commanding 32 soldiers. On the seventh day, the Jaredites' once huge population was reduced to the two warrior commanders; Coriantumr and Shiz. Exhaustion and loss of blood finally brought Shiz to unconsciousness, whereupon Coriantumr raised himself up and cut off Shiz's head.

Then God told Ether to go and witness how his words of prophecy had been fulfilled [550 BC].

Ether finished his records and hid them away, where they would eventually be found by the people that God sent next to receive this promised land.

Ether's closing words were, "It doesn't matter to me whether I am taken directly up to God before death, or whether I physically die in the flesh, as long as I am saved in the kingdom of God."

THE FIRST BOOK OF NEPHI — 600 BC TO 588 BC
From Plates Inscribed by Nephi[1] then Abridged and Later
Inscribed onto the Book of Mormon Plates by Mormon

An account of the exodus of the family of Lehi[1] from Jerusalem in 600 BC and their transoceanic emigration to the Western Hemisphere in 589 BC. Both Lehi and his son, Nephi[1], receive numerous visions from God.

THE FIRST BOOK OF NEPHI SUMMARY

The First Book of Nephi is the story of Nephi's family emigration to the Western Hemisphere, beginning with his family's exodus from Jerusalem while Nephi[1] was still an adolescent. Nephi's father Lehi[1] had a vision in which God warned him that Jerusalem was about to be conquered and destroyed. He and his family were commanded to leave their home and set out on a journey. God told Lehi that he would guide them to a promised land that was the choicest place on earth.

Shortly after their departure, Nephi and his older brothers were sent back to Jerusalem twice on assignments from God. They returned the first time to acquire the records of their ancestors that were inscribed on brass plates. On this trip, Nephi had to murder Laban, the record keeper, in order to fulfill his mission. The records that were retrieved are known to us as those portions of the Old Testament that were written prior to 600 BC.

On their second trip back to Jerusalem, they gathered together the family of Ishmael to accompany them in their exodus. The inclusion of this second family provided wives for Nephi and his brothers.

When Nephi and his party departed on their journey through the wilderness, God provided Lehi with a magical brass ball, called the Liahona, which worked as a divine compass and as a conveyance of God's words. The Liahona pointed the way as long as they observed God's will. Over the course of the next eight years, the party traveled 1,500 miles through the uninhabited wilderness of the Arabian Peninsula, suffered hardship, and had children before finally reaching the shores of the Indian Ocean.

When they arrived on the coastline, Nephi received another vision from God, in which he was commanded to build a boat in which the group could cross the ocean to the promised land. With the reluctant help of his brothers, Nephi managed the construction, through regular instructions from God. When it was ready, the party boarded the ship and set sail for America via the Indian and Pacific Oceans.

After a hazardous and mutinous 19,000-mile ocean journey, they arrived safely on the west coast of the North American continent and began to farm the land. They easily domesticated cows, oxen, horses, and goats that they found in the forest.

Interwoven with this story of their journey is an account of the growing conflict between Lehi and his two wicked older brothers, Laman[1] and Lemuel. On several occasions, Laman and Lemuel conspired to kill Nephi, only to back down when God revealed his protective powers and support for Nephi.

Also woven into the story are the many dreams and visions of both Nephi and Lehi, in which God shows them the correct path for life, the heavenly rewards for obedience to God, and the punishment of eternal hell for disobeying God's words. In one of Nephi's visions, an angel of God showed him the birth, mission, and crucifixion of Jesus Christ; and the arrival and visitation of Jesus Christ to Nephi's descendants in America 600 years in the future. Nephi was shown the unfortunate destruction of his own descendants at the hands of his brothers' descendants in America, the discovery of the New World by Christopher Columbus, the arrival of European immigrants, the American Revolutionary War, and the founding of the United States of America more than 2,300 years in the future.

In his visions, Nephi was also shown the formation of the Roman Catholic Church by his angel guide, who described it as the "great and abominable church" and "the whore of all the earth." The angel told Nephi that this abominable church would be led by the devil, and that this church would deliberately corrupt the Old Testament Gospels, and also corrupt the New Testament Gospels after they'd been written, hundreds of years in the future. He was told that the reason for this corruption was to purposely lead men astray so that the devil could more easily capture them. Nephi was told that the records that he and his descendants kept would be critical in the restoration of the true gospels, and ultimately in the salvation of the world. The angel told of a final conflict between the true church of Jesus Christ and the devil's abominable church. In this climactic battle, the devil's church would be destroyed, and Jesus Christ would reign supreme.

Chapters 20 and 21 of the First Book of Nephi match up nearly word for word with Isaiah 48 and 49, in the Old Testament, from the *King James Version of the Bible*. In the context of the story, Nephi read these two chapters to his brothers from the brass plates he retrieved from Jerusalem, as evidence of the truth of Jesus Christ's coming. Afterwards, he liberally interpreted Isaiah's words to reinforce the visions he had received concerning the destiny of his brothers' descendants, and the end of the world.

THE FIRST BOOK OF NEPHI - TRANSLATION

Chapter 1. 1830 and 1981 Versions

I am Nephi. Like my father, Lehi, I was born and raised in Jerusalem by caring parents. Like my father I was also educated to read and write, and learned the history of the Jewish people. My life has been filled with trials, but I have always been graced by God of whom I have learned much, and about whom I have much to tell. Here I begin an historical account of my life, written in the Egyptian language and inscribed on metal plates that I've made with my own hands.

During my childhood, a new king of Judah named Zedekiah came to power in Jerusalem. In the first year of his reign, many prophets came to Jerusalem, warning the people to repent or our great city would be destroyed. [600 BC]

Hearing these prophecies, my father Lehi was greatly troubled for his family and friends. He went into the desert to seek guidance through prayer to God. While in prayer, he had a vision in which a pillar of fire appeared on a rock in front of him. He was shown and told many disturbing and astonishing things. Lehi was so overwhelmed and stunned by what he had seen and heard that he returned to his home and lay down on his bed to recover. He was then carried away in yet another vision, in which he saw the heavens open and witnessed God himself sitting on a throne surrounded by countless angels singing their praise to God.

He saw a single man, as bright as the sun, descend from heaven. Behind him were twelve others, whose bodies shone like stars, who came and stood before him. The leader gave my father a book and commanded him to read it. As he read, Lehi was filled with God's spirit.

The book confirmed the prophets' warnings that Jerusalem was doomed for the sinful and evil ways of its people. Jerusalem was to be invaded by an army and destroyed. Many would die fighting, and many more would be taken away to Babylon as slaves. Lehi saw and read about many other amazing and marvelous things, and he proclaimed the greatness of God. He had seen that those who obeyed God would receive his mercy, be saved, and not perish as was foretold. Lehi rejoiced in the salvation that God had shown to him.

Following and trusting in this vision, Lehi went out to warn the Jews of Jerusalem about what he'd seen and heard. He told them about the coming destruction of Jerusalem, about the coming Messiah, and of God's mercy to those who obeyed Him. Rather than listening to his warnings, the people ridiculed and attacked Lehi instead. They threatened him with death, instead of acknowledging him and changing their evil ways. Many prophets before him had been cast out and killed, they pointed out, for displeasing the people. But Lehi knew that God protected and delivered the people he chose, and made them mighty.

Chapter 2. 1981 Version

God came again to Lehi in a dream saying, "You are blessed, Lehi, because of the things you've done. You have faithfully conveyed my words to your people as you were commanded to do. Because of this your neighbors seek to kill you."

God told Lehi to gather his family and travel to the wilderness. Lehi then abandoned his home, property, money and riches. Following God's advice, he brought only his family, tents and traveling supplies. Our family of six was comprised of my parents, Lehi and Sariah, my older bothers Laman and Lemuel, my younger brother Sam, and me.

We traveled south from Jerusalem for three days, following a river valley which flowed into the Red Sea. Upon our arrival we set up camp there. Laman and Lemuel were not at all happy about leaving Jerusalem and thought Lehi was a fool. They complained about being abducted from the comfort and easy life of the city to die stupidly and unnecessarily in the wilds. They both disbelieved that the great city of Jerusalem could be destroyed, prophecies or not. Lehi named the river where we camped after Laman and the valley after Lemuel, hoping to transform their resistance into participation. When this was unsuccessful, Lehi prevailed upon them by invoking the spirit of God, and filled them with fear, until they relented.

Like Lehi, I wanted to know God's will. When I prayed, God gave me understanding, and I came to trust my father's vision. When I told my brother Sam about this, he also believed, but Laman and Lemuel continued to complain and disbelieve. On their behalf I again prayed to God, who answered me saying, "Because of your faith, Nephi, you are blessed. I will lead you to the choicest lands on Earth. If your brothers continue disobeying my will, I will cut them off from my blessings while you will become their ruler and teacher. They and their descendents will be cursed and be deprived of power over you and your descendants. However, if your descendants also rebel against my will, they too will lose my protection and good will."

Chapter 3. 1981 Version

When I returned to camp after speaking with God, I learned that my father had received yet another dream in which God had appeared to him. "I have dreamed a dream," he said, "in which God has commanded me to send you and your brothers back to Jerusalem. You are to go see the record keeper, Laban, and bring back some brass plates on which the genealogy of our ancestors, and a history of the Jewish peoples, are written. I have already talked with your brothers about this and they have complained, saying that what I ask is much too hard to do. I have reminded them that it is not my request, but a commandment from God. Because you have not complained, I ask that you do this. Doing so will earn you favor with God."

"I will do as God has ordered," I replied. "God would not command us to do this unless he also made it possible to fulfill his will." This pleased my father greatly because he knew that I was blessed by God.

So, my brothers and I traveled back to Jerusalem. When we arrived, we conferred with one another and decided to cast lots to determine which of us would go see Laban. The task fell to Laman. When he visited Laban and asked him for the brass plates, Laban angrily refused. Laban threw him out, called him a thief, and threatened to kill him; Laman fled.

Laman returned and told us what had happened. Discouraged, my brothers were ready to return to the wilderness empty handed.

"By the life of God," I said, "we will not return to our father in the wilderness without

accomplishing what God has sent us to do. In his wisdom, God requires that we obtain and preserve these records for our children. These records contain the words of the holy prophets since the beginning of the world."

We returned to our own home in Jerusalem and gathered together the gold, riches, and treasures that we had left behind. Together, we all went to Laban's home again, this time offering to give him all of our wealth in exchange for the records. Laban wanted our wealth — but not at the cost of giving up the brass plates; so he told his servants to kill us. Our only escape was to abandon our wealth and run to the wilderness, where we hid in a cave.

Laman and Lemuel were now extremely angry with my father, Sam, and me. They proceeded to beat us with a stick until an angel of God came and stood before them. "What are you doing?" the angel demanded. "God has chosen Nephi to lead and rule. Return to Jerusalem at once and God will deliver Laban into your hands."

After the angel vanished, Laman and Lemuel complained further about our mission. "Laban will meet us with fifty armed servants," they argued, "who will be well equipped and ready to kill all four of us."

Chapter 4. 1981 Version

"Let's go back to Jerusalem," I said to my brothers, "and faithfully fulfill God's commandments to us. God is mightier than all the earth, mightier than 50 of Laban's servants, or even 10,000 armed men. Let's go and be strong like Moses who ordered the Red Sea to part, let our ancestors pass, and afterwards drowned the Pharaoh's army. How can you doubt the certainty of our success when an angel of God has spoken to you? God will deliver Laban to us just as he destroyed the Egyptians."

In spite of my brothers' complaints and anger, we returned to Jerusalem that night. While they hid themselves outside the city walls, I crept into the city and back to Laban's home, led by the Spirit of God. When I approached Laban's home, I saw a drunken man fall down on the ground and on approach, found it to be Laban himself. When I saw his beautiful sword, I pulled it from its sheath to marvel at it, and the Spirit told me to quickly kill Laban.

"I have never spilled the blood of anyone," I said silently to myself.

When I hesitated to do as I was told, the Spirit again spoke to me saying, "As promised, God has delivered Laban into your hands." I remembered that Laban had refused to listen to God's warnings, had refused God's will to give us the plates, had stolen all of our family's wealth, and had even tried to kill my brothers and me. Now he lay at my feet, unconscious. Again the Spirit spoke to me, "Kill him," he said. "It is better that one wicked man should die than that a nation should falter and perish in disbelief." Hearing this, I was reminded of God's promise to create a great nation in the promised lands. I recognized the need to have Laban's brass plates with God's commandments to Moses inscribed upon them. I grabbed Laban by the hair and cut off his head with his own sword.

After removing Laban's clothes and armor, I put them on myself and went into his treasury. Acting and speaking as if I were Laban, I got one of Laban's servants to give me access to the treasury. He helped me to obtain the plates and we returned with them to my brothers, who were waiting outside Jerusalem's walls. When my brothers saw me approaching, in Laban's clothing and armor, in the company of the servant, they panicked and ran away in fear. They assumed that I was dead and that Laban was coming to kill them, too. I called after them and they came back, after recognizing my voice.

The servant who had helped me now understood the actual situation. He became frightened and prepared to run. I grabbed hold of him and said, "God has commanded us to do this and we are diligently doing as we have been instructed. If you come to the wilderness with us, you will have a place among our family." I told him that I had no desire to kill him but would spare his life and give him freedom if he would listen to my words and come to obey God's will. I didn't want to alert the Jews and have them come chasing after us. His name was Zoram, and he accepted our offer with a promise of allegiance. The five of us then returned to the wilderness with the brass plates in hand.

Chapter 5. 1981 Version

Both of my parents were filled with joy when we returned. While we were gone, my mother Sariah was convinced that our lives had been lost on our quest to regain the brass plates. She had complained bitterly to my father, saying he was a dreamer. "You have taken us from our homes, my sons have died, and surely we will also die in this wilderness," she said.

"I know I am a dreamer," my father replied, "but if I hadn't seen God in a vision, I wouldn't have known of his goodness. We would have stayed in Jerusalem and died with everyone else. But now we will obtain a land of promise, and I know that God will return our sons unharmed."

After we returned my mother said, "Now I know for sure that God has commanded us to leave our home, has protected my sons, and given them the power to accomplish their mission."

Sacrifices and offerings of thanks were made to God for our safe return.

Lehi read the plates and determined that they were a true record of God's creation of the Earth. They told of the creation of our earliest ancestors, Adam and Eve, and gave a history of the Jewish people from the beginning of the world to the present time of King Zedekiah. They also contained the prophecies of the holy prophets since the beginning of the world. We learned from a genealogy in the records that our family was descended from Jacob's son Joseph[1] who had been sold into slavery in Egypt. God had saved Joseph and put him in a position to preserve his family and their household from perishing during the famine that followed many years later. We learned that Joseph's descendant, Moses, had led his people out of Egypt, guided by the same God that now guided our family.

When my father saw all of this, he was filled with the Spirit and began to prophesy. "These records will go forth to all nations and races who are descendants of mine. They will not perish or be dimmed by the passage of time."

We came to see the wisdom of God's command that we retrieve and safeguard these records so that we could bring them with us on our journey through the wilderness to the promised land. We would now be able to teach our children and their children the accurate history of the Earth and of God's commandments.

Chapter 2. 1830 Version

Chapter 6. 1981 Version

As a descendant of Joseph of Egypt, I write these things to persuade men to come to the God of Abraham, Isaac, and Israel to be saved. It is my wish that my descendants continue to keep this record of things that are important to God and pass them on to their children and to all the children of mankind.

Chapter 7. 1981 Version

God then told Lehi not to continue the journey to the promised land until his sons had found women they could marry, and with whom they could have children themselves. God commanded that my brothers and I again return to Jerusalem, and this time bring Ishmael and his family back to the wilderness with us.

When Ishmael and his family heard our story, they were sympathetic and agreed to come because they saw God's hand in this venture. On our journey back to the valley, however, Laman and Lemuel again rebelled against the will of God and convinced two of Ishmael's daughters and both of his sons that this was a fool's journey and should be abandoned. All six wanted to return to Jerusalem.

"It is a sad thing when I, your younger brother, need to set an example for you," I said to my bothers. "How could you have forgotten that we are traveling at God's command, that we have seen an angel of God who has come down and spoken to us, that God delivered Laban and the records into our hands, that the destruction of Jerusalem is imminent? Let us be faithful to God's will and go to this promised land towards which he guides us. If you return to Jerusalem, you too will perish. The people there have forgotten God, rejected the prophets, and tried to kill our father. In so doing, they have lost God's protection."

At this they became very angry, beat me with their fists and tied me up with ropes. They intended to kill me and leave my body to be eaten by wild animals; but I prayed to God to burst the ropes that bound me. And so it happened. The ropes were loosened and fell from my hands and feet, and I was able to stand before them again and speak.

All of this did nothing to dissipate their anger or change their minds about killing me, so they came at me again. But one of Ishmael's daughters, one of his sons, and his wife intervened until my brothers relented in their intention to take my life. After having lost their anger, Laman and Lemuel felt foolish and regretful, and asked for my forgiveness. Accordingly, I forgave them. I encouraged them to accept God's will in prayer, which they did.

And so we proceeded to travel again toward Lehi's camp in the wilderness, in the Valley of Lemuel. When we arrived, Lehi gave thanks unto God, made sacrifices, and gave offerings.

Chapter 8. 1981 Version

Before we left on our long journey we gathered together the seeds of all the grains and fruits we knew of so that we could plant them upon our eventual arrival in the land that God had promised to us.

While out walking in the wilderness Lehi had another dream. "I have dreamed a dream," he said. "Or in other words I have seen a vision. Because of what I've seen I have reason to I rejoice for Nephi and Sam. I believe their descendants will be saved. I fear greatly, though, for Laman and Lemuel whom I saw I saw in a dark wilderness."

"A man in a white robe appeared and asked me to follow him. For many hours we traveled through a dark, dreary wasteland. Eventually we arrived in a broad field that held a beautiful tree with white fruit. When I tasted the white fruit I was instantly filled with joy and wanted to share it with my family. It was truly the best fruit imaginable. Beside the tree ran a river and beside the river, a little ways off, stood Sariah, Sam, and Nephi who all looked as if they didn't know where to go. When I called to them, they came and also tasted the fruit. I looked further and saw Laman and Lemuel. But they would not come to me and taste the fruit.

"Also along the river's bank was an iron handrail leading directly to the tree, and a straight and narrow path beside the handrail leading to a large fountain. I saw multitudes of people groping their way towards the tree, trying to stay on the narrow path. A great mist of darkness arose causing many who were on the path to lose their way, wander off, and become lost. Those who held onto the handrail tightly managed get to the tree and taste its fruit. Many who tried the fruit acted ashamed afterwards.

"Across the river there was a great building so tall that it seemed to float high in the air above the earth. It was filled with people of all ages who were finely dressed, pointing their fingers and mocking those who were sampling the fruit. This was what was causing the people to act ashamed, fall away, and become lost on forbidden paths."

There was much more to my father's vision, but I'll be brief. In addition to the multitudes groping their way toward the tree there were other multitudes making their way to the great building. Many were drowned in the fountain and many were lost from view wandering down strange roads. The multitudes who entered the great building all pointed their fingers of scorn at those who tried the fruit. Lehi saw that those who followed the words of scorn were lost and fell away, while those who ignored the scorn and ate the fruit were saved.

Because Laman and Lemuel had refused the fruit Lehi was deeply concerned for them. He feared that they might be lost to God and cast away from his grace. So he pled with them, as a loving parent, that they should pay attention to his words and obey the commandments of God, so as to not be cast off and lost from God's grace.

Chapter 9. 1981 Version

During our journey, much more happened to us than can be written upon these plates. This record is not meant to be a complete history of my people, but rather to be a record of God's commandments to use in the ministry to my descendants. Because God has commanded me to make this record, I know that his purpose is wise and his words will be fulfilled.

Chapter 3. 1830 Version

Chapter 10. 1981 Version

Lehi went on to speak and prophesy about the coming destruction of Jerusalem and the scattering of the Jewish people. After Jerusalem fell, many of the people would be carried away in slavery to Babylon. In God's time they would return again and come to occupy the lands from which they would be driven, this land of their inheritance. Six hundred years following our departure from Jerusalem, a prophet and Messiah of God would arise among the Jews as a Savior of the world. Because all of mankind was in a lost and fallen state, they would rely on this Savior as their Redeemer. Many other prophets, he reminded us, had also foreseen the coming of this Messiah.

Lehi said a prophet would precede the Messiah to prepare the way, and baptize him with water in Bethabara, beyond Jordan. After baptizing the Messiah, this prophet would make a record that he had baptized the man who would remove the sins of the world. This Messiah would be disbelieved, would be slain, would arise from the dead to be seen, and afterwards would redeem the sins of mankind.

The family of Israel, he said, is like an olive tree whose branches will be broken off and scattered across the face of the Earth. "We are," he said, "like branches broken off from a natural tree. Our journey from Jerusalem to the promised land is a fulfillment of the prophecy that the Jewish people will be scattered."

In the last days, after the Gentiles have received the full and true gospel of Jesus Christ, the scattered branches will be gathered together again and grafted onto the tree which is the knowledge of the true Messiah.

Having heard my father's words, I also wanted to see and hear these things for myself, about the mysteries of God. So God gave me the authority to speak of these things and tell anyone who seeks diligently for God that he will be rewarded by finding the mysteries laid bare. I also want to remind those who would listen that all of our doings will be brought to judgment. Those who have sinned in their lives will be forever cast off.

Chapter 11. 1981 Version

I believed that God could show me what he'd shown my father. As I sat pondering all that I had heard from Lehi, I was swept away by the Spirit of God to a high mountaintop. The Spirit asked me, "What do you want?"

"I wish to see the things my father saw," I replied.

"Do you believe in the tree of which your father has spoken?" asked the Spirit.

"Yes. I believe everything my father has said," I answered.

"Praise to God," cried out the Spirit, "for he is God over the Earth, and God over all else. You are blessed, Nephi, because you believe in the Son of God and will be shown that which you desire to see. After I've shown you the tree whose fruit your father tasted, I will give you a sign. You will see a man descending from heaven. Afterwards, you will bear testimony that it was the Son of God whom you saw."

I looked, and saw the tree that Lehi had spoken of. It was whiter than freshly fallen snow. "I have seen the tree that you have shown me, and it is precious above all else," I said to the Spirit.

The Spirit of God now asked, "What else do you wish for Nephi?"

"I want to know the meaning of this," I replied, as I would to any other man — all the while knowing that while he appeared as a man, he was nonetheless the Spirit of God.

"Look," he replied, but the Spirit had vanished, and I was shown the city of Jerusalem and other cities including Nazareth in which I beheld a beautiful white virgin.

The heavens opened and an angel descended to come stand by me saying,

"Nephi, what do you see?"

"A virgin," I replied, "who is more beautiful than all other virgins."

"Do you know the meaning of God's condescension?" he asked.

"I know that God loves his children," I said, "but I don't pretend to know the meaning of all things."

"The virgin you see is the mother of God* in flesh," the angel stated. And then she was carried away in Spirit.

*In subsequent versions of *The Book of Mormon,* the "mother of God"

is changed to the "mother of the Son of God."

"Look," said the angel. And again the beautiful virgin appeared before me, this time holding a child in her arms. "Look, Nephi, and see the Son of God, the Eternal Father.* Now do you understand the meaning of the tree that you and your father have seen?"

*In subsequent versions of *The Book of Mormon,* the "Eternal Father" is changed to the "Son of the Eternal Father."

"Yes," I replied, "the tree is the love of God, which is the most desirable thing in the world."

"That's right," said the angel, "and the love of God is also the thing most joyous to the soul."

"Look," said the angel. When I looked, I saw the Son of God walking amongst the people, who fell down at his feet to worship him. I saw the iron handrail that my father had spoken of. I came to understand that it was the word of God which led to the tree of God's love, and to the fountain of God's waters beside it.

"Look and see the condescension of God," the angel commanded. I looked again and saw the Son of God being baptized by the prophet my father had spoken of, and acknowledged before God. And then I saw the Son of God walking and preaching amongst multitudes of people, who then rejected his messages and sent him away. I also saw that there were twelve who followed him and believed in his messages. Then I was shown angels descending from heaven to help the people with understanding.

"Look," said the angel. I looked again and now saw the Son of God healing the sick and the dispirited. Then the Son of God, the Everlasting God,* was taken prisoner, judged, and killed on a cross. And the people rallied to oppose the Son of God's twelve apostles who had believed in him.

*In subsequent versions of *The Book of Mormon,* the "Everlasting God" is changed to the "Son of the Everlasting God."

Now, I saw the large building that Lehi had spoken of from his vision. The people inside included many people of Israel, and they were gathered to fight against the word of God.

The building then collapsed on all those inside. "This will be the destruction of all nations and peoples that oppose the twelve apostles of the Son of God," the angel said to me.

Chapter 12. 1981 Version

"Look," the angel said again, "and see the descendants of you and your brothers." I saw countless people who would be descendants of mine and descendants of my brothers, living in cities spread across the promised land to which we traveled. I saw wars and many generations of people killed in these conflicts. Ultimately, I came to see a mist of darkness fall across the face of the promised land, followed by huge storms and earthquakes that tore the mountains to pieces and broke the plains apart. Many cities were sunk, burned, and collapsed.

As the darkness lifted, I saw many people arise from the ruins who were not destroyed by God's terrible judgment. To these people the Son of God appeared, descending from heaven. The Spirit of God fell upon twelve of these people and they were blessed. The angel said to me, "These twelve disciples are chosen to minister to your descendants and judge them, because of their faith in the Son of God. Do you remember the twelve apostles you were shown earlier? Those twelve apostles will judge the twelve tribes of Israel. Their judgments will extend to these twelve disciples who will minister to your descendants, because they are also descendants of Israel. They are righteous forever. Because of their faith in God, their garments are made white with his blood."

"Look," said the angel, yet again. I saw three generations come and go, living in righteousness and following the word of God. Their garments were pure white, like the garments worn by the Son of God and his disciples.

"Their garments are made white by the blood of the Son of God," the angel said, "because of their faith in him."

Four generations after the visitation of the Son of God, I saw that many people still lived their lives in righteousness.

"Now look at your descendants and the descendants of your brothers," the angel commanded. When I looked this time, I saw these descendants gathered together in huge numbers, in preparation for war.

"Look now," the angel said, "and see the fountain of dirty water, and the river that your father spoke of, the depths of which are the depths of hell. The mists of darkness are the temptations of the devil that blind the eyes and close the hearts of men. These temptations lead men down broad roads where they become lost and perish. The great building that your father saw represents vanity and pride. An enormous gulf divides this building from the tree of life to which you aspire. This gulf is the justice of God as recorded since the beginning of time, and extending throughout all eternity."

As the angel spoke, I watched as the descendants of my brothers overpowered my descendants and spread forth across the land. I saw many more generations of war, and saw my descendants falter in their belief. As their belief failed, I saw them become dark and loathsome people who were filthy, idle, and abominable.

Chapter 13. 1981 Version

"Look again," said the angel. "What do you see now?"

"I see many kingdoms and nations," I replied.

"These are the nations and kingdoms of the Gentiles," he said.

Among these many nations I saw the formation of a great church.

"Look now, and see the formation of a church that is more abominable than any other church," said the angel. "It kills, tortures, and imprisons the saints of God."

I saw that this great and abominable church was founded and led by the devil himself. I saw gold, silver, and expensive red clothing made from fine silks and linens. I also saw many prostitutes.

"As you can see," the angel said, "this church distinguishes itself with its desire for riches, fine clothing, and whores. In pursuit of these worldly excesses, they destroy and enslave the saints of God."

When next I looked, I saw a great ocean that divided the Gentile nations from the descendants of my brothers. "Look and you can see that the anger of God has fallen upon your brothers' descendants."

Next, I was shown a single Gentile man on the Old World continent opposite the ocean from my brothers' descendants. The Spirit of

God came upon him, and inspired him to cross the ocean and discover the promised land in which my brothers' descendants lived. After this discovery, many others from the Gentile nations were also filled with the Spirit of God, and followed him to the promised land seeking freedom from abuse and slavery. They became the instruments of God's anger for the punishing and scattering of my brothers' descendants. The Spirit of God blessed these Gentiles in the promised land. Like my own slain and exterminated descendants, they were white skinned, fair, and beautiful. These Gentiles were humble before God and received his blessings because the power of God was with them.

The angel showed me a gathering of Gentile armies from the kingdoms of the Old World across the ocean that came to do battle with the New World Gentiles. Because the blessing and power of God was with the New World Gentiles, they were guided to victory and delivered from freedom and slavery at the hands of all other nations. The people of the New World prospered and carried a book with them as they spread out across the promised land.

"Do you know the meaning of this book?" the angel asked.

"I do not," I replied.

"The book you see," said the angel, "is a record of the Jewish people and contains the commandments of God to the descendants of Israel. It contains many prophecies from the holy prophets. It is a record like the brass plates you have brought with you from Jerusalem, except that many parts of the holy record are missing from it. It is of great importance to the Gentiles. Before this book was first adopted by the Gentiles, it contained the full and complete gospel of God. The twelve apostles testified that it bore the complete and truthful record of Jesus Christ."

"After the Gentiles adopted it," the angel continued, "the great and abominable church that you saw began removing important parts of it, including many of the covenants made with God. This was done purposefully to pervert the true ways of God, blind the people's eyes, and close the hearts of men and women. You can see for yourself how the great and abominable church has corrupted the holy scriptures of Jesus Christ. Because of these corruptions, many Gentiles stumble on the path and are overpowered by Satan."

"God has promised your father that his descendants would have this promised land for their inheritance. So he will not allow the Gentiles who come later, and are also favored by God, to utterly destroy them. Neither, in his great mercy, will he permit these Gentiles to remain forever blinded because of the corruptions introduced by the great and abominable church."

"Jesus Christ has said," the angel continued, "that when he brings his great judgment and mercy to your father's descendants, he will also bring with him a restoration of the true gospel that has been lost. Your descendants will witness his visitation, teachings, and mercy. They will write this down and hide it away before their descendants falter in unbelief. After they are destroyed, your descendants' words will eventually be given to the Gentiles as a gift from God. From your descendants, these Gentiles will receive God's true Gospel and salvation. Those who embrace this Gospel will have God's gift and be saved in the everlasting kingdom of God."

I was then shown how the true Gospel would come to the Gentiles in the New World. From them, I saw how it came to my brothers' descendants, whom God would not allow to perish completely. This Gospel would convince those who could hear the truth, Gentiles, Jews, and descendants of my brothers' alike, that the records of the prophets and the twelve apostles of Jesus Christ are true.

"These last records that you have seen," the angel said, "will reestablish the truth that has been lost, and establish to all peoples that Jesus Christ is the Eternal Father,* and the savior of the world. All men must come to him, or they will not be saved. And they must come to him according to the words and records of your descendants, and the true records of the twelve apostles of Jesus Christ. The time will come, in the last days, when God will again make himself visible and evident to the nations of the world and to the Jews and Gentiles, and the last will be first, and the first will be last."

*In subsequent versions of *The Book of Mormon,* "Eternal Father" is changed to "Son of the Eternal Father."

Chapter 14. 1981 Version

The angel continued to explain things to me. "If the Gentiles listen to the word of Jesus Christ when he comes in those last days, and do not turn away from him, they will also be included with the family of Israel and be blessed. If they do this, they will overcome their ignorance and live in freedom in the promised land.

"On the other hand, those who refuse God and maintain their allegiance with the abominable church of the devil's, will be eternally committed to the great pit of endless hell. This captivity by the devil will be God's justice to those who are offered blessing and turn away from him.

"Jesus Christ has promised that he will implement a mighty and everlasting transformation of his people involving either deliverance into eternal peace, or consignment to eternal slavery to the devil. Do you remember the covenants that God made with the family of Israel?"

"Yes," I replied.

"Look," he said, "at this great and abominable church that is led by the devil. There are really only two churches in the world. One is the church of Jesus Christ, and the other is the church of the devil. Whoever does not belong to the church of Jesus Christ belongs to the church of the devil, which is the whore of all the earth."

I looked and saw that what the angel said was true. Because of its wickedness, the great abominable church of the devil, the whore of all the earth, spread its influence and abominations across the oceans and nations of the world, gathering unto itself far greater numbers of followers than the church of Jesus Christ.

As I watched, the angel of God showed me multitudes of people gathering to fight with the abominable church against Jesus Christ. I watched as Jesus Christ invested those scattered people who believed in him with his righteous and almighty power. As God's anger poured out upon the followers of the great abominable church of the devil, wars erupted everywhere on Earth between the Gentile nations.

"Look and see," said the angel, "how the day will come when God will pour his anger onto the devil's great and abominable church. When this war begins, the work of God in fulfilling his covenants with the family of Israel will also begin.

"Look," said the angel.

The angel of God then showed me a man dressed in a white robe and identified him as one of Jesus Christ's twelve apostles, named John, who would see and write clearly about the end of the world for all to heed. I, too, was shown the end of the world, but was forbidden to write about it. What I have written about here is a small part of what I was shown by the angel of God in the visions that were given to me.

Chapter 4. 1830 Version

Chapter 15. 1981 Version

When I returned from my visitation with the Spirit of God, I went to my father's tent and found my brothers arguing with one another about the things my father Lehi had told them. Because they had little faith in God, our father's words were difficult for them to take seriously or to find meaning in.

Because of what I'd just seen regarding the fall of their progeny and the destruction of mine at the hands of their descendants, I was saddened by the hardness of their hearts. I asked what they were arguing about.

"We cannot agree on what father means when he talks about the branches of the olive tree and the Gentiles."

"Have you thought to ask God about the meaning of this for yourselves?" I asked.

"No," they replied, "God doesn't talk to us of such things."

"How can you fail to keep God's commandments?" I asked. "Do you want to perish because your hearts are closed to him? God has said that if you humble yourself before him and have faith, keep to His commandments and maintain belief, you will receive God's blessings and all things will become known to you. The olive tree is a metaphor for the descendants of Israel. Our family is descended from Israel, yet now we are broken off from it, as a branch is broken from an olive tree. We are to be transplanted in the promised land to which we travel.

"Many generations from now, a Messiah will reveal himself to the world and introduce a gospel of God's commandments, and many generations after that, the descendants of Gentiles will introduce this full and true gospel to our descendants in the promised land. The grafting on of the olive branch will be complete when this gospel is known to all. Our descendants will then come to recognize that they are remnant descendants of Israel. They will see how our descendants came to be in the promised land, and will have the opportunity to be saved. In these latter days, God, in his power, will also give his blessing to those Gentiles who receive him because the Jewish people will have rejected him. Our father speaks not only about our descendants, but about the entire family of Israel and the fulfillment of the covenant that God made with Abraham that all of his descendants would be blessed."

I explained how in the latter days the Jewish people would be restored to the land of their inheritance, and rescued from their confusion as described by the prophet Isaiah. When I finished explaining these things, my brothers calmed down and became humble again before God. Then they asked, "What then is the meaning of the tree, the iron handrail, and the river that father has seen in his vision?"

"The tree is the tree of life," I explained. "The iron handrail leading to the tree is the word of God. If you hold fast to God's word, you will not perish or be led astray, which can happen if you let go. The river of filthy water is the gulf between you and God that separates the wicked from the tree of life, and from God. The river is a representation of hell in which lost souls will drown forever.

"Our father," I told them, "has seen God's justice as a bright, blazing fire, forever ascending to God that divides the wicked from the righteous."

"Does the fire represent the burning of our bodies, as torment, during this life?" they asked. "Or does it signify the state of our souls after death?"

I explained that it represented the passing of earthly things and also the spiritual trials which await us. "A day will come," I said, "when we will be judged by how we've lived

our earthly lives. If we die in wickedness, we will be cast away from God. Filthy people will not be fit to live with God, for there is no filth allowed in his kingdom. A place for filth has been prepared. It is called Hell, and the devil is its proprietor. God's great justice calls for all souls to either live with him in his kingdom, or be cast away from it in judgment. This is how the wicked are separated from the righteous and also separated from the tree of life whose fruit is the most desirable of all things known, and the greatest of God's gifts."

Chapter 5. 1830 Version

Chapter 16. 1981 Version

My brothers protested against my words, declaring, "What you say is very harsh, and hard for us to bear."

"People who are guilty of wickedness," I replied, "will see the truth as harsh. The righteous will be lifted up, and the guilty will be cut down. If you were willing to be righteous, willing to listen to the truth, and live your lives as God wants you to, you wouldn't complain about the harshness of my words." After this explanation, my brothers repented again and gave me hope that they had finally relented in their opposition to God's will.

We had been staying in the Valley of Lemuel since leaving Jerusalem and having twice returned, for Laban's brass plates and again for Ishmael's family. During this time my brothers, Zoram, and I had each made matches with Ishmael's five daughters and married them. One night, God spoke again to my father Lehi, and commanded him to gather up his party and continue our journey on the following day.

When Lehi got up in the morning, he discovered that during the night God had left a magical object at the doorway of his tent. It was a finely made brass ball with two spindles. It was named the Liahona. One of the spindles acted like a compass, and pointed in the direction we were supposed to go. And so, that morning, we left our comfortable valley and crossed the river in the southeasterly direction that the Liahona indicated. As we traveled we hunted for wild game with our slings and arrows. We followed the fertile eastern shoreline of the Red Sea and found ample food as we went.

One day while I was out hunting, I broke my steel bow, and my brothers' bows lost their camber, making them useless for further hunting. Tired from traveling, hungry, and in the middle of the wilderness, our party became dissatisfied and began dissenting against God's plan. Even my father was now grumbling and feeling let down by God. Rather than doing nothing, I fashioned a new bow and made arrows from available materials. When I was armed, I approached my father and asked where he thought I should go in search of food.

Again God spoke to Lehi and reprimanded him for his loss of faith. This caused my father to have much regret and sorrow. "Look at the brass ball that I have given you," commanded God, "and read what is written on it." In addition to being a compass pointing the way, the Liahona also conveyed God's intents and guidance in writing, according to the faith and diligence that we brought to it. When my father read the words God had written on the ball, he and the rest of our party were humbled with fear. As we went, the writing changed from time to time to provide us with more help in fulfilling God's plan for us.

Following the written instructions on the magic brass ball, I went up alone on a mountaintop and successfully hunted plentiful wild game with which to feed our party. With our stomachs full and our faith restored, we all humbled ourselves to God and gave thanks.

We continued our long arduous journey, traveling and resting, then traveling and resting again. One night, Ishmael died in his sleep; we buried his body in the wilderness. In grief, Ishmael's daughters blamed my father for this fool's journey which had cost their father's life. "We have suffered hardships, hunger, thirst, and endless weariness," they complained. "We are fearful that this journey will go nowhere except to our own deaths also. We want to return to Jerusalem."

My brothers and the sons of Ishmael also wanted to return to Jerusalem. "Let's kill our father and our brother Nephi," my brother Laman said. "Who does our younger brother Nephi think he is, to set himself up as our ruler and teacher? He says he talks with God and with angels, but we know that it is all a pack of lies to deceive us and make us submit to his will. He seeks to take us into some strange wilderness and make himself king over us."

Before their group anger could bring about our deaths, God appeared to them also. In convincing and no uncertain terms he reproached them for their plotting against Lehi, against God, and against me. Hearing this, they repented, and agreed to continue on our journey, receiving God's blessings of guidance and food.

Chapter 17. 1981 Version

We journeyed eastward through the wilderness for eight years under the guidance of God and endured great hardship and suffering. During this time, our wives bore children in the wilds and grew as strong as the men, bearing all the difficulties without complaint. Also during the journey, my mother gave birth to two more sons, who were named Jacob and Joseph[2]. Our survival on this journey became proof that God keeps his promises to his people, if his people honor his commandments.

Eventually, we arrived at the coastline of a great ocean in a place we named Bountiful for its abundance of fruits and wild honey. At Bountiful, we pitched out tents, rested, rejoiced, and gave thanks to God for bringing us here safely.

Many days after our arrival, God's voice came to me, saying, "Arise and go to the mountain."

When I arrived on the mountaintop, God spoke to me again. "You must build a ship according to instructions that I will give to you," he said. "After that, I will carry your people across the ocean."

"Where will I go to find iron ore with which to make the tools necessary to build a ship?" I asked. After God told me where to find the ore, I made bellows from the skins of animals and began to make my tools from the molten rocks.

My brothers mocked and ridiculed me when they saw me beginning the task of building an ocean-going ship. "Our brother is a fool," they said, "if he thinks he can build a ship and cross the ocean." They, of course, refused to help in any way, and disbelieved that I was being instructed by God.

Again, I was deeply saddened by their lack of faith in God and by the hardness of their hearts. My sadness pleased them because they thought that I had been defeated. "We knew this was too large a task for you," they said. "You are too much like our foolish father who has brought us to this distant, dreadful place. It would have been far better if we had stayed in Jerusalem enjoying our wealth and possessions, than to endure the hardships we and our women have had to put up with. It would have been preferable to have died. If we'd stayed, we could have been happy. The people of Jerusalem were good people who were wrongly judged by our father, who has brought us to ruin." On and on they went, complaining about my father and me.

"Do you believe that our ancestors would have ever escaped their enslavement in Egypt if they hadn't listened to the words of God?" I asked. "Do you think they could have been freed if Moses hadn't led them out of their slavery? You know it was a good thing for them to have escaped from Egypt. You know that Moses was commanded by God to lead them. And you know that God parted the waters of the Red Sea, allowing them to escape. You know that the Pharaoh's army was drowned. And you know that Moses' people were fed manna from heaven in the wilderness. You know that Moses, through the power of God, struck a rock to provide drinking water in the desert.

"In spite of being led and upheld by God, Moses' people complained about and criticized both him and God. According to his word, God destroyed those who opposed him and led those who obeyed him. God did everything according to his word.

"After Moses and his people crossed the Jordan River, he empowered them to drive the inhabitants from the land, scattering and destroying them. Do you think that those people who occupied the promised land were righteous? No. Do you think that our ancestors would have been more favored people if the inhabitants of the land had been righteous? No. God made all men equal, but he favors those who are righteous in his eyes. The people inhabiting the promised land had rejected him and were full of sinfulness. Because of this, God brought his anger to bear upon them, and blessed our ancestors for their righteousness.

This is what gave them the power to obtain the promised land for themselves.

"God made the earth for the possession of his children, but he supports the nations that are righteous, and destroys the nations that are wicked. God rules from the throne of heaven. This earth is his foot stool. He loves those who choose him as their God. He loved our ancestors Abraham, Isaac, and Jacob, and remembered his promises to them. That is why he brought them out of slavery in Egypt.

"When his people closed their hearts to him as you are doing now, he straightened them out in the wilderness by sending flying, fiery serpents among them. When they were bitten, he prepared a way for their healing. In spite of the simpleness of his plan, many people perished because they were too stubborn to follow his path. Even after their episodic opposition to Moses and God, these people were still led by God to the promised land.

"Now the time has come when the wicked people in Jerusalem are about to be destroyed. Only a few will be delivered from certain slavery and death. God has commanded our father to journey in the wilderness. Now you plot to kill him just as the people in Jerusalem did. Just like them, you are murderers in your heart. You are quick to sin, and slow to remember your God, even though you've seen an angel who spoke to you. He still speaks to you in your conscience. Are you so deaf that you cannot hear his words unless he thunders at you? You know that the power of God's word can bring about the end of the earth. You know that he can make the rough places smooth, and the smooth places rough. Why then are your hearts so closed?

"My soul is broken with grief because of you. My heart is in pain. I am terrified that you will be forever cast out. Look at me. I am filled with the Spirit of God to the limits of my strength."

Having said all this, my brothers became very angry with me and wished to throw me into the sea to drown. When they approached to do their deadly work, I cried out to them, "In the name of Almighty God, I order you not to touch me. I am filled with the power of God. Whoever lays a hand on me will wither and perish by the power of God." I further commanded them to discontinue their complaining and plotting against our father, and contribute their efforts to help construct the ship that God had commanded me to build.

"I can do whatever God commands me to do," I said. "If he ordered me to turn water into earth, I would be capable of doing it. Given all the miracles that God has shown us so far, how can you doubt that he will guide me to build a seaworthy ship?"

My words and declarations of power confused and frightened my brothers so much that they decided against trying to harm me, for the time being. Shortly after this incident, God spoke to me and said, "If you stretch out your hands towards your brothers, I will give them a shock so that they will know that I am their Lord and God. This will convince them of the seriousness of your words."

When I did as God had commanded me to do, my brothers were shocked just as he had promised. They fell down before me, saying, "We now know for sure that God is with you because we have been stunned by his power."

When they tried to worship me, I refused to let them. "I am only your younger brother," I said. "Worship God, and honor our father and mother instead. Pray that you will live long in the promised land that God is about to give to us."

Chapter 18. 1981 Version

All of us then joined together to build the ship. I was guided by God on the particulars of its design and the shaping of the timbers. I climbed the mountain often in order to receive specific instructions from God as to how the ship should be constructed, and was also shown many great visions. When it was completed we saw that it was of good design and fine workmanship. In thanks, we humbled ourselves before God's will and guidance.

After the ship's completion, God came and spoke to Lehi again. He told him that it was time to load the ship with our provisions that we had gathered. After that, we boarded the ship with our wives and children, set out to sea, and were driven by the wind towards the promised land across the ocean. [590 BC]

Many days into our sea journey, things were going well and my brothers, the sons of Ishmael, and their wives decided it was time to party. They danced and sang and acted rudely, forgetting that we were carried across the ocean by the will of God. I became afraid that God would take offense at our disrespect and destroy our vulnerable boat in the sea, so I spoke out very directly, admonishing them for their behavior.

"We will not have a younger brother acting as ruler over us," they said, angrily. Laman and Lemuel grabbed me harshly, dragged me to the ship's deck and tied me tightly to the ship's mast. God tolerated this because he wanted to demonstrate the seriousness of violating his will, and used the opportunity to show his power when confronted by such wicked behavior. Immediately, our magic compass that God had prepared for us quit pointing the way, and my brothers no longer knew in which direction to steer the ship. A great storm arose across the ocean and we were driven backwards for several days. While my brothers were terribly concerned about all of this, they still did not untie me or loosen the bindings that caused me great swelling, soreness, and pain.

When my father, my wife, my children, and Ishmael's sons spoke out against my brothers' harsh treatment of me they were rebuffed and threatened with harm. In the storm my old parents nearly died from the violence of the sea and from sorrow at the behavior of their sons. On the fourth day, the storm became so bad that our ship was threatened with imminent destruction, and my brothers realized that their decision to tie me up was the direct cause of our peril. The harsh judgment of God was upon them, and they realized that unless they repented, we would all be swallowed by the ocean and die. Again, my brothers realized the error of their ways, and untied me.

After being released, I took the magic compass Liahona in my hands and prayed to God. My prayers were answered when the storm abated and our magic compass again showed the way to the promised land. I then steered the ship and we sailed onward again towards our destination. Many days later, we arrived on the coastline of the promised land and went ashore to pitch our tents. [589 BC]

We tilled the earth and planted the seeds that we'd brought with us from Jerusalem. Our crops grew well and we were blessed with abundance. We discovered animals of all kinds in the forests including cows, oxen, horses, and goats for our domestication and use. We also found gold, silver, and copper ore.

Chapter 19. 1981 Version

After arriving in the promised land, God commanded me to engrave two sets of plates to pass on to my descendants. The first set concerned my father's genealogy, the story of our travels in the wilderness, a detailed account of the wars, conflicts, and past destructions of our people, and the many prophecies of my father and me. These, the second set of engraved plates, are intended to be an ongoing sacred record of our people. They are meant to be handed down from generation to generation, from one prophet to another, and added to until God commands otherwise. Accordingly, I don't write anything upon these plate except what is sacred. Some people will consider these records of priceless value, while others may consider them to be worthless. Some people even consider God's word to have no value, and don't listen to what he says.

The angel who spoke to me said that in six hundred years the God of the Jewish people will be born as a mortal man, rejected, suffered, and abused. The Old World prophets Zenock*, Neum*, and Zenos* say that he will be crucified, buried in a sepulcher, and lifted up afterwards.

*Zenock, Neum, and Zenos are Old World Hebrew prophets for whom all historical references are lost outside The Book of Mormon. Nephi's knowledge of these prophets comes through Laban's brass plates brought from Jerusalem.

Zenos prophesied that three days of darkness would be the sign of the Messiah's death to the family of Israel who live beyond the sea. He says, "The Lord God will surely visit all the family of Israel on that day. Some will hear his voice because of their righteousness. Others will see the thunder and lightning of his power in the form of great storms, fire, smoke, darkness, the earth splitting, and the lifting up of mountains. As the rocks break and the earth groans the Spirit of God will fall upon the kings across the seas. 'The God of nature suffers,' they will exclaim.

"The people of Jerusalem and their descendants will be punished and plagued by all people for turning their hearts aside, rejecting the signs and wonders, and crucifying the God of Israel. Because of this they will be forced to wander the world and be despised among all nations. When the day comes that these people have a change of heart, God will again remember the promises he made to their ancestors. He will also remember his people across the seas who are descendants of Israel. 'I will gather them in,' said God, 'from the four corners of the earth.' All the people of earth will see the salvation of God, and be blessed."

I write all of this to remind my people to remember their God. I write this also to all the descendants of Israel who have been scattered.

My spirit is weakened by the knowledge of those who were left behind in Jerusalem. If God had not been merciful to us and shown us the way, as he also showed the way to the ancient prophets, we too would have perished. I am thankful for what I have learned about the ancient prophets from the brass plates we brought with us. I have shared the knowledge from the brass plates with my brothers and I have taught them about the ways in which God has delivered his blessings and his anger upon people in the past.

Chapter 6. 1830 Version

I have attempted to convince my brothers of the importance of believing in God by reading to them from the books of Moses. In order to help them understand Jesus Christ, I have taught them about Isaiah and asked them to apply his prophecies and lessons [from 720 BC] to our own lives and circumstances now, on this new continent [588 BC].

"Listen to the words of the prophet, Isaiah," I said to them. "We are broken branches from the tree that is the family of Israel. Isaiah speaks to us of hope, as well as to our brothers who have been left behind."

Chapter 20. 1981 Version

[*Chapter 20 of the First Book Nephi is virtually indistinguishable, word for word, from Chapter 48 of Isaiah from the Old Testament.*]

Isaiah carries God's words to the people of Jerusalem in Babylon, and chastises them for saying that they live by the word of God, while failing to do so in actuality. He reminds them that he had made predictions and that the people had seen these prophecies fulfilled. In spite of their stubbornness, God withholds his anger and does not cut them off or destroy them. God reminds them that he is first and last, that he created the heavens and earth. "If you would only listen to my word," God says, "peace would flow like a river and your people would become too many to count. Go now, leave Babylon singing, and I will satisfy your thirst in the desert. But there will be no peace for the wicked."

Chapter 21. 1981 Version

[*Chapter 21 of the First Book Nephi is virtually indistinguishable, word for word, from Chapter 49 of Isaiah from the Old Testament.*]

Isaiah explains how God has chosen him to be his spokesman and prophet. God promises to keep the people of Israel from harm, and to get them released from bondage; and he promises that their present captors will become their slaves. God reminds them that he can no more forget them than a mother can forget her child. When God does this, the world will know that he is the almighty God of Israel.

Chapter 7. 1830 Version

Chapter 22. 1981 Version

After I read Isaiah's prophecies to my brothers, they asked, "What is the meaning of this? Are these words to be understood as spiritual or worldly?" they asked.

"They were told to Isaiah by the voice of the Spirit," I answered, "and the Spirit speaks to prophets about worldly events. What I have read pertains to things both spiritual and worldly. It appears as though the family of Israel will be scattered across the face of the earth. Many of Israel's descendants have already been scattered to the point where no one knows where they all are. After the family of Israel is completely scattered and confused, God will help raise a mighty nation among the Gentiles on this new continent. These Gentiles will then scatter our descendants even further.

"After God has scattered our descendants, he will do something amazing among the Gentiles which will be of great value to our descendants. It will be as if the Gentiles lifted our descendants up on their shoulders, carried them away in their arms, and nourished them by restoring their knowledge of God. This will be of great value to the Gentiles and all the descendants of Israel as well. By making the promises between God and Abraham known to everyone, all the people of the world will be blessed.

"The descendants of Israel will be gathered together in their lands of inheritance, knowing that God is their Savior. When that happens, the followers of the great and abominable church, the whore of all the earth, will fight amongst themselves. They will become drunken with their own blood. Every nation that fights against the family of Israel will end up falling into a pit of their own digging. All who oppose God will be destroyed. That great whore of an abominable church that has perverted the right ways of God will tumble heavily into the dust.

"The prophet says that the time quickly comes when Satan will have no more power over the hearts of men. The proud will be like stubble in the field that must be burned. God will pour out his anger because he will not permit the righteous to be destroyed by the wicked. Through his power, the righteous will be preserved while his enemies are destroyed by fire. Everyone who is righteous has nothing to be afraid of. Everyone who fails to listen to the warnings will be cut off.

"Moses said, 'A prophet of God, like me, will rise up among you. When he does, you must listen to everything he says. Those who do not will be destroyed.'

"This prophet about whom Moses speaks is Jesus Christ, and he will exercise righteous judgments on all men. The righteous will not be afraid or confused. It is the followers of the devil who should be afraid. Churches that are built for the purpose of gaining wealth and power over people, or satisfying lust and worldly desires, should tremble and quake in fear for they are instruments of the devil. This is what the prophet Isaiah has to say.

"The righteous will be gathered from all corners of the earth and counted as one people, to find comfort, and nourishment under the one God, while Jesus Christ will rule in might, power, and glory. Satan will have no power over the people who live in righteousness.

"All these things written on these plates of brass are true and will shortly come to pass in the world. All people of the world who repent and are obedient to God will find safety and

security in him. Don't you believe for a moment that it is only your father and I who say these things are true. If you are obedient to God's will, you too will be saved on the day of judgment."

THE SECOND BOOK OF NEPHI — 587 BC TO 545 BC

from Plates Inscribed by Nephi[1] then Abridged and Later Inscribed onto the Book of Mormon Plates by Mormon

This is an account of Nephi's life in the Western Hemisphere from 587 BC until the time of his death around 545 BC. After Nephi's father Lehi dies, the family breaks into to two opposing factions, the Nephites and the Lamanites. God becomes so displeased with the Lamanites that he curses them and turns their skin color from white to dark. Lehi's and Nephi's visions and prophecies continue.

SUMMARY OF THE SECOND BOOK OF NEPHI

The Second Book of Nephi continues directly from the First Book of Nephi's conclusion and completes the story of Nephi's life in the Western Hemisphere. This book represents Nephi's account of three groups of people: the Lehites, the Nephites, and the Lamanites. The Lehites are comprised of the whole party that followed Lehi's command from God to migrate from Jerusalem to the New World. After Lehi's death, the Lehites broke into two splinter groups led by Lehi's son Nephi[1] (the Nephites) and Nephi's older brother Laman[1] (the Lamanites). The Lamanite people are identified by The Book of Mormon as the principal ancestors of the Native Americans.

Nephi began the story by describing another of Lehi's visions. God showed Lehi that Jerusalem had, in fact, been destroyed since their departure, as had been predicted.[1] He prophesied that their new land would be a protected place of liberty as long as people lived by God's commandments. If they didn't follow God's laws, they would be destroyed. He predicted the eventual discovery and

---

1. In 599 BC, the Babylonian King Nebuchadnezzar's army took the city of Jerusalem, with little destruction. Afterwards, around 10,000 of Jerusalem's most prominent citizens were removed as captives to Babylon. This removal of and displacement of local peoples was a common practice of conquest at the time. It was believed that the conquered people were less likely to rebel if they were removed from their homelands and scattered elsewhere among the conqueror's empire. Several years later, the new kings rebelled, and Nebuchadnezzar sent an army to reconquer Jerusalem. In 586 BC, after a two-year siege, the Babylonian army prevailed, and destroyed the city of Jerusalem and its Temple. Almost all of its surviving citizens were taken away as slaves. The first conquest would have occurred the year following the Lehi family departure from Jerusalem. The second conquest and destruction would have occurred three years after the Lehi family arrived in the New World.

bloody conquest of their new land by European immigrants after the people's faith in God failed.

Before he died, an aging and weakened Lehi gave the Lehite people, both individually and collectively, warnings and blessings. He passed the mantle of spiritual authority on to his son Nephi, who had diligently observed God's commandments. He asked the entire party to listen to Nephi and to obey his commands as if they were the word of God. Lehi predicted the trials and tribulations of his sons and their descendants, and prophesied the coming of Jesus Christ and Joseph Smith. Lehi predicted that his descendants would write The Book of Mormon, and that Joseph Smith would eventually discover and reveal this knowledge to the world. He used these blessings as a platform for reviewing and describing the theology that he wanted his party to follow. His religious discourses covered the range of time from the fall of Adam through the future resurrection of Jesus Christ, and continued with prophecies into contemporary times. Lehi's central message to his people was to obey God's commandments, devote themselves to Jesus Christ, and be saved. Failure to do this, he said, would result in their destruction.

During his blessings, Lehi quoted Abraham's grandson, Joseph[1] of Egypt, who was one of Israel's twelve sons. Joseph of Egypt prophesied the coming of Moses and also a descendant, Joseph Smith, in the latter days. He predicted that Joseph Smith would bring forth great knowledge, convince people of its truth, and preserve Joseph of Egypt's descendants forever.

Shortly after he conferred all of his blessings, Lehi died. After his death, the Lehites lacked a central unifying figure, and conflict followed.

Nephi's older brothers conspired again to kill him and take control of the Lehites, but God warned Nephi to take his followers and flee into the wilderness. After packing some minimal possessions, including the brass plates from Jerusalem and the magic compass Liahona, the Nephites departed to establish a new nation elsewhere. Due to their unity and hard work, the Nephites were immediately successful in growing crops, producing metals, and building a city. Their numbers multiplied quickly and the new community thrived. Knowing that the Lamanites bore his people great hatred, Nephi began producing weaponry and prepared to defend his people against the inevitable and anticipated attacks from the Lamanites.

After Nephi's departure, the Lamanites rejected God, who in turn cursed them. He miraculously transformed their physical appearance from handsome, white people, into loathsome people, permanently marked with God's curse by dark skin color. They became increasingly lazy and mischievous, and abandoned their cultural habit and identity as a civilized people.

God warned Nephi that the Lamanites would become the enemy of the Nephites, and that if the Nephites ever wavered in their devotion to him, his people would be destroyed by them. Approximately 40 years after leaving Jerusalem and 30 years after their arrival in the New World, the first of the ongoing Lamanite wars began.

Nephi and his brother Jacob[2] preached to the Nephites. They told them that God had affirmed the destruction and conquest of Jerusalem, as had been prophesied. Had they stayed behind, they too would either be dead or enslaved. Consequently, their people owed everything they now had to God. They spoke of living in alignment with God's plan, and finding salvation, or alternately discovering the eternal hellish torment if God was rejected.

Nephi prophesied more about the coming of Jesus Christ, his death, and his visitation with the Nephite people after his resurrection. He foretold of the time, four generations after Jesus Christ's visitation to the Nephites, when the Nephites would fall into apostasy and be destroyed by the Lamanites. Nephi prophesied about the latter days, when the Gentiles would come to America. He talked about the conquest of the Lamanites' descendants (the Native Americans) by these Gentile immigrants. He foretold the discovery, translation, and distribution of *The Book of Mormon* by Joseph Smith, which would bring the gospel of the Nephites to all the people of the world, long after the Nephites had passed away.

Nephi told of a day when many false churches would be established that would compete with each other to proclaim themselves as the true church of God. Most of these churches, he said, would teach false doctrines, corrupt the words of God, engage in secret conspiracies with the devil, build fine churches, act in their own special interests, and pursue material wealth. In the last days, Nephi predicted that the "great and abominable church, the whore of all the earth" (the Roman Catholic Church) would fall to the ground. God told Nephi that in the latter days two testimonies of his word, from two separate nations (the Bible and *The Book of Mormon*), would run together to form his complete and true gospel.

Nephi prophesied that after *The Book of Mormon* was delivered to the world by future Gentiles who were converted to its truth, his words would be carried to the Native Americans. Those Native Americans who believed in Jesus Christ would, after several generations, be transformed from dark and loathsome people back into white and beautiful people again, by the power of God.

Nephi prophesied that God would do a marvelous thing in the last days, and deliver his believers from darkness into peace and light. Nephi told how God had shown him of Jesus Christ's baptism in water by John the Baptist, and advised his people to follow this future example to achieve a remission of their sins. First, God told Nephi to be baptized in the name of Jesus Christ. Then Jesus Christ told Nephi that whoever is baptized in his name would receive the Holy Ghost, and commanded Nephi to follow this example.

In closing, Nephi testified that his words were true, and that this truth would be clear to everyone when they stood before God on the day of judgment.

Sixteen of the 33 chapters of the Second Book of Nephi are direct recitals of the Old Testament prophet Isaiah, whom Nephi and his younger brother Jacob quote from the brass plates that Nephi retrieved from Jerusalem. Fifteen of the 16 chapters of Isaiah match up nearly identically, word for word, with their counterparts from *The King James Version of the Bible.*

The 16th of these Isaiah chapters (Chapter 27 of the Second Book of Nephi) is similar to, but significantly different from, the text of Chapter 29 of Isaiah found in the Bible. In this chapter, Isaiah is said to have prophesied that during the last days a book whose words have long been hidden in the ground (presumably *The Book of Mormon*) would be delivered to a man (presumably Joseph Smith). Isaiah prophesied that this sealed book would be unsealed and translated by the power of God and then broadcast to the people of the world. He foretold that after this book was discovered by the designated man it would remain hidden, except to three witnesses who would be allowed to see it and testify to its truth. Through this book, the faithful from the past would speak as if they had arisen from the dead. The book would contain revelations from God, and those who rejected this word of God, Isaiah said, would be cursed.

Further chapters in the Second Book of Nephi are devoted to Nephi and his younger brother Jacob's liberal interpretation and commentary on Isaiah's words.

By the time the Second Book of Nephi has reached its conclusion, *The Book of Mormon* and Joseph Smith have been prophesied by Joseph of Egypt, and by the Old Testament prophet Isaiah, and Lehi, and Nephi.

THE SECOND BOOK OF NEPHI - TRANSLATION

Chapter 1. 1830 and 1981 Versions

After I spoke to my older brothers about Isaiah's prophecies, I warned them to be obedient to God's will. Our father Lehi told them how fortunate we were to have been guided by God out of Jerusalem, and into this promised land. Lehi reminded them of their rebellions during the ocean crossing and the great mercy of God, who had spared their lives.

"I've had another vision," Lehi told us, "in which I've seen that Jerusalem has been destroyed. Had we remained there we would certainly have died. In spite of the troubles of our long journey, we have been given this land of promise to populate with our progeny, and to share with those who will also be led here by the hand of God. If the people of this land remain faithful to the commandments of God, it will be a place of liberty to those people, and protected from conquest. To protect the land from being overrun, God has promised me that it will be hidden safely forever from other nations as long as his will is being kept."

"But," continued Lehi, "when the time comes that our people's faith in God fails, and they reject the Messiah Jesus Christ, after having been given so much, the judgments of God will fall heavily upon them. After that time, other nations will also be guided to this promised land and God will give them power to take the promised lands for themselves. Those who have failed God will be killed and scattered. As generations pass, there will be bloodshed, and great visitations, so it is important that you listen to and remember my words.

"Awaken, my sons, from the deep sleep of hell, and cast away the chains of misery. Awaken and pay heed to an aging parent who will soon die. God has redeemed my soul and I pray that you also will remember the commandments of God. My worry and fear is that God's anger will fall upon you and your future descendants, that you will be forever destroyed by famine and war, and be led into captivity by the devil. How I wish that these things would not happen, and that you would remain in God's grace. The choice is yours, to keep God's commandments and prosper, or fail God and be cut off from me. Please don't let me die in grief and sorrow.

"Your brother Nephi has kept his commandments since we left Jerusalem, and has been an instrument of God's will in bringing us to this promised land. Stop rebelling against him. Were it not for him, we would have perished from starvation in the wilderness. Yet you sought to kill him and brought him suffering and sorrow. I am fearful that he will suffer at your hands again because you accuse him of seeking power and authority over you. I know that his only wish is to serve the glory of God and assist you, his brothers, in your own welfare. He has only been direct with you to help you see and understand the perils that you face. Because the power of God is with him, you must obey his commands as you would the word of God."

Lehi then spoke to all of his sons, as well as the sons of Ishmael, saying, "If you listen to Nephi, the generations that follow will not perish. If you will follow him, I will leave you with my first blessing. To those who do not follow Nephi, I remove this blessing."

Turning to Zoram, Laban's former servant whom Nephi had brought with them from Jerusalem, Lehi said, "Zoram, you are a true friend of my son Nephi. Because of your faithfulness to him, you and your progeny will be blessed with prosperity as long as you and they follow the path of Nephi and God's will."

Chapter 2. 1981 Version

Lehi now spoke to his second youngest son and said, "Jacob, you are the first of my two sons to be born during our journey through the wilderness. Throughout your childhood you have suffered greatly because of your brothers' rudeness. Nonetheless, you know the greatness of God, who can turn suffering into strength. Your soul is blessed because you can and will follow Nephi. I know that you will be redeemed because you have seen the time when God brings salvation to men. Your redemption will come through the Messiah Jesus Christ, who will offer himself as a sacrifice to sin for those who honestly repent, and through whom men may be resurrected from death after his first example. Those that believe in him will be saved. Whoever stands in opposition to him will be punished.

"There is an opposition in all things," Lehi continued, "and men need to choose between right and wrong, between holiness and wickedness, between happiness and misery. Without opposites there would be no opportunity for choice. Without opposites life would be no different from death, and mortality no different than immortality. Without God's laws there is no sin. Without sin there would be no righteousness or happiness, and no punishment or misery. Without these things there is no God. And without God there would be no earth, for there would have been no creation. There would be nothing."

Then, speaking again to all of his sons, Lehi said, "For your benefit I say that there is a God, and that he created all things in the heavens and of the earth, both to act and be acted upon. God has also created the forbidden fruit in opposition to the tree of life, so that man could act for himself and choose between the opportunities offered.

"According to what has been written, an angel of God sought that which was evil, and fell from heaven to become a devil. Because he fell from heaven and became miserable forever, he also sought the misery of all mankind. Through the serpent he said to Eve, 'Come, eat of the forbidden fruit and you will not die. You can be like God, knowing both good and evil.' After eating the forbidden fruit, Adam and Eve were driven from the garden and forced to till the soil, and bring forth the children who now populate the earth.

"Our time here has been prolonged by God so that we can repent while we are mortal, according to his commandments. Had Adam and Eve not defied God's words and fallen, they could have remained in the garden of Eden, and things would have remained as they were, in innocence, with no children. Having no joy, they knew no misery. Doing no good, they knew no sin. But as you can see, in God's wisdom that is not the way things happened. Adam fell so that men might know joy.

"The Messiah will come," Lehi continued, "to redeem the fallen people. Once redeemed, they will be free forever, knowing good from evil. Therefore, men are free to act and choose liberty and immortality through Jesus Christ, or to choose slavery to the devil, and death. The devil wishes for us to be as miserable as he is, while God wishes for us to be faithful to his laws and choose eternal life. My sons, I want you all to choose God's will and listen to his commandments, be faithful to him, and live eternally. Do not choose eternal death and alignment with the evil that allows the devil to hold you captive in his kingdom of hell.

"My sons, these are the last days of my life and I have chosen the path of God according to the words of the prophet. My final wish is for the everlasting welfare of your souls."

Chapter 2. 1830 Version

Chapter 3. 1981 Version

My father Lehi next addressed his youngest son. "Joseph[2], you were born in the days of my greatest sorrows while we traveled through the wilderness. May God bless you and your progeny forever, if you, too, keep the commandments of God. You are a descendant of Joseph[1] who was sold off by his brothers and taken to Egypt as a slave. He was a prophet who saw our present time. Like us, Joseph of Egypt was promised many things by God. One of those promises was that his descendants would become a mighty branch of the family of Israel which would be broken off and remembered when the Messiah Jesus Christ becomes manifest in the world in the latter days. He promised that our descendants will be brought out of the darkness into the light, and out of captivity into freedom.

"Long ago our ancestor, Joseph of Egypt, declared that God had said to him, 'Joseph, from your descendants I will raise up a great prophet, seer, and revelator. He will be highly regarded among your descendants. I will command him to do great work among your descendants by bringing to them the knowledge of the promises that I have made to your ancestors. Just as I will raise up and bring forth Moses to deliver your people out of the land of Egypt, so too will I raise up the great prophet of which I speak. He will not only bring forth my word, but convince people of its truth. In the latter days, he will bring knowledge of my covenants and expose false doctrines, bring peace among your descendants, and restore the entire family of Israel.'

"Joseph has prophesied," said Lehi, "that, 'The great prophet whom God will raise up in the latter days will be blessed by God, and will confound all those who oppose him. His name, like mine, will be Joseph, and Joseph will also be the name of his father.* He will bring my people into salvation. I am as sure of this prophecy as I am sure of the prophecy of Moses, because God has promised to preserve my descendants forever.'

*Joseph Smith's father was also named Joseph Smith.

" 'I will bring forth a Moses,' God said to Joseph of Egypt, 'and give him a rod of power, and give him written commandments to follow. Likewise, in the last days I will bring forth the prophet Joseph who shall write the words of your descendants that are necessary to be heard.' "

Lehi continued his prophesying to my brother Joseph. "Because of these promises you are blessed and your descendants will not be destroyed, because they will listen to the words that the latter day prophet Joseph shall bring to them in a book. Among your descendants, this mighty one will rise up and be an instrument of God's hand, who will work wonders towards bringing restoration to all the family of Israel, and to the descendants of your brothers.

"You are still young, Joseph; therefore, listen to the words of your brother Nephi. If you do this, all of my blessings will come true. Above all, remember the words of your dying father."

Chapter 3. 1830 Version

Chapter 4. 1981 Version

There are a few things I want to say regarding the prophecies made by Joseph of Egypt, of which my father has spoken. We know these to be true prophecies about his descendants because they were written on the brass plates we have carried with us from Jerusalem, and because many of these prophecies have already come true. Long ago, he truly prophesied about his descendants, and about our future generations.

When Lehi finished speaking about the prophecies of Joseph, he gathered to him the sons and daughters of Laman, and said to them, "God has said that if you keep his commandments you will prosper in this land, and if not, you will be cut off from him. Before I die, I want to leave you with a blessing. I know that if you are brought up properly, you cannot fail. My blessing is this — that if you do fail, that rather than being cursed yourselves, that curse will fall upon your parents for failing to bring you up properly. My blessing is that God will have mercy on you and your descendants."

Lehi then brought the sons and daughters of Lemuel before him and said the same thing to them that he'd said to the children of Laman. Following that, he gathered the household of Ishmael to him and said likewise to them.

Finally, Lehi spoke to his son Sam, saying, "You and your descendants are blessed. You and your brother Nephi will inherit this land. Your descendants will be counted with his descendants and will be blessed for all their days."

After having given his blessings to all of our party who had traveled with him from Jerusalem, Lehi aged quickly, died, and was buried.

Shortly after our father's death, Laman, Lemuel, and Ishmael's sons grew angry with me when I was compelled to speak to them about God's warnings. I found it impossible not to remind them of what our father had said before he died.

In response to their anger, I have turned inward and found solace in writing on these plates the words that I can share, and that might benefit my descendants. In repose, I see how I could have been better, and am saddened. God has supported me and led me through my troubles in the wilderness. He protected me on the long ocean crossing. He has filled me with love and bewildered my foes. He has heard my anguish by day and answered me with visions at night. His angels have answered my prayers. Having seen all of this, why do I still sometimes yield to temptations and anger? I must awaken my soul and refuse to be angered, or saddened, by my troubles. In my heart, I rejoice in God, who is the rock of my salvation. Oh, God, will you redeem me, deliver me from my enemies, and protect me from sin? My heart is broken and my spirit is remorseful for my shortcomings. Oh, God, guide me on the path to righteousness and help to clear the way. Oh, God, I have trusted in you and will do so forever. I know that to listen to my own flesh, or put my trust in men, is to invite your curse. I know that God gives to those who ask, so I raise my voice to you as the rock of my everlasting faith.

Chapter 4. 1830 Version

Chapter 5. 1981 Version

I cried before God because of the anger of my brothers; but their anger only grew, as they plotted to kill me. They spoke out against me, saying that I sought to rule over them and that I was the source of their troubles. "Let us kill him," they said, "and we will no longer be bothered by his lectures. Then we, as the older brothers, shall rightfully rule this people."

God came and warned me that I should leave, and flee into the wilderness with those among us who still listened my words. So I gathered up my family, the families of Zoram, the families of my brothers Sam, Jacob, and

Joseph, my sisters, and those who believed in the warnings and revelations of God. We packed up the possessions that we could carry and traveled for many days before we stopped and rested in a place we called Nephi. The people who came with me called themselves the people of Nephi, or Nephites.

Because we kept the commandments of Moses, God was with us and we prospered. We planted our seeds, raised flocks and herds of animals, and reaped abundance. I brought with us the brass plates from Jerusalem and the magic compass, Liahona, which God had given to my father to guide us in the wilderness. Our people multiplied and we thrived in the new land.

I knew that the Lamanites, as Laman's people were now called, harbored great hatred towards me and my people, the Nephites. Because of this, it became necessary to undertake preparations for our defense against them. I still carried with me the sword of Laban, that I had used to kill Laban back in Jerusalem. Because I knew that the Lamanites might come to destroy us and try to steal our prosperity, I used Laban's sword now as a model from which to fashion many similar swords.

I taught my people how to construct buildings and work with wood, iron, copper, brass, steel, gold and silver. The ores for these metals were found in great abundance. I built a temple fashioned after Solomon's great temple and guided the Nephites to industry and hard work. We became great craftsmen. As our community took hold, the Nephites wanted me as their king, but I declined, arguing that no king was necessary. I promised to help them to the limits of my abilities.

For the Lamanites, the warnings of God were fulfilled, and they were cut off from him. Because of their wickedness and the hardness of their hearts against God, a great curse fell upon them. The Lamanites were physically transformed by God so that their appearance would not in any way be enticing to my Nephites. Where before they had been handsome, white people, their skin became dark and their features loathsome. They would remain this way, God said, until they repented of their sins. God further warned us that if any of the Nephites should marry and couple with any of the Lamanites, the children of such a

union would be similarly cursed in appearance. Because of these curses which fell upon them, they became lazy, mischievous people who fed themselves on wild beasts of prey instead of growing plants for harvest or raising livestock.

God said to me, "Nephi, these Lamanites will be the enemy of your descendants, and a reminder of my covenants with you. If your descendants should ever forget me and my commandments, these Lamanites will destroy them."

Thirty years had now passed since we left Jerusalem, and we Nephites had found great happiness in this promised land. My brothers Jacob and Joseph were blessed by me as priests and teachers of my people. In keeping with the word of God, I continued to keep a record of my people on the plates, and another record of God's will for my descendants. [569 BC]

By the time forty years had passed, our first wars with the Lamanites began. [559 BC]

Chapter 5. 1830 Version

Chapter 6. 1981 Version

My brother Jacob said these words to our people.

"I have been called upon by God and ordained by my Brother Nephi whom you look upon as your king and protector. In the past, I've spoken to you of many things from the time of the world's creation through the present time, including the recent words of my father Lehi. I speak to you today for the welfare of your souls. Nephi has asked me to read to you the words of the old prophet Isaiah regarding the destiny of the house of Israel, of which we are a part, and how it may be applied to us.

"These, then, are God's words, as spoken to Isaiah. 'Gentiles in the future will bring the symbol of God to the people of the world and they will then support your sons and daughters. Kings and queens will prostrate themselves before your descendants.'"

Commenting on this quotation of God by Isaiah, Jacob said, "God has shown me that the people of Jerusalem whom we left behind have been either killed or carried away as slaves to Babylon. God has also shown me that they will return to Jerusalem in the future. God has further shown me that his son Jesus Christ will manifest himself to their descendants, who will torture and crucify him. Those whose hearts are so hardened that they act like this against God will be judged, tormented, hated, and scattered. But God will be merciful, and these descendants of Israel will not be destroyed. When they come to realize that God is their redeemer, they will again be gathered together in the lands of their inheritance.

"Those future Gentiles of whom Isaiah has written, who do not oppose Zion, and who do not align themselves with the great abominable church, will be saved, because this is what God has promised us. Those who oppose Israel and who oppose the keepers of God's promises will grovel in the dirt at their feet. The people of God are the ones who wait patiently for the coming of the Messiah. According to the words of the prophet Isaiah, the Messiah will return a second time, in power and glory, to redeem his people and destroy their enemies. When that day comes, those who believe in him will be saved. Those who do not believe in him will perish by fire, great storms, bloodshed, disease, and starvation. They will be made to know that Jesus Christ and God are one. If the people of God are oppressed or imprisoned, they will be set free."

Chapter 7. 1981 Version

[Chapter 7 of the Second Book of Nephi is virtually indistinguishable, word for word, from Chapter 50 of Isaiah from the Old Testament.]

Jacob reads Isaiah's words from the plates brought by the Nephites from Jerusalem. God speaks through Isaiah and places responsibility for their captivity on the people of Israel's own unfortunate behavior. God reminds the people of his ability to redeem them and his unwillingness to do so if they abuse and scorn God for their predicament.

Chapter 8. 1981 Version

[Chapter 8 of the Second Book of Nephi is virtually indistinguishable, word for word, from Chapter 51, and Chapter 52: Verses 1–2, of Isaiah from the Old Testament.]

Jacob continues reading Isaiah's words to the Nephites. Speaking through Isaiah, God reminds the people of Israel that he has blessed

and protected them since the time of Abraham and Sarah. He reminds them that in the days of Moses, he helped them to defeat the pharaoh of Egypt and to escape from bondage. God declares Israel's children as his people, and promises them freedom again. God's anger with his people is now spent. The recent desolation and destruction that has been the lot of Israel's descendants will now fall on the backs of their tormenters. "Rise up," God says, "and you will soon be free from slavery."

Chapter 6. 1830 Version

Chapter 9. 1981 Version

"I've read these of words of Isaiah," Jacob said to the Nephites, "to show you the covenants God has made with the descendants of Israel. God has spoken to the Jews through his prophets since the time of Adam and Eve, from generation to generation, until the time comes that his people are restored to the true church of God. At that time, they will be gathered home to the lands of their inheritance. We know that God will appear in Jerusalem, our former home; that he will suffer under the hands of men and die, so that all men will become subject to him. Since the fall of Adam and Eve, men have become cut off from God, and subject to death. To fulfill his merciful plan there needs to be a power of resurrection after death. Unless amends are somehow made for this fall, our deaths will be permanent and our spirits will be forever subject to the devil. Without resurrection, our spirits will become like the devil's, filled with misery, lies, murder, and secret works of darkness.

"But the goodness of our God," Jacob continued, "has prepared a way for our escape from the grasp of this monster of death and hell that I shall also call the death of our bodies and also the death of our spirits. The death of Jesus Christ in Jerusalem, of which we are foretold, will make death temporary only. His death and resurrection will yield up and restore the captive spirits of hell, as well as their bodies, where they will become immortal and face the judgment of God.

"At that time, we will have full knowledge of guilt, dirtiness, and nakedness, as well as of our goodness and purity. Having passed from death into immortality, people will appear in judgment before Jesus Christ. As surely as Jesus Christ lives, and as God has spoken, those who have been righteous will remain righteous, and those who have been filthy will remain filthy. The filthy are the people of the devil, and they will go with him into everlasting fire and torment without end. Because this is God's justice, and these were his words, the law must be fulfilled.

"Those who are righteous, who have believed in Jesus Christ, who have endured the troubles of the world, and who have despised the shame of it, will inherit the kingdom of God which was prepared for them. Their joy will be full forever. This is the great mercy of our God, Jesus Christ, for he will deliver his saints from the devil and hell. He will come into the world with a willingness to suffer all the pains of all the descendants of Adam and Eve, if only they will listen to his words. His commandment is that men must repent, have faith in him, and be baptized in his name or they cannot be saved. Those that will not repent, believe in him, and be baptized in his name must be damned, for this is the word of God. This is God's law.

"However, people who have not heard God's law will not be condemned, but will be redeemed by Jesus Christ's mercy. Only those who have heard and rejected or ignored this law will be condemned. For them, there is only delivery to the devil, death, hell, and the eternal torment of fire. Those men who think of themselves as educated and wise in the ways of the world, and who listen to their own thinking minds instead of listening to the word of God, will perish. In such cases all of the knowledge, education, and worldly wisdom is foolishness and will not benefit them beyond their mortal lives. Learning and knowledge are only good when people also heed the laws of God.

"The rich are cursed, because they despise the poor and persecute the humble. Because they worship their treasures, their treasure is their God. But their treasure will also perish with them. Those who will not listen and will not see are cursed, and they will perish. Those with unclean hearts are cursed, and they will perish. Those who lie, who murder, and who fornicate are also cursed, for they will perish and be sent to hell. Those who worship false idols are cursed, because the devil takes particular delight in them. Those who die in their sins are cursed, for they will return to God to see his face with their sins intact.

"Beloved brothers, remember the dangers in opposing God and yielding to the enticements of the devil. Always remember that to be carnally minded is to die, while being spiritually minded is to find eternal life. I have not said any of these things against you personally, but have only spoken the words of God. The words of God are harsh to those who sin, but the righteous will not fear them for they love the truth and cannot be shaken. The path I describe is straight and narrow, and at the end of that path is a gate, whose gatekeeper is Jesus Christ. Remember to be careful, because God cannot be deceived. He will open that gate to anyone who knocks, but those who come to him inflated with their knowledge or wealth, he despises. Unless they put aside their foolishness, they may not pass; and the happiness of life eternal which is prepared for the saints who believe in God, will remain hidden from them forever.

"I've done all that I can to help save you. You must help yourselves, now. I can only hope that you will turn away from sin and not have to concede your depravity before God when your time of judgment comes. If you were holy, there would be no need to be clear with you about the dangers of sin. But as a teacher, I must teach you about the consequences of being unholy in the eye God.

"As you can see, I detest sin and take delight in holiness, by praising the name of God. If you thirst, you too can come with me to the waters of God's mercy and drink, for free. Likewise, there is no need to spend money on things of no value, or to work for that which cannot satisfy. Come feast with me on that which will not perish or be corrupted. Remember the words of God and pray to him by day, and give thanks by night.

"God's promises to us are great, and because of his greatness he has promised that our descendants will not perish but will, in future generations, become a strong branch among the descendants of Israel. I could say more, but that is enough for now."

Chapter 7. 1830 Version

Chapter 10. 1981 Version

Jacob addressed the Nephites again on the following day.

"As I said, we, and our descendants, are a great branch of the people of Israel. It has been revealed to me that many of our descendants will perish eternally because of their refusal to believe in God's word. But God will also be merciful to many others of our children, who will come to accept the knowledge of Jesus Christ. As I have said, it is necessary that Jesus Christ come in flesh to the wicked Jews of Jerusalem to be crucified, because who but they would kill their God? Any other nation on earth would recognize him as God, repent, and worship him. Because of their transgressions, destruction, hunger, disease, and bloodshed will befall them and those who are not killed will be scattered across the face of the earth. But, God has also said that when these people come to recognize Jesus Christ as God, they will be restored according to his promise to their forefathers, and given the lands of their inheritance. These scattered descendants of Israel will be gathered from all corners of the earth and the Gentile nations will have his blessing because they will help in this gathering. This is God's word, so who can doubt its truth?

"God has said that this new land will be the land of your inheritance," Jacob related, "and that Gentiles will also be welcomed and blessed on it. This land will be a land of liberty for the Gentiles because there will be no kings in it. God will fortify this land and those who fight against it will perish. God has said, 'The promises I have made will be fulfilled to the people of the world and I will destroy the secret works of darkness, murders, and abominations. Any of those who fight against Zion, whether they are Jews or Gentiles, men or women, will perish because they are the whores of the earth. Any who are not for me are against me.'

"God has also said," continued Jacob, "that he will torment our descendants at the hand of the Gentiles who will come to this land. These Gentiles will become as fathers to our descendants and be counted also among the descendants of Israel. God has promised this land to your descendants and also to the Gentiles who will be counted among your descendants, and all of those who live here who worship God. Let us then remember God's will and lay aside our sins, because he has brought us across the sea to this promised new land. Lift your hearts and remember that you are free to act for yourselves, to choose eternal death or eternal life. It is only by reconciling yourselves with the will of God that you will be saved. By the power of resurrection, may you be raised from death and find your way to the eternal kingdom of God."

Chapter 8. 1830 Version

Chapter 11– 1981 Version

Jacob said many more things to my people than I can write down, but what I've related seems sufficient.

I, Nephi, will now relate more of the words of Isaiah from the plates brought with us from Jerusalem, because he also saw Jesus Christ as my brother Jacob and I have seen him. These ancient words of his prove the truth of what I have said. If Jesus Christ should not come, all men would perish. Without Jesus Christ, there would be no God. Without God, there would be no creation, and we would not exist. But there is a God and he is Jesus Christ, who will come to us in a time of his own choosing, Isaiah writes to all people.

Chapter 12. 1981 Version

[*Chapter 12 of the Second Book of Nephi is virtually indistinguishable, word for word, from Chapter 2 of Isaiah from the Old Testament.*]

Isaiah predicts that in the last days God's temple in Jerusalem will be earth's greatest attraction, and that people will come from everywhere to pay homage to it because in those days the world will be ruled from Jerusalem. God will settle disputes between nations, wars will end, and weapons of war will be converted into instruments of peace. People who have worshipped wealth, false prophets, and idols will cower in fear, and try unsuccessfully to hide from God's judgment. God will not forgive them for these sins. Idols will be abolished and only God will be held on high. Isaiah admonishes people to stop putting faith in men and doing those things which displease God.

Chapter 13. 1981 Version

[Chapter 13 of the Second Book of Nephi is virtually indistinguishable, word for word, from Chapter 9 of Isaiah from the Old Testament.]

Isaiah predicts that God will deprive Jerusalem and Judah of food and water, kill their leaders, and destroy their armies and judges. Anarchy will be the rule. God will do this because, as in Sodom, the people have shamelessly refused to abide by his laws and have instead chosen evil. God is angry because the poor have been abused and defrauded by rulers who enrich themselves. The haughty women of Israel who vainly worship their own beauty and ornamentation will be exposed naked, condemned to baldness, and caused to stink. Their husbands will die in battle, leaving them crying in the dirt.

Chapter 14. 1981 Version

[Chapter 14 of the Second Book of Nephi is virtually indistinguishable, word for word, from Chapter 4 of Isaiah from the Old Testament.]

Isaiah predicts that those who are saved from the destruction will be God's holy people and will live afterwards in bounty. God will provide a canopy of smoke and cloud over the land to shade it during the day and shelter it from rain and storms.

Chapter 15. 1981 Version

[Chapter 15 of the Second Book of Nephi is virtually indistinguishable, word for word, from Chapter 5 of Isaiah from the Old Testament.]

Isaiah tells a parable that compares Israel to a vineyard. He describes a lovely fenced garden on the hillside, with rocks removed from the soil, and planted with the best vines. In the end, despite his best efforts, it only grows wild grapes. In anger, he tears down the fence, and allows it to be trampled and eaten. He discontinues pruning, allows weeds to overtake it, and deprives it of water.

The vineyard of God, Isaiah tells us, is a representation of the descendants of Israel. Instead of good leaders and good people, God finds oppressors and cities crammed with wealthy people who offer no place for the humble people to live. Like the gardener, God will tear down the fence and deprive the unthankful people of protection and nurture. God, says Isaiah, is angry at the injustice and abuse, the drunkenness and the partying, and will therefore bring exile and starvation. Just as fire consumes withered plants, so too will Israel be consumed by ignoring God's laws. To cleanse the people, God will signal distant nations and invite them to invade, capture, and kill those who have transgressed against his word. The high and mighty will be brought down and the faithful will eat in their places.

Chapter 9. 1830 Version

Chapter 16. 1981 Version

[Chapter 16 of the Second Book of Nephi is virtually indistinguishable, word for word, from Chapter 6 of Isaiah from the Old Testament.]

Isaiah relates how he came to see God and was purified in God's presence by an angel. God then asked Isaiah to be his messenger and prophet to the people, and give him advice on how to send his message. Isaiah is commanded to relate this message until the cities are destroyed and the country is laid waste. God tells Isaiah that a tenth of his people will survive and Israel will grow again from this remnant.

Chapter 17. 1981 Version

[Chapter 17 of the Second Book of Nephi is virtually indistinguishable, word for word, from Chapter 7 of Isaiah from the Old Testament.]

Isaiah recounts how he was asked by God to meet with King Ahaz of Judah, and of how God predicted, for Ahaz, the coming of a Messiah born of a virgin who will know to choose good from evil as a young child. Isaiah also predicts how a curse from God will bring the coming of armies and the destruction of the land.

Chapter 18. 1981 Version

[*Chapter 18 of the Second Book of Nephi is virtually indistinguishable, word for word, from Chapter 8 of Isaiah from the Old Testament.*]

Isaiah predicts that because the people refuse God's care, Assyria will invade Israel. He warns against consulting with sorcerers and those who would blame their misfortunes on God.

Chapter 19. 1981 Version

[*Chapter 19 of the Second Book of Nephi is virtually indistinguishable, word for word, from Chapter 9 of Isaiah from the Old Testament.*]

Isaiah recounts the wars and ruinous condition of the lands between the Red Sea and Assyria, and predicts the coming of a Messiah whose reign of justice and peace will be everlasting. He criticizes, rages against, and warns those whose behavior strays from God's will, promising punishment and devastation.

Chapter 20. 1981 Version

[*Chapter 20 of the Second Book of Nephi is virtually indistinguishable, word for word, from Chapter 10 of Isaiah from the Old Testament.*]

Isaiah predicts that God will send desolation to the people of Israel because of the unfair laws and the immoral behavior of his people. God will stand by without helping when the Assyrians invade and cleanse the land, as an instrument of God's anger. After using Assyria, God will turn and punish them also, destroying their armies. Afterwards, those who are left in Israel and Judah will again come to trust in God. Isaiah warns those who have faith not to be afraid, because the Assyrian oppression will not last very long.

Chapter 21. 1981 Version

[*Chapter 21 of the Second Book of Nephi is virtually indistinguishable, word for word, from Chapter 11 of Isaiah from the Old Testament.*]

Isaiah predicts the coming of a glorious Messiah from the descendants of David who will rule in fairness and truth. Nations will rally to this Messiah, and the children of Israel will be gathered again in the nation of Israel.

Chapter 22. 1981 Version

[*Chapter 22 of the Second Book of Nephi is virtually indistinguishable, word for word, from Chapter 12 of Isaiah from the Old Testament.*]

Isaiah predicts that when the Messiah comes, the people will bow down in thanks because God's anger will have been converted to salvation for all.

Chapter 10. 1830 Version

Chapter 23. 1981 Version

[*Chapter 23 of the Second Book of Nephi is virtually indistinguishable, word for word, from Chapter 13 of Isaiah from the Old Testament.*]

Isaiah predicts the merciless destruction of Babylon as punishment for its wickedness.

Chapter 24. 1981 Version

[*Chapter 24 of the Second Book of Nephi is virtually indistinguishable, word for word, from Chapter 14 of Isaiah from the Old Testament.*]

Isaiah predicts that after Babylon has fallen, God will again have mercy on the children of Israel and return them to their lands. Other nations, Isaiah foretells, will help in their return. Those who enslaved Israel will in turn be enslaved. The king of Babylon will be sent to hell and his country will be ruined.

Chapter 11. 1830 Version

Chapter 25. 1981 Version

I, Nephi, have some commentary to make regarding these words of Isaiah. I recognize that many of his words are hard to understand for those who do not comprehend the nature of prophesying among the Jews. I have not previously spoken a great deal about the prophecies of the Jews because so much of their works lie in the realm of darkness, and so many of their actions are ones of abomination. But now I write these thoughts onto my plates so that future generations of people and nations will know what Isaiah has predicted, and also know that they are true prophecies from the Jews. Like Isaiah, I too grew up in Jerusalem and understand the ways of the Jews.

You, my people, are also children of Israel and so I give you this prophecy. As Isaiah's prophecies are fulfilled, everyone will understand them, including my own descendants, and Isaiah's words will be of great value to them in the latter days.

Even though many generations of Jews have been destroyed because of their failure to follow God's rules, God has always warned them beforehand, as he did to my father before we left Jerusalem. Because they didn't listen to God, they were destroyed or carried away as slaves to Babylon. My prophecy is also that they will return again to their land and be subject to more wars, until the day comes when Jesus Christ appears to them in the flesh. Because their hearts are hardened, they will reject and crucify him. But three days after he is laid in the grave, he will rise again from the dead and all of those who believe in him will be saved in the kingdom of God. I have seen this day, and this prophecy is the delight of my heart. I further predict that, after Jesus Christ has arisen, Jerusalem and Babylon will again be destroyed, and the Jews who have opposed God will be scattered among all nations of the earth.

Many generations will pass and the scattered Jews will be tormented by the nations to which they have fled, until such time as they believe in Jesus Christ and recognize him as the true and only Messiah. At that time God will again gather and restore them. There is only one Messiah spoken of by the prophets, and he is the one whom the Jews will reject. Any other Messiahs will be false. This true Messiah will come to Israel six hundred years after my family left Jerusalem, and according to the prophets his name will be Jesus Christ, the Son of God. I say that these things are true and that there is no one who can save man except this Jesus Christ of whom I have spoken.

Now then, God has promised me that these things that I write will be kept and preserved, to be handed down from generation to generation so that the promises made to Joseph[1] of Egypt will be fulfilled, and that his descendants will never perish as long as the earth stands. In waiting, we observe the laws of Moses and look forward to the coming of Jesus Christ and the fulfillment of the law. In so doing, we will work diligently to write, to persuade our children and brothers to believe in Jesus Christ, and to be reconciled to God, because it is only by his grace that we are saved. By talking of Christ, rejoicing in Christ, preaching of Christ, and prophesying of Christ, our children will know where to look for the remission of their sins.

These words I speak will stand as testimony against your stubbornness, because they show you the right way to believe in Christ; by denying him, you would also deny the prophets and the law of God. Bow down before him, worship him with all your might, all your mind, all your strength, and all your soul. If you do this, you will not be cast out.

Chapter 26. 1981 Version

I have seen many future generations of our people come and go, bringing with them great wars and conflicts. I have seen that after Jesus Christ has arisen from the dead in Jerusalem, he will come to this land and show himself to a future generation of our descendants. When this Messiah, Jesus Christ, is born into the world there will be signs given to my people of his birth, his death, and his resurrection. This will be a mighty time of reckoning. The wicked among my people will die as punishment for having disregarded, abused, and killed the prophets and saints among them. They will die by fire, be swallowed by the earth, buried in landslides, blown away by great storms, and crushed by falling buildings.

I am nearly consumed with sorrow and pain for the destruction of these people, but I also know that God's ways are just. I also see that those who listen to the prophets and look forward to the arrival of Jesus Christ will not perish, because he will heal them. The descendants of those who are healed will have peace for three generations, but four generations after the appearance of Jesus Christ my people will have again forgotten God's spirit and his will. After yielding to the dark works of the devil, through their pride and foolishness, they will be punished with destruction and sent to hell. This I have seen, and it grieves my soul.

Just as the Jews need to be convinced that Jesus Christ is the Son of God, so too do the Gentiles need to learn this. In his own way Jesus Christ will come to every nation and all people, working miracles and giving signs according to their faith.

Listen, this is my prophecy. During the last days, our descendants will have dwindled from disbelief, and the descendants of the Lamanites will be oppressed, overrun, and killed by the Gentiles who will come to this land. This will happen because of their failure to remember and believe in the word of God and the words of Jesus Christ. Even after these people have been brought low and humbled, the prayers and history of their faithful ancestors will not be forgotten. God will help them to be heard. As if whispering from the ground, a book concerning our people will be written, sealed, buried, and hidden so that our story here is not destroyed and lost.

The proud and self righteous Gentiles that come to this new land will subdue the remaining descendents of our family of Israel that have come with us from Jerusalem. They will compete with one another to build many churches and faiths that fail to faithfully promote the miracles and power of God. They will build churches that promote their own special interests at the cost of the poor, causing envy, strife, and ill will. There will be secret conspiracies with the devil, who seeks to bind their souls to him and lead them astray.

But listen, my people; God does not work in darkness. He loves the world and only seeks to help it by laying down his own life and offering salvation for all. He asks that everyone join him in salvation and repentance.

God prohibits his people from priestcrafts in which men seek personal fortune and fame over the welfare of Zion. God commands that all men have the charity of love. Without that, they are nothing. People who labor for Zion will not perish, while those who labor for money will die. Further, God commands that men should not murder or lie, not steal or curse, not harbor envy or ill will, not fight with one another or fornicate. Those who do so will perish. God will remember and embrace all who come to him to receive his goodness, whether they are black or white, free men or slaves, men or women, heathens, Jews, or Gentiles.

Chapter 27. 1981 Version

[Chapter 27, the Second Book of Nephi, embodies much of the same text found in Chapter 29 of Isaiah from the Old Testament , but also expands upon it significantly. Verses 2–5 slightly rephrase Isaiah 29: Verses 6–10. Verses 6–24 expand greatly upon Isaiah 29: Verses 11–12. Verses 25–35 are virtually indistinguishable, word for word, from Isaiah 29: Verses 13–24.]

In Chapter 29, Isaiah predicts the future destruction of Jerusalem. God accuses its people of being blind and stupid. Isaiah relates that these future events have been recorded, but when seers go to read about them, they find that their eyes have been closed by God and the books appear to be sealed. God chastises the people as fools for refusing to obey him and swears to take awesome vengeance. God tells of a future time when the deaf will hear the words from a book, the blind will see, justice will prevail, and those living in error will believe the truth.

[The Second Book of Nephi, Chapter 27, expands on, and deviates from Isaiah's prophecy in Isaiah, Chapter 29, as follows.]

Isaiah predicts that in the last days, or the days of the Gentiles, the nations of the world will become filled with all manner of abominations. At that time God will bring forth a book comprised of words that have lain asleep for a long time. This book will be sealed. In it will be a revelation from God, from the beginning of the world until its end. Because of the unfaithfulness of the people, the book will be kept hidden from them until the last days.

At God's chosen time this book, whose words have long lain sleeping in the ground, will be delivered to a man who will in turn deliver these words to others. The book will be unsealed and translated by the power of God. A day will come when these words will be revealed and broadcast to all the people of the world.

The book itself will be delivered to the man whom I've spoken of and will remain hidden from all other men, except for three witnesses who will be allowed to see it and testify to its truth. No one else will be allowed to see the book except by the grace of God. Through this book the faithful from the past will speak as if they had arisen from the dead. Those who reject this word of God will be cursed.

God will say to this man, "Give some of the unsealed words to another. Have him take these words to an educated man, and ask him to read them."

The educated man will respond by saying, "Bring me the whole book and I will read them." When he is told that book is sealed, he will say, "Then I cannot read it."

The man who will be given the book will protest his ability to read the words, saying, "I am not an educated man."

And God will say to him, "The educated may not read the book because they have rejected it. Through me you will be able to read. Do not touch the books which remain sealed because I will bring them to the world in my chosen time. When you have translated the words that I have asked you to read, and have obtained the witnesses that I have promised to you, seal up the book again and hide it. I will preserve the parts that you have not read until it is time to reveal it to the people of earth. I am a God of miracles. I will show the world's people that I am the same God past, present, and forever."

Chapter 12. 1830 Version

Chapter 28. 1981 Version

I, Nephi, have written to you as the Spirit of God has asked me to do, and I know that these prophecies of Isaiah will certainly come true. The book that will be written, which will include these words I now inscribe, will be of great value to all men, and especially to our remnant descendants in this new land because they will be descendants of Israel.

In the last days, church after church will be built up, with each one saying that it is the true church of God. The priests will all compete with other priests to teach their way. But in spite of what they say, all of these churches and all of these priests will not serve God. These priests will say, "Listen to us, because God and Jesus Christ have come and gone, giving us their powers. God no longer does miracles. If someone tells you so, don't believe them."

In the last days, many people will say, "Life is brief, so eat, drink, and be merry. Don't be too afraid of God. Lie a little, take advantage of others when you can, because there is no harm in this. God may slap our wrists, but we will still be saved in the kingdom of God." Many will teach such false, vain, and foolish doctrines, and be proud of themselves for it. These corrupt teachers will try to hide their works of darkness from God, but the blood of dead saints will cry against them from the ground. To build their fine churches and wear their fine clothing, they rob the poor and persecute the humble. Except for the humble followers of Jesus Christ, many people will deviate from God's will. Those who are proud and stubborn, who preach false doctrines and pervert the true way of God, and who live immoral lives will be cursed and cast down to hell. But those who truly repent their evil acts will not be destroyed.

In the last days, the great and abominable church, the whore of the earth, will fall to the ground. In so doing, the devil's kingdom will be shaken and those who belong to it will be moved to repent before the devil lays his everlasting claim to them. In the last days, the devil will incite people to anger against all that is good. Others, he will seduce with a false sense of security, and lead them benignly to hell. To some he will offer flattery, and deny the existence of hell until they are trapped by his trickery. In the end, people will die and be judged by the acts of their lives before God. Those who have been seized by the devil must go to the place prepared for them, a place with a lake of fire and eternal torment. Those who think that all is well in the world, and who listen to men instead of God, will be cursed. Those whose lives are aligned with God will be glad, and those aligned against God will be sorry. Those who say that they've received the word of God and need no more of it will be cursed.

Listen to what God says: "I will ration my words to my people a little bit at a time, bless those who listen, and give them more so they can learn. Those who close their ears to me, thinking they've heard enough, will receive no more of my teachings and will lose what they already have. Do not put your trust in men or listen to them except those who teach by the power of God. I will curse the Gentiles who refuse to listen even after I have held out my arms to them and shown them my mercy, unless they repent and come to me to be received."

Chapter 29. 1981 Version

"In the last days," God has said, "I will do a marvelous thing in remembrance of my promises, and for a second time will deliver my people who are descendants of Israel. Also, in remembrance of my promises to you and your father Lehi, I will not forget your descendants. This I will do by bringing them the words of their ancestors, which will spread to all corners of the earth like a banner among my people, the descendants of Israel. Many Gentiles will say that they already have a Bible and that there cannot be any more Bibles. But do the foolish Gentiles even thank the Jews for the Bible they have, that has come from them? Do they remember the suffering of the Jewish people, or recall their diligence in bringing salvation to the Gentiles? Rather than thank the Jews, who are my ancient promised people, the Gentiles curse them, hate them, and refuse to help them. But I have not forgotten them, and what they do to the Jews will also be done to them.

"Remember that I have created many nations and have created all men to receive my word. In the last days, two testimonies of my word from two nations will come forth, because I have said the same thing to both nations. When the two nations run together, their two testimonies will also run together. I will bring forth both testimonies to bear witness that I am the same God, past, present, and forever, and that I have spoken of these things twice. My work is not yet finished, nor will it ever be finished. Just because the Gentiles have some of my words in their Bible, they should not suppose that they have all of my words, or imagine that I have not caused more words also to be written. Everywhere I speak, I command that people should write the words I speak to them, because I will judge men on the basis of what I have commanded to be written. I will speak to the Jews, the Nephites, the other tribes of Israel, and to the other nations of earth, and command that they write down my words also. In the end, the Jews will have the words of the Nephites, and the Nephites will have the words of the Jews. Just

as my people, the descendants of Israel, will be gathered home to their own lands, my words will also be gathered into one book. I will show those who fight against me that I am the same God who promised Abraham that I would remember and shelter his descendants forever."

Chapter 30. 1981 Version

I, Nephi, do not want my followers to think that they are any more righteous than the Gentiles that I've spoken of. Unless you obey the commandments of God, you are just as likely as they are, to perish. Any Gentiles or Jews who repent and accept Jesus Christ are as likely to be as saved as any of you who do likewise.

I predict that the book that I've spoken of will be delivered to the future Gentiles of this land who will be converted by its words, and then those words will be carried to the remnants of our descendants. Those remnant people of this new land will then learn how their ancestors came from Jerusalem, and that they are descended from the Jews. Like their ancestors they will also learn of Jesus Christ and be blessed. If they receive Jesus Christ, darkness will fall from their eyes, and after several generations pass they will again become white* and beautiful people.

> *In subsequent versions of *The Book of Mormon* the word "white" has been changed to "pure."

In the last days, the scattered Jews will also begin to believe in Jesus Christ and begin to gather. Like our descendants, those Jews who believe in Jesus Christ will become fair and beautiful people. At this time, God will begin his work among all nations and peoples to restore and reward his people. The people will be fairly judged and divided by God into those who are faithful and righteous, and those who are not. Those who oppress the poor and meek, and those who have failed him, will be destroyed.

After the judgment, the wolf and lamb will live together in peace and leopards will lie down with newborn goats. Lions and calves will lie side by side and baby children will lead them. No harm will come to any of God's children because his knowledge will wash over them as water covers the sea. All things will be made known and no secrets will be withheld. Darkness will come into the light, seals will be broken, and Satan will have no power over the hearts of the people for long time to come.

Chapter 13. 1830 Version

Chapter 31. 1981 Version

God has shown me that Jesus Christ, who will remove the sins of the world, will first be baptized by a prophet. If Jesus Christ in his holiness needs to be baptized by water in the name of God, then surely those of us who are unholy have even greater need of baptism ourselves. By humbling himself before God, Jesus Christ bears witness that he will keep God's commandments, and the Holy Ghost descends upon him in the form of a dove. By performing this act, Jesus Christ shows us the example which we should follow. The voice of God came to me saying, "Repent and be baptized in the name of my Beloved Son." And the voice of the Son, Jesus Christ came to me saying, "He who is baptized in my name will receive the Holy Ghost. Follow me, and do the same things that you've seen me do."

My brothers, I know that if you follow Jesus Christ's example with all the purpose of your heart and repent your sins without deception, taking the name of Jesus Christ in baptism, then you will receive the Holy Spirit of God. But if, after having done this, you should deny God's commandments, then it would be better if you had never known of me. God has told me that those who endure with him to the end will be saved, and those who cannot endure to the end will not be saved. Therefore, it is important that you do as I have been shown. You must pass through the gate of repentance through baptism with water, and then comes a remission of your sins by fire and by the Holy Ghost. Pass through this gate and the straight path before you will lead to eternal life. By keeping God's commandments, and enduring to the end, you will have eternal life. This is the way. There is no other way under heaven whereby you can be saved. This is the doctrine of Jesus Christ and of the Father and

of the Holy Ghost, which is one God without end.

Chapter 14. 1830 Version

Chapter 32. 1981 Version

Now, brothers, what should we do after we've been baptized? By the power of the Holy Ghost, angels will speak the words of Jesus Christ and will tell you what to do. If you don't understand something, you can ask God, and his angels will answer. This is the doctrine of Jesus Christ and no more will be revealed until he comes to you himself, in the flesh.

This is all that I can say. I can only mourn for those who stubbornly will not listen. If you listen to the Holy Spirit, you will know that you must pray. Pray to God about all things in the name of Jesus Christ and God will bless your lives.

Chapter 15. 1830 Version

Chapter 33. 1981 Version

I wish that I were a better writer and could convey the power of God as well in writing as I can in speech. But do not cast aside my writings, because I believe them to be of great value to all people, and especially to my descendants. I pray that my words will be made strong so that those who read them will know about their ancestors, be persuaded to do good, and believe in Jesus Christ till the end of time which is eternal. Because I speak harshly against sin, only the spirit of the devil can be angry at my words.

I speak in kindness to my people, to the Jews whose heritage I've come from, and to the Gentiles who will come to this new land. You will know that these words are true when you stand before God in judgment, and learn that they are his words also. I pray that many of us will be saved by God on the last great day. And so I finish speaking, as the voice of an ancestor whispering to you from the grave, and bid you farewell until the great day of judgment comes. My words will either save you or condemn you. So says God, and I must obey.

THE BOOK OF JACOB — 544 BC TO 500 BC

From Plates Inscribed by Jacob[2], the Brother of Nephi[1] then
Abridged and Later Inscribed onto the Book of Mormon Plates by
Mormon

*Jacob[2] succeeds Nephi as the Nephites' main prophet and preaches to them about the
future coming of Jesus Christ. He recites a parable comparing the family of Israel to an olive
tree, works to restore his people's declining righteousness, and describes the continuing conflict
between the Nephite and Lamanite peoples.*

SUMMARY OF THE BOOK OF JACOB

Nephi's younger brother, Jacob[2], was born while Lehi's family traveled in
the wilderness on their journey from Jerusalem to the Western Hemisphere.
Jacob described how Nephi[1] assigned him the task of keeping a sacred record for
future generations so that there would be an awareness among the Nephites of
the coming of Jesus Christ, hundreds of years in the future, and a record of
Jacob's ministry to Nephite people.

When Nephi died, new political leaders were chosen and Jacob succeeded
Nephi as the primary prophet for the Nephites. After Nephi's death, the
Nephites forgot about God's commandments and lapsed into sins of pride, the
pursuit of wealth, self-importance, and fornication. Jacob was commanded by
God to admonish them for their immorality and sins. He warned them of the
price they would pay if they rejected the words of God, and he encouraged them
to repent their abominable ways while they still could. He reminded them about
the coming of Jesus Christ, the opportunity for eternal life in the kingdom of
God, and the possibility of eternal torment in hell.

Jacob reminded the Nephites of the Parable of the Olive Tree, as written by
the martyred Old World prophet Zenos. In the parable, an old olive tree in a
vineyard struggled to thrive against adversity with the help of a master and his
servants. Branches were grafted onto the tree and also were cut from it to be
planted elsewhere. Later, the cut branches were grafted back onto the original
tree and its life was renewed. Ultimately, Jacob told his people, the restored olive
tree symbolized the family of Israel, with its many branches scattered across the
earth that would be gathered together in the last days.

Jacob recorded an incident involving a stranger named Sherem, who visited
the Nephites and told them false stories to dissuade them from believing in Jesus
Christ. When God struck Sherem down, the Nephites repented and were
restored to God's good will.

The Book of Jacob concludes with the futile attempts of the Nephites to
reconcile their differences with the Lamanites and the passing on of Nephi's
legacy as prophet and scribe to Jacob's son Enos.

THE BOOK OF JACOB - TRANSLATION

Chapter 1. 1830 and 1981 Versions

Fifty-five years after our family left Jerusalem my older brother, Nephi, assigned me the task of inscribing and adding my record to the metal plates that he'd begun. Without dwelling too much on the history of the Nephites, of which he had written, he wanted me to write about what I considered to be most sacred and precious; so, here, I make a record of sermons, revelations, and prophecies to pass on to future generations, for the sake of Jesus Christ and for the sake of our people.

Revelations and prophecies made us aware of the future coming of Jesus Christ, and of future events concerning our people. Because these prophecies are a source of anxiety and concern, we sought to persuade our people to seek Jesus Christ's kingdom and God's good favor to come. The alternative was to be cast out and denied God's blessings, as happened when the family of Israel fell into temptation in the wilderness. We argued that they should not rebel against God or anger him, but that they should believe in Jesus Christ — who would suffer and die on the cross, bearing the sins of the world. I have taken it upon myself to follow Nephi's instructions and write of the these sacred things.

When Nephi grew old and saw his death coming, he assigned a man to carry on his reign as king of the Nephites. Because the people loved Nephi as a protector and defender who had labored tirelessly on their behalf, they chose to honor him by calling their future kings by the name of Nephi also, regardless of what their former names may have been. When Nephi died, the next King Nephi began his reign and the people grew selfish and wicked. They indulged themselves with many wives and mistresses, as David and Solomon had done long ago. They sought gold and silver and puffed themselves up with pride.

Since God had called me and my brother Joseph to be priests and to lead our people, I spoke out to them from the temple. We were responsible for bringing them the word of God, so that their sins would not fall on us when the day of judgment came.

Chapter 2. 1830 and 1981 Versions

"My brothers," I told the Nephites after Nephi's death, "I have come to the temple today to fulfill my responsibility to God and bring you His word, so that later I will not have to answer personally for your sins. As you know, I have been diligent in teaching you the ways of God, but now I am deeply troubled about the welfare of your souls. Until now, you have observed the word of God as I have taught you; but, now you are beginning to stray into sinful ways which are an abomination to me and an abomination to God. It breaks my heart and embarrasses me before God that I must speak to you about the wickedness I see. It saddens me deeply to speak of these sins so directly in front of your wives and children, when so many of them remain pure before God and have come today to hear God's healing words.

"Nonetheless, I am strictly commanded by God to admonish you for your crimes and to aggravate your wounds, not to heal them. And I am regrettably obliged to wound those without crimes with my harsh words, rather than feed them with the pleasing words of God. For God has told me, 'Jacob, go to the temple and give the people my words.'

"Many among you have begun searching for the riches of gold and silver and some of you have found more of these riches than others. The richer ones among you have inflated your importance with expensive clothing and put yourselves above those with less, imagining yourselves to be better than they are. Do you think God justifies you in doing this? No; he condemns you for it, and wants you to know that if you continue, his judgments will be swift. If God wanted to, he could destroy you with a single glance from his eye. I wish that he would do this and rid you of your sins and abominations. I wish you would listen to his commands and give up the pride that is destroying your souls.

"If you share your riches with your brothers and think as much of them as you do of yourselves, you will be on the pathway to the kingdom of God. Christ wants you to have riches if your intent is good, so that you can clothe the naked, feed the hungry, liberate the debtors, and relieve the sick.

"For those of you who are filled with pride, who oppress and despise your neighbors because of your greater possessions, I ask, what do you have to say for yourselves? Don't you suppose that this behavior is abhorrent to the God who has created you, who asks you to keep his commandments, and sees all of his people as equally precious?

"Now, I am finished speaking about your pride because there is an even grosser crime that needs to be addressed. God has told me, 'Your people are falling into sin because they misunderstand the scriptures. They make excuses for their promiscuity because they read of David and Solomon's many wives and mistresses. Even while these things were written, they were abominable before me. I have led your people out of Jerusalem by the power of my hand, to raise up a mighty branch of the family of Joseph, and will not tolerate this behavior.'

"So, my brothers, listen to me and hear the word of God. You may not have but one wife, and further, you must have no mistresses at all. God has said, 'I am pleased when women are chaste, because sexual fornication is an abomination to me. I hereby order your people to keep my commandments or I will curse the land for their sins. Unless I command otherwise, they must obey this law. I have seen and heard the suffering of my daughters, both in Jerusalem and in this new land, because of their husbands' promiscuity; and I will have none of it. If men seduce my daughters into sin because of their innocence, I will curse them into destruction. Men will no longer be allowed to be sexually promiscuous as David and Solomon were.'

"My brothers, all of us know that these commandments were given to Lehi and that God condemns you now for doing what you already know is wrongful. Your fornication is a greater sin than the sins of the Lamanites, for you have broken the hearts of your loving wives and lost the confidence of your children, through your bad examples before them. The sorrow in the hearts of your wives has been heard by God, and God's strict judgment has come down upon you."

Chapter 3. 1981 Version

"Now, I want to speak to those of you whose hearts are pure. If you look steadily to God and pray with faith, he will console you in your trials and send justice to those who torment you. Because of your purity, you may feast on his love forever.

"Those among you who are filthy before God will find that the land is cursed because of you, and a time will quickly come when you will be destroyed by the Lamanites. When that time comes, only the righteous among you will be saved by God. While the Lamanites, whom you hate, are cursed and their skins have been turned to the color of filth, they have not forgotten the commandment to keep but one wife and to have no mistresses. In this regard, you are filthier than they are. Because of this observance, God shows them mercy and they will one day become a blessed people. If you look at them, you will see that their husbands and wives love each other, and that they also love their children. Their hatred for you arises from their fathers' mistakes, not their own. How can you think that you are much better than them in the eyes of God? Oh, brothers, I am afraid that unless you repent your sins and fornications, that their skins will be whiter than yours when you approach the kingdom of God.

"I command you to abandon your hatred of the Lamanites because of their skin color and filthiness, and remember that their filthiness is inherited from their fathers. Look to yourselves, now, and ask whether you also want to have your children cursed for your sins and the sorry example you set for them, just as the Lamanites are cursed for their fathers' sins? Do you want your children destroyed for your filthiness and the responsibility for their destruction laid on your heads on the day of judgment? Oh, brothers, awaken yourselves from the sleep of death and listen to my words. Release yourselves from the embrace of the devil so that you are not cast down into the eternal death of hell."

Chapter 3. 1830 Version

Chapter 4. 1981 Version

Because of the great difficulty of engraving my words on these metal plates, I cannot write but a small portion of what I'd like to say to future generations. I also recognize that any easier form of writing would not endure the test of time; so I pass along what I can and hope that these words from the past will be received with thanks and joy for the knowledge they impart, and not with contempt or sorrow for the ancestors whose story they tell.

I have made this record so that future generations will know that we recognized Jesus Christ and his glorious mission hundreds of years before his coming. Great prophets before us also knew of Christ's coming and worshipped God in his name. We honor the law of Moses because it directs our souls to Jesus Christ. We honor Abraham and his obedience to God's commands in surrendering his son Isaac for sacrifice, as a symbol of God and his only Son, Jesus Christ. Likewise, we study the prophets' writings in search of revelations and witnesses for hope, so that our faith may remain unshakable. Through the strength of our faith we can command the trees, the mountains, and the waves of the sea to obey us in the name of Jesus Christ.

God also shows us our weakness, so that we will know that only by his grace do we have these powers. For this reason it is imperative that we listen to his revelations. The ways of God and the depths of his mysteries are impossible for men to fully know, but the power of his word created the earth and all men upon it. So, brothers, seek not to advise God, but rather to receive advice from him because his counsel is filled with wisdom, justice, and mercy in all his works.

By reconciling ourselves to the atonement of Christ, we can be resurrected through his power, and be among the first to receive God's blessings, even before Christ physically comes to earth in the flesh. Rather than marvel at my words, take it upon yourselves to know of our potential for resurrection and of the world to come.

When the Spirit speaks through God's prophets, men need to understand that this is the truth, and not a lie. These prophecies speak of how things really are, of how they will be, and of the salvation of our souls. These prophecies do not stand alone, but rather stand in the company of prophets from the past also. Because the Jews were stubborn people, they rejected these words, killed the prophets, and looked for things they didn't understand. Because of their blindness, God has removed his clear messages to them, and they will fall.

Because I am led by the Spirit into prophecy, I see that the Jews will reject the only stone upon which they might ever build a safe foundation for themselves. Even so, the Spirit shows me how it will become possible for them to build a foundation upon this rejected cornerstone. Let me unfold this mystery for you.

Chapter 5. 1981 Version

Do you remember the words of the prophet Zenos* to the family of Israel?

> *Zenos is a martyred Old World Hebrew prophet for whom any historical references outside The Book of Mormon are lost. Jacob's knowledge of Zenos comes through Laban's brass plates, brought from Jerusalem to America with the Lehites in 600 BC. Zenos' martyrdom is referred to later in The Book of Mormon text, in the *Book of Helaman*, and tells of his murder for boldly testifying about the coming of Jesus Christ.

The family of Israel, says Zenos, is like a cultivated olive tree in a man's vineyard.

When the olive tree grew old and began to decay, the devoted vineyard master attempted to preserve its life. He pruned, cultivated, and fertilized the ground around it. Many days later, the tree began to sprout a few tender new branches, while the top of the tree began to die.

When the master saw this, he directed his servant to go gather fresh branches from a wild olive tree, to graft on and replace the dying branches. The dying branches were then removed and burned so that they would not clutter the grounds of the vineyard. In addition, the master collected some healthy new shoots from the favored tree and planted them himself, in hidden places around the vineyard, in order to preserve the fruit in case the favored tree's roots should die. Having done this, they continued to prune, cultivate and fertilize the favored tree in hopes of preserving its life.

After a long while, the master and servant came again and surveyed the vineyard to see the results of their efforts. The wild olive branches that had been grafted onto the favored tree had thrived and now began to bear fruit that resembled the tree's former fruit. The master told his servant that if they hadn't grafted on the wild branches, the favored tree would have surely died, but now would yield good olives. There would be an abundance for them to gather, preserve, and enjoy.

When they went into the far reaches of the vineyard to observe the branches from the favored tree that had been planted, they saw that the first of these branches thrived and also brought forth abundant fruit. The servant asked why the master had chosen this particular location, as it was one of the poorest places in the vineyard. The master replied that he knew it was a poor spot, but told the servant to look for himself, and notice that because of the master's efforts the branch had taken hold and given good olives to be gathered.

The next branch had been planted in an even worse spot, but it too thrived and bore good olives because of the master's efforts. Gather up these olives also, the master directed.

The last branch had been planted in good ground and had been equally cared for, but only a part of the tree brought forth good olives, while the rest of it gave wild fruit that was of no value. The master then directed the servant to remove the branches from this tree that yielded the wild fruit and burn them. But the servant suggested that they should prune, cultivate, and fertilize the tree instead, and see if giving it more time would bring better fruit. Accordingly, all the trees were then equally nurtured.

After another long stretch of time, the servant and master again visited the vineyard to survey the trees and gather up the olives for storage. The favored tree, onto which the wild branches had been grafted, now bore fruit in abundance, but none of the olives were any good. The master asked the servant what he thought should be done to get harvests of good olives. The servant observed that even though the olives were bad, the grafting had preserved the roots of the tree from dying. The master replied that the living roots did him no good if the tree brought forth bad fruit. Even though the roots were good now, the tree had brought forth so many wild branches and so much bad fruit that it was again beginning to die. Unless

something was done to save the tree, it would end up in the fire.

They went out into the far reaches of the vineyard to visit the branches from the favored tree that had been planted. They found that all of them now bore bad olives, also. They found that the bad branches from the last tree had overpowered the good branch and caused it to die. In anguish, the master cried aloud, asking what more could he have done? All of his olives were now bad and the olive trees in his vineyard were good for nothing except burning.

The master now lamented the fact that he had not cut off the bad branches from the last tree which had been planted in good ground, as they had overwhelmed and destroyed the good branches. "How has my good vineyard become so corrupted that it now needs to be destroyed and burned?" cried the master.

Again, the servant intervened, and pointed out that the wild branches were overwhelming the good roots, and taking their strength for bad purposes. When the servant asked the master to wait a little longer before destroying the olive trees, the master conceded. He directed the servant to remove the best branches from the planted trees and graft them back on to the favored tree to replace the worst of the favored tree's branches, for its roots were still strong. Perhaps this would restore good olives to the vineyard and they might yet overcome the bad ones.

So the master and all of his servants went again and labored in the vineyard, knowing that this was the last time that an attempt would be made to restore the favored olive tree. When the branches were grafted, the last ones to be removed were the first to be replaced, and the first ones removed were the last to be replaced. All the trees were again pruned, cultivated, and fertilized for the last time. As the newly grafted branches began to grow, those that brought forth bad olives were cleared away at once so that they could not overpower the good roots. Room was made for the good branches to thrive as the bad branches were cleared away and burned.

The branches that had been removed from the favored tree were brought back and grafted together again. The favored tree began to thrive as the bad branches were destroyed. Through diligent effort, the good branches and the good roots were kept in balance so that the bad branches no longer overwhelmed the favored tree's vitality. In the end, the branches of the favored tree were restored and all the branches yielded good olives again.

Seeing the success of their final effort, the master called all the servants into the vineyard and said to them, "Look, the vineyard has been restored according to my will and the olives are as good now as they were in the beginning. I bless you for your diligence in carrying out my instructions, and share with you my joy at our success. For the last time I have pruned, cultivated, and fertilized the vineyard. When the time comes that bad olives again present themselves, both will be gathered, but the good olives will be preserved, while the bad ones will be cast into the fire and destroyed at the end of the season."

Chapter 4. 1830 Version

Chapter 6. 1981 Version

Now, my brothers, Jacob continued, I have told you this story from the prophet Zenos because the favored olive tree in the vineyard is truly the family of Israel, and my prophecy to you is that this parable of Zenos will surely come to pass. In the latter days, God will again extend his hand to recover his people. Through the help of his servants, he will nourish and prune his vineyard. And after that, the day of final judgment will come. Those who have labored diligently in his vineyard will be blessed and saved, while those who refuse his call will be cursed and burned in the fire.

In his mercy, God remembers the roots and the branches that are the family of Israel, and extends his hands outward to reach for them. While the stubborn and difficult people turn away, those who don't close their hearts will gain entry into the kingdom of God. Brothers, I beg of you to repent and come cleanly to God's embrace. After having been nourished by God's hand for so long, how can you possibly wish to become bad fruit to be cut down and thrown into the fire? Will you reject this warning? Will you reject all the prophets who have foreseen the coming of Jesus Christ, and mock the salvation that has been prepared for you? If you reject God's plan, you need to know that you will stand in front of God in shame and guilt

before being sent away to the lake of fire and sulfur, the place of eternal smoke and endless torment. Be wise and choose the straight and narrow path to eternal life. What more can I say?

Chapter 5. 1830 Version

Chapter 7. 1981 Version

A few years later, a man named Sherem came among the Nephites and preached that Jesus Christ wasn't coming at all. Using flattery as a tool, he worked to undermine Jesus Christ's doctrine, and succeeded in convincing many people that the prophecies were false. Knowing that I was the most faithful to the prophecy of Christ's coming, he sought out an audience with me, also. He spoke with the skill and artistry of the devil to try and shake my belief and have me deny the revelations and visions of angels I'd seen. But I couldn't be budged, because I'd heard the voice of God speaking to me.

"Brother Jacob," Sherem said to me, "while you go around talking about this so-called doctrine of Jesus Christ, you are leading your people away from God and the law of Moses. You ask that they worship this being who is supposed to show up some hundreds of years from now. That's blasphemy. No one can know these things or predict the future."

With the help of God, I contested his words, and asked if he denied that Christ was coming.

"I know there is no Christ, and there never will be," Sherem responded.

"Do you believe in the scriptures?" I asked.

"Yes, I do," he said.

"Then you must not understand them," I replied, "because they testify about Christ and prophesy his coming. I have seen him myself, and I know that without his atonement all of mankind will be lost."

"Show me some sign of this Holy Ghost whom you claim to know," he demanded, insolently.

"Who am I," I responded, "to command signs from God on your orders? You know that what I say is true, but deny it because you are of the devil. Nonetheless, if God chooses to strike you, let that be your sign that Christ is coming. But let that be God's will, not mine." After I'd spoken these words, Sherem fell to the ground, too weakened to get up.

Many days later Sherem, declared that he was about to die and asked for the people to gather so that he could speak to them. On the following day, he confessed to everyone who came that he had spoken falsely. He affirmed the truth of Jesus Christ, the angels, and the power of the Holy Ghost, telling of how he'd been deceived by the power of the devil. Now that he was dying, he was afraid, because he knew the truth of hell and the reality of eternal punishment. "I fear that I have committed the unpardonable sin of lying about God, of denying Christ, and of denying that the scriptures foretell his coming. But, now, I confess before God."

Having said this, Sherem died and the people all fell on the ground, overcome and astonished by the power of God. Because my prayers had been answered by God, I was pleased when peace and love were again restored to my people. The Nephites soon forgot the words of this wicked man, and they returned to the scriptures of God.

Fresh attempts were made to regather and restore the Lamanites to the knowledge of truth but it was useless because their minds were set on wars, bloodshed, and their eternal hatred of us. Try as we might to help them, they continued in their efforts to destroy us by force of arms; so, we Nephites did our best to fortify ourselves against their onslaughts, and trusted in God to help us defeat their attacks.

As I grow old and approach my death, I conclude my record on these plates by saying that I've done my best to pass along the knowledge of God. Our lives have passed by like dreams in this lonesome new land where we wander as solemn outcasts from distant Jerusalem. We've been born in the wilderness into trial and tribulations, hated by our warring and contentious brothers, mourning for a peace that we've never known.

Before going to the grave, I have spoken with my son, Enos, and given him these plates. I've told him what my brother, Nephi, instructed me to do. He has promised to continue these records and also to pass them along as I have done. And so, I make an end to my writing and bid you farewell hoping that many of my brothers will come to read these words.

THE BOOK OF ENOS — 499 BC TO 421 BC

From Plates Inscribed by Enos, the Son of Jacob[1] then Abridged
and Later Inscribed onto the Book of Mormon Plates by Mormon

Enos' faith in Jesus Christ is affirmed by God. The Nephites become increasingly successful farmers while the Lamanites become increasingly bloodthirsty and savage. The ongoing wars with the Lamanites intensify.

SUMMARY OF THE BOOK OF ENOS

When Jacob[1] died, the legacy of the records was passed on to his son Enos, the grandson of Lehi[1]. Enos was among the first generation of Nephites to be born in America. He told of his personal revelations from God about the coming of Jesus Christ and the preservation of the Nephite record, which would later become The Book of Mormon.

By the time of Enos, the Nephites had become proficient at farming, growing abundant grains and fruit, and raising up herds of cattle, goats, and horses.

Futile attempts were made to restore the fierce and savage Lamanites to the one true faith in God, while the ceaseless wars between the Lamanites and Nephites continued. Enos describes how the Nephites continued to develop their agricultural-based civilization, and his struggles against his people's inherently stubborn nature.

At the end of his life, Enos passed the tradition of the engraved plates on to his son, Jarom.

THE BOOK OF ENOS - TRANSLATION

My father Jacob was a good man, who taught me to read and write and to honor the name of God. I struggled to receive God's blessing and be forgiven for my sins. One day, while out hunting in the forest, I considered deeply my father's words about eternal life and the joy of saints. I kneeled down before God and cried out to him in prayer for my soul. I prayed all day long, and when night came I raised my voice to reach the heavens.

A voice came to me saying, "Enos, your sins are forgiven and you are blessed." Because I knew that God couldn't lie, my sense of guilt vanished.

"Dear God, how does this happen?" I asked.

"Because you have faith in Jesus Christ, whom you've neither seen or heard," God replied. "Go in peace, Enos, because your faith has made you whole."

Having heard God's words, a desire stirred in me to help my Nephite brothers. I prayed more to God, on their behalf. Again, the voice of God came to me, saying, "To the degree that your brothers keep my commandments, I will visit them also. I've given them this holy land, but I stand ready to curse it if they fall into wickedness. I will come to your brothers; but when I do, I will bring sorrow upon them for their gross violations."

After hearing these words, my faith was strengthened and I prayed further for the benefit of my brothers. Again, God's voice came to me. "Because of your faith, I will grant your desires," he said. My main desire had been the preservation of the Nephite records in the event that our people were destroyed by the Lamanites. Restoring them to the true faith was impossible at this time, as they had sworn to destroy us and our records. If the Lamanites

destroyed us but this record survived, it could be revealed in the future and prove to be the salvation of the Lamanites' descendants.

I cried out in thanks and relief, knowing that God was willing and able to preserve our records regardless of what became of us. He had told me, "Whatever you ask in faith, in the name of Jesus Christ, you will receive." So I knew that our records would not perish, but would come forth to the Lamanites in God's own time because God had promised this to me as he had to my fathers before me.

After I went among the Nephites and testified about these prophecies, our people went out among the Lamanites again. They tried tirelessly to restore them to the one true faith in God; but it was to no avail, because their hatred of us was so strong and they were led by their evil nature. They had become wild, ferocious, and bloodthirsty people who were filled with idolatry and filth. Skillfully using bows and arrows, axes, and swords, the Lamanites fed themselves by killing wild beasts and often eating them raw. They lived in tents instead of building homes, and wandered the wilderness in loin skins instead of wearing clothing. These wild brothers of ours continually sought to destroy us. During my years, we saw many wars between the Nephites and Lamanites.

The Nephites, on the other hand, farmed the land, raising grains and fruit. We raised up herds of cattle, goats, and horses. Even though there were many prophets among us, the Nephite people remained stubborn and difficult for me to understand. Without our harsh preaching, prophecies of wars and destruction, eternal damnation, and God's judgments to keep them in line and in fear of

God, they would have quickly destroyed themselves.

But I am old now. A hundred and seventy nine years have passed since my grandfather left Jerusalem, and I will soon die. It has been my honor and privilege to be a prophet of God and a preacher to my people, the Nephites. All my days I have rejoiced in the truth of Jesus Christ above all else in the world. When I pass, I go to rest with Jesus Christ, my Redeemer. I rejoice in the certainty that one day my mortal body will become immortal, when I stand before him. He will look on my face with pleasure and say, "Come, be with me and be blessed; I have prepared a place for you in my Father's mansions." [420 BC]

THE BOOK OF JAROM – 419 BC TO 361 BC
from Plates Inscribed by Jarom, Son of Enos then Abridged and Later Inscribed onto *The Book of Mormon* Plates by Mormon

The Nephites dramatically increase in population, build great fortified cities to protect themselves from the warring Lamanites, and become skilled metal workers. Many Nephites receive revelations of Jesus Christ's coming.

SUMMARY OF THE BOOK OF JAROM

Jarom was the son of Enos, grandson of Jacob[1], and great-grandson of Lehi[1]. He was among the second generation of Nephites to be born in America. Two hundred thirty-eight years after the Lehites left Jerusalem, Jarom wrote of their exponential increase in numbers and prosperity. The Nephites built great fortified cities to resist the endless Lamanite attacks, and developed highly refined metalworking technologies in steel, iron, gold, silver, brass and copper.

Jarom testified that he and many others had also received revelations regarding the future coming of Jesus Christ. The Nephites during Jarom's time had maintained the commandments of God, and so God had protected them from destruction at the hands of the Lamanites, as had been promised.

At the end of his life, Jarom passed on the keeping and recording of the metal plates to his son, Omni.

THE BOOK OF JAROM - TRANSLATION

I accept the legacy that my father Enos has passed on to me and hereby maintain the sacred records for the benefit of the Lamanites' future descendants. I don't have a lot to say and will not write of the prophecies or revelations that I've received because they are the same revelations that my forefathers have already written of, concerning the plan for our salvation.

For the most part, the Nephites have become as hard in their hearts, as stubborn, as deaf to the truth, and as blind in their minds as ever. That they have not been thrown off the land by God is a testimony to his mercy. But there are also many among us who have given up their stubbornness and demonstrated their faith in God. These people find themselves in communion with the Holy Spirit and have many revelations of their own.

The Nephites have grown strong after being in this land for 200 years. They have observed the law of Moses and kept the

Sabbath sacred unto God. Because our laws are strict, there is no profanity or blasphemy among us. [399 BC]

As both the Lamanite and the Nephite populations have grown greatly, we have spread ourselves broadly across the new land. Even as our Nephite numbers grow, the number of murderous Lamanites increases faster. In frequent battles with the Lamanites, our defenses have so far held because of the fortifications we have built around our cities, and because our kings and leaders have maintained their faith in God.

As our numbers have grown we have become rich in silver and gold, and developed the capacity for fine workmanship in wood, iron, copper, brass, and steel. We have constructed great buildings and created

machinery for making all kinds of tools to farm with, as well as making weapons of war. And so we have been well prepared to repel the Lamanite attacks.

Because our prophets have been vigilant in their warnings the Nephites have kept God's commandments to their forefathers and, as promised to us, we have prospered on the land. We are also very aware that if we stray from God's commandments the Lamanites will destroy us. So our prophets and priests have kept us intensely focused on the coming Messiah, as if he were already here.

Since our people left Jerusalem, 238 years have now passed. It is now time for me to pass on the legacy of the plates to my son Omni, so that this record may be continued as our forefathers have instructed us to do. [361 BC]

THE BOOK OF OMNI — 359 BC TO 130 BC

from Plates Inscribed by Omni, Amaron, Chemish, Abindom, and Amaleki then Abridged and Later Inscribed onto the Book of Mormon Plates by Mormon

The Nephites discover the Mulekite people, another group of emigrants who had escaped the destruction of Jerusalem. The Nephites also learn of the presence of the Jaredite people in the Western hemisphere long ago.

SUMMARY OF THE BOOK OF OMNI

Omni was the son of Jarom, grandson of Enos, and great-grandson of Jacob[1]. Omni declared that he had practically nothing to add to the story before passing the records on to a succession of other heirs, who also declared that they had nothing significant to say. Four generations later, the records ended up in the hands of Amaleki.

Amaleki related the story of King Mosiah[1] and his time, when God warned the Nephites to leave the land of Nephi and escape the Lamanites, or be destroyed. They journeyed through the wilderness to a land called Zarahemla, where they encountered another group of people known as the Mulekites, who were also refugees from Jerusalem. Under the leadership of Mulek, this group had been contemporaries of Lehi's and had traveled separately to the Western hemisphere hundreds of years earlier, under God's guidance. Although the Mulekites were more numerous than the Nephites, they lacked a written record of their history and thus welcomed the Nephites. Both groups united under King Mosiah's rule.

The Mulekites brought King Mosiah a large stone engraved with an unknown language, and with the gift and power of God, he translated it. It told of the story of a previous people, the Jaredites, who had also journeyed across the ocean to America during the time when the Tower of Babel was being constructed. The stone described a man named Coriantumr and the destruction of his people. The Mulekites knew of Coriantumr, because their ancestors had met and sheltered him until he died.

When King Mosiah died, he was succeeded by his son King Benjamin. Amaleki affirmed the truth of Jesus Christ and the power of revelation; then he passed the records on to King Benjamin, before he died.

TRANSLATION OF THE BOOK OF OMNI

My father Jarom instructed to me to preserve and add my record to these sacred plates. Most of my life has been spent wielding a sword against the Lamanites in protection of my people, the Nephites. I want you to know that I am not the righteous man that I am supposed to be, as I have not kept the laws and commandments of God. I have seen seasons of peace and seasons of war. Two-hundred-eighty-two years have now passed since my forefather Lehi gathered up our family and left Jerusalem behind. And now I pass the plates and the continuity of our records onto my son, Amaron. That's all I have to say. [317 BC]

I, Amaron, now add my words to this record. I'm afraid I don't have much to say, either. After 323, years most of the wicked Nephites have been killed off by the Lamanites. This fulfills the covenants given to our fathers, that the people who follow God's laws would be preserved, while those who don't would be destroyed. Having written this, I pass the plates on to my brother Chemish. [279 BC]

(Chemish adds nothing to the record, and passes the plates on to his son, Abindom. Likewise, Abindom passes the keeping of the records on to his son, Amaleki, adding only his affirmation to the prophecies and revelations that have already been written before him.)

I, Amaleki, will now write about King Mosiah, who governed over the land of Zarahemla during my time. God had warned King Mosiah to flee from the land of Nephi into the wilderness, along with all the people who would listen to his warning. As they left, the people were led by prophecies and revelations that admonished them to follow the word of God. Through God's power, we were led through the wilderness and into the land of Zarahemla.

When our people arrived, we discovered it was occupied with people led by a man named Zarahemla. He rejoiced at receiving us and the brass plates that our forefathers had brought with us from Jerusalem. As it turned out, the forefathers of Zarahemla had also come out of Jerusalem at the time that King Zedekiah of Judah was captured and carried away to Babylon in bondage.* Like us, they were descendants of Jews who had left the Old World under the guidance of God. They had traveled across the ocean and arrived here around the same time that our ancestors, the Lehites, had.

*Subsequent *Book of Mormon* references to the people of Zarahemla identify them as originally having been led by Mulek, one of King Zedekiah's sons. Consequently, these people are referred to as the Mulekites.

The Mulekites had lived in this same area since their arrival in this new land. When we met them they had been through many wars, but were still very populous. They had brought no records with them, carried no knowledge of

God as creator, and their language had been corrupted as well, so that it was impossible for us to understand them. Mosiah therefore decreed that they should be taught our language. Afterwards, Zarahemla was able to give us an oral genealogy of his ancestors, to the best of his memory. The Mulekites then united with us and acknowledged Mosiah as their king.

A large stone with engraved writing, found by the Mulekites, was brought to King Mosiah for interpretation. By the gift and power of God, King Mosiah translated the writing on the stone. It told the story of a man named Coriantumr and the destruction of his people. The stone also told about Coriantumr's forefathers, who had lived in Babylon at the time of the construction of the great tower. God had confused the languages of the people working on the tower in order to halt its erection, and scattered the people far and wide. Many of Coriantumr's people had been severely judged by God, the stone said, and their bones could be found lying around on the ground in the north. It also turned out that this man Coriantumr had been discovered by earlier Mulekites, and had lived with them for a period of nine months before he died.

I want to tell you about a group of stubborn Nephites who returned through the wilderness to our original land of Nephi. They hoped to reclaim possession of that land. Because their leader was a contentious man, they fought amongst themselves until there were just fifty of them left alive. When they returned to Zarahemla, they recruited new members for their campaign, including a brother of mine. After they departed, we never heard from them again.

I, Amaleki, was born in the days of King Mosiah, and have lived to see his death. King Mosiah was succeeded by his son, King Benjamin. During King Benjamin's reign the Lamanites followed us into the land of Zarahemla, and brought more warfare and bloodshed upon us. But we were successful at driving them away. Now, I am old and have no children to pass these records along to, so I give them over to King Benjamin instead, because I know that he is a man of God and will keep them safe. In closing, I want to say that all men should come to God and the Holy One of Israel. I believe in prophesying, revelations, the help of angels, the gift of speaking in tongues, and the gift of translating alien languages. All good things come from God, and all that is evil is the product of the devil. If you come to Jesus Christ, the Holy One of Israel, and offer your souls in fasting and prayer, and endure to the end, you will be redeemed in his salvation. The plates are full, my writing is done, and now I can prepare to die.

THE WORDS OF MORMON — AD 385
Inscribed and Added to the Book of Mormon Plates by Mormon

Mormon explains his abridgement of the Nephite records and adds some missing parts from the story of King Benjamin.

SUMMARY OF THE WORDS OF MORMON

Writing in AD 385, Mormon described the near destruction of his people that he'd witnessed, and predicted their complete and imminent destruction at the hands of the Lamanites. He acknowledged that he had put his soul into completing the records that were destined for the Lamanites' descendants in the future. Mormon described how he had merged and abridged the records from Nephi through King Benjamin. Two sets of plates were handed down to him across many hundreds of years, during which time the prophesied arrival of Jesus Christ had come and gone.

Mormon also completed the story of King Benjamin's reign that was left untold, following Amaleki's death in the Book of Omni.

TRANSLATION OF THE WORDS OF MORMON

I, Mormon, have watched the destruction of almost all my Nephite people and I am preparing to deliver this record to my son, Moroni. I think that he will see the complete destruction of our people. But, hopefully, he will survive long enough to complete this record concerning Jesus Christ for the benefit of the Lamanites' descendants.

Hundreds of years have now passed since the coming of Jesus Christ and I want to talk about what I've written. I have found two sets of plates from which I've made abridgements — a set of small plates and a set of large plates. After completing the abridgement from the plates of Nephi, through the reign of King Benjamin, I found the small plates on which Jacob, Amaleki and other prophets including Nephi had briefly written. In particular, I've been pleased to read these small plates from Jacob through Benjamin, because they include many prophecies and revelations from our forefathers about the coming of Jesus Christ. The messages on these plates will be of great value to future Lamanites because they contain prophecies which have long since been fulfilled and other prophecies which will surely also be fulfilled.

After Amaleki gave the small plates to King Benjamin, they were combined with the other large plates which contained the records passed from king to king until the time of King Benjamin. All these plates were then passed down, from generation to generation, until they reached me. I pray that they will continue to be preserved from this day forward for there are many things written on them about the judgment of people, by God, in the last days.

The rest of my record is taken from the large plates, but will only be a brief account. My abridgement is perhaps a hundredth of what was originally written. I know that this is the wise and right thing to do, because the Spirit of God whispers to me, telling me what to do. I pray that someday the descendants of the Lamanites will come to the knowledge of God, and through the redemption of Jesus Christ will again become fair and righteous people. Now, I proceed to finish my record according to the knowledge and understanding that God has given to me.

During the time of King Benjamin, the people fought intensely among themselves, and the Lamanite armies came into Zarahemla to destroy them. But Benjamin gathered his armies and personally wielded the sword of Laban from Jerusalem. With the help of God, they fought mightily against the Lamanites, killing thousands of them and driving them out of the land.

False prophets pretending to be Jesus Christ came forward, creating dissension and defections to the Lamanites; but their mouths were sealed shut and they were punished for their crimes, because King Benjamin and his prophets were able discern their lies. King Benjamin was a holy king and reigned in righteousness over his people. With the help of many holy men who sharply spoke the word of God, with power and authority, he was able to keep the stubborn people in line and once again established peace in the land.

THE BOOK OF MOSIAH — 200 BC TO 91 BC

From Plates Inscribed by Zeniff, Limhi, Alma[1], Benjamin, and Mosiah[2] then Abridged and Later Inscribed onto the Book of Mormon Plates by Mormon

All of King Benjamin's Nephite subjects assemble, accept Jesus Christ as their savior in a mass conversion, and adopt the name "Children of Christ." The Nephites discover and translate the written record of the destroyed Jaredite civilization. Alma[1] repents and reforms himself, founds the Church of Christ, and leads his people out of slavery to the Lamanites. King Mosiah[2] institutes a political system ruled by democratically elected judges. Alma[2] experiences a miraculous conversion to Christ and becomes the first democratically elected leader of the Nephite people.

THE BOOK OF MOSIAH SUMMARY

Mosiah[2], after whom this book was named, was the son and heir of King Benjamin and the grandson of Mosiah[1] mentioned in the Book of Omni. The Book of Mosiah tracks the intricate and interrelated choreography between five different groups of Nephite peoples. It also connects the record of the Jaredite people from the Book of Ether with the Nephites' history. The Book of Mosiah is abridged and written by Mormon from the writings of five different authors. Parts of the Book of Mosiah overlap with the part of the Book of Omni that was written by the prophet Amaleki.

The first group of Nephite people chronicled in this book are the ones living in the land of Zarahemla. The Book of Mosiah begins with an account of King Benjamin's final sermon to his people regarding the future coming of Jesus Christ, as told to him in a vision by an angel of God. The angel tells King Benjamin of the importance of believing in Jesus Christ, of repentance for sin, and of following the laws of God in order to be redeemed and live eternally in heaven. The angel tells Benjamin that whoever believes in Jesus Christ will receive remission for their sins, the same as if Jesus Christ had already come. Following this sermon, all of King Benjamin's subjects accept Jesus Christ as their savior and accept a new name for themselves, the Children of Christ. King Benjamin passes the crown and the keeping of the sacred records on to his son, Mosiah. King Benjamin dies several years later, about 125 years before the birth of Jesus Christ.

At the time of King Benjamin's death, King Mosiah became curious about a legendary party of lost Nephites who had traveled back to the land of Nephi long before Mosiah's birth. (The land of Nephi was the land from which their Nephite ancestors had come before they were driven into the land of Zarahemla by hostile Lamanites.) This party, mentioned by Amaleki in the Book of Omni, had left Zarahemla about 120 years earlier under the leadership of a man named Zeniff. King Mosiah directed a man named Ammon[1] to go search the land of Nephi and determine the fate of Zeniff's group. Ammon's party is the second group of Nephites described in the Book of Mosiah.

One of King Noah's priests, Alma[1], knew that Abinadi was telling the truth, and led a group of people into the wilderness to establish a new church based on the laws of God. This fourth group of Nephites named themselves the Church of Christ.

Ammon finds Zeniff's descendants enslaved by the Lamanites in the land of Nephi and full of stories to tell. These people, under the leadership of Zeniff's grandson, King Limhi, are the third group of Nephite people recorded in the Book of Mosiah. In their records, Zeniff described how his group established themselves in the land of Nephi and of their difficult relationship with the Lamanites. Zeniff was succeeded by his son, Noah, who turned his back on God and led the kingdom into corruption. A prophet of God named Abinadi arose in Noah's time and prophesied that unless the king and his people repented their sins, and restored their relations with God, they would all be destroyed. When King Noah heard this, he and his corrupt priests had Abinadi burned to death.

One of King Noah's priests, Alma[1], knew that Abinadi was telling the truth, and led a group of people into the wilderness to establish a new church based on the laws of God. This fourth group of Nephites named themselves the Church of Christ.

Soon after Abinadi's death, a destroying Lamanite army attacked Noah's kingdom. In their retreat from the Lamanites, the people of King Noah separated into two groups. One group was comprised of King Noah, his priests, and men who were only interested in their own survival. The other group was comprised of women and children who weren't strong enough to make the escape, and of those men who preferred to die with their families than survive at any cost. When the Lamanite army overtook this second faction of Nephite refugees, they agreed to spare those who would become willing slaves.

After escaping from the Lamanites, the first faction divided again — between the men who regretted having left their families behind, and King Noah and his priests. When King Noah attempted to interfere with the men's decision to return and avenge their families, the men turned on King Noah and burned him to death. His renegade priests fled, before the same fate befell them, and became the fifth group of Nephite people in the story.

King Noah's son Limhi became the nominal king of the enslaved Nephite people. King Limhi recognized that their destruction and enslavement were the result of the kingdom's corruption, so he repented and asked God to deliver his people from slavery. God, of course, was still angry with these people and was slow to answer their prayers. Meanwhile, King Limhi authorized an expedition to attempt finding the way back to Zarahemla, so they could escape their enslavement. Instead of finding Zarahemla, the expedition discovered the ruins of the Jaredite civilization, which they presumed to have been the ruins of Zarahemla. At these ruins, they found the golden plates on which Ether had earlier written the history of the Jaredite people. However, the inscriptions were in a language the Nephites could not read. The expedition returned to King Limhi and reported that Zarahemla had been destroyed.

Shortly after that, Ammon and his group arrived. The King and his people then learned that the people of Zarahemla were actually alive and well, and that the ruins that had been found were not those of Zarahemla. Ammon and King Limhi then organized an escape and returned safely to the land of Zarahemla. In their exodus, they were pursued unsuccessfully by an army of Lamanites, who got lost.

The lost army of Lamanites found and absorbed the renegade priests, and then found and enslaved Alma and his Church of Christ people. The renegade priests became cruel jailers and the overseers of Alma's people on behalf of the Lamanites. In answer to their prayers, God delivered Alma's people from the Lamanite slavery and guided them to Zarahemla.

King Mosiah welcomed first Limhi's and then Alma's people to his kingdom. Alma's Church of Christ took hold and became firmly established in the kingdom.

Through the gift of God, King Mosiah translated Ether's golden plates with the aid of magical translation devices in his possession. Through the golden plates, he learned of the Jaredites' history, and told his people about it.

King Mosiah's four sons and Alma's son, Alma^2, experience a miraculous conversion from their sinful and destructive ways. Afterwards, Mosiah's sons ask for and receive permission from their father to return to the land of Nephi in hopes of converting the Lamanites to the Church of Christ. This leaves the kingdom without royal heirs; so King Mosiah institutes a new form of democratic government, ruled by elected judges. Alma's son, Alma^2, becomes the first chief judge and also the keeper of the sacred records.

THE BOOK OF MOSIAH - TRANSLATION

Chapter 1, 1830 and 1981 Versions

Peace prevailed during the reign of King Benjamin. He bore three sons, named Mosiah, Helorum, and Helaman^1, who were educated in reading, writing, and the history of their ancestors. They were taught about the prophecies, God's covenants with their ancestors, and the plates brought from Jerusalem by Nephi.

"My sons," Benjamin said to them, "I want you to remember that if it were not for these plates that record God's commandments, we would suffer in ignorance and not know the mysteries of God. Without the plates, Lehi could not have remembered all of this to teach to his children, nor could they have passed it on to their children. Without the plates, our belief would have failed us and we would be as the Lamanites are, lost, without knowing the way.

I want you to know that these plates are truthful records from our distant history before Lehi left Jerusalem, and the history of our ancestors since we arrived in this new land. Read them diligently and keep the commandments of God, so that we may prosper in this land according to the promises made to our forefathers by God."

As Benjamin grew old, he chose his son Mosiah as his successor. "My son," he said, "I want you to gather the people of Zarahemla together tomorrow, so that I can make a proclamation to them about your succession as King. I also want to give them a new name by which they will be distinguished above all other people and forever remembered. I offer this new name as a remembrance of their diligence in keeping God's commandments. However, if these favored people of God should transgress and fall into wickedness and adultery, God will weaken them by withdrawing his protection. Without God's preservation, we will be destroyed by the Lamanites as surely as our ancestors would have been if they hadn't also been protected."

Benjamin told Mosiah all that he knew about being king and managing the affairs of the kingdom. He also gave Mosiah custody of the brass plates from Jerusalem, the plates of Nephi, Laban's sword, and the magic compass, Liahona, which had led their ancestors through the wilderness according to their devotion to God. [124 BC]

Chapter 2, 1981 Version

On the following day, people from throughout the land gathered at the temple to hear King Benjamin speak. So many people came that it was impossible to count them all. They brought offerings and sacrifices, according to the law of Moses. They gave thanks to God, who had brought them from Jerusalem, who had protected them from their enemies, and who had given them good leaders and teachers. They gave credit and thanks to King Benjamin for the peace and prosperity they had enjoyed. They thanked him for helping them keep the commandments of God that brought them love and well being.

The people placed their tents around the temple, with the openings facing inward so they could hear King Benjamin speak. There

were so many people that he had a tower built so more could hear. Recognizing that even this would be insufficient, King Benjamin wrote down his address and distributed it, so that even those who couldn't hear him would be able to receive his words.

"My brothers," said King Benjamin, "I have important things to say to you about the mysteries of God. I am a mortal man, like yourselves, who has been chosen by the people, blessed by my father, and accepted by God to be your ruler and king. As king, I have never sought to make myself rich at your expense. I have never imprisoned you in dungeons. I have not allowed men to enslave one another, commit murder, theft, or adultery. In all ways, I have asked you to keep the commandments of God.

"With my own hands I have labored to serve you, so that you would be free from the burden of taxes. I haven't done all of this so that I could brag to you. I've done this so that I could come before God with a clear conscience. I do all of this in service to God, so that you might also learn this wisdom — that serving your fellow beings is also working in service to God. Just as I serve you and God, I ask that you serve each other and God.

"If you are thankful to God, who has created you in the beginning and who preserves you from day to day in peace, then you should also be willing to serve him without any hesitation. All that he requires is that you keep his commandments. If you do this, you will prosper with his blessing. You owe God your lives, because he created you. When you try to repay the debt by keeping his commandments, you immediately receive his blessing back in payment, so the debt can never be repaid.

"How important do you think you are? You are no better than the dust from which God created you. Look at me, your old king, who is about to die. I am no better than any of you, because I am also created from that dust.

"I have asked you to gather with me today as I end my rule as your king. I wish to leave this service with a clean conscience that I have done all that God has commanded of me regarding you. I want to stand blameless before God, so that I may die in peace and my immortal soul will join the choirs above in singing praise to God. Since I can no longer be your teacher and king, God has commanded me to declare my son Mosiah as your new ruler and King today. My request is that you continue living under my son as you have under me. As you've kept my commandments and God's commandments, you've prospered and have been protected from your enemies. I ask that you keep my son Mosiah's commandments as well.

"But, be aware of the conflicts that may rise up among you if you listen to the voice of the evil spirit, for there is a curse on those who listen to that spirit. If you know God's laws and disobey them, an everlasting punishment and damnation of your soul awaits you. Except for the young children, you already know about your eternal debt to God, about giving him all that you have, about giving him all that you are, and about the prophecies in the holy records from the prophets who lived before us. The prophets who spoke for God were virtuous and true.

"Having been taught all of this, if you disregard these words and live against what has been said, you will lose the guidance of wisdom in which you've prospered and been preserved. Men who live against God's laws live in open rebellion against God and are enemies to all righteousness. If they fail to change their ways and repent, before their death, they die as enemies to God. Divine justice will awaken their souls to their guilt and provide eternal pain and anguish like an eternal fire that burns forever and ever. There will be no mercy for such a man and his payment will be the endurance of never ending torment.

"Awaken, all of you, and see the consequences of disregarding God's laws. I pray that you will accept the blessed and happy state that comes with keeping the commandments of God. Those who obey will be blessed in all things, of the earth and of the spirit. If they are faithful to the end, they will be received into heaven and live with God in a state of never ending happiness. Remember that these things are true because God has spoken it."

Chapter 3, 1981 Version

Benjamin continued, "An angel of God visited me and said, 'Awaken and hear the words I have to say, because I bring good news

of great joy. God has heard your prayers and judged you favorably. I have been sent to tell you that in the near future our eternal God will come down from heaven to live among men. He will work mighty miracles such as healing the sick and diseased, raising the dead, restoring the lame to walk, giving vision to the blind and hearing to the deaf. You may rejoice in this news and tell your people, so that they will also be filled with joy. He will cast out devils and the evil spirits that reside in the people's hearts.

"He will suffer temptations, pain, hunger, thirst, and fatigue just as mortals do,' the angel said, 'but to an even greater depth because of his anguish over the wickedness and abominations of his people. Because of the people's disregard for his laws, he will bleed from every pore. He will be called Jesus Christ, the Son of God. His mother will be named Mary. Though he brings salvation to his people through faith in his name, he will be named as the devil, tormented, and crucified.

"But on the third day, he will arise from death and judge the world. His blood and self-sacrifice will atone for Adam's fall from grace that has been conveyed to his descendants. His resurrection will save the people who have sinned and died in ignorance of God's laws. But those who knowingly violate God's laws are cursed, unless they repent and put their faith in Jesus Christ. For this reason, God has sent his holy prophets out among all men to proclaim that whoever believes in the coming of Jesus Christ will receive remission for their sins, as if he had already come. For this you may rejoice.

"Because God saw that his people were a stubborn lot, he gave them the law of Moses. God has given you many signs and prophecies of his coming, and yet, the people don't understand that the law of Moses is meant to prepare them for his arrival and his atonement. Even sinless children could not be saved without his atonement, because they are children of the fallen Adam. Except for the blood atonement of Jesus Christ, there is no other way for the salvation of man.

"Behold, God's judgments are fair. Children who die in infancy will not perish. Likewise, unless men humble themselves and become as little children, they cannot receive salvation through the atoning blood of Jesus Christ. People have all fallen from salvation through their common ancestor, Adam. But if

178

they become submissive, meek, humble, patient, filled with love, and willing to submit themselves to God, as children submit themselves to their parents, they will become saints instead of men through the power of Jesus Christ.

"The time will come when knowledge of Jesus Christ will spread through all nations and peoples,' the angel concluded. 'When that time comes, only young children will be held blameless and all others may only be saved through repentance and devotion to God.'

"I, Benjamin, have now spoken the words that God has commanded me to speak. He has told me that this message will stand as a testimony on judgment day. You will be judged for your actions that are good as well as your actions that are evil. If they are evil, you will be witness to your own profound guilt and abominations, and will fall from God's presence into eternal torment and misery. If you choose to disregard God, you drink from the cup of God's wrath as surely as Adam, who ate the forbidden fruit. For those of you who choose this course, there will be no mercy. Your torment will be like a lake of eternal fire and burning sulfur with smoke ascending forever and ever.

"This is what God has commanded I say to you."

Chapter 2, 1830 Version

Chapter 4, 1981 Version

When King Benjamin finished telling the Angel of God's message, he looked out across his people. They had all fallen to the ground because the fear of God had come upon them.

They had seen themselves at their worst and witnessed their own guilt. They knew that they truly were less than the dust of the earth. With one voice, they all cried out, "Have mercy and give us the atonement of Jesus Christ's blood, so that we may be forgiven for our sins. Purify our hearts. We believe in Jesus Christ, the Son of God, who created heaven and earth and all other things. We believe that he will come and live among men and bring with him our salvation."

After the people had spoken these words, the Spirit of God came upon them and they were filled with joy. Their sins had been forgiven and peace of mind had been granted to them.

King Benjamin said, "If the knowledge of God's goodness has made you feel small and worthless in your fallen state, then you can also understand his power, his wisdom, his patience, and his suffering for his people. The atonement which has been prepared is for all who put their trust in God and keep his commandments until the end of their mortal life. This is the only path to salvation available to you. To be saved, you must believe in God's power, give up your sinful behavior, repent your past sins, and humble yourself before God; then ask sincerely for his forgiveness. If you believe this, then act accordingly.

"Once you have known God's goodness and tasted his love, you've felt the joy that comes from being forgiven. You are nothing before him, but his goodness will save you, anyhow, if you humble yourself to the truth that was brought from his angel. If you follow his laws and allow yourselves to be filled with the glory of God, you will live in peace without hurting one another. If you follow God's laws, your children will not go hungry or naked, fight with each other, or be led astray by the devil. You will teach your children the wisdom of truth and sobriety, to love one another, and serve one another. Without judgment you will help those among you in need. Aren't we all beggars? Don't we all depend on the same God for food, clothing, and everything we have? Even now, you call upon him, begging for remission of your sins. Has your begging been in vain? No. God has filled you with his love and his spirit so that you can be filled with indescribable joy.

"Just as God has given you all that you have, you should give what you have to each other. If you deny your brother's needs and condemn him for it, you are only condemning yourself by adding to your sins. In the end, you will die and all your possessions will be lost to you anyhow. The poor who would have given but have nothing to give, are without guilt. But the poor who covet wealth are as guilty as the rich who give nothing. To sustain the remission of sins you've received, help your poor fellows by giving according to your ability to give. Feed the hungry, clothe the naked, visit the sick, and give them relief from their wants.

"Do all of this in wisdom and order. No one is expected to do more than he can. When you borrow from your neighbor, always remember to return what was borrowed. To keep what was borrowed is a sin and might also cause your neighbor to sin. There are so many ways to sin that I cannot mention or even count them all. Watch yourselves, your thoughts, your words, your actions, and observe the commandments of God. Do this for the rest of your lives and you will not perish."

Chapter 3, 1830 Version

Chapter 5, 1981 Version

When King Benjamin finished speaking, the people cried with a single voice, saying, "We believe everything you've told us and we know it is true because the spirit of God has changed our hearts. Our inclination to do evil is gone and we desire to be good, forever. Because of the prophecies, we know what is coming and embrace it. Our faith in what our King has told us has brought us great knowledge and joy. We are willing to enter into a promise with God to obey his words and commandments for the rest of our lives. We do not want to end up in the eternal torment that the angel has spoken of and receive God's anger instead of his love."

"Those are the words I wanted to hear," said King Benjamin. "The covenant you've made is a righteous one. Now, I want to give you a new name that will identify and distinguish you. Because you have accepted this covenant with Jesus Christ, you will be called the Children of Christ. You are his sons and daughters, because today he has conceived you spiritually. If you tell me that your hearts are changed through your faith in Jesus Christ, then I say that you have been born of him. Only through him can you be free; so I implore you to take the name of Christ with you everywhere, to remember your covenant for as long as you live. Whoever does this will find himself on the right-hand of God.

"On the other hand, whoever does not take on the name of Christ must take some other name and stand on the left-hand side of God. As Children of Christ, you will carry this name as long as you do not sin. Write it in your hearts and carry it with you always, so that you will know when he calls to you. How can you

know a master whom you haven't served? Does a man take care of his neighbor's ass? No. He doesn't want to feed someone else's animals along with his own, so he drives it away and casts it out. This is how it will be for you if you don't remember the name you are called. Be steady and immovable in attending to the works of Jesus Christ. Receive eternal salvation through the wisdom, power, and justice of the God who created everything."

Chapter 4, 1830 Version

Chapter 6, 1981 Version

King Benjamin had a record kept of all the people who had made a covenant to keep God's commandments. Except for little children, it turned out that everyone had accepted the covenant and taken upon themselves the name of Christ.

King Benjamin blessed his son Mosiah and crowned him as king, appointed priests to remind the people of their promises to keep the commandments of God, then dismissed the crowds. On the day that King Mosiah was crowned, he was 30 years old and 476 years had passed since Lehi's family had left Jerusalem. [124 BC]

Three years later, Benjamin died. Like his father, King Mosiah also kept the commandments of God and did as God commanded him to do. He farmed the earth with his people and for several years there was peace in the land.

Chapter 5, 1830 Version

Chapter 7, 1981 Version

After three peaceful years, King Mosiah grew curious about a legendary group of Nephites who had returned to the land of Nephi long ago, before his father's reign. Nothing had been heard of them since they had left. King Mosiah assigned sixteen strong men to visit their old Nephite homeland and see what had become of this expedition. The group was led by a big, strong, man named Ammon, who was a descendant of Zarahemla. [121 BC]

Ammon's expedition wandered in the wilderness for 40 days, without being at all certain where to find the lost party they were looking for. When they came to a hill which overlooked the city of Shilom, in the land of Nephi, Ammon took several others with him and went down to the city to investigate.

They shortly met up with the king of the land of Nephi, outside the city walls. His guards surrounded them, tied them up, and put them in prison. Two days later, they were brought out of prison to see the king again, and were ordered to answer his questions.

The King said, "I am Limhi, the son of Noah, and grandson of Zeniff who came here from the land of Zarahemla many years ago to take possession of this land of our inheritance. I am the King of my people by their choice. I demand to know why you have come so boldly to our city. I have preserved your lives to hear your story, so speak."

Ammon came forward and bowed before the king, saying "Thank you for sparing our lives. I am Ammon, a descendant of Zarahemla. I have come looking for our lost brothers who left the land of Zarahemla many years ago with Zeniff."

When King Limhi heard this, his attitude changed remarkably and he welcomed the strangers. He said to them, "Now that I know that my brothers in Zarahemla are still alive, I rejoice. Tomorrow, my people will rejoice with us. Times are difficult here. We live in slavery to the Lamanites, who tax us heavily. Will you help us to escape our bondage and let us be your slaves? It would be far better to be slaves to you Nephites than continue paying tribute to the king of the Lamanites."

The Nephite party was released and allowed to return to the hill above the city, where the rest of their party was encamped. The entire group then returned to King Limhi's city where they ate, drank, and rested from the effort and privations of their journey. The following day, King Limhi sent a proclamation out to his people that they should gather at the temple to hear him speak.

"My people," King Limhi said, when they had gathered. "Lift up your heads and be comforted because the time is at hand when we will be liberated from slavery to our enemies. Although our past efforts to free ourselves have failed, I have new faith that this time it will be different. Put your trust in the God of Abraham, Isaac, and Israel, who brought his children out of Egypt, opened the Red Sea for them, and fed them manna in the wilderness.

"That same God," King Limhi continued, "brought our fathers out of Jerusalem and preserved his people. The reason that we are in slavery now is because of our disregard for God's laws and the abominations we have become. When Zeniff came to restore our inheritance of this land, he was deceived by the cunning of King Laman[2]. In trying to make peace, he entered into a treaty with him that gave us land but forced us to pay more in taxes than we can afford to pay; so now we have become slaves. We pay taxes of half the corn, barley, and grain we grow, half the animals we raise, and half of all that we own. This is too much and is the source of our despair.

"So many have been killed and so much blood has been spilled in vain because of our disregard for God. If we had not violated God's laws, this evil would have never come upon us. Instead of listening to God, we have fought with one another. We have even killed one of our own prophets, who warned us of our abominations and foretold the coming of Jesus Christ. Because of his prophecies he was killed. We have also committed many other violations that have angered God. After all of this, it is no wonder that we live in slavery and torment.

"God has told us, 'I will not protect my people if they violate my laws, but will withdraw my support and watch them stumble over their mistakes. If my people sow filth they will reap the poison of my judgment.'

"Now look at us. We are stricken and tormented people and God's words have been fulfilled. But it is not too late to turn to God, with all our purpose, and put our trust in him. If we do this, we will be delivered out of slavery."

Chapter 8, 1981 Version

King Limhi then asked Ammon to address his people. Ammon told them what had happened to their brothers in the land of Zarahemla since the time that Zeniff had left for the land of Nephi. Ammon told them about King Benjamin's last public address and explained the significance of Jesus Christ to the gathering of King Limhi's people.

Ammon was brought the plates which contained the records of King Limhi's ancestors since their departure from Zarahemla. After Ammon had read the record, King Limhi asked him if he knew how to translate languages. Ammon said that he did not. King Limhi related a story of how he'd directed 43 of his people to take a wilderness journey to reconnect with Zarahemla again in hopes of relieving their oppression at the hands of the Lamanites. The expedition got lost and failed to find Zarahemla, but instead discovered a land filled with lakes and rivers. In this land they also found the ruins of a huge earlier civilization. The ground was covered with bones of men and animals. They discovered buildings of all kinds, perfectly preserved copper and brass armor, rusted swords, and most important of all, 24 golden plates covered with curious engravings that were incomprehensible to any of their people.*

*These are the 24 gold plates on which Ether had recorded the history of the Jaredite people.

"Do you know of anyone who might translate these golden plates?" asked King Limhi, "For I am very curious to know what they say. Perhaps they will give us an understanding of these people who were destroyed, and from whence they came."

"My king, Mosiah, is a prophet, seer, and revelator of God," answered Ammon, "and could certainly translate these golden plates. He possesses a certain gift from God which are called interpreters. God permits people to use the interpreters to translate ancient writing. People who use them without God's permission can die by seeing things they weren't meant to see."

Ammon explained that a seer is the greatest position a man can have with God. Seers are prophets and revelators. They know hidden and secret things from the past, present, and future. Seers bring things to light which would not otherwise be known. Through the gift of God, seers work miracles to benefit their fellow men.

When Ammon was finished talking, King Limhi rejoiced and gave thanks to God. "A great mystery is hidden within these plates," he said, "and these divine interpreters were undoubtedly created for the purpose of revealing this kind of hidden knowledge. The works of God and his patience with his children are great. With our lack of understanding and wisdom, we are like herds

of sheep fleeing from the shepherd. He tries to protect us from being scattered and devoured by wild beasts."

Chapter 6, 1830 Version

Chapter 9, 1981 Version

[The following chapters (numbered 9 through 21 in the current version of The Book of Mormon, and 6 through 10 in the original 1830 version) are the record that Limhi gave Ammon to read. They are a history of the people led by Zeniff, who left Zarahemla for the land of Nephi about 80 years before their rediscovery by Ammon. The departure of Zeniff's group was briefly mentioned by the prophet and scribe Amaleki in the Book of Omni.]

I was part of two expeditions to the land of Nephi to reclaim the land of our forefathers from the Lamanites, wrote Zeniff. On the first expedition I was assigned the job of spying on the Lamanites, because I knew the country. In the course of my spying I had an opportunity to see a lot of good things about the Lamanites. I quit wishing for their destruction, and thought we should make a treaty with them. My views were not popular with many of my companions, and when conflict arose over this matter, our leader ordered me killed. This order led to even greater conflict. Members of our party began killing each other, until most of us were dead. Those of us who returned to Zarahemla told a sorry story to the wives and children of our fallen friends. [200BC]

In spite of our first failure in the land of Nephi, many of us still believed in the idea of returning to our ancestor's lands and gathered together another group for a second attempt. During our journey through the wilderness, we met with trouble and starvation because we were slow to remember God. After many days of wandering, we found ourselves near the land of Nephi and back in the place where our previous party had camped and battled with each other.

This time, our group supported my idea of a treaty with the Lamanite king, so I went to his city with four of my men. We asked if we could live in the land of Nephi in peace with them. King Laman² agreed and ordered his people to move out of the land of Nephi so that we could possess it. We constructed buildings and repaired the walls around the city of Nephi and the city of Shilom. We farmed the land, growing crops of corn, wheat, barley, peas and many varieties of fruit. We multiplied and prospered.

The reason that King Laman had so easily assented to our occupation of the land was because he had a tricky plan to bring us into bondage. We lived in peace for 12 years. During that time, King Laman grew uneasy with us because as we grew stronger, his ability to overpower us diminished. Because the Lamanites were lazy, idolatrous people, they wanted to have us work the land for them as slaves. If their plan succeeded, they could glut themselves on the fruits of our farms and the livestock from our fields. [188 BC]

In the 13th year of my reign in the land of Nephi, King Laman stirred up his people to fight with us, and the wars began. A large party of Lamanite warriors attacked a group tending plants and feeding flocks of animals. They began to kill us, and took the harvest and the animals for their own. Those who were not killed fled to the city, asking for my protection. I armed them with bows and arrows, swords, scimitars, clubs, slings and other kinds of weapons. Then we went into battle, praying to God for support against our enemies. Just as he had delivered our ancestors from their enemies, God answered our prayers and helped us to defeat the Lamanites. In a single day we killed 3,049 of them and drove them from our land. With my own hands, I helped to bury the Lamanites, along with our own 279 dead. [187 BC]

Chapter 10, 1981 Version

After that, Zeniff continued, a time of peace came to the land. I made certain that we would be prepared the next time the Lamanites came against us. I had many weapons made and set out guards to protect our fields, our flocks, and our people so that the Lamanites could not surprise us again. With these protections in place, we lived in peace and prosperity for 22 years. [171 BC]

When King Laman died, his son became king and began stirring up his people to make war with us. My spies discovered their preparations for war and we prepared to protect ourselves as well. Their army came to us from the north, armed with bows and arrows, swords, scimitars, and slingshots. Their heads were shaved and they clothed themselves only with leather loin skins around their waists.

I had hidden the women and children in the wilderness. All men and young boys were ordered to be armed and ready for war. With the strength of God, we met the Lamanites on the battlefield. The Lamanites knew nothing of God and they relied on their own considerable strength. They were wild, ferocious, and bloodthirsty people who believed in the story of their heritage and their grievances with us. They were told that their ancestors had been unjustly driven from Jerusalem, and that their fathers had been abused in the wilderness and during the ocean crossing. They believed they had been cheated by the brothers of their fathers after their arrival in the new land, because Nephi had been treated preferentially by God. They didn't know that Nephi had been chosen because he kept God's commandments, while his brothers had not. Nephi's brothers were angry with him because they didn't understand the ways of God, and had closed their hearts to him. They thought Nephi had wished to rule over them. The Lamanites were also angry because, when Nephi left his brothers behind, he'd taken the brass plates with him. The Lamanites believed their fathers had been robbed by Nephi.

The Lamanites taught their children to hate the Nephites. They were taught to murder them, steal from them, plunder their cities and fields, and do all they could to destroy them. There has been profound hatred of the Nephites by the Lamanites ever since. I was deceived by King Laman to think we could live in peace, but now I resign myself to despair because I have brought my people to this land to suffer and be destroyed.

When the battle came, I told my people to put their trust in God. We fought the Lamanites face to face, and drove them again from the land. We killed so many that we didn't bother to count the dead. Afterwards, we returned to farming the land and tending our herds.

Now I am old, Zeniff concluded, and have already passed the reign of our kingdom on to one of my sons. [161 BC]

Chapter 7, 1830 Version

Chapter 11, 1981 Version

Zeniff was succeeded as king by his son Noah, who did not respect or obey the laws of God. He had many wives and mistresses and allowed his people to live in sin and abominations. The people fell into all forms of fornication and wicked behavior.

King Noah imposed a tax on the kingdom and demanded a fifth of all wealth, livestock, and harvests. With these riches he supported his wives and mistresses in luxury while the rest of the people worked to provide the goods. He deposed all of the humble priests whom Zeniff had installed and replaced them with new ones who were filled with pride and self-importance. King Noah and his lazy retainers led a life of idol worship and fornication at the expense of the people who paid for their wickedness with their heavy taxes. Following this example, the people also became immoral and corrupt.

King Noah built elegant and spacious buildings adorned with fine woodwork, gold, silver, iron, brass, and copper. An imposing throne and decadent seats were made for the king and his priests to amplify their importance and vanity. A high tower was built near the temple where the king could look out across his kingdom and into the land of the Lamanites. King Noah's heart was consumed with the pursuit of riches and sumptuous living with his wives and mistresses. His priests consorted with whores. Extensive vineyards were planted around the land and wine was made available in great quantities to the king and all his people.

The Lamanites began to sneak back into the kingdom and kill outlying herders and farmers. King Noah tried to send out guards to protect the people, but the efforts were too little. The Lamanites killed the guards and stole the livestock in a fresh attempt to destroy the hated Nephites. When King Noah sent out his army, the Lamanites withdrew. The kingdom celebrated and boastfully exaggerated their military capabilities against the Lamanite multitudes. They reveled in their power and took delight in bloodshed.

A prophet arose in the kingdom and said, "God has commanded me to speak on his behalf. He curses this kingdom because of the abominations, fornications, and wickedness of the people. Unless you repent, you will receive his anger." His name was Abinadi. [150 BC]

"You will be delivered into the hands of your enemies as slaves. You will come to know God as a jealous master, who is intolerant of your sinful living. When you come crying to him about the ill treatment you receive from your enemies, he will be slow to answer. Unless you humble yourselves before God and repent your ways, you will be punished. God has commanded me to say this to you."

After hearing this, the people were angry with Abinadi. When they tried to have him killed, God intervened and protected him. When King Noah heard about Abinadi's words, he was furious. "Who is this Abinadi," he asked, "that we should be judged by him? Who does God think he is that can bring troubles on my kingdom? Bring Abinadi to me now, so that I can personally kill him. I will not tolerate his attempts to stir up my people."

Because the people were blinded by the leadership of King Noah, they rejected Abinadi's warnings and sought to help their king destroy him. No one repented.

Chapter 12, 1981 Version

After two years, Abinadi came again to the kingdom, in disguise, to deliver his prophecies. "God has commanded me to tell you about the punishment that awaits you if you do not relent in your disobedience to his laws and repent your evil ways. God curses this generation of people. You will be hunted and killed by the Lamanites before being delivered to them as slaves. When King Noah's life is worth less than garments burning in a fire, he will know who God is. God will punish his people with such troubles, starvation, and disease that they will howl in sorrow all day long. Their backs will be loaded with burdens and they will be driven like donkeys. Bitter winds and insects will afflict their crops and steal their grain. This will be done in retribution for your sins and abominations. Unless you repent, you will be utterly destroyed from the face of the earth. Only your records will be left behind to show that you ever existed, and these will be used as an example to other nations." [148 BC]

Abinadi was bound up and brought before King Noah as a prisoner. "This man is out prophesying evil about our people and says that God will destroy us," they said. "He says that your life is as worthless as a dry stalk trampled underfoot. He pretends to speak for God, saying that great harm will befall us unless we repent. What sins have we done that we should be condemned or judged critically by this man or by God? We are guiltless and this man lies about all of us, making false prophecies. We are far too strong and prosperous to be become slaves of the Lamanites, as he predicts. We give this man to you, to do what you think is best."

Sometime after Abinadi was cast into prison, King Noah's priests brought him out for questioning. During the interrogation, the priests hoped to confuse him and to have good reasons to condemn him for heresy. But Abinadi answered boldly and confounded them with his words. One of his questioners asked him about the meaning of an old scripture of prophecy from Isaiah.

"How can you priests pretend to teach your people," asked Abinadi in response, "about the spirit of prophecy, if you ask me for the meaning of your scriptures? You are perverting the ways of God. Even if you do understand the scriptures, they certainly aren't what you teach. What do you teach your people?"

"We teach the law of Moses," they replied.

"If you teach the law of Moses," Abinadi said, "why don't you keep it? Why do you devote yourselves to wealth and fornication? Why do you allow your people to live in sin? God has sent me to expose this evil against his people. You know that I speak the truth and that you should tremble before God. You will be punished for your crimes, because you say you teach the law of Moses. Doesn't the law of Moses say that salvation comes from observance of God's commandments?"

When the priests affirmed that salvation did come from observance of the law of Moses, Abinadi said to them, "If you keep the commandments of God, you will be saved. God said to Moses, 'I am the god who brought you out of slavery in Egypt. You shall have no other gods but me. You shall not worship any idols or graven images.' And yet you have done exactly that and taught the people to do these things. You have not obeyed the law of Moses at all."

Chapter 13, 1981 Version

When King Noah heard what Abinadi had said to his priests, he ordered Abinadi's execution, saying, "We don't need to worry about him. He's crazy."

When the priests attempted to seize him, Abinadi declared, "Don't you touch me. If you do, God will strike you down. Because I'm here to deliver God's message, he will not allow me to be destroyed at this time. Even though I've only told you the truth, you're angry with me now and have decided that I'm crazy."

After Abinadi spoke, the guards were afraid to touch him, because it was evident from his shining face that the spirit of God was upon him. "You can see that you have no power to kill me," he said, with the authority of God. "I will finish delivering my message even if it hurts you to hear the truth about your sins. By the time I finish, my words will fill you with wonder, amazement, and anger. After that, it doesn't matter whether or not I live. Whatever you do to me will be a preview of what will happen to you and your people.

"Now, I want to remind you about God's commandments, because you don't seem to know them. For most of your lives, you have taught heresy, instead. God has said that you must not make or worship idols or graven images. You must not use the name of God as a curse. You must remember to keep the sabbath holy by using it for rest and worship. You must honor your father and mother. You must not kill. You must not have sexual relations with anyone except you spouse. You must not steal. You must not lie about your neighbor. You must not covet your neighbor's possessions, wife, or anything else of his."

Chapter 8, 1830 Version

"Have you truly taught your people to observe these commandments?" Abinadi asked. "No, you haven't. If you had, God would not have sent me to prophesy the destruction of your people. You say that salvation comes from the law of Moses? Then do it. A time will come when following these laws will not be enough on its own because without God's atonement for our sins, we are doomed to perish even if we observe the laws of Moses. The day-to-day remembrance of Moses' simple laws are necessary for a stubborn people to maintain God's favor. Ever since Moses, prophets have foretold the coming of a Messiah who would redeem God's people. This Messiah will be God himself who will become mortal, walk among us, be tormented, slain, and resurrected so that we may be forgiven for our sins."

Chapter 14, 1981 Version

"Didn't the prophet Isaiah speak of the Messiah?" Abinadi asked, quoting Isaiah.

[Chapter 14 of the Book of Mosiah is virtually indistinguishable, word for word, and verse for verse, from Chapter 53 of Isaiah from the Old Testament.]

Isaiah talks about the burdens the Messiah will have to endure because of the sinful nature of God's children. He predicts that the Messiah will be rejected, imprisoned, tried, and executed, even though he will do nothing wrong. He foretells that it is God's plan to send someone who will bear the sins of mankind.

Chapter 15, 1981 Version

"You need to understand," Abinadi continued, "that God himself will come down among men and redeem his people. The one who will come among us in the flesh will be called the Son of God, but because he will be conceived by God, the Son will be one with the creator of heaven and earth. In his earthly life he will be subject to temptation, to which he will not succumb. He will suffer and will be mocked, tormented, and disowned by his people. He will work miracles, and be led to die on the cross without complaint. Afterwards, he will rise from death and make this release from death open to all who believe in him. This is his compassion toward men: to defeat death, take their sins upon himself, redeem them, and satisfy the demands of justice.

"So, I say to you, who will help me tell the people what will come? Who will save himself? Who will help his descendants be redeemed? All those who receive this message and believe in the power of God to save will be heirs to God's kingdom. After having been saved, are we not God's children? Who will listen to what the prophets have said? Throughout time, they have declared that God reigns. This redemption

has been planned since the beginning of the world, because without it we would all perish. When God comes amongst us, the first resurrection will be at hand and those who have believed in him before he comes will be a part of it. They will be raised up to live with God who has saved them, and have eternal life.

"At the time of this first resurrection, those people who died before Jesus Christ comes and who were ignorant of his salvation will have a choice to join him. Little children will be given eternal life. But God will not save those who rebel against him during their life and die with their sins intact. Those who willfully disobey God's laws will have no part in the first resurrection. Don't you think you should be frightened? God will not save you, because justice must be done. A time will come when the salvation of God will be declared to all people in all nations who will sing his praise when they see his hand in their redemption."

Chapter 16, 1981 Version

Abinadi reached out his hand and said, "When this time of salvation comes, everyone will see eye to eye and concede that God's judgments are fair. The sinners will be cast out, howling and weeping, wailing, and gnashing their teeth because they have disregarded God's words and could not be saved. The devil will have gained power over them just as the snake gained power over Adam and Eve, and caused their fall. From this fall, man has become lustful, hedonistic, and devilish by choosing evil over good and by making alliance with the devil. In the absence of God, man would remain forever lost in this fallen state.

"When man persists in his sinful nature, he is in rebellion against God and the devil holds him captive. If he remains in this state, no redemption is possible for him. Likewise, if Jesus Christ does not come as foretold, no redemption is possible. If he does not rise from the dead after his death, there cannot be resurrection. But, there will be a resurrection, and the finality of death is withdrawn through Jesus Christ.

"Jesus Christ is the endless light and life of the world that can never be darkened or ended by death. Mortal men may become immortal by setting corruption aside and choosing purity. Then God will judge each person by his actions

186

to see whether he is good or evil. Those who are good will be rewarded with eternal life and happiness. For those who are evil, their punishment will be endless damnation and delivery to the devil. Everyone will know ahead of time both the rewards and the punishment. God's arms are open to receive those who repent and closed to those who refuse him.

"Shouldn't you tremble and repent your sins?" Abinadi asked the priests. "Remember, only through Jesus Christ can you be saved. If you teach the law of Moses, you should also teach that it is just a shadow of things to come."

Chapter 9, 1830 Version

Chapter 17, 1981 Version

When Abinadi was finished speaking, King Noah ordered him put to death. But there was one young priest, named Alma, who believed what Abinadi said and knew it was true. Alma was a descendant of Nephi's. He pled with King Noah to set aside his anger and let Abinadi leave in peace. This caused the King to be even angrier and he ordered Alma immediately removed from his circle of priests. After Alma left, the king sent servants out to kill him; but Alma fled from the city and hid from the King's anger. In hiding, he wrote down what Abinadi had said.

Abinadi was thrown into prison and King Noah consulted with his priests. After three days, the King ordered Abinadi brought before him again. "Abinadi, you have declared that God himself will come down among the people. Unless you retract this declaration and reverse your accusations against me and my people, you will be put to death for heresy."

"I will not recall my words concerning you and your people," stated Abinadi, "because they are all true. In order to be in a position to declare their truth to you personally, I have even allowed myself to be captured and imprisoned. I would rather die than recall my words, because they will stand in eternal testimony against you. If you kill an innocent man, this also will stand as testimony against you on the day of judgment."

At this point King Noah, was thinking of releasing Abinadi because he was afraid of the judgments of God that Abinadi had foretold; but the priests argued against his release. They wanted him dead; so, the king ordered Abinadi put to death. They tied him to a stake and set the wood beneath him ablaze. When his flesh was burning, Abinadi said to Noah and his priests, "Just as you do this to me, your descendants will also cause others who believe in God to suffer as I do. Because of your sins, you will become diseased, be stricken, and become scattered like wild animals chased by ferocious beasts. You will be hunted, taken into slavery by your enemies, and suffer the pain of death by fire. God avenges himself on those who destroy his people."

After saying these words, Abinadi died in the fire because he would not retract the commandments of God. In his death, the truth of his words were sealed.

Chapter 18, 1981 Version

After fleeing from King Noah, Alma repented his sins and began teaching Abinadi's message about the coming of Jesus Christ, his resurrection into heaven, and the resulting redemption of people from his suffering. He privately taught those who showed interest, hoping to pass unnoticed by the king. Many believed his words.

He found a place in the woods named Mormon, where a fountain of pure water arose from the ground. This is where he taught and where people came to hear him speak. One day, a large number of people had gathered to hear him. [147 BC]

"Here are the waters of Mormon," he said. "If you wish to enter the community of God and lighten one another's burdens, you have come to the right place. You must be willing to share the grief of others, and stand as witnesses to God to be redeemed and live eternally in the first resurrection. If this is your desire, you must be baptized in the name of God. We do this as witness to your promises that you will keep his commandments and receive his Spirit."

Hearing these words, the people clapped their hands in joy, saying, "This is our heart's desire."

Alma took a man named Helam into the water and said, "Oh, God, pour your Spirit into this servant so that he may do your work with a holy heart. Helam, I baptize you by the authority from Almighty God as testimony that you have entered into a promise to serve him as long as you live. May the Spirit of God enter you and grant you eternal life through the redemption of Jesus Christ." After saying this, Alma submerged Helam and himself in the waters of Mormon. They arose rejoicing and full of the Spirit.

Alma baptized the people in this way, one after another, until 204 people had all been filled with the grace of God. They called themselves the Church of Christ, from that day onward. As more were baptized, after that day, they were also added to the church.

For every 50 members, Alma was given authority from God to ordain new priests. He commanded that they teach only the things which he'd been taught about repentance, redemption, and faith in God. He commanded that they should all work together as one people, without conflict. They should see with one vision, keep one faith, connect with one baptism, and knit themselves together in unity and love towards one another. And so they became the children of God.

Alma commanded that the sabbath be set aside from work days as a holy day in which they would assemble and offer their thanks to God. Alma's priests were told not to rely on the people for their support, but rather to work, using their own efforts to sustain themselves and impart the knowledge of God. Alma commanded that his people give part of their food and possessions, in accordance with their ability, to help the people in need. Having given, the people could stand tall before God, knowing that they had helped their brothers both tangibly and spiritually.

All of this was done secretly in the place by the water named Mormon. When King Noah discovered this secret movement, he sent his servants to spy on the church and report back to him. When he heard of their large assembly, the king accused Alma of rebellion and sent his army out to destroy the church. Alma and his people learned of the king's plan in advance, and 450 of them slipped out of King Noah's grasp, into the wilderness.

Chapter 19, 1981 Version

King Noah's army searched in vain and returned empty-handed. The kingdom was divided and splintered with dissent. Some even whispered against the king and conflicts broke out everywhere. [145 BC]

Among the dissenters was a strong man named Gideon, who swore in anger that he'd kill King Noah, himself. During a fight between them, Gideon was about to prevail when an army of Lamanites arrived. The king pled with Gideon to spare him so that he could help fight the enemy and save the people. Gideon knew that the king was far more concerned with his own life than with the safety of his people, but let him live, anyhow.

King Noah led the people in a hurried retreat into the wilderness in an effort to escape from the pursuing Lamanites. When the enemy caught up with the king's people and began slaughtering them, the king ordered the men to abandon their wives and children so that they could retreat more quickly. Some men followed King Noah's orders and ran away to save their lives, while others preferred to stay and die with their families.

The beautiful daughters of those left behind pled with the Lamanites and charmed them into sparing all of those who hadn't run away with King Noah. Instead, they were taken as captives and brought back to the land of Nephi, where they were allowed to stay, subject to two conditions. The first condition was that they would hand King Noah over to the Lamanites. The second condition required them to pay tribute to the Lamanites of half of everything they owned and produced, on an annual basis.

One of the captives was Limhi, son of King Noah. He became the new leader. Without Limhi's knowledge, Gideon made secret plans to organize a search party to find King Noah in the wilderness. He found the refugees who'd fled with King Noath in the forest, but the king and his priests were not with them. These people had sworn to return to the land of Nephi to avenge their dead families. When the king had ordered them not to return, they turned on King Noah and burned him to death. As they prepared the same fate for the king's priests, the priests had run away.

When Gideon's search party found them, the refugees were preparing to return to the land of Nephi. When they learned the fate of their families and the conditions of the peace settlement, the men were overjoyed because their families were still alive.

With King Noah dead, the new King Limhi made an oath with the Lamanites to live according to their conditions. To ensure that they honored the treaty and didn't run away, the Lamanites posted guards and paid them from the taxes. The kingdom recovered and there was peace for two years between the people of King Limhi and the Lamanites.

Chapter 20, 1981 Version

It regularly happened that young Lamanite women gathered to sing and dance together in a place called Shemlon. One such day, King Noah's renegade priests discovered them and secretly watched their merriment. Because they were ashamed of themselves and were justifiably afraid of being killed by the angry people if they returned to their families in the city, they roamed the woods as fugitives. Because they had no female company in their exile, the priests decided to abduct the women and carry them into the wilderness with them.

When the angry Lamanites discovered that 24 young women were missing, they assumed that the blame lay with King Limhi and his people, so the Lamanite King sent his army to destroy the kingdom. King Limhi saw the preparations for war, from his tower, and set up an ambush for them.

When the Lamanites arrived at the place of ambush, the Nephites emerged from their hiding places and attacked. The Lamanites had twice as many warriors, but the Nephites fought like dragons for the lives of their wives and children and drove the Lamanites back.

Among the fallen Lamanites, the Nephites found the wounded Lamanite king. He had been left behind by his fleeing warriors. They tied him up and brought him to King Limhi. "Why have you started a war between us?" King Limhi asked. "We have honorably kept all of our promises to you. Why do you break your promises to us?"

"Because your people have stolen our women," the Lamanite king replied.

King Limhi was perplexed, because he knew nothing of this. "I will get to the root of this," he said. "If any among us have done as you say, I will have them killed."

Gideon, the king's captain, said he didn't believe that the people of the kingdom were responsible. He reminded the king of the outcast priests still out roaming in the wilderness. "We must tell the Lamanite king about this," King Limhi responded, "before their armies return and destroy us. If we cannot make peace with them, we will be defeated by their huge numerical advantage. It is as Abinadi foretold. All of this is happening because we wouldn't obey God's laws and abandon our sinful lives. Let's go talk to the Lamanite king, because it is better to keep our promises and live under him in slavery than to die. Let's put an end to this bloodshed."

When they told the Lamanite king about King Noah's renegade priests and of their innocence in the abduction of the women, the Lamanite king agreed to persuade his people to accept a peace treaty. "If you and your people come out with me unarmed, to meet my army, I swear that I will not kill you," he said. When they did this, the Lamanite warriors had compassion and peacefully disbanded their war party without incident.

Chapter 21, 1981 Version

The peace didn't last long. Before many days had passed, the angry Lamanites began harassing the Nephites again. Their king had forbidden his people to kill them, but had said nothing about abusing the Nephites. The Lamanite guards began treating the Nephites like prisoners. They were beaten, ordered about, loaded with burdens, and treated like pack animals. The prophecies of God were being fulfilled.

The Nephites were heavily guarded, now, and unable to escape the adversity imposed upon them. Things got so bad that they tried to drive the Lamanites out by force, but the Lamanites were too strong and retaliated by killing many of them. It was a grievous time. Wives mourned for their dead husbands and children cried for their dead fathers. Everyone lived in fear.

The fear gave way to anger and the Nephites tried once more to defeat the Lamanites, and again failed, suffering heavy casualties in the attempt. They even tried a third time to relieve themselves from slavery and failed yet again. There was nothing left for them to do but to submit to the slavery and allow themselves to be beaten and driven by their enemies, so they humbled themselves before the Lamanites and cried out to God all day long for deliverance.

God was slow to hear their cries, because he remembered how they'd turned away from him in their time of prosperity. Nonetheless, he did hear them and began to ease their burdens by softening the Lamanites' anger towards them; but, he didn't release them from their slavery. Slowly, they began to prosper again. As their harvests became more abundant and their livestock thrived, the kingdom was relieved of constant hunger. As a result of the wars, the women greatly outnumbered the men; King Limhi ordered that his people should support the widows and fatherless children so that they wouldn't starve.

The renegade priests who had stolen the Lamanite women and caused so much trouble were now stealing the kingdom's harvests from the fields, and whatever else they could take. The Nephites watched their lands carefully, hoping to capture and punish the priests.

When Ammon and his party from Zarahemla were discovered outside the city's walls, they were thought to be these renegade priests. That is why they were bound, imprisoned, and so badly mistreated. Had they been the priests, they would have been put to death. When King Limhi found out that they were his relatives from the land of Zarahemla, he was overjoyed.

In the depths of their slavery, King Limhi sent an expedition out to find the land of Zarahemla, in hopes of leading his people out of their captivity. When the party found the ruins of the Jaredite people, they had mistakenly believed them to be the ruins of Zarahemla. This expedition had returned to the land of Nephi in despair, just a few days before Ammon and his party arrived.

Now, King Limhi was doubly blessed. His brothers in the land of Zarahemla were alive and well, and King Benjamin* had a gift from God that would enable them to translate the strange writing on the Jaredites' golden plates.

*In subsequent versions of *The Book of Mormon,* King Benjamin has been changed to King Mosiah. At the time that Ether's golden plates were discovered, King Benjamin was dead and his son Mosiah was the king and translator. King Benjamin never knew of the existence or the content of Ether's plates.

Ammon was sorry to hear about the Lamanite wars, the death of so many brothers, the sins and troubles with Noah and his priests, and the unfortunate death of the prophet Abinadi. He was gladdened to hear of the church that Alma had been inspired by Abinadi to establish, but saddened to hear about the disappearance of Alma and his blessed people.

No one knew where Alma and his followers had gone. The kingdom's people would have gladly followed them because they had since entered into a similar covenant themselves, to serve God and honor his commandments. They wished for Alma's return because now they, too, wanted to be baptized in God's name, but none of them was authorized by God to perform this rite. Ammon also declined to baptize the people, saying that he was too unworthy a servant of God's to do this for them. Their desire to be baptized as a testimony of their willingness to serve God, and form a church as Alma had, would have to wait. For now, all of their efforts would have to be applied toward delivering themselves from their enslavement to the Lamanites.

Chapter 10, 1830 Version

Chapter 22, 1981 Version

Ammon and King Limhi began plotting and planning their escape from the Lamanites. They invited thoughts and ideas of all the people. It was no small task. It seemed impossible for themselves, their families, and their herds of livestock to flee from the Lamanite lands without a terrible fight, because there were so many Lamanites to contend with. [121 BC]

Gideon, the king's captain, had an idea. "You've listened to me in the past," he said to King Limhi, "and I ask that you listen again. There is a gate through the back wall of the city that is guarded lightly. At night, the guards at that gate get drunk and are inattentive. I propose that we secretly organize all of our people and their herds of livestock for a stealthy, late night exit through that gate and out into wilderness beyond. If you agree with this plan, I will personally go and give the guards some extra wine to ensure that they are asleep when we pass through. If we move quickly, we can outflank the Lamanite lands and escape with all our people and all our livestock."

The king was pleased with Gideon's idea and the plan was secretly passed along to all the Nephites. The guards were delighted with the gift of extra wine, and drank it greedily. On the designated night, the people of King Limhi gathered themselves and their livestock and silently passed through the gate without being observed by the sleeping guards. They traveled widely around the Lamanite lands and set their course for Zarahemla. They were led by Ammon and his party, who knew the way. Along with their animals, they took whatever wealth and provisions they could carry.

After many days of travel through the wilderness, they arrived in the land of Zarahemla and were received warmly by King Mosiah and his people. King Limhi and all his people became grateful subjects of King Mosiah.

When the Lamanites discovered that King Limhi and his people had escaped, they sent an army out to pursue them; but after two days, the Lamanite army lost the trail and went astray in the wilderness.

Chapter 11, 1830 Version

Chapter 23, 1981 Version

After God warned Alma to flee from King Noah, he had taken the people of his church and fled into the wilderness with their livestock and provisions. After eight days, they came to a beautiful place where the water was pure and King Noah wouldn't find them. They settled, and began diligently building a community in which to live.

Although the people wanted Alma as king, he declined. "I doubt the wisdom of having a king," he said. "God doesn't want one man putting himself above others. As you've seen with King Noah and his priests, kings can become corrupt and forgetful of God's laws. I, myself, was caught in the trap and did many things as his priest that I now regret. Fortunately, God heard my cries and answered my prayers. He made me an instrument to bring you to his knowledge and truth. I neither want nor deserve any glory.

"As subjects of King Noah, you were caught and dragged down into the oppression of the kingdom. Now that you've been freed by the power of God, do you really want another king to rule over you? I want you to stay free, and trust no one as king. Likewise, you shouldn't trust anyone to be your teacher or priest unless he is a man of God who dutifully follows his commandments himself."

Alma taught that if each person would love each other as he loved himself, there wouldn't be conflicts. As the founder of their church, Alma decreed that only God could convey the authority of any man to become a priest or minister to the people. Accordingly, only men of God were ordained by him as ministers. As the people were spiritually nourished, they prospered and flourished. They built a city in the wilderness and named it Helam.

As God scolded them and tested them from time to time with hardships and trials, they grew stronger in their faith. The people of Alma's church were keenly aware that only the power of God could have delivered them and led them to this place. In this, they rejoiced.

One day, while the people were out tending their fields, an army of Lamanites unexpectedly appeared. The people fled the fields in fear and gathered together in the city of Helam. Alma stood before them like a rock and reminded them to call on God for deliverance from danger. In response to his certainty, the people quieted their fear and prayed to God, asking him to send out his compassion to the Lamanite army. They prayed for the lives of themselves, their wives, and their children.

God conferred upon the Lamanites the compassion that Alma's people had prayed for. Alma and his people went forward and delivered their city of Helam and themselves into the hands of the Lamanite army.

This was the same army of Lamanites who had gotten lost, chasing after King Limhi's people after their exodus from the land of Nephi. Before stumbling onto the city of Helam, they had also discovered the land of Amulon, where King Noah's priests had settled with the Lamanite women they'd kidnapped earlier.

Amulon and his fellow priests had married the Lamanite women whom they had abducted. These wives of theirs now pled with the Lamanite army not to destroy their husbands. Because of the women's intercession, the

Lamanites spared their husbands and allowed them all to join their lost army.

It was this entire lost group who discovered the city of Helam and Alma's people. The Lamanites promised Alma that if he could lead them back to their homeland, his people's lives would be spared and they would be given their freedom. In trust and faith, Alma did as he was asked. But the Lamanites then decided to dishonor their promise. They set guards around Helam to insure that Alma's people didn't escape. The Lamanite king then gave Amulon the title of King over Helam as long as he obeyed the will of the Lamanites.

Chapter 24, 1981 Version

Amulon became a trusted retainer of King Laman, the new Lamanite king who was named after his father. He taught them how to write and keep records. This enabled the Lamanites to greatly increase their wealth and trade with each other. As they became more powerful, they also became more overbearing.

As king of Helam, Amulon became the overseer of Alma and his people, whom he took delight in persecuting. Alma and Amulon had once been fellow priests under King Noah. While Alma had been inspired and transformed by Abinadi's words, Amulon held them both in contempt. Amulon blamed Alma for the fall from his previous status as high priest in the kingdom of Noah to his present status as subject of King Laman, so he worked Alma's people like animals and put them under the constant supervision of heavy-handed taskmasters. The hardships imposed on Alma's people became so great that they cried out to God for help. Amulon ordered them to stop their crying and instructed their guards to kill anyone they found praying to God.

Alma and his people then prayed to God in silence. "I hear your silent prayers," God said to them. "I know of your covenants to me. You may be comforted in your torment by knowing that I promise to deliver you from your slavery. Until then, I will ease your burdens so that you won't even feel them. I do this so that you will know that I am with you in your hardships."

With the weight of their burdens lifted by God, the people of Alma submitted cheerfully to the circumstances. Their faith and their patience was so great that God again came to them saying, "Tomorrow I will deliver you from slavery."

During the night, Alma's people gathered their livestock and provisions. The next morning, God induced a deep sleep upon the Lamanites and all their taskmasters. While they were asleep, the people of Alma fled the land of the Lamanites. After traveling a day in the wilderness, they rested and gave thanks to God for his mercy in delivering them from slavery. They knew that no one but God could have freed them.

God told Alma to make haste and get his people out of the Lamanites' land, because their presumptive masters were now awake and in angry pursuit. "When you move on," God said, "I will stop them here and let them chase you no further."

After twelve more days of travel in the wilderness, they reached the land of Zarahemla and were received joyfully by King Mosiah. [120 BC]

Chapter 25, 1981 Version

When King Mosiah gathered all of his people together, he found two separate groups standing before him. The smaller group was comprised of the descendants of Nephi. The larger group were descendants of Mulek. Both of these groups together were only half as many as the Lamanite people. He read aloud the accounts of Zeniff from the time of his departure until the return of his descendants. Then he read the account of Alma.

The people were thunderstruck, filled with wonder and amazement. When they saw the people who'd been delivered from slavery, they were joyful. When they thought of their relatives who'd been killed by the Lamanites, tears of sorrow came over them. When they thought of the goodness and power of God, they gave thanks out loud. When they thought of the sinful Lamanites to whom they were related, they were filled with anguish over the state of their souls.

Before Amulon and the other priests had become renegades, they had lived among the other Nephite families in the land of Nephi. After hearing about the sins and treachery of the renegade priests, all of those who were related to the priests disowned them, and changed their names to Nephi.

When King Mosiah finished reading the accounts of Zeniff and Alma, he asked Alma to speak to his people. Alma spoke of repentance and faith in God. To all of those who had been delivered from slavery, he stressed that it was God who had delivered them. When he was through speaking, Limhi asked to be baptized by Alma, as the other members of his church had been baptized. Then all the people who had escaped from the land of Nephi clamored to be baptized by Alma also. By this baptism, all the people became united in the Church of God, because they believed in the words of Alma.

King Mosiah granted Alma a charter to organize churches throughout the land of Zarahemla and gave him power to ordain priests and teachers for every church. This had become necessary because there were too many people to assemble in one place and hear the word of God. There came to be seven churches all united as one Church of God through Alma. The same message of repentance and faith was taught in all of them. People who wanted to take the name of Jesus Christ or God joined the churches and were called the people of God. The people were blessed by the Spirit of God and prospered in the land of Zarahemla.

Chapter 26, 1981 Version

The new generation of young people didn't understand the words of the late King Benjamin and didn't relate to the tradition that their fathers had adopted. They didn't believe in the coming of Jesus Chris and his resurrection from the dead, so they disrespectfully turned away from the words of God. They refused to be baptized or join the church and pursued a lustful, sinful life.

At first, the young dissenters were not too numerous, but as they undermined the faith of the believers, their numbers became greater than those who followed God's laws. As church members became influenced by the deceptions and fell into sinful ways, the church struggled with how to respond. Because Alma had been given authority over the church, the priests brought their unfaithful members before him. Nothing like this had happened before, so Alma didn't know what to do, either. When he had them brought before King Mosiah, the King didn't want to judge these people any more than Alma did; so, he handed them back over to Alma for judgment and discipline.

Alma was deeply troubled by the predicament, and didn't want to do the wrong thing, so he asked God what to do. "You are blessed, Alma," God told him, "because you have established a church among your people. The people who maintain faith in the words of Abinadi and honor my name are also blessed. I bless you for asking me what to do with the unfaithful members of your church. You may serve me by gathering my sheep to your flock and receiving them. I am happy to receive and to forgive all of those who hear my voice, because I have taken on the sins of the world that I created. Those who believe in me will live eternally and have a place at my right hand. Those who don't hear my voice are not my sheep, and will not be redeemed on the day of judgment. Those who turn away will be consigned to eternal fire and the company of the devil.

"So go back to your people," continued God, "and judge your people according to the sins they've committed. If they confess their sins and sincerely repent, they will be forgiven. They must also forgive those that have abused them, because those who refuse to forgive may not be forgiven. Those who will not repent their sins must be excommunicated from your church and cast out. From this time forward, this is what you must do."

After Alma heard these instructions, he wrote them down and prepared to judge his people according to God's commands. Those who repented were taken back into the church and those who did not were cast out and their names were erased.

Under Alma's management of church affairs, things went well again. There were many new baptisms and there was better compliance with God's laws. There was peace in the church and prosperity for its members. Alma and his priests worked hard to keep their brothers on the path of God, in spite of persecutions from those who didn't believe as they did. They taught, guided, and helped their brothers by prescribing thankfulness and unceasing prayer to God. [100 BC]

Chapter 27, 1981 Version

The persecutions endured by the faithful at the hands of the unbelievers became so great that Alma complained to King Mosiah. After consulting with his priests, King Mosiah sent out a proclamation throughout the kingdom that forbade the persecution of members of the Church of God. Another command was issued within the churches, ordering all people to treat one another with equal respect and love. There was to be no more arrogant pride among them. Unless they were ill, people were admonished to support themselves with the labor of their own hands. This included priests as well. By acting this way, the people of faith were promised the grace of God.

Peace came to the land of Zarahemla again as the people grew in population and spread themselves across the land. They built villages and large cities, and by God's grace, they prospered and grew wealthy.

Among the people who disbelieved in God were King Mosiah's sons, and one of Alma's sons who was also named Alma. Alma^2 was an immoral and idolatrous young man who spoke with a silver tongue and persuaded others to join him in his sinfulness. He became a festering sore to the Church of God by stealing the faithfulness of others and causing dissension among the people. He opened doors that the devil could not have opened otherwise. He and Mosiah's sons had a secret plan to destroy the church by leading people astray, and by turning them against the commandments of God and King Mosiah.

One day when they were going about their deviltry, an angel of God appeared before them, descending from the sky, and speaking with a thundering voice that made the earth shake. They were so astonished that they fell to the ground and couldn't understand what the angel had to say.

The angel cried out again, saying, "Alma, get up off the ground and tell me why you abuse the Church of God. This church has been established by God and nothing will overturn it except the sins of his people. God has heard his people's prayers and also heard your father's prayers about your behavior. I have come here to try and convince you of the power and authority of God, and show you that the faithful prayers of his servants are answered.

Seeing me, how can you dispute the power of God any longer? I have been sent here by God so that you can personally see me and hear me. Now, go and reflect on the slavery that your father's people endured in the land of Helam and remember how many great things were done to deliver them into freedom. Alma, stop your efforts to injure the church any further and demonstrate that the prayers of your father and his people are answered."

After delivering his message, the angel disappeared, leaving Alma and King Mosiah's sons so shocked that they fell to the ground again. Alma was so stunned that he became unable to speak or move afterwards. His companions had to carry him back, helpless, to his father. When they told his father what had happened, Alma rejoiced because he knew that this had happened by the power of God.

Alma gathered a crowd together to witness God's response to their prayers. The priests assembled themselves and began to pray that God would now show his strength by restoring Alma to consciousness, and by demonstrating to the people his power and goodness once more. After two days of prayer, Alma recovered and proclaimed that he had sincerely repented of his sins and been redeemed by God and reborn in Spirit.

"All mankind must be born again," young Alma told them, "in order to transform themselves from their sinful state and become sons and daughters of God. Unless they become new beings, they cannot inherit the kingdom of God. Otherwise, they will be cast off from God's grace, as I was. I have been saved, through great effort, from the fires of hell. Now, I am reborn to God. In ignorance I rejected God and denied the truth of what our ancestors have spoken. Now, I know that God will come and show himself to everyone. On judgment day, everyone will acknowledge God and tremble before his gaze."

From that day forward, Alma and the sons of King Mosiah began to travel and teach the people about what they'd seen and heard. Ironically, they were now the recipients of the same sort of abuse that they had once showered on others who professed faith in God. Their conversion was a great consolation to the church and confirmed the people's faith in honoring the laws of God. Alma and the king's sons worked hard to repair the injury they'd previously done to the church, by confessing their sins and explaining the prophecies and scriptures to those who wished to receive them. They became great instruments in God's hands, bringing knowledge and peace to the people of Zarahemla.

Chapter 12, 1830 Version

Chapter 28, 1981 Version

After the king's sons traveled and taught across the land, they came to their father and asked his permission to go to the land of Nephi and teach their relatives, the Lamanites. They thought it possible that the Lamanites could be cured of their hatred toward the Nephites and be restored to God. The notion that anyone would have to endure the endless torment of hell that awaited unbelievers was unbearable to them. [92 BC]

The Spirit of God had converted them from the worst of sinners to the most faithful of believers, but they still suffered anguish for their past and were concerned about the sufficiency of their repentance. After they had pleaded for many days with King Mosiah to go teach among the Lamanites, the King sought guidance from God. "Let them go, because many will believe them," God said to the King. After they'd left, King Mosiah had no one to pass the kingdom on to. All of his sons had declined his offer.

For solace, King Mosiah brought out the golden plates with the ancient writing that Limhi had brought with him. Using the magic seer stones, he translated the Jaredite records from the time of the Tower of Babel through the total destruction of the Jaredite people. His people had been anxious to know what was written on the golden plates. When he told them the story of the Jaredites, they felt sorrow for the deaths of so many, but glad to have the knowledge of God that the records contained.

Chapter 13, 1830 Version

King Mosiah took out all the records that had been preserved and saved by his ancestors: the brass plates from Jerusalem, Nephi's large and small plates, the Jaredite records, and the records of Zeniff, Alma and Limhi, and gave them to Alma's son, along with the magic seer stones that permitted interpretation. The king commanded the younger Alma to also keep and preserve them, add his own records, and hand them down safely to the next generation as had been done since Lehi left Jerusalem.

Chapter 29, 1981 Version

After passing the accumulated records on to Alma, King Mosiah sought guidance from his people as to who should succeed him as king. The response was unanimous. The people wanted his son Aaron[1] to be the next ruler. But, Aaron had not wanted to be king, and had gone to the land of Nephi.

He let the people know that Aaron was neither available nor willing to take his place. "Now that I've asked you and cannot give what you request," he said, "I'm afraid that conflicts will arise over anyone else I choose. The last thing I want is bloodshed or wars over the royal succession. Let us be wise and figure out how to sustain the peace.

"I will remain king for the rest of my life," King Mosiah decided, "but let's appoint judges, instead of kings, to keep the law and rule the people according to God's commandments. Men make mistakes in their judgment, but God's judgments are always pure. If we could always have honorable men to be king, as my father Benjamin was, then having kings would be fine. But, remember what happened when corrupt men like King Noah ruled? Remember the destruction and slavery that he brought upon his people?

"Without the intervention of God, Limhi's people would still be enslaved. Because they humbled themselves before him and cried out for his help, they were delivered into freedom. This is how God uses his power. He supports those who put their faith in him. I have learned that you cannot depose a bad king without tremendous conflict and bloodshed. Bad kings surround themselves with bad people and hold onto power by revoking fair laws, trampling on God's commandments, and destroying those who oppose them. Corrupt kings corrupt the righteousness of their people. I don't want these things to happen to my people ever again.

"I want you to choose your own judges so that you can be ruled by the laws of God that have been passed down to us from our ancestors. I trust the collective voice of the people to choose what is right, and make the laws accordingly. If the time comes that the people choose evil over good, then God will bring his anger down and destroy them as he's done before. If the judges you select violate God's laws, make them answer to higher judges that you also select. If the higher judges also violate God's laws, they should be judged by the voice of the people.

"Therefore, I command that you have no king," he concluded, "but instead become responsible and answerable for ruling yourselves. I want you to live in equality and freedom forever. I want every man to enjoy his rights and privileges as long as God lets us live."

King Mosiah wrote about the burdens of trying to be a righteous king and the benefits of spreading that burden among all the people. He expounded upon the liabilities of having bad kings, and in the end the people saw the truth of his words, and abandoned their desire to be ruled by a king.

The people gathered together throughout the land and cast votes for whomever they wanted to be their judges and rule over them. They came to see the wisdom of this, and were happy with their freedom of choice. They now loved and respected King Mosiah more than ever. He had ruled them fairly, established peace, and delivered them from the rule of kings.

The judges who were selected to rule were headed by Alma^2, who was also the head of the church. Alma observed the laws of God and judged the Nephite people fairly. The peace of King Mosiah was sustained throughout Zarahemla under the new reign of judges.

Alma's father, the founder of their church, died at the age of 82, having lived to see the commandments of God fulfilled. King Mosiah died at the age of 63, after having ruled for 33 years. Five hundred nine years had now passed since Lehi and his family left Jerusalem. The reign of kings had ended, and the Nephite people now ruled themselves through their selected judges. [91 BC]

THE BOOK OF ALMA — 92 BC TO 52 BC

From Plates Inscribed by Alma^2, the Son of Alma^1, and his sons, Helaman^2, and Shiblon then Abridged and Later Inscribed onto the Book of Mormon Plates by Mormon

The newly established practice of electing rulers takes hold, although competing interests continue to cause conflict. Alma^2 and the four sons of King Mosiah^2 evangelize among the Nephites and the Lamanites. The term "Christian" is used for the first time to describe followers of Jesus Christ. The wars between the Nephites and Lamanites intensify, claiming hundreds of thousands of casualties.

THE BOOK OF ALMA SUMMARY

The Book of Alma chronicles a 40-year period of upheaval and change for the Nephites. Upon King Mosiah's death, Alma^2 became the head of the church, the elected chief judge, leader of the government, chief warrior of the Nephite army, and keeper of the sacred records. Persecutions of devout church members became rampant. Shortly after the king's death, individuals and groups arose who challenged the rule of the judges. They tried to use the newly established democratic process to subvert the law of God and weaken the church. Failing that, they tried rebellion in an attempt to restore leadership by imperial rule. This, too, was defeated.

Alma appointed a new chief judge to succeed him as political leader, and devoted himself to the role of spiritual leader. He worked to heal the fractures and divisions within the church. Alma traveled broadly, repeating his Christian evangelist theme in one community after another. He preached tirelessly to the Nephite people, and tried to convince them of the importance of following God's laws.

After a 14-year absence, Mosiah's four sons returned to Zarahemla from their mission to convert the Lamanites. They told stories of successes, failures, miracles, and baptisms. They also brought with them a band of Lamanite converts who became Nephites.

The Nephite population expanded greatly and splintered into many special interest groups and factions in different areas of settlement. Some of the Nephite people fell out of righteousness, some maintained their righteousness, and some restored their righteousness through repentance.

The progression of prosperity, peace, sinful living, rejection of God's laws, and repentance ebbed and flowed across the land like tides along a ragged coastline. This upheaval was a backdrop for repeated sermons imploring the Nephite people to follow God's laws or be destroyed, and to maintain faith in the imminent coming of the savior Jesus Christ. Miracles were performed to demonstrate God's power. People who defied or ignored God's laws were destroyed. There is a tremendous repetition of the sermons heard in previous times imploring people to follow the will of God and believe in Jesus Christ. In 72 BC, the term "Christian" is first coined and used as a descriptive name for the people who follow the future teachings of Jesus Christ.

It was a period of intense and repeated wars between the Lamanites and the Nephites, and conflicts between competing Nephite factions. It was a time of Nephite defections to the Lamanites and conflicts between different Lamanite factions. Some former Nephites became Lamanite kings and leaders, through deception and cunning. In general, the Nephites wanted peace and prosperity, while the Lamanites wanted warfare and bloodshed. These two related peoples were in constant conflict. Throughout this period, armies were repeatedly mobilized and hundreds of thousands of people were killed, in alternating periods of peace and war.

The Nephites continued to build great cities and an extensive civilization. The Nephite armies used armor, swords, scimitars, bows and arrows. They organized themselves into military units with a hierarchical chain of command. The Nephites continued their extensive agricultural and animal husbandry practices.

The Lamanites used horse-drawn chariots for transportation and possessed the same sort of weapons and armor as the Nephites. The Lamanites also adopted the practice of tending domesticated livestock and possessed large flocks of animals.

Alma passed custodianship of the records on to his son Helaman[2], and departed on another of his solitary missions to evangelize among the Nephite people. On the way to this last mission, he vanished, never to be heard from again, and legends arose around his disappearance. Some said that he was taken directly up into heaven by the Spirit of God. After his disappearance, Helaman took over as head of a weakened and struggling church.

Around 55 BC, a large northward migration of the Nephite people began. Practically surrounded by an ever-expanding Lamanite population, thousands of men, women, and children left Zarahemla on foot. Thousands more sailed north on ocean-going vessels that were constructed for this purpose.

Helaman passed custodianship of the records to his brother Shiblon. Before Shiblon died, he passed the original set of records on to his nephew, Helaman's son, Helaman[3]. Multiple sets of the sacred records were made and distributed across the land so that all Nephites would be able to remember the words of God.

THE BOOK OF ALMA - TRANSLATION

Chapter 1, 1830 and 1981 Versions

The Nephites were ruled by elected judges after the death of King Mosiah, and Alma was chosen as the first chief judge. Within the first year of his reign, a physically powerful man named Nehor was brought before Alma for judgment. Nehor was charged with priestcraft, coercion, and murder.

Nehor had been preaching an alternate doctrine of God to the Nephites that ran contrary to the teachings of the church. He said that priests should be supported by the people and not have to work personally with their hands. He taught that everyone would be saved on judgment day, and that to live in fear of God's punishment was unnecessary. He said that because God had created all men, all men would be redeemed and live eternally, regardless of how they behaved during their mortal lives. Many people believed Nehor and supported him. Their support inflated his self-importance, purchased his expensive clothing, and allowed him to establish a church of his own.

On his way to preach one day, he met and argued with an older man who belonged to the church of God. As it turned out, this older man was Gideon, who had been instrumental in delivering the people of Limhi from slavery. In a heated debate, Gideon defended the church and criticized Nehor for his impertinence. In anger, Nehor drew his sword and killed Gideon on the spot.

In spite of Nehor's vigorous defense of himself, Alma declared, "Not only are you guilty of priestcraft, you are guilty of trying to enforce your views through violence. If this is allowed to stand, it will result in our complete destruction. Nehor, you have shed the blood of a great man who has done good things for us. If we don't avenge his death, his blood will seek vengeance on us. Therefore, you are condemned to die according to the laws of King Mosiah that have been ratified by the people." Nehor was taken to the top of Manti Hill, where he confessed that his teachings were contrary to the word of God, and was executed.

Unfortunately, this did not put an end to the teaching of false doctrines. There were still plenty of people who delighted in vanity and wealth, and richly supported the priests who condoned their pretensions. Although liars were punished, the false priests claimed protection under the rules allowing freedom of belief.

Robbery and murder were punished harshly, but persecutions of church members by non-members became a rampant problem. Because of the members' humility and free declaration of the word of God, they were verbally abused by those who didn't agree with them. While the rules of the church of God forbade its members from fighting with their persecutors, many did so, anyhow. In this way, the church was challenged from the inside and the outside. Some members were rejected and some left of their own accord. Those who remained became steadfast in keeping the commandments of God, and bore their persecutions with patience.

When the priests set aside their work to preach the word of God, the people set aside their work to listen. Afterwards, everyone including the priests returned to their labors. No one was above anyone else. The teachers were no higher than the learners. Men gave to their brothers according to what they had. The poor, the needy, and the sick were supported, and all were equal. This is how the church operated. Except for the occasional persecutions, there was continual peace among the people.

Due to the great cooperation and steadiness of their church, the members became rich in livestock, grains, gold, silver, silk and fine linens. They shared with one another in such a way that all were clothed and fed, and none of them stood in need.

Those who did not belong to the church indulged in sorcery, idolatry, idleness, gossip, envy, and strife. They wore expensive clothing and puffed themselves up with self-importance. These were the persecutors, liars, thieves, adulterers, and murderers.

To the degree that it was possible, the laws were enforced and people's behavior improved. By the fifth year of elected judges, the Nephites were at peace. [90 BC]

Chapter 2, 1981 Version

Another challenger to Alma's reign came along five years after Nehor. His name was Amlici, and he wanted to be king.

Amlici was a shrewd and persuasive politician who gathered support from people who opposed the church. His political agenda was the destruction of the church of God. When an election was held, the people rejected Amlici's aspirations as king. This was a great relief to those who opposed him but, regrettably, it was not end of the matter.

Amlici's followers anointed him as their king in spite of the electoral loss, and Amlici ordered them to take over by force of arms. This split the country into two factions, the Amlicites and the Nephites (or people of God). Both sides mobilized and prepared for war.

The opposing armies, led by Alma and Amlici, met in battle on a hill above the Sidon River. Because God supported and strengthened the Nephites, a great slaughter of the Amlicites ensued. As the Amlicites fled, the Nephites pursued and killed them. At the day's end, 12,532 Amlicites and 6,562 Nephites lay dead.

That night, Alma sent spies to follow the remnant of the Amlicites' army and discover their enemy's plans. The following day the spies returned, and reported that the Amlicites had joined forces with large numbers of Lamanite warriors. This combined army was now marching across the land toward the Nephite capital city of Zarahemla. Unless Alma's army responded quickly, the city would be overrun, and their families would be killed.

Alma's army broke camp and raced to meet the enemy. As they crossed the Sidon River, they were met by countless Amlicite and Lamanite forces, determined to destroy them. But because God had heard the Nephites' prayers for deliverance from their enemies, the Amlicites and Lamanites fell before them.

When Alma found himself in hand-to-hand combat with Amlici, he cried out, "Spare my life, God, and I will be an instrument in your hands to preserve my people." Having said this, Alma was strengthened and he killed Amlici with his sword. Then Alma went after the Lamanite king, who was defended by his guards. Their attack on the Lamanites was so ferocious that the Lamanites turned and fled, in spite of their numerical advantage.

Alma's army threw the enemy's dead bodies into the river, and crossed it in pursuit of the fleeing Lamanites and Amlicites. The enemy forces were killed, scattered, and driven into the wilderness before the advancing Nephites. For many years afterwards, the enemy's bones could be found heaped in piles upon the earth. [87 BC]

Chapter 3, 1981 Version

The Nephites buried their dead and returned to their homes and families. So many had been killed in the war with the Lamanites and Amlicites that the exact numbers of dead were never known. The casualties included warriors on both sides, and Nephite women, children, and livestock. Vast fields of grain had also been destroyed.

The Amlicites who joined the Lamanites were cursed by God and marked accordingly, as the Lamanites had been, so that they would be forever separate from the Nephites. The Amlicites had condemned themselves by rebelling against the word of God and became Lamanites also. By their example, every man who is cursed by God does so through his own voluntary choice.

Shortly after the defeat of the Lamanites and Amlicites, the Lamanites raised another army with which to make war against the Nephites. Because Alma had been wounded in the previous battle, he didn't personally go to fight this time but sent out an army out to defeat the enemy again. The victorious Nephites drove the Lamanites out of their lands and reestablished peace, for the time being.

Tens of thousands were killed and consigned to their fate. According to their good acts or bad, they were rewarded with eternal happiness, or punished with eternal misery. [87 BC]

Chapter 2, 1830 Version

Chapter 4, 1981 Version

The sixth year of elected judges was free of war, but the Nephites were burdened by the loss of so many people, livestock, and crops. Some wondered whether God had sent these burdens to them as a sign of his displeasure with their sinfulness. As a result, there was a flurry of baptisms and a renewal of the church. In the seventh year of elected judges, peace prevailed, and 3,500 souls were baptized in the church of God. [85 BC]

In the eighth year of elected judges, members of the church displayed signs of pride because of their restored wealth. They wore fine silks and linen, and decorated themselves with gold and silver. Alma, the priests, and the elders of the church were troubled to see these signs of wickedness emerging. The people became ostentatious in their displays of wealth, arrogance towards each other, and abusive responses to those who questioned their behavior. These changes brought about dissension, envy, mean and petty behavior, persecutions, and pridefulness that was often greater within the church than outside of it. Because of this the church began to fail.

In the ninth year of elected judges, Alma saw these examples set by church members extending beyond the church and leading towards the destruction of the people. Great inequalities were developing. The rich turned their backs on the poor, the needy, and the sick. The righteous and faithful members of the church were saddened by what they saw, did what they could to redress these grievances, and looked toward the joy of Jesus Christ and his deliverance from death. Alma remained steadfast in his faithfulness to God. He resigned from his position as the chief judge so that he could devote himself to the affairs and needs of the church.

A new chief judge, named Nephihah, was appointed by the people to rule the land. Acting as the high priest in the church, Alma went out evangelizing among the people and asking them to remember their duties to God. He hoped to reverse their slide into sinfulness and to reclaim their devotion to the church through his direct testimony to them. [83 BC]

Chapter 3, 1830 Version

Chapter 5, 1981 Version

Relieved of his position as chief judge, Alma began preaching to the Nephite people. This is a sermon that he delivered in the city of Zarahemla.

"I have been consecrated by my father Alma as high priest in the church of God. My father was given this authority by God himself as the founder of our church in the land of Nephi. He baptized his brothers in the waters of Mormon. He delivered them first from the wicked King Noah, and then from slavery to the Lamanites through the mercy and power of God.

"In this land of Zarahemla, the church of God has grown and spread among the Nephite people. As members of this church, do you sufficiently remember the slavery of your fathers? Have you sufficiently remembered God's mercy to them? Do you remember that God delivered their souls from hell? God changed them. He has brought them from darkness into the light of his everlasting word. Where before, they were captured by death and the chains of hell, they were released by God, and saved.

"How did this come to happen? It happened because my father believed in the word of God, spoken by the prophet Abinadi. His faith changed my father's heart just as the hearts of your fathers were changed by the words of my father. They humbled themselves before the true and living God, were faithful throughout their lives, and so were saved.

"Don't you know that God has created you in his image? Have your hearts been changed? Do you have faith in God's power to redeem you? Do you look forward to standing before God and being judged by your actions during your lifetime? Can you imagine God saying to you on judgment day, 'Come to me and be blessed for the righteousness of your acts during your mortal life'? Do you think you can lie to God and tell him that your acts have been righteous when they have not been, and that he will save you?

"When that day comes and you stand before God's judgment, you will remember perfectly every unrighteous act that you have committed. You will remember every time that you have defied the commandments of God. Do you think that God will save you, then, if you yielded to the devil and became his subjects? I will tell you now that you cannot be saved unless you are willing to be cleansed of sin. If you have lived a filthy life, you will appear as filth and your appearance will testify against you. If you have murdered, you will be covered with blood.

"Do you suppose that you can hope to join the spotless white company of God, Abraham, Isaac, and Jacob[1] if you are covered with filth? I say, No, you may not, unless God has lied to us

from the beginning. You will be cast out if you are children of the devil.

"Do you want a change of heart? Do you want your sins cleansed white by the blood of Jesus Christ, who will redeem his people from sin? Are you ready to give up your pride? If so, you need to act now, because the kingdom of heaven is coming soon and your mortal life is not eternal.

"Are you willing to give up your envy? Then, do so now, because the hour of judgment is close at hand, and none of us knows when it will come. Do you mock or abuse your brother? If so, then you are not ready to be saved unless you repent. All sinners need to repent because God has told us so. He has opened his merciful arms and said, 'Repent and I will receive you. Come to me and eat the fruit from the tree of life. I freely give you bread to eat and the water of life to drink. Come to me in righteousness and you will not be cast into the fire'.

"The time is at hand for those who have not been righteous to wail and mourn. If you've been sinful, inflated with vanity, or led astray as unwatched sheep, it is time to listen when the shepherd, Jesus Christ, calls out to you. If you are not the sheep of God, you are the sheep of the devil and part of his flock. Those who do good are children of God and those who do evil are children of the devil.

"I have been commanded by God to stand before you and testify of these things to come. I personally know them to be true. I know this because God has answered my prayers and has given me revelations. Our fathers before us have also been given these revelations and told that they were true. I know that Jesus Christ will come to redeem the sins of the world for those who steadfastly believe in him.

"So I say to all of you, repent and be born again. And the Spirit of God says, 'Repent for the kingdom of heaven is soon at hand and the Son of God is coming. Unless you repent, you cannot inherit the kingdom of heaven. Those who do not repent will be cut down and cast into the eternal fire'.

"I ask, how can you set these words aside and trample upon the will of God? How can you allow yourselves to be inflated with pride? Will you persist in wearing expensive clothing and setting your hearts on riches? Will you persist in thinking of yourselves as better than your neighbors, and abusing your brothers who remain humble before God? Will you persist in turning your backs on the poor and withholding your support from them? Unless you quickly repent your sins, you will be cast into the fire.

"Become righteous, I say, and honor the word of God so that you will be saved. The names of the righteous will be written in the book of life and the names of the sinners will be blotted out. God calls out to you. If you listen, he will bring you into his flock and you can become his sheep where the ravenous wolf cannot hurt you.

"I command you now, in the same language that I have been commanded, to do as I have said. I command you to come be baptized and seek repentance so that you may eat the fruit of the tree of life." [83 BC]

Chapter 4, 1830 Version

Chapter 6, 1981 Version

By the laying on of his hands, Alma ordained priests and elders to watch over the church. Those who did not belong to the church and wanted to repent were baptized and received into the church. Those church members who did not repent were rejected from the church, and their names were erased so that they would not be confused with the righteous. Everyone had an opportunity to join the church and receive the word of God.

The followers of God were commanded to gather to fast, and pray often, for the welfare of those who didn't know God. After setting forth these instructions and rules, Alma moved on to other cities, delivering his message and restoring the church of God in other places. [83 BC]

Chapter 5, 1830 Version

Chapter 7, 1981 Version

This is the sermon that Alma delivered to the people of Gideon.

"Now that I have retired from political leadership, I am able to come and speak with you about matters of God. I have come hoping to find you humbled and blameless before him, and not in the horrible state that our brothers in Zarahemla were. They have now repented and been restored to righteousness. I trust that you have not fallen as far as your brothers in

Zarahemla have and that you look forward to the remission of your sins that will come. The time when Jesus Christ the redeemer will come and live among people is not far away.

"The Spirit has told me to prepare the way for God, and walk the straight path, because the kingdom of heaven is at hand when the Son of God comes to earth. He will be born of a virgin named Mary and will be conceived by the power of the Holy Ghost. The Son of God will be born in Jerusalem, in the land of our ancestors. During his mortal life he will suffer pain, abuse, and temptation of every kind. He will take upon himself the pains and sickness of his people. He will take death upon himself so that he may release his people from the bondage of death. He will take upon himself his people's sickness so that he may be filled with mercy and the knowledge of how to heal them. He will take upon himself the sins of his people so that they may be delivered from them. This is my testimony.

"If you want to be born again, you must repent. If you are not born again, you cannot inherit the kingdom of heaven. Come be baptized and cleansed of your sins, and have faith in Jesus Christ, who will take away the sins of the world. Set aside your sins and show God of your willingness to repent. Make a covenant with God to keep his commandments, and witness it by being baptized in water. Whoever does this will have eternal life.

"Do you believe these things? I know that you do believe, because your faith is strong. I perceive that you do walk the straight path of righteousness that leads to the kingdom of God. You know that you cannot walk on crooked paths or live in filth, and be received into the kingdom of God. When the judgment day comes, those who have lived in filth will remain in filth.

"I have said these things to awaken you to your sense of duty to God at all times, giving thanks to God for whatever you receive. I want you to see that if you have faith, hope, and charity that you will always be fulfilling the good work that is asked of you. May God bless you and keep you clean so that you may sit down with Abraham, Isaac, Jacob[1], and the holy prophets who are also clean. I rejoice because of the attention you've paid to receiving my word. May the peace of God rest upon you, your houses, lands, livestock and all you possess, your women and children, from this time forever forward." [83 BC]

Chapter 6, 1830 Version

Chapter 8, 1981 Version

After Alma had restored the church in Gideon, as he had in Zarahemla, he returned home to rest. In the tenth year of elected judges, Alma traveled to the land of Melek to preach and restore the church. Again, people came to him and were baptized.

After he finished his work in Melek, he traveled to the land of Ammonihah to preach the word of God. But Satan had taken hold of the people there, and they refused to listen to him. Alma prayed mightily to God that the people would repent and be baptized. Still they rejected him, saying, "We know you are the high priest of the church in other places, but here we do not believe such foolish traditions. Because we aren't part of your church, you have no power over us. You are no longer chief judge over us, either. Go away."

The people of Ammonihah rebuked Alma, threw him out, and spat upon him. He left Ammonihah discouraged, and continued his mission, traveling next toward the city of Aaron. He was traveling in sorrow and anguish because of the horrible treatment he'd received from the unrepentant and wicked people of Ammonihah, when an angel of God appeared to him. "You are blessed," the angel said, "so lift up your head and rejoice. You have been faithful in keeping the commandments of God ever since you first received God's message. I know this, because I am the same angel who delivered that message to you, long ago. God has sent me now to command that you return to Ammonihah and deliver his word to those people. Tell them that unless they repent, God will destroy them. They threaten to destroy the freedom of your people by violating the laws and commandments God has given to his people."

With the angel's words to spur him on, Alma wasted no time returning. When he reached Ammonihah he was hungry, so he identified himself as a servant of God to a man whom he met, and asked for something to eat. "I am a Nephite," the man answered, "and I know you are a holy prophet of God. An angel came to me in a vision and told me that you would be coming. I would be honored if you would come and eat with me at my home." The man's name was Amulek.

After a good meal, Alma blessed Amulek and his house, and gave thanks to God. He told Amulek of his mission, his previous reception by the people of Ammonihah, and God's command that he return to testify against their sinfulness. Having fasted while he'd traveled, Alma spent many days resting with Amulek before he began his preaching.

Alma received a revelation that Amulek should help him preach to the people of Ammonihah. They were told to relate the prophecy given by the angel: that the people had better repent, or God would demonstrate his fierce anger with them. To show his power, God would make it impossible for him, or Amulek, to be imprisoned or killed by their enemies. As they preached and prophesied, they were filled with the spirit and power of God that had been given to them. [82 BC]

Chapter 7, 1830 Version

Chapter 9, 1981 Version

When Alma went out and preached to the people of Ammonihah again, he was challenged.

"Who are you," they asked, "that we should believe in your testimony, even if you tell us that the world will end? If you tell us that our great city will be destroyed in a single day, we won't believe it. Who is God to send you among us and declare the truth of such things?"

When the people of Ammonihah tried to seize Alma, they found that they could not do so. "You are a wicked and perverse generation of people to have forgotten the tradition of our ancestors," Alma said to them. "Do you forget how God led them through the wilderness? Have you forgotten how many times God delivered our ancestors from their enemies and saved them from destruction at the hands of the Lamanites? If it had not been for his unequaled power and mercy, we would have been swept from the earth long before now. Without his mercy, we might have been consigned to eternal suffering.

"God commands you to repent. If you don't, you cannot inherit the kingdom of God. But that is not all. If you don't repent, God will utterly destroy you, and nothing can turn his fierce anger away. Don't you remember the words he said to Lehi? 'If you keep my commandments, you will prosper. If you do not keep my commandments, you will be cut off.'

"I want you to remember that the Lamanites have not kept God's commandments and have been cut off just as God said. Even so, they will be shown more tolerance than you, if you remain in your sins without repentance. God will show their descendants mercy because they have been born into ignorance through the tradition of their ancestors. At some time, they will come to believe in God's word, to know the error of their ancestors. Many of them will be saved who believe in his name. But, if you persist in your sinfulness, your days will not be long. The Lamanites will suddenly and unexpectedly be sent to utterly destroy you. This will happen according to God's will and anger. After having given you so much, he will not tolerate your sinfulness, and would rather see you destroyed.

"You have been a highly favored people of God. You have been favored above all other people. You have had things made known to you, and have been shown that which is to come. Your ancestors have been visited by the Spirit of God, visited by angels, and seen the spirit of prophecy and revelation. They have been delivered out of Jerusalem, saved from starvation, and sickness, protected from destruction in battles, and delivered from slavery time after time. Because of this, you have prospered and become rich.

"Having received so many blessings, if you should now reject God's light and knowledge, you will be far worse off than the Lamanites. God has made promises to them that do not apply to you. He promises that if you don't repent, you will be utterly destroyed. God has sent out angels among us saying, 'Repent now, because the kingdom of heaven is at hand. Soon, the Son of God will come in his glory, full of grace, equity, truth, patience, mercy, and suffering, eager to hear the cries of his people and answer their prayers. He will come to redeem those who are baptized and repent in his name. Prepare the way of God, for the time is at hand when men will reap a reward

according to how they have been. If they have been righteous, they will find salvation of their souls according to the power and deliverance of Jesus Christ. If they have been evil, they shall find damnation of their souls and slavery to the devil.' This is what the angel has said.

"You are my beloved brothers. I want you to repent and see that your hearts have been hardened against the word of God. I want you to see that you are a lost and fallen people."

The people were angry with Alma when he finished because their pride and stubbornness had been inflamed. As stirred up as they were, the people of Ammonihah were still unable to seize and imprison Alma. They found that God's protection made it impossible for them to even touch him.

Amulek then stepped forward, and he, too, preached to the people of Ammonihah. [82 BC]

Chapter 8, 1830 Version

Chapter 10, 1981 Version

This is what Amulek said.

"I am Amulek, the son of Giddonah, who was descended from Nephi, who was a descendant of Manasseh, the son of Joseph[1] of Egypt. You all know me well. I have many friends and relatives among you. As you know, I've worked hard for my prosperity.

"Until now, I have paid very little attention to the mysteries of God. I see now that this was a mistake, because I have seen his power and how he preserves our people. My heart was closed and I couldn't hear when I was called. I would have continued rebelling against God, except that something happened to me recently when I traveled to see a relative. An angel of God appeared to me and said, 'Amulek, go back to your home. You need to meet and feed a holy prophet of God, who will come to you. He will be hungry after fasting for many days, and I want you to take him home with you. He will bless you and your home, and the blessings of God will also rest on you and your home.' On my way back, I found him. He is this man, Alma, who has just spoken to you. I know that he is a holy man because the angel of God told me so. I know what Alma says is true, because God has sent an angel to my home and told me so. Alma has blessed my entire household."

When Amulek had spoken, the people were astounded to hear that one of their own people validated Alma's words. There were slick and skillful lawyers among the people who tried to trick Alma and Amulek into saying something incriminating enough to justify imprisonment or death. They wanted to force Alma and Amulek to contradict themselves, and thus to condemn them as liars. Amulek knew their intentions, because he perceived their thoughts. "You are a wicked and perverse generation of people," he said. "You lawyers and hypocrites are laying the foundation of the devil when you try and set traps to catch God's holy servants. Your attempts to pervert the ways of righteous people will result in bringing down God's anger and the destruction of our people.

"Our late King Mosiah foresaw that, if the time came when the people chose sinfulness, they would be ripe for destruction. God says to us through his angels that the kingdom of heaven is at hand, and commands us to repent. He will come down to us with justice in his hands. If it were not for the prayers of the righteous among us, we would be destroyed by starvation, disease, and warfare. It is only by the prayers of the righteous that you are spared. If you throw out the righteous among us, nothing can stop God's anger. Repent, before it is too late."

"This man violates our laws and slanders the wise lawyers that we have selected," the people responded angrily.

"How has Satan come to have such a great hold on your hearts?" Amulek asked passionately. "Will you yield to his power and let him blind your eyes? Won't you please listen to the truth that I've spoken? I have not testified against your law, but rather have used it to condemn you. Your sinful lawyers and judges are the very ones who prepare your destruction."

When Amulek finished, the people cried out against him. "You are a child of the devil," they said. "You lie to us. You speak against our laws and then deny it. You vilify our esteemed lawyers and judges."

The offended lawyers marked Amulek's words. They would be ready to oppose Alma when the opportunity presented itself. These lawyers were looking out for what was good for them, regardless of the truth. Foremost among

those to take offense was a man named Zeezrom, who stood to gain the most by Amulek's demise. [82 BC]

Chapter 11, 1981 Version

The law of Mosiah provided that judges would receive a wage according to the time they spent on the cases before them. If someone refused to pay a debt, he was called before a judge, who heard the evidence. When the evidence was ruled upon, people were compelled to pay what they owed or were cast out as thieves.

For many judges, the sole purpose of taking the job was to get paid. They conspired to create riots and disturbances to get more employment from the resulting lawsuits brought before them. Now, they conspired against Alma and Amulek.

Zeezrom was very skilled in the ways of the devil and sought to destroy that which was good. He asked Amulek, "Will you answer a few questions for me?"

"Yes," Amulek replied. "But I will say nothing contrary to the spirit of God which is in me."

"Here is a small bag of silver. I will give this to you if you will deny the existence of God," Zeezrom said.

"Why do you tempt me, you child of hell?" Amulek asked. "The righteous do not yield to temptations. You know there is a God, but unfortunately you love money more than him. You have no intention of giving me this money, anyhow. You just want to see if you can buy my denial of God so that you can destroy me. For this evil, you will receive your just reward."

"So, you say there is a true and living God?" asked Zeezrom.

"Yes, there is a true and living God."

"Is there more than one God?" asked Zeezrom.

"No," replied Amulek.

"How do you know this?"

"An angel has told me," said Amulek.

"And who is it that will come, the Son of God?" asked Zeezrom.

"Yes."

"Will he save his people in their sins?" Zeezrom inquired.

"He will not. It is impossible for him to violate his word," answered Amulek.

Zeezrom turned to the people and said, "Remember his answer. He has said there is but one God. He says that the Son of God will come, but will not save his people. Amulek, here, seems to think he has authority to command God."

"That is a lie," Amulek responded. "You said that I spoke as if I had authority to command God, because I said he would not save his people in their sins. What I said was that he cannot violate his word. God has said that no unclean thing can inherit the kingdom of heaven. How can you be saved unless you inherit the kingdom of heaven? Therefore, you cannot be saved in your sins."

"Is the Son of God the very Eternal Father?" asked Zeezrom.

"Yes. He is the very Eternal Father of heaven and of earth, and all things in them. He is the beginning and the end, the first and the last," answered Amulek. "He will come to the world to redeem his people and he will take upon himself the sins of those who believe in his name. Only those who believe in him will have eternal life and salvation. The wicked will remain as they were, but will not die. Everyone will arise from the dead and stand in judgment before God according to their actions. Jesus Christ's death will raise the dead from their temporal death. The spirit and the body will be reunited in perfect form. We will be brought to stand before God just as we are now, knowing everything, and in perfect remembrance of all our guilt. This restoration will come to all, young and old, enslaved and free, men and women, wicked and righteous. Not even a hair of their heads will be lost. Each of us will be arraigned before the court of God's justice to be judged according to our actions, whether they are good or whether they are evil. Our mortal bodies will be raised to immortal bodies with their spirits united together, never to be divided. The whole will become spiritual and immortal. There will be no more corruption."

When Amulek finished speaking, the people were astounded and Zeezrom began to tremble. [82 BC]

Chapter 9, 1830 Version

Chapter 12, 1981 Version

Zeezrom was silenced because Amulek had caught him in his attempts at lying and deception. Zeezrom's efforts to destroy Amulek had failed, and now he trembled at the consciousness of his own guilt. Seeing this, Alma explained the scriptures and expanded on what Amulek had said. Many people were gathered around to listen.

"Zeezrom," Alma said, "you have lied to your people and you have lied to God, for all of your thoughts have been revealed to us by the Spirit of God. As you can see, we know all about your devil's plan to deceive the people and turn them against us. The devil has a hold on you and exercises his power through you. What I'm going to say to you, Zeezrom, also applies to all the rest of you. You are caught in a trap that the devil has laid to catch people. He seeks to bind you with his chains and tie you down to eternal destruction and slavery."

After Alma spoke, Zeezrom trembled even more, because he'd become convinced that Alma and Amulek spoke through the power of God, and that they truly knew his thoughts and intentions through the spirit of prophecy. "What did Amulek mean when he spoke of the resurrection of the dead? He said that both the good and the evil would rise from the dead and stand in judgment before God according to their actions."

"The mysteries of God are revealed to many, but the understanding of his word is withheld according to the degree of people's devotion to him. Those who are closed to God are able to receive less of his word, and therefore become easy prey of the devil. These are the chains of hell.

"Amulek has spoken truthfully about death, about being raised from death, and about judgment by God according to your actions. Those who rebel against God's word will be condemned by their own words, thoughts, and actions. In this depraved state you cannot look at God, and would prefer to hide from his presence. But you cannot hide from God's judgment. When you stand before him in his glory, power, majesty, and dominion, and acknowledge your shame, you will see that his judgments are fair. He has the power to save any man who believes in his name, who does good work, and who seeks repentance.

"Those who die in sinfulness will experience a second death, or spiritual death. They will find themselves in a place of eternal fire and burning sulfur. They will be chained down in slavery to eternal destruction under the power of Satan's will. They cannot be redeemed by God's justice and they cannot die."

The people were astounded, when Alma finished speaking. A ruler among them came forward and asked, "Are you saying that men will rise from the dead and be changed from mortals to immortals who will never die? What, then, does the scripture mean that says, an angel and flaming sword will be placed by God on the edge of the garden of Eden to prevent Adam and Eve from returning to eat from the tree of life, and thus live forever?"

"I was just about to explain that," said Alma. "We know that Adam fell by eating the forbidden fruit of knowledge. Because of his fall, we have all fallen, and become lost people. If Adam had eaten also the fruit from the tree of life, he wouldn't have died and God's word would have been meaningless. This would have made God a liar for having said, 'If you eat, you will surely die.'

"We can all see that death comes to mankind. But you can repent during your life and prepare to meet God's redemption after your resurrection from death. If, when the world was created, there was no plan for redemption, there would be no resurrection from death. But there was such a plan laid out, and the resurrection that we speak of will occur.

"If Adam and Eve had eaten from the tree of life, they would have been miserable forever, without God's redemption. But this is not the way it is. Men must die and then, after their death, be judged. In order to let men know where they stood, God sent angels to tell them his plan, and show them his glory. From that time forward, God let them know of his plan for their redemption according to their faith, repentance, and good works. He gave them his commandments and showed them the difference between good and evil, the penalty for ignoring his word, and the reward for their compliance with his laws. Without such a plan, redemption would have no power and

justice could not be served according to the supreme goodness of God.

"God called on men through Jesus Christ saying, 'If you repent and open your hearts, then I will have mercy on you through my son Jesus Christ, and grant you a remission of your sins. Whoever closes his heart to me through sinfulness will receive my anger and be cast out.'

"So, my brothers, I say to you that if you close your hearts to God, you will not enter into eternal rest with God. If you provoke him, he will send down his anger in provocation according to the promises he's made, and consign you to the everlasting destruction of your souls. Since you now know these things, I beg you to repent so that you don't receive his anger. Receive the blessings that he has prepared instead." [82 BC]

Chapter 13, 1981 Version

"I want you to think ahead to when God gives these commandments to his people," Alma continued. "God ordained priests based on the holy order of Jesus Christ to teach these things to his people, so that they would look forward to his Son for redemption.

"This is how God's priests came to be ordained. They were called and prepared from the beginning of the world, based on God's foreknowledge of their great faith and good works. Then, they were left to choose between good and evil. Their choice of good then became a demonstration of their holy calling and their preparation to be priests. Their purpose for being called and ordained into the high priesthood and holy order of God is to teach his commandments to his people, so that they might also enter into heaven. This high priesthood is an order that has always been here, since the beginning of time, and will always be here, through eternity. Ordained high priests therefore become high priests forever in the order of Jesus Christ."

Chapter 10, 1830 Version

"After being ordained and sanctified, high priests are cleansed by the blood of Jesus Christ," Alma continued. "After being cleansed, they cannot look upon sin without revulsion. Now, I ask that you should humble yourselves before God and offer up your repentance so that you may enter God's place of rest.

"I ask that you humble yourselves, as the people did in the days of Melchizedek. Melchizedek was a high priest from the order of which I've spoken, to whom Abraham paid tithes in the amount of one tenth of all that he owned. The people who followed these ordinances did so in order that they could look forward to Jesus Christ, a remission of their sins, and the opportunity to enter the resting place of God. During Melchizedek's time as king of Salem, the people were filled with all manner of sinfulness and abomination.

"Melchizedek exercised great faith and was ordained as high priest in the holy order of God. When he preached repentance to his people, they repented, and Melchizedek established peace in the land during his time. And so he became known as the prince of peace. There were many high priests before him and many afterwards, but none of them was greater. The scriptures are before you. If you refuse their message, it will be the cause of your own destruction.

"Now is the time to repent, because the day of salvation approaches. The angels of God are declaring this good news to all nations across the face of the earth. They have also come to us and made it known in no uncertain terms that we are highly favored people in this distant land. They ask us to prepare our hearts to receive the word of Jesus Christ in his coming glory. We can only wait to hear the good news from the angels, because I don't know how soon he will arrive. It might be any day. Whether he comes sooner or later, I still rejoice in it. When he does come, good and holy men will hear of it from the mouths of angels because that is the prophecy which will be fulfilled.

"From my innermost heart, I wish that you would listen to my words. My anxiety is so great that I am in pain. Do not procrastinate. Cast off your sins. Humble yourselves before God, call on his holy name, pray continually, and do not be tempted beyond your ability to resist. Allow yourselves to be led by the Holy Spirit to become humble, meek, submissive, patient, filled with love, and long suffering. Have faith in God that you will receive eternal life and the love of God in your hearts, so that you will be lifted up on judgment day and enter God's place

of rest. May God grant you repentance so that you are spared his anger and consignment to the second death of hell." [82 BC]

Chapter 14, 1981 Version

Many people believed Alma's words and began to repent. They went home and read the scriptures.

Most people in Ammonihah, though, were angry with Alma and Amulek for their criticisms and accusations of sinfulness. They argued that their laws, lawyers, and judges had been vilified. These people wanted to destroy Alma and Amulek. They tied them up with strong ropes and brought them before the chief judge.

Many people testified against Alma and Amulek, and the officials charged them with slander and violation of laws. They were also accused of heresy for saying there was only one God, who would send his Son Jesus Christ among them, but would not save them all.

When Zeezrom heard the accusations, he was upset, because he knew he'd been instrumental in blinding the people's minds with his lies. The awareness of his own guilt created within him the pains of hell; so he went before the court proceedings and said, "It is me who is guilty, not them. Alma and Amulek are spotless before God." When he pled in their behalf, Zeezrom was vilified and spat upon by the people. He was accused of being possessed by the devil.

Those who believed Alma and Amulek were cast out, and men were sent to throw stones at them. The believers were then gathered up as a group and set on fire, along with all their scriptures. As the people were being burned to death, Alma and Amulek were brought forward to witness their destruction.

Amulek saw the suffering of the women and children being consumed by the fire, and suffered also. "How can we stand by and watch this atrocity?" he asked. "Let us extend our hands to exercise the power of God within us, and save them from the flames."

"The Spirit prevents me from interfering," Alma said, "for behold, God receives them in glory. He suffers that anyone would do such a thing. The judgments that he will exercise in his anger against the oppressors will be just, and the blood of the innocent will be witness against them on their judgment day."

"Perhaps they will burn us, too," said Amulek.

"Only if it is the will of God," said Alma. "But our work here is not finished, so we will not be burned."

When the bodies and the scriptures had been consumed in the fire, the chief judge stood before them and struck them in the face, saying, "After seeing this, will you dare to preach to our people again about being cast into lakes of fire and burning sulfur? Neither you nor God had any power to save those we threw in the fire, even though they believed in your faith."

He hit them again, and asked "What do you have to say for yourselves?" When they didn't answer, he hit them yet again, and ordered his officers to throw them into prison.

Three days later, Alma and Amulek were taken from their prison cell and interviewed by antagonistic lawyers, judges, priests, and teachers. But they said nothing in response to their interrogation.

The next day the inquisitors came again. The judge hit them in their faces. Others came forward and struck them, and spat upon them. "Will you stand and judge this people again? Will you condemn our laws? If you have such great power, then why don't you try delivering yourselves? How will we look when we are damned?" They were mocked and deprived of food and water for many days. Their clothes were stripped from them and they were left naked, bound, and imprisoned.

Many days later, the chief judge came and hit them again. "If you have the power of God, deliver yourselves and we will consider believing that God will destroy us, as you've described." Then all of their tormentors proceeded to hit them, and said the same thing.

When the last of them had finished their foul work, the power of God filled Alma and Amulek. They rose to their feet and Alma cried out, "How long, God, must we suffer this abuse? Give us the strength according to our faith in Jesus Christ, to deliver ourselves." Thereupon they snapped the ropes that bound them. When their tormentors saw this, they fled. The fear of destruction overcame them and they fell to the ground. The earth shook powerfully and the walls of the prison collapsed around them. Everyone inside, except Alma and Amulek, was killed.

The roar of the prison's collapse brought people into the streets. When Alma and Amulek stepped forth from the wreckage, unhurt, the people saw what had happened and ran from them in terror.

Chapter 15, 1981 Version

After the destruction of the prison, Alma and Amulek were ordered to leave the city of Ammonihah. When they proceeded to the land of Sidom, they found the people of Ammonihah who had been cast out and stoned for believing in their words. The people related stories of what had happened to them and of how they had been delivered.

In Sidom, Zeezrom lay sick with a burning fever caused by his remorse. He presumed that Alma and Amulek had been killed, and he assumed personal responsibility for it. The accumulation of his multiple sins was driving Zeezrom insane with guilt and scorching him internally. When Zeezrom learned that Alma and Amulek were alive, and in Sidom, his heart was encouraged. He sent a message asking them to come to him.

Alma and Amulek found Zeezrom sick in bed and burning with fever because of his past sinfulness. When he saw them, he stretched out his hand and asked them if they could heal him. Alma took him by the hand and asked, "Do you believe in the power of salvation through Jesus Christ?"

"Yes," Zeezrom answered, "I believe in everything that you've taught."

"If you believe in the redemption of Jesus Christ, you can be healed," said Alma.

"Yes, I believe in accordance with your words," said Zeezrom.

"Lord God," Alma cried out, "have mercy on this man, and heal him according to his faith in Jesus Christ." When Alma said this, Zeezrom leapt to his feet and began to walk. News of this astonishing recovery quickly spread throughout Sidom. Afterwards, Alma baptized Zeezrom and he became a preacher of God's word from that time forward.

Alma established a church in Sidom, and consecrated priests and teachers to give baptisms. People flocked from all around the region to be baptized.

The people of Ammonihah never repented, and attributed Alma's power to the devil.

Amulek was rejected by his family and friends in Ammonihah, and gave up his wealth for the word of God. After establishing the church firmly in Sidom, Alma returned again to Zarahemla. He took Amulek with him into his own house, where he counseled him, and strengthened his faith in God. [81 BC]

Chapter 11, 1830 Version

Chapter 16, 1981 Version

Zarahemla was at peace when Alma and Amulek returned; but in the 11th year of elected judges, another war with the Lamanites began. The Lamanites attacked along the border lands beside the wilderness starting at Ammonihah. By the time the Nephites raised an army to defend the land, Ammonihah had been destroyed and all the people had been killed. In other lands, the Lamanites took captives with them back into the wilderness.

The chief captain of the Nephite army came to Alma to ask whether or not the captives might be recovered. Engaging his spirit of prophecy, Alma inquired of God, and learned that the Lamanite war party would cross the Sidon River in the south wilderness. God told Alma that if they met the Lamanites at that point, the captives could be delivered from their bondage through the power of God; so the Nephite army went to the appointed place.

When the Nephite army came upon the Lamanites, they scattered them and drove them back into the wilderness. All of the captives were recovered without a single loss.

Except for the people of Ammonihah there were no casualties, and the captives were all able to return to their homes. The people of Ammonihah had believed that their great city could not be destroyed, but in a single day it was leveled. The dead were mangled by dogs and wild beasts, and their bodies heaped in piles were covered only with a shallow layer of dirt. Because of the stench, the area remained desolate and uninhabited for many years to come.

For several years, there was peace between the Nephites and Lamanites. Alma and Amulek continued to preach about the importance of repentance, in the temples, sanctuaries, and synagogues that were built. Throughout the Nephite lands, the church was restored among the Nephite people. There was equality among the people and God poured out his Spirit across the land. The minds of men were prepared to receive the word about the coming of Jesus Christ.

The priests spoke out against lies, deception, envy, conflict, hatred, theft, plunder, murder, adultery, and lust. They spoke also about the coming of Jesus Christ, his suffering, death, and resurrection. Many of the people wanted to know where he would appear, and were told that he would come to them after his resurrection. The people were glad and joyful to hear this. In the 14th year of elected judges, the word of God was preached in its purity throughout the Nephite lands and God poured his blessings down upon his people. [78 BC]

Chapter 12, 1830 Version

Chapter 17, 1981 Version

Alma was traveling southward from Gideon to Manti when he unexpectedly met Mosiah's four sons returning to Zarahemla from their travels in the land of Nephi. These were the same companions who had been with Alma when the angel appeared, that had changed all of their lives. Alma was pleased to learn that they were still his brothers in God. Their faith had grown stronger through prayer and fasting. Because they possessed the spirit of prophecy and revelation, they had taught with the power and authority of God. For 14 years they preached the word of God among the Lamanites. They had great successes and made many converts through the power of their words. They had also met with great troubles, and had suffered physically and mentally in their labors.

After declining King Mosiah's offer to rule, the four brothers had traveled into the Lamanite lands with the intent to be instruments of God's hand in bringing the Lamanites to a correct understanding of the truth, and the incorrectness of their ancestors' traditions. God answered their prayers and fasting with a personal visit, in which he said, "Be comforted. Go among the Lamanites to establish my word. Your mission will require patience in suffering. If you act as good examples to them, your efforts will be the salvation of many." Hearing this, Mosiah's sons and their party were encouraged.

When they reached the borders of the Lamanite lands the brothers disbanded and went their separate ways. They trusted in God to bring them together again at the end of their mission. They had chosen to do the work of bringing the word of God to the wild, hardened, and ferocious Lamanites. These were people who took pleasure in killing Nephites. They robbed and plundered them for their coveted riches of gold, silver, and precious stones. The Lamanites were lazy people who worshipped idols and didn't want to bother producing riches for themselves. Since they followed the sinful tradition of their ancestors God's curse had fallen upon them, until such time as they repented. Mosiah's sons brought them word of God's plan, the opportunity for repentance, and redemption.

Ammon[2] was the leader among Mosiah's sons. He blessed his brothers on their missions and went alone into the land of Ishmael, named after the sons of Ishmael from Jerusalem who had also become Lamanites. He was soon discovered, tied up, and brought before King Lamoni, who would decide whether he would be killed, enslaved, freed, or imprisoned.

The king asked whether Ammon wished to live in the Ishmaelites' lands or the Lamanite lands. Ammon replied that he wanted to live among the Ishmaelites, maybe even for the rest of his life. King Lamoni accepted Ammon, released him, and asked him to marry one of his daughters. Ammon declined the offer of marriage but volunteered to become King Lamoni's servant.

Ammon was assigned the task of herding sheep along with some of the king's other servants. Several days after his assignment, King Lamoni's servants and some Lamanite shepherds all were driving their flocks to water at the same time and place. The Lamanites scattered King Lamoni's flocks, so that the sheep took off in all directions. King Lamoni's servants were horrified and wept in fear of losing their lives. "The king will kill us," they said, "as he killed others who allowed his flocks to be scattered and lost."

When Ammon saw this he was filled with joy. He knew that this apparent tragedy gave him an opportunity to show his power by restoring the king's flocks, and winning the trust of his fellow servants. He said to them, "My brothers, be cheerful and let's go look for the flocks, gather them up, and bring them back to the water. If we do this, the king will not kill us."

Following Ammon, they quickly gathered the flocks together and returned them to the water to drink. When the Lamanite herders tried to scatter their flocks again, Ammon directed his fellow shepherds, saying, "Encircle our flocks to ensure that they do not get away, and I will go contend with these men who attempt to scatter them."

The Lamanite herders were numerous and had no fear of Ammon. They thought they could kill him any time they wanted to. They didn't know that God had promised Mosiah that he would deliver his sons from harm. They didn't know anything about the ways of God. They took delight in scattering King Lamoni's flocks and got ready to do it again. But Ammon stood his ground and used his sling to cast stones at them with great power and accuracy, killing six of the Lamanite herders. The Lamanites were astonished with his power, and angry because of their dead brothers. The Lamanites tried to cast stones at Ammon and kill him, but failed. Then they came at him with clubs; but Ammon cut the arm off every man who lifted his club against him. When the leader was killed by Ammon's sword, the attackers fled in fear of his strength.

Ammon returned to water the flocks and bring them to pasture again.

His fellow herders collected the severed arms and later presented them to the king, and bore testimony as to what they'd seen. [90 BC]

Chapter 18, 1981 Version

After King Lamoni's servants testified about what they'd seen, the king learned of Ammon's faithfulness in protecting his flocks, and his prowess and power in defending himself against those who sought to kill him. He was astonished. "Surely this is more than a man," he said. "Is this the Great Spirit who avenges the Lamanites because of their murders?"

"We don't know whether he is the Great Spirit or a man," they answered. "What we do know is that your enemies cannot kill him. Neither can they scatter your flocks when he is with, us because he is strong and highly skilled. Therefore, we know that he is a friend to the king. And because he cannot be killed, his powers seem greater than a man's."

After listening to his servants, the king said, "Now I know that he is the Great Spirit whom our fathers have spoken of. He has come down at this time to preserve your lives, because if you had allowed my flocks to be scattered again, I would have had you killed as I did others before you."

The Lamanite king suddenly questioned his wisdom in killing those other servants who'd allowed his flocks to be scattered. He became fearful that he might have to answer to this powerful new man for this past killing. "Where is this man with so much power?" he asked.

He was told that Ammon was dutifully feeding the king's horses, and was even further astonished. Before the incident with the sheep, he had ordered his servants to prepare his horses and chariots for a visit to his father in the land of Nephi. King Lamoni's father, who was king over all the land, was hosting a great feast.

"No one else among you is as faithful to my commands as this man, who remembers and executes them," the king said. "Surely this is the Great Spirit. I'd like to talk with him, but I don't dare to."

When Ammon had prepared the horses and chariots, he went in to see the king. Judging by the look on the king's face, he thought perhaps he should leave, but the servants said to him, "Great One, the king would like you to stay."

Ammon turned to the king and asked, "What can I do for you, my king?"

The king didn't know what to say, and so an hour went by without him responding. Again, Ammon asked what he could do, and again the king was unable to answer. But Ammon was filled with the Spirit of God and he was able to read the king's thoughts. "Are you speechless because you've heard how I defended your flocks and servants with my sling and sword?" he asked. "Do you marvel that I was able to kill seven of your enemies and cut the arms off of many others who sought to injure you? What have I done that was so great?

I'm a man, your servant. Whatever you want that is right, I will do."

The king heard Ammon's words and was astounded that he could read his thoughts. "Who are you?" he asked. "Are you the Great Spirit who knows all things?"

"I am not," Ammon replied.

"How do you know my thoughts?" the king asked. "Tell me about this, and tell me how you killed and maimed the Lamanites who scattered my flocks. If you tell me, I will guard you with my armies even though I know you are more powerful than all of them. Whatever you want of me, I will grant to you."

"Will you listen to my words," Ammon asked, "if I tell you about the power by which I do these things? This is all I want from you."

"Yes," answered the king, "I will believe whatever you say."

"Do you believe there is a God?" asked Ammon.

"I don't know what you mean," replied the king.

"Do you believe there is a Great Spirit?" Ammon asked.

"Yes," the king said.

"That is God," Ammon responded. "Do you believe that this Great Spirit, or God, created everything in heaven and earth?"

"I believe he created all things on earth," replied the king, "but I don't know what heaven is."

"Heaven is a place where God lives with all his holy angels," Ammon explained.

"Is it above the earth?" the king asked.

"Yes," answered Ammon. "God looks down on man, and knows the intents and thoughts of everyone because he created them in the first place."

"I believe what you say," the king said. "Are you sent by God?"

"I am a man, and man was originally created in the image of God," Ammon said. "I am called by his Holy Spirit to teach these things to your people so that they many learn what is honest and true. Some of God's spirit resides in me, giving me knowledge and power according to my faith in him."

Ammon talked about the creation of the world, Adam, and the fall of man, to the king and his assembled servants. He recited the holy scriptures and the words of the prophets from the past through the time when their common ancestor, Lehi, had left Jerusalem. He told the story of Lehi[1] and his family's journey through the wilderness and the hardships they had endured. He spoke of the rebellion of Laman, Lemuel, and the sons of Ishmael. Ammon recited the records and prophecies of his people from the time of Lehi's departure through the present time. He told them about the plan of redemption that had been prepared for them since the founding of the world. He told of the coming of Jesus Christ. When he was finished speaking, the king believed it all.

"Oh, God," the king cried out. "Have mercy on me and my people, as you have shown to the people of Nephi."

Having said this, the king fell down as if he were dead. His servants carried him to his wife and laid him on his bed. For two days and two nights his wife, sons, and daughters were distraught, and mourned for him in the tradition of the Lamanites. [90 BC]

Chapter 19, 1981 Version

After two days and two nights, King Lamoni's family prepared to bury his body. Having heard of Ammon's fame, the queen sent for him. Ammon arrived and asked the queen what he could do.

"My husband's servants say that you are a prophet of God," the queen said, "and that you have the power to do great works in his name. If this is true, please go see my husband. Some say he is dead, but others say that he is not. Some say that he stinks of death and should be buried, but I don't think so."

This is what Ammon had been hoping for, since he knew that King Lamoni was under the power of God. He knew that the dark veil of disbelief was being removed from the king's mind, and that his soul was being illuminated by the glory, joy, and goodness of God. When he entered the king's bedroom, he could see that he was alive.

"He is not dead," said Ammon. "He is sleeping in God. Tomorrow he will rise again, so do not bury him. Do you believe this?"

"Other than your word, I have no basis for believing," she replied. "Nevertheless, I believe what you say."

"You are blessed because of your faith," Ammon said. "Among all the Nephites, there is no faith as great as yours."

The queen stayed by the king's bedside through the following day until the king arose, as had been foretold by Ammon. When he arose, the king said to her, "Blessed is the name of God, and blessed are you. I have seen the Redeemer. He will come forth, born of a woman, and he will redeem all mankind who believe in his name."

Having said this, the king was filled with joy and the queen was overpowered by God's Spirit. Ammon fell to his knees in thanks and joy. His prayers had been answered. The Lamanites had been filled with God's Spirit. The king, the queen, and Ammon were all so overpowered by God's presence that they fell to the ground. When the king's servants saw this, they cried out to God because the fear of God had come upon them, also. All of the king's servants called upon God and fell to the ground, except a Lamanite woman named Abish. Because her father had had a vision, she was already a secret convert to God.

When Abish saw the king, queen, their servants, and Ammon fall to the ground as if dead, she knew this was caused by the power of God. She saw this miracle as an opportunity to convert others to God by having them witness this scene. She ran from house to house, telling the people what had happened, and asking them to assemble in the king's house.

As the number of witnesses grew, some began to suggest that this was an act of great evil that had come upon them, because the king had allowed Ammon (a Nephite) to live in their land. Others claimed that the king had brought this upon himself by killing the servants who had allowed his flocks to be scattered. Others, who had scattered the king's flocks, were also present. They were angry with Ammon because he had killed or maimed their companions while he was defending the king's flocks.

One of those present was the brother of the leader whom Ammon had killed with his sword. This man drew his sword and stepped forward to kill Ammon, but he instantly fell dead before the crowd of witnesses. Ammon was protected by God as had been promised to his father, King Mosiah. When the crowd saw this, they were overcome by fear and wonder. They asked themselves about the meaning and source of these great powers they witnessed. No one dared to touch any of the fallen people.

Some said that Ammon was the Great Spirit. Some said he was sent to them by the Great Spirit. Others said he was a Nephite monster sent to torment them, or that he had been sent by the Great Spirit to punish them for their sinfulness. The Great Spirit had always favored the Nephites and intervened when the Lamanites attacked. These interventions had already caused the destruction of many Lamanites. The arguments among the crowd were harsh and angry.

When the servant woman, Abish, saw the arguments and commotion she'd aroused by bringing the crowd together, she burst into tears. She took the queen's hand, hoping to raise her from the ground. As soon as she touched her, the queen arose and stood.

"Oh, blessed Jesus," the queen cried out loudly, "who has saved me from an awful hell. God have mercy on this people."

The queen was filled with joy. When she took the hand of King Lamoni, he also arose and saw the argumentative crowd surrounding him. He immediately reprimanded his people and taught them about what he'd learned from Ammon. Because of what they'd seen and heard, many people believed Ammon's words, and were converted to God. Many others would not believe, and went away.

When Ammon arose, he ministered to those who stayed. The servants who had fallen down declared that their hearts had been changed. They no longer felt inclined to do evil had passed. They declared that they'd seen angels who had talked with them, and told them about God and his righteousness. Those who believed were baptized, became righteous, and established a church. This is how the work of God began among the Lamanites. It demonstrates that God reaches out to all who repent and believe in his name. [90 BC]

Chapter 20, 1981 Version

After establishing a church in King Lamoni's land, the king asked Ammon to go with him to the land of Nephi to meet his father. But Ammon received a message from God, saying, "Do not to go to the land of Nephi because the king there will try to kill you. Your brother Aaron and his companions are imprisoned in the land of Middoni. Go there, instead."

When Ammon told King Lamoni that he wanted to go to Middoni to free his imprisoned brother, the king offered to help. "I know that God gives you strength to do all things," he said, "but let me go with you because the king of Middoni is a friend of mine. If I flatter and plead with him, he will release your companions. Who told you that your brother was imprisoned?"

"God has told me," Ammon answered. "I am to go there and deliver them."

When King Lamoni heard this, he ordered his servants to prepare his horses and chariots for immediate departure. On their way to Middoni, Ammon and Lamoni met Lamoni's father, the king of all the Lamanite lands.

"Why didn't you come to the great feast in honor of my sons and my people?" Lamoni's father asked. "And where are you going off with this lying Nephite?"

King Lamoni told his father where they were going, and why, because he was afraid of offending his father. He also explained why he'd had to stay in his own kingdom and miss the great feast.

Lamoni's father was angry. "These Nephites are the descendants of liars," he said. "Their ancestors have robbed us, and now their descendants come to deceive and steal from us again. Why would you want to help deliver them from prison?" Lamoni's father ordered his son to kill Ammon, abandon his journey to Middoni, and return to the land of Ishmael.

"I will not kill Ammon," Lamoni stated, "nor will I return with you to the land of Ishmael. I am going with Ammon to Middoni to help release his companions because I know that they are holy prophets of the true God."

Lamoni's father drew his sword to strike his son. But Ammon stepped in, saying, "Do not kill your son — even though it would be better that he die than you. He has repented his sins, and can be saved. If you were to die, on the other hand, nothing could save you. If you kill your innocent son, his blood will cry from the ground to God for vengeance and you will lose your soul."

"I know that my son is innocent," said the father. "It is you who have sought to destroy him." And he turned on Ammon, intending to kill him instead. Ammon not only withstood the blows directed at him, but disarmed and wounded Lamoni's father. When it became obvious that Ammon could kill him, Lamoni's father begged for mercy.

"If you free my companions from prison, I will not kill you," said Ammon.

"Spare me and I will give whatever you ask," replied Lamoni's father. "I will even give you half of my kingdom."

"Give my companions their freedom; let Lamoni retain his kingdom, and do what he wants; and I will not kill you," said Ammon. "Otherwise, I will kill you."

The old king rejoiced when he saw that his life would be spared. He was also astonished to realize that Ammon's love for his son Lamoni was genuine. "I will grant your requests," he said. Because he was interested in hearing more, he said, "I would also like to have you and your companions come visit me in my kingdom so that I might learn more about you."

Ammon and Lamoni continued their journey to Middoni, and Lamoni was able to persuade his friend to release Ammon's companions from prison. When Ammon saw his brother and his companions, he was filled with sadness to see what poor treatment they had endured. They were naked. Their skin was raw from the ropes that had bound them. And they had patiently endured hunger, thirst, and other abuses. It was their misfortune to have fallen into the hands of hardened and stubborn people who wouldn't listen to their words. [90 BC]

Chapter 13, 1830 Version

Chapter 21, 1981 Version

When King Mosiah's sons and their missionary companions entered the Lamanite lands and went their different ways, Ammon's brother Aaron went to the great city called Jerusalem. The Lamanites who lived there were known as Amalekites and Amulonites (named after Amulon the leader of King Noah's renegade priests). These apostate Nephites were even more stubborn, sinful, and abominable than the average Lamanites.

When Aaron began preaching to the Amalekites in their synagogue, one of them began arguing with him. "Are you telling us you've seen an angel? We don't see them. Do you think you are better than us? You tell us that unless we repent, we will perish. How do

you know our thoughts and intents? How do you know we have any reason to repent? What makes you so sure we aren't righteous people? Look around you. We've built this synagogue to gather in and worship God. We believe that God will save us all."

"Do you believe that the Son of God will come to redeem mankind from their sins?" asked Aaron.

"We don't believe you know anything about this," the man replied. "We don't believe in your foolish traditions. We don't believe you or your ancestors know the future."

As Aaron explained what the scriptures said about the coming of Jesus Christ, the resurrection of the dead, the redemption of mankind through the death and suffering of Jesus Christ, and the atonement of his blood, they became angry with him. They made fun of him and wouldn't listen to what he had to say. When Aaron saw that he was getting nowhere, he left, and went to a village named Ani-Anti. There he found his missionary companions Muloki and Ammah, who were preaching to the local villagers. No one would listen to them there, either, so they went next to the land of Middoni. Again, very few people listened to them or believed what they said. When Aaron and some of his companions were arrested and thrown in prison, the rest of their party fled.

Aaron and his companions suffered in prison until his brother Ammon and King Lamoni arrived to free them. Afterwards, they were led by the Spirit of God to preach in all the Amalekite synagogues and assemblies of Lamanites where they were allowed. Because God blessed Aaron's mission, many people became convinced of their sins and the incorrect traditions of their ancestors.

After a short time, Ammon and Lamoni returned to the land of Ishmael, and Lamoni refused to allow Ammon to be his servant any longer. Lamoni began a campaign to build synagogues for his people where they could gather and learn about God. Lamoni's father had granted him the right to reign in the land of Ishmael, and so Lamoni declared that his people were also free to worship God according to their own wishes. Ammon preached to King Lamoni's people and they became vigilant in their devotion to the commandments of God.

Chapter 22, 1981 Version

Some time after Ammon left, Aaron and his companions traveled to the land of Nephi where Lamoni's father was king. They presented themselves at the king's palace and Aaron introduced themselves as the companions of Ammon, who had been freed from prison. "If you will spare our lives," Aaron said, "we will be your servants."

"I will grant you your lives," said the king, "but I don't want you to be my servants. However, I do want to understand the generosity and great words of your brother, Ammon. I also want to know why he hasn't come from Middoni with you."

"The Spirit of God has called Ammon to go another way," said Aaron, "to teach to the people of your son Lamoni in the land of Ishmael."

"What do you mean by the Spirit of God?" the king asked. "This is what troubles me. And what did Ammon mean when he said, 'If you repent you will be saved, and if you don't repent you will be cast off on the last day?'"

"Do you believe that there is a God?" asked Aaron.

"I know that the Amalekites say there is a God," replied the king. "I have allowed them to build sanctuaries where they can gather to worship him. If you say there is a God, I will believe you."

Aaron rejoiced when he heard this. "Assuredly," he said, "there is a God."

"Is he the Great Spirit who brought our ancestors out of Jerusalem?" he asked.

"Yes," said Aaron, "he is that Great Spirit. He created everything in heaven and earth. Do you believe this?"

"I believe that the Great Spirit created everything," said the king. "I want you to tell me everything you know, and I will believe your words."

Aaron read the scriptures describing God's creation of Adam in his own image, how God had given him commandments, and how because of Adam's disregard for the commandments man had fallen. Aaron expounded upon the scriptures and described the plan for redemption which had been prepared from the beginning, through Jesus Christ and all who believed in him. He described man's fallen state, how the suffering and death of Jesus Christ were required to atone for the sins of mankind, and how Jesus Christ would put an end to death through faith and repentance.

When Aaron had spoken the king asked, "If I want this eternal life, what do I have to do? How may I be born of God, and root this wicked spirit out of me? I want to be filled with joy and not be cast off on the last day. I will give up everything I have to receive this."

"If you want this," Aaron replied, "you need to bow down before God. You need to repent for all of your sins, call on his name in faith, and believe that you will receive what you hope for."

Accordingly, the king bowed down before God and cried out, "Oh, God, Aaron has told me that you will make yourself known to me if I repent my sins before you and ask to know you. He says that I will be raised from the dead and be saved on the last day." When the king said these things, he was struck down as if he were dead.

The king's servants ran out and told the queen what had happened. When she came to see for herself, she saw the king lying on the ground as if he were dead and Aaron and his companions standing around as though it was they who had knocked him down. The queen became angry and ordered the servants to take them away and kill them. Because the servants had seen what caused the king's fall, they didn't dare to touch Aaron and his companions. Instead, they pleaded with the queen. "Any one of these men is mightier than all of us," they said. "If we try to kill them, we will fall, too."

When the queen saw the fear of the king's servants, she became frightened, too. She ordered the servants to go call in more people to kill Aaron and his companions.

Aaron saw danger in the gathering mob, so he put out his hand and raised the king, saying, "Stand." When the king rose from his apparent death, in the presence of his queen and servants, they were all astounded and fearful. Afterwards, the king's entire household was converted to God.

As people gathered in compliance with the queen's orders, they raised their voices against Aaron and his companions. But the king reassured them, and the tension eased. Later, the king called upon Aaron and his companions to preach the word, and sent a proclamation out among his people throughout all his lands.

Chapter 14, 1830 Version

Chapter 23, 1981 Version

The Lamanite king's proclamation said that none of his people should harm any of Mosiah's sons, Ammon, Aaron, Omner, Himni, or any of their missionary companions, as they traveled about his lands to preach the word of God. They were to be treated well, granted access to all places, and given the freedom to preach the word of God, because the king and all of his household were now converted. The king asked his people to become convinced of the sinful traditions of their ancestors, as he had been. He asked them to become convinced that they were all brothers and that they should not murder, plunder, steal, commit adultery, or sin in any way.

Following in the wake of the king's proclamation, Aaron, his brothers, and his missionary companions went from city to city. They preached the word of God, taught about the scriptures and prophecies, established churches, and consecrated priests and teachers throughout the Lamanite lands. They had great success. Thousands were converted to the Nephite traditions and learned about God. These converts were so faithful that they never fell away, and became righteous people. They laid down their weapons and quit fighting with their brothers.

The Lamanite people who were converted included those who were in the land of Ishmael, the land of Middoni, the city of Nephi, the land of Sidom, the land of Shemlon, the city of Lemuel, and the city of Shimnilom. Only a single person among the Amulonites and Amalekites was converted, and the rest of them remained in their disbelief of Jesus Christ. The Lamanite king wanted to give his converted people a new name to distinguish themselves from the unconverted Lamanites, Amulonites, and Amalekites. In consultation with Aaron and their priests, they renamed themselves the Anti-Nephi-Lehies, and were no longer considered Lamanites. They became a very industrious people who were friends to the Nephites. Because of this, the God's curse was lifted from them.

Chapter 24, 1981 Version

The unconverted Amalekites, Amulonites, and Lamanites rebelled in anger and hatred against their converted king and his Anti-Nephi-Lehi people. When the old king died that year, he was succeeded by his son, who assumed the name of Anti-Nephi-Lehi.

As the remaining Lamanites began to prepare for war against the people of God, Ammon and his brothers met with King Lamoni and his brother King Anti-Nephi-Lehi to decide how to defend themselves. Among the converted people, there was not a single person willing to take up weapons to defend themselves or make any preparation for war.

The king decreed that they should not fight against their former brothers. "I thank God that these Nephites were sent to us to preach the word of God and show us the error of our ancestral traditions," he said. "I am also thankful that God has given us a portion of his Spirit, allowing us to receive the truth from our Nephite brothers. Through this communication we've learned about our sins and the wrongness of the many murders we've committed. I am thankful that God has given us the opportunity to repent these things and be forgiven through his son Jesus Christ.

"We were the most lost people of all mankind," the king continued. "Now that we've repented and been forgiven by God, let us never again stain our swords with the blood of our brothers. If we stained them again, we might never be able to cleanse ourselves through the blood that Jesus Christ will shed for the atonement of our sins. God has had mercy on us by making these things known so that we will not perish. He loves our souls as he loves our children. He has sent angels to visit us so that his plan of salvation may be known to future generations. Let us bury our swords deep in the earth so that they will remain unstained as a testimony that we never used them again. If our brothers destroy us, we may go to our God and be saved."

When the king finished speaking, all of his people joined together and buried their weapons. They decided that they would prefer to lay down their lives than to take the lives of their brothers, and they would prefer to work

217

hard on their own than to take something away from their brothers.

The unconverted Lamanites, though, were intent on destroying the king and putting another in his place. They wanted to destroy or drive the Anti-Nephi-Lehi people from the land. When the people saw the Lamanite army coming against them, they went out to meet them and lay down before them, unarmed. They called on the name of God as the Lamanites began to kill them. Without any resistance, the Lamanites killed 1,005 of them, all of whom were blessed by God and went to live with him.

When the Lamanites saw that their brothers would not run from death, and that they cried out to God as they were being killed, they stopped the killing. Many of the Lamanites now regretted their acts, and repented what they had just done. They too threw down their weapons, full of remorse for the murders they had committed and hoping for mercy from those who remained armed. At the end of the day, more Lamanites were converted to God than the number who had been killed. God works in many ways to bring about the salvation of his people.

The majority of the killing that day was done by the Amalekites and Amulonites, none of whom had joined the people of God. These were people who had once been Nephites and had become apostate. This plainly shows that once people have received enlightenment by the Spirit of God, and then turn away into sin, they are even worse off than those who had never known these things.

Chapter 25, 1981 Version

Because the Lamanites had now killed many of their own relatives, they became even angrier with the Nephites and swore vengeance against them. They took their armies across the border and into the land of Zarahemla, where they destroyed the people and city of Ammonihah. In subsequent battles with the Nephites, they were killed and driven out. Most of the Lamanites killed were Amulonites, the descendants of Noah's renegade priests.

Many Lamanites witnessed so much suffering and loss that they began to remember the words that Aaron and his companions had preached. They began to doubt their Lamanite

traditions, and to believe in God. Many were converted. But their new Amulonite rulers would have none of it, and had them burned to death. This martyrdom then caused great dissension and anger among the Lamanites, who began hunting down and killing the Amulonites. And so the prophecies of the martyr Abinadi, whom Amulon and Noah's priests had burned to death, were fulfilled as their descendants were hunted down and destroyed.

When the Lamanites saw that they could not defeat the Nephites, they returned to their own lands and joined with the remnants of the Anti-Nephi-Lehi people. Many of them converted to God, and buried their weapons. They became righteous people who kept the commandments and laws of Moses, and looked forward to the coming of Jesus Christ. They knew better than to suppose that salvation came from the law of Moses, but those laws strengthened their faith in Jesus Christ whose coming was foretold.

Mosiah's sons and their missionary companions rejoiced for the success they'd had among the Lamanites. They saw that God had fulfilled their prayers and honored his word in every way.

Chapter 26, 1981 Version

"My brothers, we have good reason to rejoice," Ammon said. "How could we have imagined when we started out that God would have granted us such blessings? The Lamanites were in darkness and we brought them the light of God. We were instruments in God's hands to accomplish this great work. Thousands of them now rejoice at having been brought into God's company. The field was ripe. We thrust the sickle and reaped the harvest. Now God will raise them up on the last day. Let us sing praise to God and give thanks to him because he does righteous work forever. Had we not come to them, these dearly beloved people would still be filled with hatred against us, and would be strangers to God."

"Your joy sounds a lot like boasting, to me," said Aaron.

"I do not boast in my own strength, or wisdom," replied Ammon. "My heart is filled with the joy of God. I know that I am nothing. I know that I am weak and do not boast of my own strength. I do boast of my God, because in his strength I can do all things. Look at the miracles we have performed in this land, in God's name. Look at how many thousands of people God has released from the pains of hell. All of this is because of the power of his word which is in us. Don't we have good reason to rejoice?

"I say we have reason to praise God forever for releasing these people from the chains of hell. They were surrounded with darkness and destruction. Now, he has brought them into everlasting light and salvation, surrounded by the bounty of God's love. We have been instruments in accomplishing this great and marvelous work. So, let us glory with God's joy and give him our praise. How could we glory too much in God? How can we say too much about his great power and mercy, about his suffering on behalf of all men? I cannot speak the smallest part of what I feel.

"Look at how he snatched us from our awful and sinful state, as well. Do you remember how angry we were when we ourselves threatened to destroy his church? Why weren't we consigned to destruction and doomed to eternal despair? I shudder at the thought. Rather than exercising his justice on us, he showed mercy and brought us across the gulf of death and misery to the salvation of our souls. Nobody knows this except those who have been saved. Those who repent, exercise faith, do good works, and pray ceaselessly are allowed to know the mysteries of God. Things are revealed to them which are hidden to others, just as we have brought thousands of souls to repentance.

"Do you remember how we were laughed at and scorned when we proposed going to the land of Nephi and preaching to the Lamanites? Do you remember what they said to us? 'Do you really think you can bring the knowledge of truth to the Lamanites? Do you really think you can convince those stubborn Lamanites that their ancestral traditions are wrong? Those people take pleasure in killing others and spend their days reveling in sin. Let's pick up our weapons and destroy them, instead. Let's drive their sinfulness out of the land before they come and destroy us.'

"But look what happened. We came not to destroy but to try and save a few souls. When we were discouraged and ready to turn back, God came and comforted us. 'Go among the Lamanites,' he said. 'Have patience with your suffering, and I will give you success.' By following his advice and working with the mercy, power, and wisdom of God to teach them, we were delivered from the suffering we were subjected to.

"We suffered patiently through all sorts of things in the hopes of finding joy through saving some of them. Now, we can look at the fruit of our labors. Are they few? No. We saved many, and can see the sincerity of their salvation through their love for one another. Has there ever been love so great in all the land? No. Not even among the Nephites, who would take up weapons to kill their fellow men. Never would the Nephites lay down their lives and allow themselves to be killed. Look at how many people we saw who laid down their lives and went to God because of their love, and their hatred of sin.

"Do we have reason to rejoice? Yes, I say to you. Never have any men had such good reason since the world began. I am carried away with joy to the point of boasting about my God because of his power and wisdom. He understands everything and shows his mercy by giving salvation to those who repent and believe in his name. If this is boasting, then I will boast. This is my life and my light, my joy and salvation, my redemption from eternal misery. Blessed is the name of my God, who has kept his people in mind, the descendants of Israel. Even we, who are a branch cut off from the main tree of Israel, are tended by God as we wander in this strange land. Likewise, God is mindful of all his people, wherever they wander on this earth. This is my joy, and my thanksgiving. I give thanks to my God, forever."

Chapter 15, 1830 Version

Chapter 27, 1981 Version

When the Lamanites realized, after many attempts, that their intentions of destroying the Nephites could not be fulfilled, they returned to the land of Nephi. The heavy losses of the Amalekite faction left them particularly bitter and angry. When they returned to the land of Nephi, they took their anger out on the Anti-Nephi-Lehi people, and began to destroy them.

The Anti-Nephi-Lehi people again refused to fight back and were slaughtered according to the whim of their enemies. When Ammon and his brothers saw this destruction among their beloved friends, they were moved to do something.

"Let's gather up your people of God," they said to the king, "and go to the land of Zarahemla. If you leave, you won't be destroyed."

"If we do as you say," the king replied, "the Nephites will destroy us because of the many murders we've committed."

"I will go and ask God what to do," said Ammon. "If he says to leave, will you go?"

"Yes," answered the king. "If God says to go, we will do so. We will be slaves to the Nephites until we have repaid them for the murders we've committed."

"It is against my father's law that there be any slaves among the Nephites," Ammon said. "If we go, we will rely upon the mercy of my people."

"Go ask God what to do," said the king. "If he says go, we will go. Otherwise, we will stay here and perish."

Ammon asked God and was answered. "Get these people out of this land so that they will not be killed off. Satan has a great hold on the Amalekites, who provoke the Lamanites to kill their brothers. This is a blessed generation of people, and I will preserve them."

When Ammon told the king what God had said, they gathered up all the people of God, along with their flocks and herds of livestock, and left the land. When they entered the wilderness that divided the Lamanite lands from the Nephite lands, Ammon had them stop. "My brothers and I will go first to prepare the way," he said. "Stay here until we return."

When they entered Zarahemla, the four sons of Mosiah encountered their old friend, Alma. It was a joyous reunion and Alma escorted his friends back to his own home. They appeared before the chief judge, and told him what had happened to them in the land of Nephi, among the Lamanites. After receiving the brothers' report, the chief judge sent out a proclamation among the people, telling them what he knew and asking for their thoughts and ideas regarding the destiny of the Anti-Nephi-Lehies. The result was a decision to set aside the land of Jershon as an inheritance for the emigrants. Furthermore, the people proposed to establish an army between the land of Jershon and the Lamanite lands so that the unarmed Anti-Nephi-Lehies could be protected from being slaughtered by the Lamanites. The Nephites proposed that the emigrants should set aside a portion of their production to maintain this protection from their enemies.

When Ammon heard this, he returned to the wilderness with Alma and told the Anti-Nephi-Lehies what had been decided. Alma also told these people the story of his conversion to God, along with the conversion of Ammon and his brothers. All of this was received with great joy, and afterwards they all went down to the land of Jershon together. From that time forward, the Nephites referred to the Anti-Nephi-Lehies as the people of Ammon, or Ammonites, and they were counted among the Nephites as members of the church of God. These people came to be recognized for their great devotion to God and other men. They were honest and upstanding in all their affairs, and resolute in their faith in Jesus Christ.

The Ammonites looked upon any violence with the greatest aversion, and would never take up arms to defend themselves. They had no fear of death because their faith in Jesus Christ, his resurrection, and their ultimate victory over death was so great. They would suffer the most horrible deaths rather than defend themselves with violence or weapons. Accordingly, they were beloved people, highly favored by God. [77 BC]

Chapter 28, 1981 Version

In the 15th year of elected judges, the Ammonites settled in the land of Jershon, where they established a church. While they were under the protection of a Nephite army, a Lamanite army came after them. The ensuing battle was bigger than any since Lehi[1] left Jerusalem. Tens of thousands of Lamanites were killed and many Nephites died, too. In the end the Nephites prevailed and drove the Lamanite army from their lands, but not without a huge loss of life. It was a time of great sadness and mourning for the Nephite people when they returned to their lands. Husbands, fathers, brothers, and sons had been killed.

Since the time of Mosiah, thousands had been buried; many thousands more were piled up to rot; and many thousands wept for their loss of their dead relatives. Many of the survivors worried that their dead had been consigned to eternal torment. Other survivors mourned for their dead while rejoicing in the fact that their dead had found eternal happiness with God. These divergent responses to death showed them the importance of living without sin, beyond the reach of the devil. Sorrow and joy can also reside side by side — sorrow at death, and joy because of the light of Jesus Christ. [76 BC]

Chapter 29, 1981 Version

If I were an angel and could have any wish, wrote Alma, I would go out and speak like a trumpet of God. With a voice to shake the earth, I would cry out for repentance among all the people. With a voice of thunder, I would declare the plan of redemption and insist upon repentance, so that sorrow would be banished from the earth.

But I am only a man, and I sin even with my wish, because I should be satisfied with the role that God has given to me. I shouldn't question God's justice because I know that he gives everyone what he deserves, whether it is salvation or destruction. I know that good and evil are presented to all men, and that each of us has an opportunity to choose for himself whether he wants joy or remorse. Knowing this, why do I want more than to fulfill the role for which I have been called?

Why should I wish to be an angel who speaks the truth to all the ends of the earth? God gives each nation an opportunity to see and know his truth. I know that God has commanded me, and I am glorified by it. I do not glory in myself, but as an instrument of God's will to bring some to repentance. This is my joy. When I see my people become truly repentant before God, I am filled with joy, and I am reminded of the merciful arm he extends to me.

I remember the bondage of my ancestors and how God delivered them out of that bondage to establish his church. I remember how God delivered his people from the bondage to the Egyptians. The same God has established his church among his people. The same God has called upon me to preach his word, and has given me so much success that I am filled with joy.

But my joy doesn't come from my success alone. I am also filled with joy at the success of my brothers among the Lamanites in the land of Nephi. Because of their diligent labors, they have brought a great harvest, and the rewards will also be great. When I think of their success, my soul is moved beyond my body because of the magnitude of my joy. May God grant them the opportunity to sit down in the kingdom of God with all whom they have saved, and praise him forever. This is my wish. [76 BC]

Chapter 16, 1830 Version

Chapter 30, 1981 Version

The Nephite and Ammonite losses during the Lamanite war were so great that their numbers were never counted. In the 16th year of elected judges, the Lamanites were driven from the land of Jershon, and the Ammonites became peacefully settled there.

The Ammonites strictly obeyed the law of Moses. According to the law, if a man committed murder, he received death. Laws were tailored to fit the crime, and people were punished for stealing, adultery, and other types of sinfulness; but there were no laws regarding people's beliefs. People were free to believe or disbelieve whatever they wanted.

In the 17th year of elected judges, the Anti-Christ appeared to the Nephite people in the form of a man named Korihor. He freely preached against the prophecies and against the coming of Jesus Christ, as was allowed by the laws.

"You people labor under a foolish and vain hope in looking forward to Jesus Christ," he said. "No one knows the future. These things you call prophecies from the past are just silly traditions that have been handed down to you. You say that Jesus Christ will come and there will be a remission of your sins. This is the effect of a frenzied mind and your inherited traditions that leads you to believe in things that aren't true."

Korihor preached that there could be no atonement for their sins. He said that people achieved things in life because of their knowledge and strength, and that whatever a man did was not a crime. Many were led into fornication by his words. He said that when people died, that was the end. When Korihor went among the Ammonites, he found that they were wiser than the Nephites. They tied him up and took him before Ammon, who was now a high priest in the land of Jershon. Ammon ordered that Korihor be exiled from the land of Jershon.

When Korihor went to preach in the land of Gideon, he was bound up again, and taken before their high priest and chief judge. "Why do you try to pervert the ways of God?" the high priest asked him. "Why do you teach that Jesus Christ will not come? Why do you speak out against the holy prophecies?"

"I say these things to free people from bondage to foolish traditions and priests who want to control them," Korihor answered. "I say that these prophecies you purport to believe in are untrue. You teach that we are guilty and fallen people because of sins committed by a distant ancestor. I say this is nonsense. Is a child guilty for the crimes of its parents? You have no way of knowing that Jesus Christ will come and be slain for the sins of the world. You mislead your people with this foolishness and keep them down. You glut yourselves with the fruit of their efforts and deprive them of their rights and privileges. You make your people feel guilty before some imaginary God who has never been seen, and never will be."

The high priest and chief judge saw Korihor's harshness and had him handed over to Alma and the chief judge in Zarahemla. There he repeated his blasphemous words again.

"You know very well," said Alma, "that we don't live handsomely on the labors of others. I myself have worked hard to support myself since the time when my father Mosiah began the reign of judges. In addition, I have traveled throughout the land on missions to declare the word of God. None of us receives anything for our efforts on behalf of the church. The payment for judges is only what is due by law. The only profit in our labor for the church is the joy in bringing the truth to our people. Do you think we deceive our people and receive wealth from them in secret?"

"Yes," Korihor answered.

"Do you believe there is a God?" Alma asked.

"No," replied Korihor.

"I know that there is a God, and that Jesus Christ will come," said Alma. "What evidence do you have, other than your word, that there is no God, or that Jesus Christ will not come? I know you believe the truth of what I say, but lie about it instead. You've cast off God and become a servant of the devil's in your attempt to harm the children of God."

"Show me one sign that demonstrates God's power," replied Korihor, "and I will be convinced."

"You've had plenty of signs," answered Alma. "Do you tempt God? Why ask for signs when you have the testimony of so many holy prophets? The scriptures are clear that God is the supreme creator of the earth and everything on it. Do you deny the truth of all these witnesses?"

"Unless you show me a sign," Korihor said, "I deny it all."

"I am saddened by your stubbornness," said Alma. "Your resistance to the truth destroys your soul. But it is better that your soul should be lost than for you to continue injuring the church of God with your lies and flatteries. Therefore, may God strike you dumb, so your mouth will never again be opened to deceive others with your lies."

"I do not deny the existence of a God," Korihor replied, "but I do not believe there is a God; and neither do you know that there is a God. Unless you show me a sign, I will not believe."

"In the name of God, you will be struck dumb," declared Alma. "That will be your sign."

And Korihor was instantly struck dumb. When the chief judge saw this, he wrote for Korihor, "Are you convinced of the power of God, now? Would you have asked God to afflict somebody else, to give the sign you asked for? Do you still dispute the truth?"

Korihor put forth his hand and wrote back: "I am now dumb. Nothing but the power of God could have done this to me. I always knew there was a God but the devil deceived me by appearing in the form of an angel, and said, 'Go reclaim my people. They have been led astray by an unknown God. There is no God.' His words were pleasing to the carnal-minded, and I was highly successful, so successful that I came to believe that the words I spoke were true. But now I have brought this curse upon myself. Will you pray for me so that this curse might be removed?"

"If your curse were lifted, you would resume your efforts to lead the people astray," said Alma. "You will be treated according to God's will."

The curse was not removed, and Korihor was reduced to begging for food. An official declaration was sent out to advise those who had believed what Korihor had said. These people were told to repent immediately or else the same fate would soon fall upon them. Everyone became convinced of Korihor's heresy and sinfulness, and all those who had been led astray returned again to God.

When Korihor went begging for food among the Zoramite people who had separated themselves from the Nephites, he was run down and killed by them. This example shows how God deals with people who oppose him. The devil cannot help them, and they are quickly dragged down to hell. [74 BC]

Chapter 31, 1981 Version

When Alma received news that the Zoramites were perverting the ways of God by worshipping idols, he was filled with sorrow at the divide between the Nephites and the sinful Zoramites. Because the Zoramites resided in the border lands between the Ammonites and the wilderness occupied by the Lamanites, Alma was concerned about the possibility of an alliance between the Zoramites and the Lamanites. He knew that preaching and persuasion were more effective than force in leading people to justice. So he took Mosiah's sons Ammon, Aaron, Omner, and Himni, Amulek, Zeezrom, and two of his own sons Shiblon and Corianton, to go preach the word of God to the Zoramites.

The Zoramites were Nephites who had formerly been followers of God. They had fallen into apostasy and would not observe the commandments of God or the laws of Moses. They no longer prayed to God daily for guidance from temptation, and in many ways perverted the ways of God.

Alma's party entered the Zoramite lands and were surprised to find synagogues in which the Zoramites gathered one day each week to make observance to God. These weekly worship services to God were like none that Alma had ever seen. In the center of the synagogue was a raised platform big enough for only one person to stand and preach with his arms outreached.

"Holy God," a man cried out, "we believe you are holy. We believe that you were, are, and will always be a spirit. Holy God we believe that you have separated us from our Nephite brothers because we do not believe in the same childish traditions as they do. We believe that we have been chosen as your holy children. We believe that there will be no Jesus Christ. We believe that we alone will be saved, while those around us will be cast down to hell. For this we thank you for choosing us. This foolish notion of Jesus Christ has led our former brothers away from God. We give thanks for being your chosen and holy people."

Alma and his party heard these prayers, and were dumbfounded. Each Zoramite in attendance went to the high platform and said the same thing in his turn. After their weekly service, the people left the synagogue and never spoke of God until the next time they gathered.

Seeing this, Alma was deeply saddened. He saw that the Zoramites were wicked and perverse people with their intentions focused on riches and fine goods. He saw their boastful pride in themselves. He cried out to God saying, "Oh God, how long do I have to suffer here as a witness to the Zoramite's sinfulness? They cry out to you but their prayers are swallowed up in their pride and pursuit of wealth. Look at their expensive clothing and adornments of gold and other precious things as they cry out to you. They say that they are your chosen people, that all others will perish.

"They say that you have told them there will be no coming of Jesus Christ," Alma continued. "How can you allow this apostasy to continue? Oh God, give me the strength to be patient with the suffering that these people cause in me. Please give me and all of my missionary companions comfort in our souls as we do this work on your behalf. Grant us success in bringing these precious Zoramite souls back to you, and to Jesus Christ."

When Alma finished speaking to God he laid his hands on the heads of all his missionary companions, and they were filled with the Holy Spirit. Afterwards they went their separate ways without a thought for their sustenance or needs. God provided them their food, drink, clothing, strength to withstand all manner of suffering, and the joy of Jesus Christ. This is what Alma had prayed for, and now his faith was rewarded. [74 BC]

Chapter 32, 1981 Version

Alma and his missionaries went into the synagogues, homes, and the streets to preach the word of God. They had great success among the poorer classes, because the wealthier people looked down upon the poor with disdain, and denied them access to their synagogues.

One day while Alma spoke on a hillside to a group of poor people, one of them asked, "What should we do? We are despised because of our poverty, especially by the priests. They have thrown us out of their synagogues that we worked to build with our own hands. We have no place to worship God. What should we do?"

Alma was pleased by this question because it showed that they had been humbled by their suffering, and were ready to receive the word of God. He held out his hand to the repentant people, and said, "I see that your hearts have been brought low, but you are blessed. You ask what you should do to worship God if you are denied entrance to the synagogues. What makes you think that God can only be worshipped in synagogues? What makes you think you can only worship God once a week? It is good that you have been denied entry to the synagogues because in so doing you have been humbled, and may learn wisdom. It is because of your poverty, your despised status, and having been cast out that you have been humbled. When men are humbled they are able to seek repentance. Those who repent will find mercy and be saved. Those who truly humble themselves to repent their sins though, will be more blessed than those who are merely humbled by their poverty."

"Blessed are those who humble themselves without being compelled to do so. Blessed are those who believe in the word of God, who are baptized without coercion or need to know before they believe. Many people say, 'Show us a sign from heaven and we will then surely believe.' Is this faith? I say no. If a man knows something, he cannot hold his belief separately.

If a man knows the will of God and doesn't heed it, is he more cursed than a man who believes and falls astray? Each are the same, and each man will be judged by his actions."

"Faith is not about having perfect knowledge of things. Faith means that you hope for things which have not been seen but are known to be true anyhow. God is merciful to all of those who believe in his name. He wants you to believe his word. He sends his word to us through angels. He gives words to men, women, and children who sometimes receive information that astounds the well educated."

"So you ask what to do because you have been thrown out and afflicted with poverty. Awaken and have faith. Believe in my words. If we compare God's word to a seed, I want you to implant that seed in your heart. If it is a good seed and you do not cast it out in unbelief, it will grow within you. It will enlarge your soul, enlighten your mind, and be delicious. As the seed sprouts and grows this will strengthen your faith, and you will know it is a good seed."

"How can you tell if it is a good seed or bad? Good seeds grow. Bad seeds don't. If you understand what I say, but don't act on it your knowledge is sound, but your faith is dormant. But as the seed grows your knowledge will become enlightened and your mind will expand."

"Can this be real? Yes, because it is light, and light is good. Is this the light of perfect knowledge? No. Until you have laid your faith aside you have only tested the experiment to see if the seed was good. But as the tree grows and is taken care of it may come to bear fruit. If you neglect the tree, and fail to nourish it, the tree will perish in the heat of the sun because its roots have withered. Now this is not because the seed was bad, but because it was planted in barren ground and never nourished. If you do not nourish God's word as his tree begins to grow inside of you, the fruit that will never come. But if you nourish God's word with faith, diligence, and patience the tree will take root and the fruit with its most precious taste will be your reward. This fruit of which I speak is sweet above anything else, whiter than anything else, and more pure than anything else will be a feast that relieves hunger and thirst forever. This fruit waiting to come to you is the

reward for your faith, diligence, and patience."
[74 BC]

Chapter 33, 1981 Version

When Alma had finished speaking his listeners asked many questions. Should they believe in one God? How could they obtain the fruit he had spoken of? How should they plant the seed, or word, in their hearts?

"You say you cannot worship your God because you've been denied entry into your synagogues," said Alma. "If you think this is true, you've made a great mistake. The scriptures say nothing of this."

"Do you remember what the old prophet Zenos said about prayer and worship?" Alma asked. "He said, 'Oh God, you are merciful for having heard my prayer even when I was in the wilderness. You were merciful when I prayed about my enemies, and you turned them toward me. You heard me when I prayed in the field, in my house, and in my closet. You are merciful to your children when they cry out to you to be heard, and you hear them. You have heard me when I cried to you from amidst great crowds. You heard me when I was cast out and despised by my enemies on whom you brought swift anger and destruction. You heard me because of my suffering and sincerity. Because of Jesus Christ you have been merciful. Because of Jesus Christ you have turned your judgments away from me. When I suffer I cry to you because you are my joy.'

"Do you believe in these old scriptures?" Alma asked his audience. "If you do, you must believe what Zenos said when he declared, 'Because of Jesus Christ you have turned your judgments away from me.' Have you read the scriptures? If so, how can you disbelieve in Jesus Christ?"

"Zenock* also spoke of these things," Alma continued. "He said, 'Oh God, you are angry with these people because they will not understand the mercies granted to them by your son Jesus Christ.' So you see a second old prophet has also testified about Jesus Christ, and because the people wouldn't listen they stoned him to death.

*Both Zenos and Zenock are identified as Old World Hebrew prophets whose words presumably come from Laban's brass plates.

Neither of them are mentioned in the Old Testament.

"But these are not the only ones who have spoken about Jesus Christ. Moses spoke of him when he brought his people through the wilderness. Those who believed and saw were healed and lived. Those too stubborn to look perished because they didn't believe. If you could be healed by merely looking wouldn't you do so? Or would you rather be lazy, not look, and perish? If so, anguish will be your reward.

"Look around and begin to believe that Jesus Christ will come to redeem his people, suffer and die to atone for their sins, rise again from the dead, and resurrect all men to stand before him in judgment according to their actions during their lives. I implore you to plant this word in your hearts, and to nourish it with your faith as it grows. If you do, it will become a tree within you to bring everlasting life. May God grant that your burdens are light through the joy of Jesus Christ. You can do all of this if you work at it." [74 BC]

Chapter 34, 1981 Version

After Alma finished speaking Amulek arose to preach. "Brothers, I know that you were taught about the coming of Jesus Christ before your division from us. When you asked Alma what you should do, he answered that you should have faith and patience, that you should try planting the word of God in your hearts and experience its goodness."

"The big question in your minds is whether or not Jesus Christ will come. Alma has shown you that Jesus Christ is our salvation. He reminded you of the words of Zenos, Zenock, and Moses to show you that what he says is true. Now I want to testify that I also know that these things are true, that Jesus Christ will come, and take upon himself the sins of the world. God has spoken it. An atonement will be made because according to the great plan of God, all mankind will perish without it. In order to accomplish this, a great sacrifice must be made. No man alive can qualify to be this sacrifice. Only Jesus Christ can make this eternal and infinite sacrifice, and in doing so bring salvation to those who believe in him. He is the means through which we are brought to faith and repentance.

"As you begin to call upon God he will have mercy on you. Cry for mercy and he will save you. Humble yourselves and pray to him. Cry out to him from the fields and from your houses throughout the whole day. Cry out to him for power against your enemies, and against the devil who is an enemy to all righteousness. Cry out to him in your secret places and in the wilderness. When you aren't crying out to God, fill your hearts with prayer to him. Do not turn away the needy and the naked, or fail to visit the sick and afflicted. Give to them. If you don't help those in need, your prayers will be empty and you will be hypocrites. Unless you are charitable, you are like waste that is thrown away.

"Now having heard so many testimonies and seeing that the scriptures verify these things I want you to come forward and repent. Quit closing your hearts because now is the time of salvation. If you repent now, you will be redeemed. It is time now to prepare for your eventual meeting with God. Whatever spirit possesses your body during life will possess it at the time of your death. If you procrastinate until the end you will belong to the devil and he will have full power over you. This is the final state of the sinner. I know this because God said he cannot be found in unholy places. Only in the hearts of righteousness can he reside.

"It is my desire that you remember what has been said, and that you work out your salvation in prostration before God. Do not deny the coming of Jesus Christ, or fight against the Holy Ghost. Humble yourselves before God and worship him wherever you are. Give thanks every day for the mercies and blessings he gives to you. If you pray continually, you will not be led into the temptations of the devil. If you don't let him in, the devil cannot overpower you and claim you as his subjects on the day of judgment.

"Have patience and stand up to life's afflictions. Refuse to hate those who have cast you out because of your poverty, or you will become sinners like them. If you persevere, one day you will find eternal rest from your troubles." [74 BC]

Chapter 35, 1981 Version

When Amulek finished preaching to the Zoramites, he and Alma returned to the land of Jershon where the Ammonites resided. There, they met up with their fellow missionaries after they too had finished their preaching to the Zoramites.

As Alma's mission had progressed, the Zoramites became angry with their missionary work and wouldn't listen to the words that were said. It would destroy their priestcraft. After Alma left the Zoramite rulers secretively canvassed their people to learn of all their people's sympathies toward his missionary work. Those who approved of Alma's teachings were thrown out of their homes and out of the land. These outcast people also came to the land of Jershon where they were ministered to and aided by Alma and his brothers.

The Zoramites then became angry with the Ammonites who sheltered the refugees, and their ruler demanded that the Ammonites also throw out the people that they had banished. The Zoramites backed up their demands with threats but the Ammonites were fearless and gladly received all the outcast Zoramites giving them food, clothing, and land to settle on.

When the Zoramites saw that their demands were being spurned, they agitated the Lamanites in hopes of provoking them into conflict with the Ammonites. As their anger smoldered, they made preparations for war against the Ammonites and Nephites.

In the 17th year of elected judges, the Ammonites moved to another area and made way for the Nephite army to occupy their land in anticipation of war. In the 18th year of elected judges, another Lamanite war began. An account of that war will follow.

Alma and his missionary companions returned to Zarahemla, having brought many Zoramites to repentance and salvation. But among his own people Alma was saddened by the conflicts and stubbornness that he saw. Many said that his words were too strict.

Alma called his three sons to him to give each of them separate guidance in matters of righteousness. The following is an account of what he said to them. [74 BC]

Chapter 17, 1830 Version

Chapter 36, 1981 Version

First, Alma spoke with his son Helaman. "Listen to me, my son. I swear to you that if you keep the commandments of God you will prosper in the land. Remember that your ancestors were once held in bondage, and that no one could free them but God. Recall that they were delivered from their trials. I want you to know that anyone who puts their faith in God will be supported in their struggles, and saved. I know this not through my earthly awareness, but through the mind of God. I know this because I was born of God, and was told these things by his holy angel.

"When we were young, Mosiah's sons and I went about trying to destroy the church of God. But an angel of God was sent down to stop us. He spoke to us as if his voice were thunder, and the whole earth shook beneath our feet. When the fear of God came upon us, we fell to the ground. The voice said to me, 'Arise.' When I did so he said, 'Unless you want to be destroyed yourself, quit trying to harm the church of God.' For three days after I heard these words I fell into a deep coma where I was racked with the torment of hell, the awareness of my failures, and sins. I had been instrumental in diverting many people away from the church and into their own destruction. At the time I wanted instant extinction. I wanted anything but having to appear before God and be judged for my deeds. For three days I suffered the pains of a damned soul.

"While I was racked with torment I also remembered my father prophesy the coming of Jesus Christ to atone for the sins of the world. As I held onto this thought, I cried out from my heart, 'Oh Jesus Christ, have mercy on me. I am bound up by the everlasting chains of death.'

"As soon as I formulated this thought I was released and couldn't even remember my previous, interminable pain. The memory of my sins also disappeared. I saw a beautiful light, and my soul was filled with joy as intense as my pains had just been. I thought that I saw our ancestor Lehi[1] sitting on a throne with God, surrounded by numberless rows of singing angels, who were praising God. I wanted to be there too. But instead, I opened my eyes and came back to consciousness. I had been born of God.

"From that moment until the present I have labored unrelentingly to bring others to the repentance that I found. I wanted them to taste the sweetness that I had tasted, to also be born again to God, and be filled with the Holy Ghost. And now, through my labors I have been rewarded. I personally know of what I speak, and the knowledge is from God. I was supported in my trials, delivered from the prison of my soul, and released from death. When I put my trust in God, he will deliver me to live in glory with him, just as he brought our ancestors out of Egypt, and buried their enemies under the Red Sea. Just as he led our ancestors out of Jerusalem to this promised land, and has also delivered them from slavery here. I never forget our slavery or God's deliverance of us. I remind you that if you keep God's commandments you will prosper in the land. If you do not keep his commandments he will cut you off from his presence. All of this is according to his promises to us." [74 BC]

Chapter 37, 1981 Version

"Helaman," Alma continued, "I want you to take possession of the engraved records of our people, and to continue this sacred record as I have done. Our ancestors have prophesied that these plates should be kept from generation to generation, and that these records will be preserved by the power of God until they are spread to every nation and people. Someday everyone will know of the mysteries contained on them. As long as these plates are kept they will retain their holy brightness. This may seem like a foolish request, but small and simple things bring great things to pass. God works to bring about his eternal purposes, and by small acts he confounds the wise and brings salvation to many souls.

"In his wisdom, God has preserved and maintained these records. Because of this, our memory is enhanced, and many people have become convinced of their errors by having the knowledge of their salvation made available to them. Without these records, Ammon and his brothers could not have convinced thousands of Lamanites of their errors. These words brought them to repentance through the knowledge of God and Jesus Christ. These words may also bring the redemption of many thousands more who close their hearts off to God. These records are being preserved and added to for a wise purpose known only to God.

"Always remember how strict the commandments of God are. If you keep those commandments you will prosper in the land. If you don't keep them, you will be cut off. God has entrusted you with the safekeeping of these sacred records that will reveal his power to future generations. If you fail to honor God's commandments these sacred things will be taken from you, and you will be delivered to Satan. If you keep the commandments of God, no power on earth can take these sacred records away from you because God is powerful in fulfilling his promises. I command that you be diligent in exercising this sacred obligation and in keeping the commandments of God.

"The 24 golden plates and their interpreting stones describe the secret works and darkness of the Jaredite people who were destroyed. These records also need to be preserved so that people can always remember the consequences of murder, robbing, plundering, wickedness, and other abominations. God saw that these people had fallen into darkness and warned them that if they didn't repent, he would destroy them all and remove them from the face of the earth. God prepared the interpreting stones so that we could understand their records and their downfall, because after their failure to repent they were destroyed as promised.

"I want you to withhold knowledge of the Jaredites' secret oaths and abominations so that our people will not discover these dark forces and fall into darkness themselves. If they did, we would all be destroyed. There is a curse on the land that will bring destruction to any who work in darkness. So make the history of the Jaredite destruction known, but do not reveal their secret plans and abominations. Tell our people that they were destroyed for their murders, wickedness, and abominations.

"Teach our people to hate sinful behavior, and to never grow tired of good works. Teach them to seek repentance and faith in Jesus Christ, to be humble, and to withstand the devil's temptations. Learn the wisdom of God's commandments. Cry out to God for support in all things. Let all of your thoughts and actions be directed towards God. Consult with God in all things and he will give you good direction. When you sleep he will watch over you. When you rise let your heart be full of thanks for God. Do these things and you will be redeemed.

"Now I want to show you the magic compass Liahona that was made by God to guide our ancestors in their travels through the wilderness. It worked for them in accordance with their faith in God. If their faith was pure, the spindles pointed the way to go. When they were forgetful of God the Liahona failed to work for them, and they could not progress. When they failed in their devotion to God, they suffered from hunger and thirst because God was not guiding them. Likewise, it is as easy to listen to the word of Jesus Christ pointing in a straight line to eternal bliss as it was for our ancestors to make the magic compass point the way to the promised land.

"If we follow the words of Jesus Christ as our ancestors followed the magic compass we will be guided to a life beyond the sorrow of this world, to a better land of promise. So do not be lazy, negligent, or forgetful of the way. The way is prepared. If we follow it, we will live forever. Take care of these sacred things, and look to God for guidance. Go now among our people, be sober, and declare the word of God. Fare well." [74 BC]

Chapter 18, 1830 Version

Chapter 38, 1981 Version

Alma spoke next to his son Shiblon. "As I told Helaman, if you keep God's commandments you will prosper in the land. If you don't, you will be cut off from him. I anticipate great joy in your steadiness and faithfulness to God. As a young man you looked to God for guidance early in your life. I hope you continue in keeping his commandments because you will be blessed if you continue. Already I have taken great joy in your faithfulness, diligence, patience, and endurance of suffering during our mission to the Zoramites. I know that you were tied up and stoned for speaking the word of God. You endured this torment because you knew God was with you, and you learned that God will deliver you.

"Now I want you to remember that if you put your trust in God, you will be delivered from your trials, troubles, and adversities. If you trust God, you will be redeemed on the last day. Don't imagine that I know these things from my earthly life. I know these things through the Spirit of God. If I hadn't been born of God, I wouldn't know what I do. God in his great mercy sent an angel to demand that I stop undermining the faith of the people. I saw that angel face to face, and he spoke to me with a voice like thunder that shook the whole earth. When I fell into a coma for three days and nights I suffered the most bitter pain and anguish imaginable until I cried out to Jesus Christ for mercy. When I did cry out I received a remission of my sins and peace in my soul.

"I want to pass on the wisdom that I've learned. There is no way that man can be saved except through Jesus Christ. He is the light and the life of the world. He is the word of truth and righteousness. I hope that you will continue to teach God's word, and be diligent and temperate in all things. Don't become inflated with pride, or boast of your wisdom and strength. Be bold, but not overbearing. Bridle your passions so that you can be filled with love. And avoid idleness. Don't labor for the praise of other men or think of yourself as better than others. Ask forgiveness for your deficiencies and remember to be merciful to others. Acknowledge your unworthiness before God at all times. May God bless your soul and receive you into his kingdom of peace on the last day. Go forward and teach the word of God unto our people. Stay sober. Fare well." [74 BC]

Chapter 19, 1830 Version

Chapter 39, 1981 Version

To his son Corianton, Alma said, "I have more to say to you than I did to Shiblon. Have you noticed his steadiness, faithfulness, and diligence in keeping God's commandments? Hasn't he set a good example for you? When we went on our mission to the Zoramites you didn't pay a lot of attention to my words. Instead, you went around boasting about your strength and wisdom.

"What most grieved me though was your departure from our ministry to chase after the prostitute Isabel. She seduces the hearts of many, but this is no excuse for you. You should have stayed with your mission companions, and the tasks to which you were entrusted. Don't you know that fornication is an abomination in the sight of God? Other than shedding innocent blood or denying God, this is the most abominable sin in God's eyes. I wish that you were not guilty of so great a crime. I wouldn't bring all of this up, and dwell on it if it weren't for your own good. You cannot hide your crimes from God, and unless you repent they will stand against you on judgment day.

"I want you to repent for your sins, and quit your immoral behavior. Unless you do this, you cannot inherit the kingdom of God. I want you to confer with your older brothers, seek their guidance in your life, and pay attention to their advice. Don't let yourself be led away into vanity and foolishness. Do not let the devil tempt you again with those wicked prostitutes.

"Look at the harm you did to our mission to the Zoramites. When they saw your conduct, they refused to believe my words. The Spirit of God has said to me, 'Command your children to do good, or else they lead many people to destruction.' In the fear of God then, I order you to quit your sinfulness.

"Turn to God with all your mind, might, and strength so that you will not be a bad example to others. Return to those to whom you've been a bad example and acknowledge your errors. You cannot carry riches and vanity with you after death, so quit chasing after them now.

"Jesus Christ will surely come to take away the sins of the world and bring good news of salvation to his people. This is the ministry to which you were called. Declare this news to the people and prepare their minds for the salvation that is to come to them and their children. Do you wonder about why these things need be known for so long before they happen? It is because the souls who are now living are just as precious to God as are the souls at the time of Christ's arrival. It is necessary that the plan of redemption be known to the people alive now, as well as to their children. This is why God sends his angel to declare this great news to us and our children at this time." [74 BC]

Chapter 40, 1981 Version

"There is more that I need to say to you Corianton," Alma continued. "I sense that you are concerned about how the dead will actually be resurrected. There will be no resurrection until after the coming of Jesus Christ. By resurrection I mean the act of becoming immortal. Jesus Christ will bring this resurrection to pass.

"Let me reveal a mystery to you. I have inquired persistently of God to discover the exact nature of how the resurrection will come about. This is what I have learned.

"There is an appointed time when all people will arise from death, but no one except God knows exactly when this event will happen. There may be more than one time when resurrections occur, but it doesn't matter to me.

"Because all men do not die at once, I asked what would happen with the souls of men between the time of death and the time of resurrection? I was told by an angel that the spirits of men who die, whether they were good or evil, are taken from their bodies and returned to the God who created them.

"Those who were righteous are received into a state of happiness called paradise. This is a state of peace, where they can rest from their troubles, cares, and sorrows. Whereas the wicked who lived evil lives have already been claimed by the devil. These people will be cast into darkness despite their weeping, wailing, and gnashing of teeth, to be enslaved by the devil. From then until the time of the resurrection these people's souls will exist in darkness, in dread of God's awful anger and fiery indignation. So the souls of the dead wait either in paradise or darkness for the time of resurrection.

"Some people think of this well deserved state of happiness or misery as the first resurrection. I can even admit that it could be viewed so. But the true resurrection happens when all the souls from Adam through the time of Jesus Christ are reunited with their physical bodies. I don't know whether all the bodies and souls are reunited at once. I do know that those who have died before the resurrection of Jesus Christ will be resurrected before those who die after him. Having given this some thought, I have come to a personal opinion that the bodies and souls of the righteous happen at the same moment of Jesus Christ's resurrection and ascension into heaven.

"In conclusion I say that there is a time between death and resurrection. The soul resides for this time either in happiness or misery. At the appointed time the souls of the dead will be reunited with their bodies, and

brought to stand in judgment before God according to how they've lived their lives. These events then fulfill the words of the prophets. The righteous will shine brightly in the kingdom of God. And an awful death comes upon the wicked. They die to all possibility of righteousness because they are unclean. Because no dirty thing can inherit the kingdom of heaven, they are cast out, and consigned to the bitter fruits of their evil earthly lives. They will drink the dregs of a very bitter cup." [74 BC]

Chapter 41, 1981 Version

"I know that this restoration of bodies is confusing," Alma continued explaining to his son Corianton. "Some people go astray by misunderstanding the scriptures, so let me make it clear. The restoration of the body is an essential aspect of God's justice because everything needs to be restored to its proper order. According to Jesus Christ's resurrection it is essential that the soul of man be restored to his complete body, down to the last detail. It is also an essential part of the justice of God for men to be judged in accordance with how they lived their lives. If they led good lives they will be restored to goodness. If they led evil lives they will be restored to evil. Everything will be restored to its proper order and mortality will be transformed to immortality. People will be raised from death to endless happiness in the kingdom of God, or will be raised from death to find themselves in endless misery in the kingdom of the devil.

"Good will be rewarded with good, and evil will be rewarded with evil. People will be their own judges as they pass through life, and choose whether to do good or evil. These are God's unalterable decrees. A pathway is prepared for everyone.

"My son, do not risk any more offenses against God. Don't imagine for a moment that you can be restored from sin to happiness. Sinful behavior is never happiness. Men that live for sexual fulfillment live in bitter sinfulness, and are without God. They live in a way that is inconsistent with the nature of happiness. Restoration does not mean that men will be raised from one state and placed in an opposite state. Restoration means bringing back evil to evil, sexual to sexual, good to good, just to just, and merciful to merciful. So see to it that you are merciful to your fellow men, deal justly with the world, live righteously, and continually do good. If you do these things you will receive your reward, and be restored to goodness. What you send out will return to you. Restoration condemns, rather than justifies the sinner." [74 BC]

Chapter 42, 1981 Version

"I sense that you are unclear about God's justice in punishing sinners," Alma explained to his son Corianton. "You seem to think that eternal misery is too great a punishment. After God banished Adam and Eve from the garden of Eden he placed an angel at the gate to prevent them from eating from the tree of life, and becoming immortal. Because they had come to know good and evil, eating the fruit would have condemned them to misery forever without a chance for repentance. Had this happened, God's great plan would have failed. Instead, fallen man was condemned to be mortal and die.

"At this time, our first ancestors were cut off physically and spiritually from God, and came to follow their own will. Because the soul is immortal it became necessary that mankind should be reclaimed from spiritual death. So earthly life became a probationary period in which man could reject or accept his sensual and devilish natures. Without the plan of redemption the dead souls would remain forever in misery and cut off from God as a result of their ancestor's disobedience. To fulfill the need for justice, a plan of redemption was brought about based on the repentance of men during their probationary, earthly lives. Without this conditional mercy, justice would be destroyed.

"After mankind had fallen they were caught in God's justice and cut off from him. A plan of mercy could not be implemented without an atonement being made, so God himself atones for the sins of man in order that justice be appeased, and that mercy can be shown. Repentance could not happen unless there was a punishment as eternal as the life of a soul. How can a man repent unless he sins? How can he sin if there is no law that defines sin? And how could there be a law unless there is also punishment? So laws were given,

punishments were fixed, and man learned remorse of conscience. If there were no punishment for murder, murderers would have no fear. Likewise, if there were not laws against sin, sinners would run rampant.

"But there is a law against sin, reinforced by punishment. Without laws and justice, punishment and mercy would be meaningless. Mercy comes because of the atonement and the consequent resurrection of the dead. Those who are resurrected from death are brought before God for judgment according to how they've lived their lives — according to the law and justice. For justice to prevail, only the truly penitent are saved. Does that mercy rob justice? Not a bit. If it did, God would cease to be God.

"This is how God brings about his great and eternal purposes that have been prepared since the foundation of the world. From this plan comes the salvation and redemption of men, but also their destruction and misery. So my son, you can see that all who live are free to choose for good or for evil, but when they are resurrected on judgment day they will find themselves restored to the conditions in which they lived. If a man has lived an evil life, and not repented during that lifetime, evil will befall him under the restoration.

"My son, don't be troubled any more by these things I've spoken of. You need to pay attention now to your own sins, and your own repentance for them. I wish you would quit questioning the justice of God. Don't excuse yourself for your sins, or deny the justice of God. Instead, let the justice of God, his mercy, and his suffering turn your heart to bring you into humility. You are called by God to preach the word to our people. Go your way now, and declare the truth of the word so that you may bring other souls into repentance and mercy. May God grant you help according to my words." [74 BC]

Chapter 20, 1830 Version

Chapter 43, 1981 Version

After Alma finished speaking with his sons, they all went out among the people to declare the word of God.

In the 18th year of elected judges, the Zoramites joined forces with, and became, Lamanites themselves. The wars between the

Nephites and the Lamanites were renewed. When the Nephites saw that the Lamanite army was coming upon them they gathered their own army and made preparation for war. The Lamanite army of thousands of warriors was led by a man named Zerahemna. He appointed Amalekites and Zoramites as chief captains because of their particularly wicked and murderous disposition. He did this by design in order to nourish his army's hatred of the Nephites. His plan was to stir up anger among the Lamanites towards the Nephites, grab more power, and reduce the Nephites to slavery.

The Nephites only wanted to live in peace, but they had to protect their lands, families, freedom, and religious convictions from the invading Lamanite army. They knew that the Lamanites would destroy anyone who worshipped the Nephite's true God. They also knew of the great hatred the Lamanites held for the Ammonites who had converted, and now would not even bear arms to defend themselves. If they fell into Lamanite hands, the Ammonites would be slaughtered. This is something the Nephites would not allow to happen because the Ammonites had contributed generously in support of their own defense.

The Lamanite army was comprised of the descendants of Laman, Lemuel, the sons of Ishmael, the priests of Noah, and former Nephites who had separated themselves. The Nephite army was commanded by Moroni[1], who was 25 years old.

When the armies met at the boundary of the Ammonite lands, the Nephites were well prepared for war with all kinds of weapons, armor, shields, and padded clothing to protect themselves. The Lamanite army was not prepared for such a force. They were armed with swords, slings, bows and arrows. Except for the Amalekites and Zoramites the Lamanites came to battle clothed in only their loin skins. Because the Nephites were so well armed, armored, and protected, the Lamanites became fearful of them in spite of their substantial numerical advantage. Seeing this great disparity of preparation, the Lamanite army dispersed back into the wilderness to attack somewhere else. They figured that Moroni would never know where they intended to go.

As soon as the Lamanite army dispersed Moroni sent spies into the wilderness to watch their camp. He also sent a party back to Zarahemla hoping that Alma might ask God for guidance as to where the Lamanite army was headed. Through Alma, Moroni's messengers learned from God that the Lamanite army was marching through the wilderness to attack a Nephite weak point in Manti.

When Moroni received this news, he left some of his army in the Ammonite lands and moved the rest of his army to Manti. When he arrived he organized the people there to defend their lands and country, their rights and freedoms. They were well prepared for battle before the Lamanites arrived. Moroni divided his army into several forces, and hid them on opposite sides of the nearby valley, beside the Sidon River. In order to attack Manti the Lamanite army would need to cross the river. Spies were positioned to alert Moroni when the Lamanites came near. With his army concealed and ready to fight, Moroni was well prepared to meet the enemy when they arrived.

When the Lamanite army approached the river and prepared to cross it, the portion of Moroni's army concealed on the far side of the river, rushed out to enclose the Lamanites from behind. The Lamanites saw the ambush and turned to fight, with the river to their backs. Because the Nephites were armored with breastplates, helmets, and shields, while the Lamanites were not, a slaughter ensued. The Lamanites fell heavily with very few Nephite casualties.

The remaining Lamanites panicked because of the enormous destruction and fled toward the river, pursued by the Nephite army. When all of the Lamanites had been driven into the river in an attempt to escape, Moroni brought his army out of hiding on the river's opposite side. The slaughter then intensified. When the Lamanites tried to flee in another direction, a third contingent of Moroni's army engaged them.

The surrounded Lamanites fought like dragons to free themselves from the trap they'd fallen into. While many Nephites were killed by the ferocity of the Lamanite defense, the Nephites were inspired by a higher cause. They were not fighting for conquest or power, but rather for the defense of their homes and families, their freedom, and the right to worship their God. They felt that it was their duty to fight because God had told their ancestors that they should not allow themselves to be killed if they were attacked. God had said, "Defend your families, even it means killing your enemies."

When the Nephites saw how intensely the Lamanites fought in their attempts to escape, many of them began to relent. Seeing this, Moroni sent messengers among his army to inspire them. "Think of your lands and your freedom," he said. So the Nephite army renewed their fighting, crying out to God for liberty and freedom from slavery.

At the onset, the Lamanite army had been twice the size of the Nephite army. Now they were reduced to a terrified group surrounded on both sides of the river. When the Lamanites' terror overcame them and they stopped fighting, Moroni ordered that his men should stop the killing. [74 BC]

Chapter 44, 1981 Version

At Moroni's command, the Nephite army stopped their combat, and withdrew one pace from the Lamanite warriors with whom they'd been fighting.

"Zerahemnah," Moroni call out to the Lamanite commander, "we do not want to be men of blood. You know we could kill you all, but we don't want to. We haven't come to battle to kill for power, nor do we want to enslave any of you. But these are the reasons you've come against us. You hate us because of our religion. But now you can see that God is on our side, and has delivered you into our hands. You need to understand that our victory was won because of our religion and our faith in Jesus Christ. Now you can see that you cannot destroy our faith."

"Therefore Zerahemnah, if you wish to live, I command you to hand over all your weapons of war. If you do this, we will spare your lives as long as you agree to go away, and quit your warring against us. I make this command in the name of that all-powerful God who has given us victory through our faith in our religion, our devotion to the rites of worship, our dedication to our church, through the support of our families, and by the sacred word of God to whom we owe all of our happiness. If you don't lay down your arms, I will order my men to exterminate all of you. Then you will see who has power over the other."

When Zerahemnah heard this he stepped forward and gave his sword and his bow to Moroni and said, "We will give you our weapons of war, but we won't make any promises to you that we, or our children, cannot keep. Take our weapons and let us go back into the wilderness, or we will keep our swords and fight to the death. We do not agree with your religion, nor do we believe that God has given you victory. We think it is your cunning and your armor that has defeated us."

Moroni gave Zerahemnah his weapons back. "Unless you promise to quit your warring against us we will destroy you," said Moroni. "Either submit to the conditions I have proposed or die."

When Moroni said this, Zerahemnah rushed forward to kill him with his sword. But as he raised it to strike, one of Moroni's guards struck Zerahemnah's sword to the ground and broke it. When Zarahemnah dodged into the midst of his armed warriors, one of Moroni's guards struck Zarahemnah and a piece of his scalp fell to the ground. The guard picked up the fallen scalp by the point of his sword and stretched it out to the Lamanites saying, "Just as your chief's scalp has fallen to the ground, so too will any of you who don't surrender your weapons and give us a promise of peace."

Hearing this ultimatum and seeing how things were, many of the Lamanite warriors were afraid for their lives. These men came forward, threw down their weapons at Moroni's feet, and made a promise of peace. All of those who did so were allowed to freely go back to the wilderness.

This made Zerahemna extremely angry. So he rallied the remainder of his army to make a mighty fight with the Nephites. By this time Moroni was angry too. He ordered his army to kill them all. Their bare bodies fell swiftly beneath the Nephite assault, just as Moroni had prophesied.

Just before they were about to be destroyed entirely, Zerahemnah cried out to Moroni and promised to end the warfare forever if their lives would be spared. So Moroni ordered his soldiers to stop the killing again. After he relieved them of their weapons and received their promises, Moroni let them go.

· There were so many dead among both the Lamanites and Nephites that no one bothered to count the bodies. The dead were thrown into the river, and carried away for burial at sea.

At the end of the 18th year of elected judges, the Nephite army returned to their homes and families. [73 BC]

Chapter 21, 1830 Version

Chapter 45, 1981 Version

After their victory the Nephites celebrated their joy, because God had once again delivered them from destruction or enslavement to their enemies. They gave thanks to God by praying, fasting, and worshipping.

In the 19th year of elected judges, Alma spoke with his son Helaman and asked, "Do you believe everything I said regarding the sacred records of our people?"

"Yes," said Helaman. "I believe."

"Do you believe that Jesus Christ will come?" asked Alma.

"Yes," answered Helaman. "I believe all the words that have been spoken."

"Will you honor my commandments?" Alma asked.

"I will do so with all my heart," Helaman responded.

"You are blessed," said Alma. "God will help you to prosper in the land. But now, I want to give you a private prophecy that I want you to write down. This prophecy must not be made known until the time it is fulfilled. Four hundred years after the time that Jesus Christ appears to the Nephite people, they will decline because of their failure to believe. Wars, epidemic diseases, and starvation will cause the Nephites to go extinct. This will occur because of their fall into darkness, promiscuity, and all forms of sinfulness. Within four generations after Jesus Christ appears to the Nephites, the people will begin their fall. When the Nephites become extinct only the Lamanites will survive, and any Nephites who survive will also become Lamanites. At that time, any believers in God who refuse to join the Lamanites will be hunted down and destroyed. Because of the Nephite's future sinfulness, this prophecy will be fulfilled."

After saying these things to Helaman, Alma blessed him. He then blessed his other sons, and blessed the earth for the sake of the righteous.

"God has said," declared Alma, " 'That every land, nation, and race of people are cursed who behave wickedly. When they are ripe, they will be destroyed.' This is both a curse and a blessing of God upon the land, because God cannot tolerate the smallest degree of sin."

Having said this Alma blessed the church and all of those who maintained their faith from that time forward. After giving his blessings Alma left Zarahemla again to go out preaching, but he disappeared, and was never heard from again.

Because he was a righteous man rumors spread that he had been taken up by the Spirit, or buried personally by God. The scriptures say that God took Moses up to join him, and people imagined that something similar had happened to Alma. But no one knew.

In the 19th year of elected judges, Helaman went out to preach among the people. Because of the Lamanite wars and the continuous petty dissensions among the people, the word of God needed to be declared and the church strengthened again. Throughout all of the Nephite lands, priests and teachers were appointed to support Helaman and re-establish the church. But the people had grown proud with their victory over the Lamanites, and sought riches over righteousness. They ignored the words of Helaman and his appointed priests. [72 BC]

Chapter 46, 1981 Version

There were a great many people who didn't want to hear what Helaman, his priests, and the church teachers had to say. Some became so angry they wanted to kill them. These people were led by a big, powerful man named Amalickiah who wanted to be king. His angry supporters included lesser judges who sought power and opportunities under Amalickiah's potential kingship. They wanted to be rulers of the Nephite people.

Amalickiah had a talent for flattery that led many church members into dissension regardless of Helaman's preaching, and the great pains he and the high priests were taking to restore the church. In spite of the recent Lamanite victory at the hand of God, the affairs of the Nephite people were precarious. It was disturbing to see how quickly the people forgot God, and how easily they were led away by an evil one. It was also alarming to see how much impact one wicked man could have on the affairs of others. Amalickiah was a slick deceiver who wanted to destroy the church of God, restrict freedom, and dismiss God's blessing on the land as unimportant.

When Moroni learned of Amalickiah's intentions, and of his success at misleading others, he became quite angry. From the fabric of his coat he fashioned a banner that read, "In memory of our God, our religion, our freedom, and our families." He attached the banner to a long pole, put on his helmet and armor, picked up his shield, and knelt on the ground in prayer. He prayed mightily to God for the freedoms his people enjoyed when Christians, as followers of Jesus Christ had come to be known, remained in possession of the land. Christians were those who were true believers in the future coming of Jesus Christ. So Moroni prayed to God that the cause of the Christians, and the freedom they had, would be preserved.

"Surely," Helaman cried out to God, "you will not let the Christians be abused or destroyed unless we bring it upon ourselves through our own sins."

Upon saying this, Moroni picked up his impromptu banner and waved it in the air as he went out among the people. "Whoever wants to hold title to this land must come forward with the strength of God," he declared, " and promise to protect their rights, their religion, and be blessed by God."

After this was said, the people did as Moroni had done, and tore off pieces of their coats as a token of their devotion to God. The symbolism of the torn coats was this. if they failed to honor the commandments of God, then God should tear them, just as they had torn their coats. This was their promise. They threw down their torn coats at Moroni's feet saying, "We understand that we will be destroyed if we violate our promises to God. If we sin, God may throw us at the feet of our enemies, just as we have thrown down our coats to be walked upon."

"We are descendants of Jacob[1]," Moroni said, "through his son Joseph[1] of Egypt, whose coat was torn to pieces by his brothers. Let us remember the commandments of God or our coats will be torn apart and we will be cast into

prison, enslaved, or killed. Before his death, Jacob saw that part of his son Joseph's coat had been preserved. He said, 'Just as a part of Joseph's coat was preserved, let a part of my Joseph's descendants be preserved by the hand of God.'"

"If we do not maintain our faith in Jesus Christ, then we may well be the part of Joseph's descendants who will perish," concluded Moroni.

Moroni sent messages throughout the land, and gathered together those who sought to maintain their freedoms, and stand against Amalickiah and the other dissenters. As Moroni's allies assembled it became obvious to Amalickiah that he had fewer followers than Moroni. He also saw that his own people were no longer so sure about the justice of his cause. In view of this, he gathered up his closest supporters and left for the land of Nephi, where the Lamanites resided.

This concerned Moroni because he didn't want to let the Lamanites become any stronger than they already were. He also knew that Amalickiah would provoke the Lamanites into a new round of wars with the Nephites in order to fulfill his ambitions. So Moroni called the army and set out to cut off Amalickiah and his followers in the wilderness, before they reached the Lamanite border.

Amalickiah escaped with a few of his men, when the armies met, and the rest of his followers were brought back to Zarahemla. Because Moroni was appointed the commander of the army by the chief judges, he had broad power to exercise his will. He ordered the execution of any of Amalickiah's people who wouldn't support the cause of freedom. In the end, very few refused.

Flags of freedom were hoisted to the top of every tower in the Nephite lands, and peace returned to the land. Helaman and the high priests restored the church, and for four years there was peace and joy within it. Many people lived to an old age and died happy in the faith of Jesus Christ. [72 BC]

Chapter 47, 1981 Version

After Amalickiah escaped into the Lamanite lands from the ambush that Moroni had set for them, he began encouraging the Lamanite king to go fight the Nephites again.

When the Lamanite king issued a proclamation throughout his lands for his warriors to gather and prepare for battle, many of the Lamanite fighters were disturbed. They didn't want to anger the king, but they didn't want to go fight the Nephites and get killed either. When the majority of his fighters refused his orders to fight, the king grew angry and placed the army's command in the hands of Amalickiah. He was told to take the loyal fighters with him, and force the rest of his warriors to join the fight.

Amalickiah had a secret plan to gain the loyalty of the dissenting Lamanites, dethrone the Lamanite king, and take power for himself. The warriors who refused to fight the Nephites were led by a man named Lehonti, and were gathered at Mount Antipas to fight the king's warriors. Amalickiah had a treacherous plan, and asked Lehonti to meet and talk with him. He proposed to make the king's warriors vulnerable to the dissenters if they came down at night and surrounded them. Amalickiah offered to deliver the entire king's army to Lehonti if he were made second in command of their combined forces.

The next morning, the king's army found themselves surrounded. The king's warriors pled with Amalickiah to join the dissenters rather than fight against their brothers. This is exactly what Amalickiah had planned and hoped for. So, contrary to the king's commands, Amalickiah surrendered his army to Lehonti in order to gain greater power for himself.

The Lamanites had a tradition of naming a second in command who would become their leader if the first man in command died. So Amalickiah had one of his servants gradually introduce poison into Lehonti's food until he died. With Lehonti out of the way, Amalickiah was appointed as chief commander of all the combined Lamanite army.

Amalickiah marched the army to the Lamanite king's city, and the king came out to greet him. He assumed that Amalickiah had fulfilled his orders and gathered up the army to go fight the Nephites. When the king arrived Amalickiah had arranged for his servants to precede him. They bowed down on the ground to him, as was their custom, in presumed reverence. When the king stretched out his hand to raise them up he was attacked and stabbed to death in his heart. The king's servants fled from this stealthy murder, and Amalickiah turned to his army behind him crying out, "The kings servants have killed him and fled. Come and see."

The army arrived on the scene and found the king lying in pool of his own blood. Amalickiah pretended anger saying, "Whoever among you loved the king, go chase down his servants and kill them." When the servants saw this turn of events, they fled into the wilderness and escaped to join the Ammonites among the Nephites.

The army returned empty handed and found that Amalickiah had gained the hearts of the people through his hidden treachery. Upon entering the city he sent messengers to the queen telling her that her husband had been brutally murdered by his servants who had then escaped. Hearing this, the queen asked that Amalickiah spare the people of the city and also bring forward a witness to testify regarding her husband's death.

Amalickiah brought the servant who had killed the king, along with his other servants who'd been a party to the murder, before the queen. Everyone testified that the king was killed by his own servants, who afterwards had run away. This satisfied the queen who trusted Amalickiah, and married him. Through this fraud the former Nephite, Amalickiah, became the ruler of all the Lamanite people. In the course of this conversion he and his followers entirely forgot about God. They became more wild, vicious, immoral, and sinful than even the Lamanites that they now ruled. [72 BC]

Chapter 48, 1981 Version

As ruler of the Lamanite kingdom Amalickiah provoked and fueled the Lamanites' hatred toward the Nephites through appointed propagandists. Now he wanted to rule over the all Nephites as well as over all the Lamanites. By the end of the 19th year of elected judges, he had succeeded in mobilizing the large Lamanite population in support of a new war against the Nephites, who he thought could be overwhelmed by superior numbers.

He appointed Zoramites as his chief army commanders because they were most acquainted with the strengths and weaknesses of the Nephites. When all was ready they prepared to march on Zarahemla.

While Amalickiah had been busy acquiring power through fraud and treachery, Moroni had been working with the Nephites to strengthen their faith in God. He also strengthened the Nephite army, built forts, protective embankments, and walls throughout the land. He placed extra soldiers at the points of weakest fortification. He worked at many levels to build support for the Christian cause of freedom, peace, and the protection of their land and families. Moroni was a strong and mighty man who did not want bloodshed, but was committed to keeping his people free from enslavement to others. He gave thanks to God for the privileges and blessings that came to his people, and worked hard to preserve these. He was solid in his faith in Jesus Christ.

The Nephites were taught to defend themselves against their enemies, but to never make unprovoked attacks against others. By fighting defensively, God supported them if they were also faithful in keeping his commandments. God would also tell them to flee or prepare for battle according to the danger involved. God made it known that when they went out to defend themselves from attack, he would deliver victory to them. This was the faith of Moroni. He gloried in preserving his people, keeping God's commandments, and resisting sinfulness. If all men had been like Moroni, the power of hell would have been shaken to its foundation, and the devil would lose his hold on the hearts of men. In this, he was like Ammon and his brothers, and like Alma and his sons. They were all men of God.

Helaman and his brothers were also busy doing their part. They preached the word of God, and performed baptisms for those who listened to their words and wished to repent. For four years the Nephites had been free from infighting. At the end of the 19th year of elected judges, the Nephites reluctantly took up arms again to defend themselves against the Lamanites. For this they were greatly sorry because they did not take pleasure in warfare. They were sorry to have to kill the Lamanites who were unprepared to meet their God. But what else could they do? If they didn't fight, their families would be slaughtered by the evil cruelty of an enemy who had once been their brothers before leaving to become Lamanites. [72 BC]

Chapter 49, 1981 Version

At the end of the 19th year of elected judges, the Lamanite army arrived on the borders of the Nephite lands, where the city of Ammonihah once stood. God had previously allowed the Lamanites to destroy this city because of the sinfulness of the people that lived there. The Lamanite army came to this city now because they thought it would be an easy conquest again. But to their disappointment the rebuilt city had been fortified by Moroni with high earthen mounds around it. These mounds shielded the Nephite soldiers from the Lamanites arrows and rocks, and the only approach was through a well guarded entrance. Moroni's defensive preparations surprised and astonished the Lamanites, who were also armored this time with shields and breastplates. Because of their superior numbers the Lamanites had imagined they could easily overpower the Nephites and take them away as slaves, or kill them according to their pleasure. But they were unprepared for Moroni's defenses.

If King Amalickiah had led his army, perhaps he would have ordered the Lamanites to attack, because he didn't care if his soldiers perished. But in his absence his commander didn't attack Ammonihah. It didn't look like an easy conquest at all. So the Lamanite army melted back into the wilderness and headed toward the city of Noah instead, in search of an easier conquest. When they arrived there, they found that Moroni had erected even greater earthworks and fortifications at Noah than he had at Ammonihah.

This was all part of Moroni's plan. He guessed that they would be intimidated at Ammonihah and would come to Noah next, because it had been the least defended of all the cities in the land. Now he had the Lamanites just where he wanted them.

The Lamanites had sworn an oath to attack Noah and brought their army forward. Once again, high earthen mounds and a moat surrounded the city, making it unapproachable except for the main entrance. The Nephites were well prepared to destroy anyone who tried to enter.

When the Lamanite army tried to force an entry at the fortified entrance they were slaughtered. When that failed, they tried digging through the mounds of earth, but were driven away by stones and arrows hurled down from the fortified city walls. The moat filled up with bodies of dead Lamanite warriors, and the Nephites enjoyed total military superiority over the Lamanite attack. When the Lamanite commanders were killed their army quit fighting. More than a 1,000 Lamanites lay dead while not a single Nephite had been killed.

The remaining Lamanite warriors fled into the wilderness and told King Amalickiah, the former Nephite, what had occurred. When King Amalickiah heard of the defeat he became extremely angry with his own people. His desire to subjugate the Nephites had not happened as planned. He cursed God. Then he cursed Moroni, and swore that he would yet drink Moroni's blood.

The Nephites gave thanks to their God for delivering them from harm at the hands of their enemies. Peaceful and prosperous times once again came to the Nephites and their church because of their vigilance in honoring the word of God. Alma's and Mosiah's sons baptized and ordained others, who spread then the word across the land to all the people. [72 BC]

Chapter 22, 1830 Version

Chapter 50, 1981 Version

Even after his victory, Moroni continued to build defensive fortifications around all of the Nephite cities. Earthen mounds were topped with a strong line of log pickets. Towers were constructed, that allowed protected defenders to rain down stones and arrows on attackers.

Moroni also directed his army to enter the wilderness to the east of Zarahemla and drove all the Lamanites back to their own lands. After clearing out the Lamanites to the eastern sea, Moroni asked the Nephites to settle this land clear down to the seashore. In so doing he eliminated the Lamanite strongholds in the eastern wilderness. To the west he fortified the border between the Nephites and the Lamanites. All of this was done to weaken and scatter the Lamanites who Moroni wanted to discourage from future attacks. New cities

were built along the Lamanite boundary all the way to the eastern coastline.

During the 21st year of elected judges, the Nephites prospered, multiplied, and became rich. Centuries previously God had told Lehi[1], "You and your descendants will be blessed as long as they keep my commandments. But remember, if they don't, then they will be cut off from my blessings." It was clear to all that the truth of God's statement could be seen. When the Nephites had fought among themselves, worshipped idols, practiced fornication and other abominations, wars and destruction had come upon them. At the same time, those who honored God's commandments were delivered from slavery and death. This period of Nephite prosperity and happiness was the greatest since the days of Nephi. These were very good years. [71 BC]

In the 24th year of elected judges, conflicts arose between the Nephites who lived in the new coastal lands of Lehi and Morianton. The people of Morianton laid claim to lands also claimed by the people of Lehi, and were willing to kill to maintain that claim. The people of Lehi appealed to Moroni because they knew they were in the right. Learning of this the people of Morianton became fearful that Moroni's army would come to the Lehites' defense, and destroy them. [68 BC]

So Morianton[2], the leader after whom the city was named, inspired his people to move north and take possession of new lands. But just before this movement was set to happen, Morianton became angry with his maid, and beat her intensely. Afterwards the maid fled to Moroni, and told him of Morianton's plans. Moroni was concerned that Morianton's influence would grow, so he sent his army out to stop Morianton's migration to the north. When Moroni's army met up with Morianton, a great battle ensued in which Morianton was killed, his army was defeated, and the survivors were returned to Moroni as prisoners. Under Moroni's leadership, the people of Morianton promised to keep the peace, and returned to their land as good neighbors to the people of Lehi.

Nephihah, the chief judge, died after many years of devoted service, and his son Pahoran[1] was appointed as his successor. Pahoran made a sacred oath to judge righteously, protect the peace and freedom of the Nephite people, maintain the cause of God, and bring the wicked to justice in accordance with their crimes. [67 BC]

Chapter 23, 1830 Version

Chapter 51, 1981 Version

The 25th year of elected judges, found the Nephites in a brief period of peace. The peace ended with complaints by a vocal, political contingent who wanted to replace the rule of judges with a restoration of monarchy. Pahoran, the new chief judge, dismissed these petitions to change the law, and refused to listen to the proponents for monarchy. This angered the king-men, as these people who wanted to dispense with free government were called.

There were also those who wanted Pahorn to remain as chief judge. These people were called free-men. They wanted judicial protection of their rights and privileges, especially the freedom of religious expression. Eventually this question was put to a vote and the people chose freedom and judicial rule. This silenced the king-men, but did not alter their desires to restore a monarchy. These king-men were themselves of royal lineage and sought to be kings. Their followers sought power and authority over other people.

At the same time, Amalickiah was provoking the Lamanites again, attempting to instigate a new war. After all, he had sworn that he would drink the blood of Moroni. The army that he was able to assemble was not as big as it had been because so many of his warriors were killed. This time though, Amalickiah led the army into battle himself. He arrived on the border of the Nephite lands just as the question of monarchy had been settled.

Because of their political loss, the embittered king-men took perverse pleasure in the new threat posed by Amalickiah's army, and refused to bear arms or defend their lands. When Moroni learned of this refusal, he got very angry with the stubbornness of the king-men. He asked the people and the governor to approve a measure that compelled the dissenters to join in the defense against the Lamanites, or be put to death. The majority of the people agreed with his petition and gave Moroni a mandate to forcefully put an end to the dissension among the Nephites.

Moroni sent his army out against the king-men and demanded their submission. All of the king-men who raised weapons against Moroni's army were destroyed immediately. 4,000 king-men were killed and many more were imprisoned. The rest of them joined Moroni's army and took up the defense of the land. After that, there were no more king-men. They were either dead, imprisoned, or fighting valiantly alongside the other Nephites for freedom.

While Moroni was busy suppressing the internal dissension, the Lamanites had entered the Nephite borders near the coastline and attacked the city of Moroni. Because the Nephites were distracted, Moroni was vulnerable to attack. Amalickiah successfully conquered the city and overcame its fortifications. Many Nephites were killed. Refugees from the city of Moroni and from the city of Lehi fled to Nephihah to prepare for battle. Amalickiah chose not to attack the strengthened city of Nephihah, but conquered the coastal cities one by one.

As the Lamanite army marched across the land, masses of Nephite refugees were driven before them, and many were killed. When the Nephite army, led by Teancum, finally caught up with and engaged Amalickiah's army, the tide began to turn. Teancum's men were seasoned soldiers, all of whom were more experienced and stronger than the Lamanites they opposed. When the armies clashed they fought until darkness, and then set camp.

That night Teancum and his servant crept stealthily into Amalickiah's camp and found his tent. The Lamanite army was so exhausted from battle that Teancum was able sneak into Amalickiah's tent and thrust a spear through his heart without awakening any of his guards. When he returned to his own camp, Teancum awakened his men and told them what had happened so that they would be prepared in case of a counter attack. [67 BC]

Chapter 24, 1830 Version

Chapter 52, 1981 Version

The Lamanites awakened the next morning to discover that Amalickiah lay dead, and that Teancum was pressing them for battle. Seeing this, they abandoned their plans of continued conquest, and retreated to the city of Mulek, to regroup behind the protective fortifications. Amalickiah's brother Ammoron was appointed as the new Lamanite king. He declared that the Lamanite army should hold on to and defend all of the Nephite cities that they had conquered at great sacrifice of their people.

Teancum saw that the Lamanites planned to keep possession of the lands they'd conquered, and determined that it would be foolish for his small army to undertake a siege of the fortified cities. Instead, he kept his army close by, and prepared places where they could defend their positions while they waited for Moroni to send a reinforcing army. [66 BC]

Moroni sent messages to Teancum advising him to hold onto any Lamanite prisoners he captured for a possible exchange of Nephites held by the Lamanites. He also ordered Teancum to secure a strategic narrow pass to the north and prevent the Lamanites from acquiring it. Because Moroni was fighting another Lamanite army on the west coast he left the fight on the east coast to Teancum. He advised him to do whatever he could to defeat the Lamanites, regain the lost cities if possible, and strengthen the cities that had not fallen.

The Lamanite King Ammoron returned home, informed the queen about the death of his brother, and raised more men with which to battle Moroni's army on the west coast. By fighting on two fronts he hoped to keep possession of the conquered cities and keep the Nephite army divided.

Early the following year Moroni advanced toward Teancum hoping to recapture the Nephite cities that had been lost to the invading Lamanite army. Until Moroni arrived it was impossible for Teancum to overpower the well defended cities. [65 BC]

When Moroni and his army arrived, they strategized on how to coax the Lamanites from the fortified cities and into the open field for battle. Since the Lamanite commander who held the city of Mulek would not be lured out by flattery or posturing, Moroni planned to trick the Lamanites into coming out using Teancum as a decoy.

Teancum took a small number of men and visibly marched down to the coast, while Moroni withdrew his army into the wilderness. When the Lamanites saw Teancum's small army in a vulnerable position they decided to attack them. This is what Teancum and Moroni had planned on. As the Lamanites advanced Teancum fled northward, which emboldened the Lamanites to chase after them. While the Lamanites were busy pursuing Teancum, Moroni emerged from the wilderness and captured the city of Mulek killing all the remaining Lamanites who attempted to resist the Nephite reconquest of the city.

After taking possession of Mulek, Moroni sent part of his army out to meet the Lamanites who were out chasing after Teancum. Meanwhile Teancum retreated as far north as the Nephite city of Bountiful, which was held by another small army led by Lehi[2]. When Teancum's force joined the army defending Bountiful, the Lamanites decided it was time for them to retreat, not knowing that Moroni's army now stood between them and Mulek.

Lehi's army pursued the Lamanites southward, being careful not to overtake them until the Lamanites were trapped against Moroni's army from behind. When the armies finally met the Nephite armies of Moroni and Lehi[2] were fresh. The Lamanite army on the other hand was exhausted and hungry from the march north to Bountiful, and then south again without resting. Moroni ordered an immediate attack. Thinking that they could break through and safely retreat to the city of Mulek the Lamanites fought ferociously. But the army of Moroni was stronger. With Moroni's army in front, and Lehi's army at their back, it was only a matter of time until the Lamanites fell and scattered. At this point, Moroni saw their confusion and said, "If you lay down your weapons, we will quit killing you."

Hearing this, the surviving Lamanite captains threw down their arms and ordered their soldiers to do likewise. But there were a great number who refused. So they were subdued by force and taken as prisoners. In the end, more prisoners were taken than the total number who had been killed on both sides. [64 BC]

Chapter 53, 1981 Version

The Lamanite prisoners were put to work digging graves for the dead. After that Teancum marched them back to the city of Bountiful, where they were forced to dig defensive ditches and build fortifications around the city. When the work was finished the Lamanite prisoners were kept in a compound within the fortified city.

Moroni gave Lehi, his fellow commander and close friend, control of the city of Mulek. Moroni and Lehi had been through so much together that they may as well have been brothers. They loved each other, and were also well loved by all the Nephites.

That year Moroni made no more attempts to attack the Lamanites, or recapture the cities that had been lost. Instead, he focused on further fortifying the Nephite cities. He made preparations for war, protected the women and children, and grew food for the people and the army.

In spite of their recent victories the Nephites were on shaky ground due to internal dissension, intrigue, and sinfulness. The Lamanites took advantage of the Nephite weaknesses wherever they could, and managed to capture a few more cities along the west coastlands.

The Ammonites maintained their pledge to never arm themselves and fight, so the Nephites moved them to Zarahemla for their own protection. When the Ammonites saw firsthand the sacrifices the Nephites were making for them, they were moved with compassion to step forward and help in their own defense. But Helaman and his brothers intervened just before the Ammonites broke their pledge. Helaman was afraid that they would lose their souls if they armed themselves and broke their promises to God. But the Ammonites had many sons who had not taken the pledge, because they had been too young at the time the promises had been made. So these sons stepped forward as the fighting contingent of the Ammonites. 2,000 of these former Lamanite sons entered the army and promised to protect the Nephite lands and their freedom. Even though their skins were still as dark as Lamanites they called themselves Nephites.

While the Ammonites had never been a liability to the Nephites they now became a great asset to them in this time of trouble. These 2,000 young men knew the commandments of God, and kept them virtuously. After choosing Helaman as their leader they marched off with courage, honesty, and strength to defend their country. [64 BC]

Chapter 25, 1830 Version

Chapter 54, 1981 Version

In the 29th year of elected judges, King Ammoron sent a message to Moroni that he wanted to exchange prisoners. This pleased Moroni for several reasons. Feeding and sheltering the Lamanite prisoners depleted his ability to provide for his own people. He also wanted the Nephite prisoners to help strengthen his army. While the Lamanites held women and children as prisoners, there was not a single woman or child among the Lamanite prisoners that he held. So Moroni developed a strategy to obtain as many Nephite prisoners in exchange as possible.

Moroni wrote back to Ammoron, saying, "I have some things to say to you about this war your brother started, and that you seem determined to continue. You should know about the justice of God, and the sword of his almighty anger that hangs over you unless you repent, quit warring on us, and remove your armies to your own lands. If you are capable of listening, you should know of the awful hell that waits to receive murderers like you and your brother have been. But since you have already rejected such warnings, and fought against God's people, I expect you will do so again."

"But be warned," Moroni continued, "that we are fully prepared to receive you and to defend our lands. Unless you withdraw, the full anger of the God whom you reject will fall upon you. This will result in your complete destruction. If you don't leave peaceably, our armies will kill you all. We will regain and protect our cities and our lands. We will maintain our religion and the cause of God. But I suspect that I talk with you about these things in vain because you are a child of the devil's who cannot hear me."

"Therefore I propose the following regarding the possibility of prisoner exchange. I will exchange one Lamanite prisoner for the safe return of a Nephite man, woman, and child. If you refuse this offer, I will set my armies upon you. I will arm women and children too. I will hunt you down, even in your own lands, until every one of you is killed. My people and I are extremely angry with you. You try to murder us while we only try to defend ourselves. If you continue to try and destroy us, you will have us working to destroy you."

Ammoron angrily wrote back, "I fully intend to avenge my murdered brother's death. I have no fear of you or your threats. You ancestors cheated and wronged our ancestors by stealing the leadership from them that was rightfully theirs. I will offer you the opportunity to lay down your weapons and become our subjects. We are the rightful governors of this land. If you do this, my people will also lay down their weapons and we can live without war. We are not afraid of your empty threats."

"Nevertheless, I will agree to your prisoner exchange proposal. We will wage an eternal war until either all Nephites are either exterminated or subjected to our authority. As to the God who you say we rejected, we know of no such being, and neither do you. If such a creator exists, he made us both. If there is a devil and hell, surely he will surely send you there for murdering my brother. But these things are of no importance to us. I wage this war to avenge the wrongs done to my ancestors by yours, and to obtain the rights of government that were stolen from them." [63 BC]

Chapter 55, 1981 Version

Ammoron's response brought Moroni to a rage. The Lamanites phony pretense for war was not honest, and everyone knew it.

"I will not exchange prisoners with Ammoron unless he ends the hostilities," Moroni insisted. "I will not give him more power than he already has. I know where the Lamanites imprison our people. Since Ammoron won't meet my conditions, we will fight until the Lamanites beg for peace."

Moroni searched among his men for a converted Lamanite who was descended from Laman. They found a man named Laman[3], who had once been a servant to the Lamanite king that Amalickiah had killed. Moroni hatched a plot using Laman[3] and a few of his fellow soldiers to pose as escaped Lamanite prisoners.

The Nephite prisoners were held in the former Nephite city of Gid. When Laman and his band approached Gid, they told the guards not to worry. "We have narrowly escaped from the Nephites," they said. "And look here, we have also stolen some of their wine and brought it with us."

Hearing this, the Lamanites guards were delighted, and ready to have their share of the wine. But Laman was sly. "We should save the wine for later, when we go to battle," he said, which only made the guards want it more.

"We want it now. We'll be given plenty when the time for battle is upon us," the guards responded.

"Whatever you want," said Laman. The wine was good, and also very strong. The guards drank freely of it. Soon they were drunk. When the drunken guards had fallen asleep, Laman returned to Moroni and told him about what had happened. It was all according to Moroni's plan. Nephites silently entered the prison while the guards slept, and armed the Nephite prisoners inside. Moroni's soldiers and the armed prisoners could have easily killed all the sleeping Lamanites, but this was not their wish. Moroni did not like killing if it could be avoided.

With the Nephite prisoners armed and loose inside the city, they were able to surround the Lamanites inside while Moroni surrounded the entire city with his army. When the Lamanites awakened in the morning they found themselves surrounded, inside and out.

Under the circumstances, the Lamanites saw that resistance was futile. The Lamanite commanders came forward, threw down their weapons, and begged for mercy. This had been Moroni's wish. So the Nephite prisoners were freed to join Moroni's army, and more Lamanite soldiers were now imprisoned. As he had done before, Moroni set the Lamanite prisoners to work strengthening the fortifications around the city of Gid.

This surprise attack and deliverance became a turning point for the Nephites. They became victorious in their successive battles to protect their rights and freedoms. The Lamanites attempted various tricks to entice the Nephites into ruin, but had no success. The Nephites owed their success to their renewed faith in God, and were not easily led astray. Moroni was vigilant in detecting any schemes designed to entrap them.

At the end of the 29th year of elected judges, Moroni judged that it was about time to attack the Lamanite stronghold in the city of Morianton. Preparations for the attack began. [63 BC]

Chapter 26, 1830 Version

Chapter 56, 1981 Version

In the beginning of the 30th year of elected judges, Moroni received a letter from Helaman. "My dearly beloved brother," Helaman wrote, "I wanted to apprise you of how the Lamanite conflicts are going in this part of the land. I have been leading 2,000 young Ammonite soldiers who took up arms to defend our land and traditions. As you remember, these are the former Lamanites whose fathers swore to refrain from killing, even in their own defense. To prevent their fathers from breaking their oaths, these sons have stepped forward to help.

"Several years ago we marched to the city of Judea to support Antipus, the regional commander whose forces had been badly decimated by the Lamanites. The cities of Manti, Zeezrom, Cumeni, and Antiparah had been conquered. The defenders of Judea were sorely depressed in body and spirit about their losses when I arrived, and were busy strengthening the fortifications of Judea. The Lamanites were determined to conquer Judea or die trying. So the arrival of my force of Ammonite sons was a great relief and blessing. [66 BC]

"When the Lamanites learned how much the defending forces had been strengthened, they were ordered not to attack Judea but to hold onto those cities that they'd taken. During the following year, we prepared the city and our army for defense. Having done that, we wanted the Lamanites to attack us rather than have to attack them behind their fortifications.

"Our spies were posted around the land to watch for Lamanite movements, and to insure that their armies did not pass Judea by to attack other cities to the north. We knew that these cities were insufficiently strong to resist the Lamanites. If they did move to attack them, we had developed a plan to fight from the rear when they were also fighting in the front. We thought that under these circumstances we could defeat them. But this is not what

happened. They just sat still, and held onto their cities.

"Some months ago we received a large delivery of provisions from the Ammonites to support their defense. We also received a detachment of 2,000 more men from Zarahemla. This resulted in a well provisioned fighting force of 10,000. As the Lamanites saw our strength grow daily they began to test our defenses to see if it would be possible to intercept our flow of men and provisions. [65 BC]

"When we saw the uneasiness that our growing strength had on the Lamanites, we developed a strategy to defeat them. My 2,000 Ammonite sons and I marched northward to a neighboring city, posing as if we were carrying supplies to them. We planned our route so that it would pass close to the city of Antiparah, where the Lamanites were strongest. When our decoy supply convoy passed them by, they came out of the city and marched to meet us. When we saw that we had drawn out the strongest portion of the Lamanite army, we quickly fled northward, bringing the Lamanite army along in tow behind us.

"Meanwhile, the army of Antipus followed behind us to catch the Lamanites from behind. When the Lamanites became aware of their mistake, they quickened their speed to catch and defeat us before the army of Antipus caught up with them. They reasoned that it would be better to take our forces on one at a time rather than being surrounded and fighting us on both sides at once.

"When Antipus saw the situation, he also quickened the pace of his army to reach and help us. At nightfall, all three armies were still separated. At dawn, we found the Lamanite army was bearing down hard upon us, and far bigger than anything we were prepared to deal with. So we turned, and escaped into the wilderness. Seeing this, the Lamanites halted their pursuit of us and laid a trap to catch anyone who might attack.

" 'Are you ready for battle?' I asked the Ammonite sons. They were ready. Never have I seen such courage. 'Our God is with us,' they said, 'and he will not let us fall. We only go forward to kill because they will not leave us alone. Let's go before they ambush Antipus and defeat his army.'

"Now these Ammonite sons had never fought before, but at this moment they thought more about the freedom of their families than they did about their own lives. Their mothers had taught them that if they didn't doubt, God would deliver them. With this in their minds, they returned to fight the Lamanites. When we arrived, we discovered that the army of Antipus had caught up with the Lamanites, and that a terrible battle had begun.

"Because of their long, fast march, Antipus' army was tired. The Lamanites had prepared well to receive them and were about to defeat the army when we returned. Antipus himself, and many of his commanders, had already been killed. Without leadership, the army was in disarray with the Lamanites were closing in for the final kill.

"My small army of 2,000 came upon the rear of the Lamanites and began methodically killing them from behind. Now, the Lamanite army turned and faced us. When this happened, Antipus' army regathered and then started attacking from what was the new rear of the Lamanite army. Together, our combined army had them surrounded. We killed so many Lamanites that the survivors were compelled to lay down their weapons, and surrender themselves as prisoners of war.

"After the battle was over I began counting my men to see how many had perished. To my joy, I discovered that not a single one of my 2,000 had died fighting. They had fought with the strength and protection of God. No one had ever seen men fight with such miraculous strength and power. They fought so ferociously that they caused the Lamanites to surrender. The prisoners were sent back to Zarahemla with some of the survivors of Antipus' army. The rest of his army joined us, and returned to Judea." [64 BC]

Chapter 57, 1981 Version

"Shortly thereafter I received a message from Ammoron, the Lamanite king," Helaman continued writing in his letter to Moroni, "that if I returned the Lamanite prisoners of war, he would hand the city of Antiparah over to us.

"I wrote back to Ammoron that we would only exchange Lamanite prisoners held by us for Nephite prisoners held by him. I told him that we were certain of our ability to take

Antiparah by force. When Ammoron refused my offer, we began our preparations for war. When the citizens of Antiparah learned of our imminent attack they fled to other cities that the Lamanites already held. So the city of Antiparah fell into our hands without a fight.

"Some time later we received generous supplies from Zarahemla along with an additional 6,060 troops. Sixty of these men were more sons of the Ammonites. After this we were a much stronger fighting force than before. So we set our sights next on recapturing the city of Cumeni, and waging war with the Lamanite army that protected it.

"We surrounded the city one night just before their scheduled supply of provisions was due to arrive. For many nights we camped outside the city walls, sleeping with our swords. We needed to be prepared for instant defense if the Lamanites attacked us while we slept. They attempted these nightly ambushes many times, but it was always at their loss. One night, the anticipated supply delivery arrived, and we successfully took the supply party prisoners, and kept the supplies all for ourselves.

"In spite of being cut off from their support, the Lamanites persisted in holding on to Cumeni. We sent the supplies back to Judea, and sent the prisoners back to Zarahemla. When the Lamanites realized that we were determined to conquer the city regardless of any resistance on their part, they surrendered. By now, the number of Lamanite prisoners was so large that it required our entire army to guard them. They tried breaking free once, fighting us with clubs and stones. By the time we subdued them, 2,000 Lamanites lay dead.

"It became necessary that we either kill them all, or bring them all to Zarahemla under heavy guard. In spite of the fact that we'd taken the supplies meant for them, keeping them all fed meant seriously depleting our own resources. In all these ways, these prisoners became a serious problem to us. We resolved to take them to Zarahemla, and sent along an army to guard and transport them.

"The next day a fresh army of well supplied Lamanites sent by King Ammon* arrived and attacked us. Just as we were about to be overpowered, the army we'd sent to Zarahemla with the prisoners the previous day, returned and saved us. We didn't have time to ask what became of the prisoners they'd taken with them.

*In subsequent versions of The Book of Mormon Ammon has been changed to Ammoron. Ammon was one of King Mosiah's sons, not a Lamanite king.

"My band of 2,060 Ammonite sons fought the Lamanites with ferocious intensity, and all those who opposed them died trying. They were precise in executing my every command. I remembered their mothers' words to them, 'that if they didn't doubt, God would deliver them.'

"Credit for our surprising victory lay with my Ammonite sons, and with the army who had been selected to convey the prisoners, but returned so quickly to us. We had regained Cumeni and driven the Lamanites back to Manti, but not without suffering great losses. As soon as the battle had been won, and the Lamanites had fled, I ordered that the wounded be gathered up for immediate treatment. 200 of my 2,060 Ammonite sons had fainted from loss of blood in the battle, and all of them were badly wounded. To my astonishment, and through the goodness of God, none of them died. The entire army was in disbelief that all of the Ammonite sons survived when 1,000 of their fellow soldiers had died. We attributed it to the miraculous power of God because of what they'd been taught to believe by their mothers — that God was just, and that whoever did not doubt would be preserved through God's power.

"After burying the dead, we asked about the fate of the prisoners bound for Zarahemla. The captain in charge was a man named Gid, and this is the story that he told. 'Shortly after we'd started out we met up with our army's spies who'd been watching the Lamanite camps. We learned from them of the imminent arrival of the fresh Lamanite army and the peril that the Nephites at Cumeni were in. The prisoners also heard of this and rose up against us in rebellion. Even though they weren't armed, they attacked us in a great rush. Most of them were killed, while a few of them broke through and ran away. Afterwards we quickly returned to Cumeni to support you. We have been delivered from our enemy's hands once again by the blessed power of God.'

"When I heard Gid's story I was filled with joy because of God's goodness in preserving us. I trust that all of those among us who have died, have gone to rest with God." [63 BC]

Chapter 58, 1981 Version

"Our next objective was to recapture the city of Manti," Helaman continued in his letter to Moroni. "Leading their army out of their fortifications by using small bands of decoys would not work again. Because their numbers were so much greater than ours, laying siege to the cities would have been suicidal. In addition, we had to deploy our troops to protect the cities that we'd regained. So it became necessary to wait, and see what came to us in the way of supplies and reinforcements from Zarahemla.

"Meanwhile, the Lamanites were also receiving supplies and reinforcements. Periodically, they would strike out at us. They tried to tempt us into attacking them at their places of greatest strength so that they could destroy us. For many months we sat and waited until we ran out of food. Eventually we received some meager food supplies and a mere 2,000 men to help defend our country from falling into the hands of our innumerable enemies.

"Our only recourse was prayer to God, asking him to strengthen and deliver us from the hands of our enemies. We asked for support to help us retain the cities and lands for the support of our people. The result of this was that God answered our prayers with a personal visit. He assured us that he would deliver us. From this visit we received renewed faith, and peace in our souls. Our small force took courage and became determined to conquer the Lamanites, maintain our lands, protect our families, and sustain our freedom.

"We gathered up our army, and pitched our tents in the wilderness near Manti. The next day, when the Lamanites saw our forces deployed around the city, they sent out spies to find out how potent a fighting force we would be. They could see that we weren't very strong in terms of numbers of soldiers, but might be capable of cutting them off from their supply deliveries. They determined that we could be easily beaten if they came out to fight us, and made preparations to do so.

"When we saw the Lamanites deploying for battle, I had two small contingents led by Gid and Teomner hide themselves in the wilderness while I remained in position with the army. When the Lamanites attacked in force, I had my forces flee to the wilderness instead of meeting the assault. The Lamanites rushed after us in haste, wanting to quickly destroy us. In so doing, they ran past the hidden bands led by Gid and Teomner, who quickly cut off the rear guard spies that kept communication with the city. They quickly ran to the nearly abandoned city, surprised and killed the guards left behind, and took possession of it. Meanwhile almost the entire Lamanite army had come after us and were chasing us around the wilderness.

"Our wilderness evasion effort traveled in the direction of Zarahemla. When the Lamanites realized this they became afraid, thinking that they might be walking into another trap. So they abandoned their pursuit of us and returned to Manti. Thinking that they'd chased our entire army, they pitched their tents for the night without a concern about Manti.

"While the Lamanite army slept, I marched my men back by another way to Manti in darkness. We arrived in Manti before the Lamanites did, and took possession of the fortified city without a fight. When Lamanite army arrived they were astonished to find us behind the fortifications and fully prepared to repel an attack. They became so afraid that they rushed into the wilderness. After that, all the Lamanites fled from our area , and abandoned our cities to us. Unfortunately they also took with them many Nephite women and children.

"Except for the stolen women and children, the people are returning to their homes. Our problem now is that our armies are too small to protect so many cities. We trust in God that we will be able to hold onto them. For some unknown reason the government is not sending us any help. Are your needs so great that all the resources are being sent to you? If this is the reason, I do not complain. If that isn't the reason we are afraid that some faction of the government is overlooking our critical needs. We know that they have much more than we do.

"In spite of the army's weakness we trust that God will deliver us from the hands of our enemies. It is now the end of the 29th year of elected judges. The Ammonite sons that I've spoken of are with me now in Manti. Although they have received many wounds, none of them have died. They know that their freedom and protection comes from God so they faithfully observe his commandments at all times. They believe strongly in the prophecies about the coming of Jesus Christ.

"My brother Moroni, may God who has redeemed us and made us free keep you always in his presence. May he also favor our people by helping you to regain from the Lamanites all that we have lost. Sincerely, Helaman, son of Alma." [63 BC]

Chapter 27, 1830 Version

Chapter 59, 1981 Version

In the 30th year of elected judges, Moroni received Helaman's letter. He rejoiced to learn of Helaman's success regaining the lost land and cities from the Lamanites. He broadcast the good news among his people so that they could rejoice too. Immediately Moroni sent a letter to the chief judge, Pahoran, and asked that reinforcements be gathered and sent to Helaman in order to keep what had been so miraculously regained. Moroni began developing plans to also regain the lost cities in his area.

As Moroni was making preparations, Nephihah and the Nephite refugees congregating there were attacked by the Lamanites. The Lamanite army had been newly strengthened with the warriors fleeing from Manti as well as through regular reinforcements received from the Lamanite king. Their armies were so large and well provisioned that they slaughtered the Nephite refugees who didn't flee, and took the city of Nephihah by storm.

Moroni was unhappy that the government had failed to send enough support to hold Nephihah. He knew how much easier it was to hold a city from falling than it was to conquer one that was in Lamanite hands. It now took Moroni's entire force to hold on to the remaining cities, and attacking the Lamanites became out of the question.

Moroni and his commanders began to suspect that the wickedness of the Nephite people was behind their recent losses to the Lamanites. They were angry at the apparent indifference of the government to the plight of their country, and the freedom that it stood for. [62 BC]

Chapter 60, 1981 Version

Moroni soon wrote again to Pahoran, the chief judge and governor of the land:

"I have some criticism for you to listen to. As you know, you and your staff have been appointed to gather and arm men to defend our lands against the Lamanite invasion. Helaman and his men, along with me and my men, have suffered great hardships in defending our country. If this were all, we'd have no room to complain. But when I learn of the slaughter of thousands of our people because of your neglect to send us troops and supplies I protest your neglect of us.

"We want to know the reason for this neglect and thoughtlessness. Do you sit on your throne in stupor while your enemies spread death all around you? The Lamanites are murdering thousands of your people. We look to you for protection and help from destruction. You withhold provisions that weaken us with hunger. Do you want to face revenge from God for the thousands who died because you failed to extend yourselves when they cried out in need of help? Do you think you can sit on your throne, do nothing, and expect God's goodness and deliverance? Do you think that our people are being killed because of their wickedness? If these are you thoughts, you are deeply mistaken. Our dead condemn us. I am deeply afraid that the judgment of God will fall upon all of us because of the negligence of a government that is supposed to be protecting them.

"If we had not been fighting among ourselves we could have withstood our enemies in the first place. If it hadn't been for the king-men who caused so much bloodshed among us, we would never have gotten into these wars in the beginning. Now the Lamanites overrun our lands, murder our people, and take them away as slaves. All of this because some wanted more power and authority.

"Why do I bring all of this up? Because now you behave as if it were you who seek power and authority. How can we be certain that you aren't traitors to your country? Or have you neglected those of us who fight because you are in the heart of our country, and surrounded by security? What possible reason could you have for failing to send us food and support? Have you forgotten the commandments of God? Have you forgotten the slavery of our ancestors? Have you forgotten the many times we've been delivered from the hands of our enemies? Or do you think that God will somehow save us again while you sit on your thrones and fail to use the means that God has provided us with?

"How long will you stand by surrounded by your idle thousands while thousands of others are dying? Do you think God will see you as guiltless in this massacre? I say no, he will not. God has said that the inside needs to cleaned first, and after that the outside will be cleaned also. Unless you repent for what you have done, and begin sending Helaman and me the supplies and reinforcements we need, it will become unnecessary to fight the Lamanites any longer. We will need to clean the inside, or the head of our great government, first.

"Unless you grant my requests to show me the true spirit of freedom and help to strengthen our armies I will leave them with the blessing of God, and come make trouble for you. I will stir up protests until any thoughts of holding personal power and authority are vanquished. I'm certainly not afraid of your power and authority. It is God who I fear. It is by his commandments that I fight to defend our country. It is because of your neglect that we suffer so much loss. Unless you join in defending the country, the sword of justice will hang over your head until it falls and brings you to complete destruction. If you don't send the assistance that I ask for I will come for you with my sword. God will not permit you to live long if you persist in your sinful neglect of his righteous people.

"How can you imagine that God will spare you while he condemns the Lamanites? Your sin is the love of glory and vain things. You well know that you violate God's laws. God has said to me, 'If those who have been appointed as governors do not repent their sins, you must go do battle with them.' I demand that you quickly comply with God's commands and send Helaman and me provisions and men. God will not let us perish from hunger when you have food to give. If you don't quickly send what we need, I will come to take it by force.

"As your chief commander, I do not seek power. I want to pull power down. I don't care about the honor of the world, but for the glory of God, the freedom, and welfare of my country." [62 BC]

Chapter 28, 1830 Version

Chapter 61, 1981 Version

Shortly after sending his letter to chief judge Pahoran Moroni received a letter in return. This is what it said:

"I want you to know that I take no pleasure in your hardships. I am deeply saddened by them. But there are many here who are pleased with your troubles, and have risen up in rebellion against me. It is these same people who are trying to depose me who are also withholding support from both you and Helaman. At this time I have been driven out of Zarahemla and have fled to Gideon with as many men as I could persuade to join me.

"I have sent out a proclamation asking people to take up arms in defense of our country. Every day brings us more supporters. The rebels are defying our authority, but seem afraid to actually attack us. They now have possession of Zarahemla, and have appointed a king who has made an alliance with the Lamanites. In exchange for managing the affairs of Zarahemla in support of the Lamanites, this new king has bargained to rule over us after we are defeated.

"I accept your criticism without anger, and take joy in your greatness. I do not seek power and authority over our people except in my role as chief judge, in which I work to preserve the rights and freedom of our people. I am resolute in defense of the freedom that God has given to us. I do not want to fight with the Lamanites or the rebels, but this is necessary because they invade our lands and try to overthrow our rightful government. If God told us to accept them as masters, I would comply. But he commands us to not submit to their rule. He asks that we trust in him for our deliverance.

"Moroni, let us resist this evil. Whatever evil we cannot resist with words, let us resist with swords. Let us retain our freedom to rejoice in the privilege of our church, in the cause of God, and Jesus Christ. Please come quickly with a few men to see me. Leave Lehi and Teancum in charge of the war under the guidance of God. I have sent them some supplies to help them during your absence.

"Gather up forces as you march to see me, and we will bring battle to this band of rebels through the strength of God and our faith in him. When we retake Zarahemla, we will be able to send more food to send to our armies, and put an end to this great injustice.

"Thank you for writing to me and helping me clarify what to do in response to the rebellion. As you have said, 'Unless they repent, God commands that you oppose them.' Tell your commanders not to fear. God will deliver them and all of those who stand strong in the freedom that God has given them." [62 BC]

Chapter 29, 1830 Version

Chapter 62, 1981 Version

When Moroni received Pahoran's letter he was encouraged, and filled with joy because of the governor's faithfulness. Pahoran was no traitor to freedom and the cause of his country after all. He was deeply saddened that Pahoran had been driven from office, and angered at those who rebelled against their country and God.

As requested, Moroni took a small group of men to see Pahoran in Gideon. They marched across the country under a banner of freedom, and gathered up an army of thousands who were willing to fight with them. When they joined forces with Pahoran in Gideon they were a stronger and greater force than that of Pachus, the king of the rebellion.

They came to battle when their combined armies reached Zarahemla. In short order Pachus was killed, his men were taken prisoners, and Pahoran was restored as chief judge and governor. Shortly thereafter a trial was held. Any of the king-men who had fought against the government, and wouldn't now take up arms to defend it, were put to death. It was necessary that the law be strictly observed for the security of the country.

In the 31st year of elected judges, Moroni sent provisions and 6,000 soldiers to Helaman, to hold that part of the country. He also sent an additional 6,000 troops, and provisions, to Lehi and Teancum. [61 BC]

Moroni and Pahoran then took an army to Nephihah to take it back. They encountered a large party of Lamanites on their march to Nephihah and easily defeated them. After taking their weapons they extracted a promise from the survivors to quit warring against the Nephite people. This group of 4,000 Lamanites was sent to live with the Ammonites, and the army continued their march to Nephihah.

When they arrived in Nephihah they pitched their tents in the plains surrounding the city. Moroni wanted the Lamanites to come out of the city and battle on the plains. The Lamanites though, had no intention of leaving their fortified city to face the stronger Nephite army on the open field. So that night Moroni went out in the darkness to the top of the city's wall, and determined that the sleeping Lamanites were all camped near the east entrance.

Moroni returned to his army, and quickly organized an invasion party, utilizing rope ladders, to gain access to the city's west side. By dawn all the Nephites were inside the city and ready to attack. When the Lamanites awoke and saw the Nephites within the city walls they ran out the east gate in terror. Rather than letting them all escape Moroni sent his army after them. Many were killed, and many more were taken prisoner. Without the loss of a single man, Moroni and Pahoran had retaken Nephihah.

The Lamanite prisoners all wanted to go live with the Ammonites and become free people. This request was granted to them. Afterwards they became diligent farmers and the Nephites were relieved of the burden of keeping them as prisoners.

After Moroni defeated the Lamanite army that held Nephihah he freed the Nephite prisoners. His own army was greatly strengthened while the Lamanite army was greatly weakened. The remaining Lamanites fled in fear when they saw that Moroni and his army was coming against them. Moroni's army chased the invaders from city to city before them. When Moroni met up with the army of Lehi and Teancum, they continued pushing the Lamanites before them until they came to the city of Moroni.

When all the Lamanites were driven into one group, led by their King Ammoron, Moroni encircled them with his army, and both sides settled down for the night. Teancum was so angry with Ammoron and his dead brother Amalickiah for starting this war that he stole into the city that night. When he found Ammoron he thrust a spear through his heart. But before Ammoron died he cried out to his guards, who chased down and killed Teancum. Lehi and Moroni were filled with sorrow when they learned of Teancum's death. He had been a great man who'd fought valiantly for his country and was a true friend of freedom.

The next day Moroni's army marched forward against the Lamanites, slaughtering and driving them from the land. This was the end of many years of war, internal conflict, famine, and hardship. More troubles did not come along for some time. In spite of the murders, injustices, and conflicts among the Nephites, the prayers of the righteous had kept them safe. The years of warfare with the Lamanites had hardened many people, and humbled others. [60 BC]

Once the frontier cities had been sufficiently fortified, Moroni and Helaman returned to Zarahemla to establish peace among the Nephites. Moroni handed over command of the army to his son, and retired in peace. Pahoran returned as the governor and chief judge. Helaman went among the people and preached the word of God. The years of wars had made it necessary to renew the church. So Helaman and his preachers began anew convincing the people of their sinfulness and need for repentance in the name of God. The church of God was reestablished throughout the land.

New judges were chosen, and the Nephite people began to prosper again. Their numbers multiplied as their riches grew, but they did not become vain or filled with pride. They were quick to remember the great things that God had done for them, and humbled themselves before him. God had delivered them from death, from slavery, from prisons, and from all kinds of hardships. They prayed to God at all times, and God blessed them according to his promises that they would prosper in the land.

In the 35th year of elected judges, Helaman died. [57 BC]

Chapter 30, 1830 Version

Chapter 63, 1981 Version

After Helaman died, his brother Shiblon took on custody of the sacred records and the other sacred objects that his father Alma had given to him. Shiblon was an honest man who stood proudly before God, always did the right thing, and kept God's commandments.

Moroni died in the 36th year of elected judges. [56 BC]

In the 37th year of elected judges, 5,400 men and their families left Zarahemla for the distant north country. [55 BC]

That same year a strange man named Hagoth built a huge ship on the western sea, and sailed north with many Nephites aboard. In the following two years after the first ship returned, he built more ships to take more Nephites northward. None of them were ever heard from again. Maybe they all drowned at sea.

It was a time of northward migration as many more people also went by land.

In the 39th year of elected judges, Shiblon died. His other brother Corianton was one of those who went north by ship and vanished. Before he died, Shiblon transferred custody of the sacred records to Helaman's son Helaman[3], who saw to it that those parts of the records that weren't forbidden to be known, were copied and distributed among the Nephite people for all to learn and know.

As had happened in the past some Nephite dissenters defected to the Lamanites to incite them to war. A war party attacked the city of Moronihah, but were beaten back and driven from the lands at great cost. [53 BC]

THE BOOK OF HELAMAN — 52 BC TO 1 BC

From Plates Inscribed by Helaman's Son, Helaman[3], and His Sons, Nephi[2] and Lehi[3] then Abridged and Later Inscribed onto the Book of Mormon Plates by Mormon

The Nephites are endangered by the ceaseless Lamanite wars and by the emergence of a new Nephite enemy, the Gadianton Robbers. Large numbers of Lamanites are converted to Christianity. A Lamanite prophet named Samuel announces that Jesus Christ will arrive in five years, and describes the signs that will accompany his arrival.

THE BOOK OF HELAMAN SUMMARY

Helaman[3], who authored part of this book, was the grandson of Alma[2], the son of Helaman[2], and the nephew of Shiblon, who were the authors of the Book of Alma. This book was also authored in part by Helaman's sons Nephi[2] and Lehi[3]. Helaman[3] was twenty-five years old when the legacy of the records was passed on to him in the 40th year of elected judges [52 BC].

The 50 year period spanned by the Book of Helaman starts with the death of the chief judge, followed by intrigue and murder over the succession of the next chief judge and ruler of the Nephite people. While the Nephites were preoccupied and consumed with this succession of leadership, the Lamanites raised an enormous and well equipped army.

Led by a renegade Nephite who was a powerful military commander, the Lamanites attacked and conquered the capitol Nephite city of Zarahemla and set out to conquer the rest of the Nephite lands. With the help of God, the Nephites defeated the Lamanite army and took back Zarahemla.

The Gadianton Robbers, a band of renegade Nephite outlaws, perpetuated governmental intrigue and murder, and became an even greater threat than the Lamanites. When Helaman became chief judge the robbers attempted to murder him also. Times of relative peace came and went as the Nephite and Lamanite people spread out and populated the continents to the south and to the north, from the sea on east to the sea on the west. Much of the northern land in the American continent was badly deforested by the previous Jaredite civilization and became known as the "land of desolation." To supply lumber for the construction of new cities in these areas a great shipping industry arose to transport materials from the areas that were still well forested.

As the Nephites prospered many of them forgot about God and become Lamanites because of their sinfulness. Others were baptized in the church and redeemed.

Helaman died at a young age and was succeeded as the chief judge by his son, Nephi. Like his father, Nephi had to contend with the conquering Lamanite armies and the internal dissension among the Nephites. During the good times the people forgot God's laws. During the bad times they begged for God's help. When the Lamanite armies took over parts of the Nephite lands the people remembered the prophecies of Alma and Mosiah. As the pendulum swung between peace and war, the Nephites swung between sinfulness and repentance.

Nephi, like his great grandfather Alma[2], decided to step down as the chief judge and spend his time preaching to the people instead of trying to rule them. When a majority of the Nephite people turned sinful, they inevitably elected corrupt leaders. Nephi taught God's laws, and of the imminent arrival of Jesus Christ. Nephi's words were so strong that he successfully converted thousands of Lamanites to the church and baptized them.

Nephi and his brother Lehi were captured by hostile Lamanites while out preaching in the Lamanite lands, and were imprisoned. Just before they were put to death God intervened and miraculously saved them. This miracle spurred on further mass conversions of the Lamanites, and the voluntary return of the Nephite's conquered lands by the Lamanite forces.

So many Lamanites were converted to the church and were convinced of the power of God and Jesus Christ that they became more righteous than the Nephites. The Gadianton Robbers, and their secret conspirators, thrived like a cancer on the general prosperity and poisoned the Nephites from within.

When another chief judge was murdered Nephi was accused of complicity. Using his power of prophecy he correctly identified the murderer as the chief judge's brother, who hoped to succeed him. Afterwards, God was so impressed with Nephi that he promised to do anything Nephi asked of him. God also assigned Nephi the role as his spokesman to the Nephite people. "Tell them that they must repent and reform their ways, or I will destroy them," God said.

The endless conflict, dissension, and wars form a backdrop against which the path to God and Jesus Christ is repeated again and again. The people's wickedness became so great that Nephi asked God for a great famine. As the people starved they remembered God again, and the famine ended.

In the 86th year of elected judges [6 BC], a converted Lamanite prophet named Samuel came to Zarahemla to preach and prophesy about repentance and the coming of Jesus Christ. Samuel wasn't allowed to enter the city, so he climbed up on the city walls and delivered his sermon to the people below. He prophesied about the future destruction of the Nephites because of their Godlessness and foretold that Jesus Christ would be born in five years, to redeem those who believed in him.

"The people will know of his arrival," Samuel said, "by the fact that an entire night will pass without darkness and afterward a brilliant new star will rise in the sky that has never been seen before. I have come to tell you of his arrival so that you will know the signs of his coming. If you repent, you will not be destroyed. If you don't repent, there will be no hope for you. When Jesus Christ dies, there will be great storms and earthquakes. Cities will be destroyed and many will die. For three days afterwards, there will be total darkness until the time of his resurrection. I urge you to repent now, while you still have the chance."

The people who heard Samuel were either afraid or angry. Many were moved to repent and be baptized. The angry people tried to kill Samuel with stones and arrows, but nothing touched him because the Spirit of God was with him. When the city guards tried to apprehend Samuel, he slipped away and was never heard from again.

When the time of Jesus Christ's arrival approached, the sinful grew more wicked. Among the godly, angels appeared, and let the people know that Jesus Christ was coming very, very soon.

THE BOOK OF HELAMAN - TRANSLATION

Chapter 1, 1830 and 1981 Versions

In the 40th year of elected judges, the chief judge and governor Pahoran[1] died, and great difficulties among the Nephites began. Three of Pahoran's many sons each thought that this position should be rightfully theirs. The contention between the brothers, Pahoran[2], Paanchi, and Pacumeni, split the Nephites into three contending factions. In the end Pahoran's son Pahoran was appointed governor and chief judge by the people's vote. [52 BC]

Pacumeni deferred to the people's choice and honorably withdrew his claim. But Paanchi and his supporters were so angry over Pahoran's appointment that they began organizing a rebellion to destroy the people's freedoms. Paanchi was arrested, tried according to the law, and sentenced to death for his treasonous actions.

When Paanchi's supporters learned of his death sentence they sent Kishkumen to assassinate Pahoran. Kishkumen was so stealthy and quick in murdering the new governor that none of guards could apprehend him, and no one knew who he was because he'd come in disguise. All of his fellow conspirators swore amongst themselves to keep his identity secret. The supporters of Paanchi then dispersed among the Nephite population so that very few of them could be apprehended. Those that were found, were tried and condemned to death.

The people then chose Pacumeni as chief judge and governor to succeed his dead brother.

In the 41st year of elected judges, King Tubaloth, a descendant of the Nephite traitor Ammoron, led the Lamanites. He organized a huge army, fully armed with swords, scimitars, bows and arrows, and equipped with helmets, body armor, and shields. The Lamanite army was led by a former Nephite dissenter named Coriantumr[2]. King Tubaloth imagined that the mighty Coriantumr would be the ideal man to lead a conquest and subjugation of the Nephites.

The Nephites were so preoccupied with their internal politics and succession of leaders that they were not prepared for a Lamanite invasion of their lands, and an attack on the great city of Zarahemla. Coriantumr's army came upon them so quickly they had no opportunity to raise a credible defense. The city was quickly overwhelmed by the well organized Lamanite attack, and everyone who opposed them was killed. When the new governor Pacumeni tried to escape, he was caught by Coriantumr and killed against the city's wall.

When Coriantumr saw how easily his army had taken Zarahemla, the Nephites' capital and strongest city, he sent his army against the large city of Bountiful next. Without giving the Nephites any time to organize, he marched his army north and cut down all resistance along the way. Men, women, and children were slaughtered, and many smaller cities were taken.

Prior to the Lamanite invasion the Nephite commander Moronihah stationed all of his strongest troops along the Lamanite border where in the past all the invasions had begun. He never imagined that the Lamanite army would bypass the border areas and quickly attack the major, central cities. When Moronihah saw this happening he immediately sent an army, under the command of Lehi[2], to intercept Coriantumr's Lamanite army before they reached Bountiful.

When the two armies met in battle the Lamanites were pushed back toward Zarahemla. The advance of the Lamanites had been stopped, but during the bloody retreat afterwards many Lamanites, including Coriantumr, were killed. When the Nephites converged on, and surrounded the Lamanite army, it was soon over for the Lamanites. Moronihah easily recaptured Zarahemla and sent the surviving Lamanites back to their own lands in peace. [51 BC]

Chapter 2, 1981 Version

In the 42nd year of elected judges, Moronihah reestablished peace between the Nephites and the Lamanites, but the position of chief judge and governor of the Nephite people still remained vacant. So again, conflicts arose as to who should lead them. [50 BC]

When Helaman's son Helaman[2] was appointed as chief judge and governor, Kishkumen began plotting his murder as well. Among Kishkumen's band of conspirators was a man named Gadianton, who was exceptional in his capacity for misleading people and in arranging the dirty work of secretive murder and robbery. The conspirators elected Gadianton as their leader.

Gadianton persuaded his band that they would be in power over the Nephites once Helaman was eliminated and he was governor. Again, the task of killing the governor fell to

Kishkumen. On his way into Helaman's chambers he encountered one of Helaman's servants, who had infiltrated the Gadianton band by disguise. When the servant showed him the band's secret hand sign, Kishkumen told him of his plans and asked for his assistance.

The servant learned of the secret plot to murder Helaman, and the conspiracy to take over the government by secret alliances, murders, and robberies. "Let us go to Helaman's chambers," said the servant. Kishkumen was pleased with the servant because he assumed that he had a fellow conspirator. But instead of helping Kishkumen, the servant pulled out a knife and stabbed him to death. Immediately thereafter the servant ran to Helaman and told him everything that he'd learned and what he'd done.

When Kishkumen didn't return Gadianton panicked and became fearful of being caught and destroyed. By the time that Helaman tried to arrest them, Gadianton's band had fled to the wilderness via a secret way and could not be found. So great was Gadianton's evil influence that over time he would come close to destroying the entire Nephite people.

Chapter 2, 1830 Version

Chapter 3, 1981 Version

In the 43rd year of elected judges, the Nephites were a united and cohesive group, with very little internal dissent. [49 BC]

In the 46th year great migrations to the north began amidst renewed conflict and dissent. These emigrants traveled great distances through areas of large lakes and many rivers, finding some occasional virgin lands that had not been deforested by the earlier inhabitants. Most of the land they passed through, was considered desolate because the former inhabitants had removed the trees and left it in such a destroyed state. In the absence of timber, the new settlers became quite skilled in building homes with rocks and cement. [46 BC]

The settlers multiplied. They spread southward and northward, from the sea on the east to the sea on the west, until they occupied all of the area in these new continents. A substantial shipping industry arose to mitigate the shortage of lumber. Many volumes of books were written about these people, their wars with the Lamanites, prophecies, the construction of great cities, temples, and synagogues, their righteousness and wickedness, murdering plundering, abominations and fornication. But it is not possible to recount all of that here. It is enough to say that the Nephites spread themselves across the face of the land. In the end they were hunted down and scattered until their descendants became mixed with, and indistinguishable from, the wicked, wild, and ferocious Lamanites.

In Zarahemla, Helaman held the position of chief judge and upholder of the statutes, judgments, and commandments of God. He raised two sons, Nephi and Lehi, who also stood tall before God. In the 49th year of elected judges, a broad peace settled across the land except for the secret conspiracies of Gadianton and his band of hidden robbers. [43 BC]

It was a year of great prosperity and success for the church. The Nephite people were showered with so many blessings that even the high priests and teachers were amazed. Tens of thousands of people were baptized and joined the church of God. So you can see how God was merciful to those who sincerely call upon his holy name. The gates of heaven are open to those who believe in Jesus Christ, the Son of God. You can see that whoever holds true to the word of God will turn away from the sneaky traps laid by the devil. They will be led by Jesus Christ along the straight and narrow path, across the everlasting gulf of misery prepared for the wicked. Those who follow Jesus Christ will find their immortal souls on the right hand of God along with Abraham, Isaac, Jacob, and all of our holy ancestors. This was a year of great rejoicing and peace for the Nephites in the lands around Zarahemla.

In the 51st year of elected judges, the peace continued, but an insidious pride crept into some people who considered themselves as members of the church of God. These people began to persecute the humble, and thought of themselves as superior. This evil was a trial for the devout members who fasted, prayed, and were ultimately strengthened in their humility and faith in Jesus Christ. The hearts of the devout were filled with joy and consolation through purification and yielding themselves to God. As prosperity and peace filled the land the people's pride grew greater, and their pursuit of wealth became more readily apparent. [41 BC]

In the 53rd year of elected judges, Helaman died and his oldest son Nephi^2 became chief judge. Like his father, he led with justice and equity and kept the commandments of God. [39 BC]

Chapter 4, 1981 Version

In the 54th year of elected judges, dissent within the church, and conflict between the people, grew so great that it resulted in rebellion and bloodshed. The Nephite rebels were killed or driven out of Zarahemla and into the hands of the Lamanites. When the rebels tried to incite the Lamanites to make war upon the Nephites, the Lamanites wouldn't listen to them at first because the Lamanites had grown to fear the Nephites' strength. [38 BC]

In the 56th year of elected judges, more Nephite rebels were driven out of Zarahemla. They convinced the Lamanites to go to war, and preparations for battle were begun. [36 BC]

The next round of the Lamanite wars began in the 57th year. In the 58th year the Lamanite army conquered Zarahemla and all the lands near Bountiful. The Nephites and the army of Moronihah were driven back by the conquering Lamanite army. Near Bountiful the Nephites made a fortified line, to defend all their lands to the north. Along this line it was a day's journey from the shores of the sea to the east to the shores of the sea to the west. An alliance of Lamanites and Nephite rebels succeeded in taking all the Nephite lands south of that line. [34 BC]

In the 60th year of elected judges, the army of Moronihah successfully recaptured many cities and lands that had been lost to the Lamanites. Some of the Nephites professed to belong to the church of God but acted otherwise. The Nephites' suffered great loss of life and property because of this. These people lost their possessions, lives, and lands because of pride in their hearts, the accumulation of wealth, the oppression of the poor, the way in which they withheld food from the hungry and clothing from the naked, the contempt they held for the truly humble, their mockery of the sacred, their denial of prophecy and revelation,

the murdering, the plundering, the lying, the stealing, the fornication, the conflicts, and the desertions to the Lamanites. They had boasted of their great strength but found that when they were left with only that strength, it was not enough to defeat the Lamanites. [32 BC]

Helaman's sons, Nephi and Lehi, and the captain of the army, Moronihah, preached to the people about their sinfulness and prophesied what would happen if the people didn't repent. When the people did repent they began to prosper again, and began driving the Lamanites from the Nephites' lands.

By the 62nd year of elected judges, Moronihah recaptured half of the lands and cities that had been taken, but he could make no further progress against the Lamanites. There were just too many of them. So he abandoned his hopes of recapturing all the taken lands and deployed his army to hold what they had. Because the Lamanite army was so strong, and so close, the Nephites lived in constant fear of being overwhelmed, killed, and destroyed. In their vulnerable situation the people began to remember the prophecies of Alma, and the words of Mosiah. They saw that they'd been stubborn and had not paid sufficient heed to the commandments of God. They saw that they had abused and corrupted the laws of Mosiah. They saw that in many ways they were as wicked as the Lamanites themselves. As their faith in prophecy and revelation weakened, the church declined. The judgment of God stared them in the face. They saw that they had become weak and that the Spirit of God no longer protected them. God wanted nothing to do with unholy people. They realized that when God quit protecting them they were no match for the numerous Lamanites, and that unless they renewed their commitment to God they would be destroyed. [30 BC]

Chapter 5, 1981 Version

In the 62nd year of elected judges, Nephi stepped down as chief judge to devote himself to preaching the word of God for the rest of his life. He despaired because the laws that empowered the people were useless if the majority chose evil over good. He saw the laws being corrupted by the people's stubbornness, and he saw how ripe the Nephites were for destruction.

Lehi joined his brother Nephi and also committed himself to preaching to the Nephite people for the rest of his life also. Together they remembered the words of their father Helaman, "My sons, I want you to remember and keep the commandments of God. I also want you to convey these words to the people. I have given you the names of our ancestors who came to this land from Jerusalem. I did this so that when you remember your own names, you will also remember them. When you remember them, remember their works. When you remember their works, know that they were good. I want you to be held in the same high regard as your namesakes are."

"I further ask," Helaman had said, "that you not boast about your good works. Your purpose in being good should be to secure the eternal place in heaven that we must presume our ancestors have received. I want you to remember the words that King Benjamin spoke to the people when he said that 'There is no other way that a man can be saved except through the atoning blood of Jesus Christ who will come to redeem the world.' I want you to remember the words that Amulek spoke to Zeezrom when he said that 'God will surely come to redeem his people, not in their sins, but from their sins.' This power of redemption comes from repentance, and through Jesus Christ. This is why he has sent angels to declare the conditions of repentance and redemption. Remember to build your foundation upon the rock of our redeemer, Jesus Christ. When the devil sends his mighty storms of hail and whirlwinds to try and dislodge you, your foundation will not fail if it is built on his rock."

Remembering these words, Nephi and Lehi went forth among the Nephites to keep God's commandments and teach his word. They traveled from one city to another until they'd visited all the Nephite cities in the south. After that they brought their missionary work to Zarahemla, which was now part of the Lamanites' lands. They preached with such power and persuasiveness that many of the Nephite rebels who had gone over to the Lamanites came forward to confess their sins, repent, and be baptized. These reformed Nephite rebels returned to the Nephite lands to restore the damages they'd done.

Nephi and Lehi spoke to the Lamanites with such authority that 8,000 of them, convinced of the wickedness of their ancestors, offered up their repentance and were baptized. The two brothers continued northward into more Lamanite lands where they were captured by the Lamanite army and thrown into prison. After having left them for many days without food the guards came to take them out for execution. When the guards arrived Nephi and Lehi were encircled in a fire that the Lamanites were afraid to touch but that left the brothers unharmed.

"Don't be afraid," the brothers said to the Lamanite executioners, "God is just showing you that we cannot be harmed or killed by you." After these words were spoken, the earth shook as if the prison might fall, and a cloud of darkness and fear descended upon the Lamanites.

"Repent, repent," came a firm, calm voice from the cloud of darkness. "Stop your attempts to harm these servants of mine. I have sent them to bring you good news."

The earth then shook again, and the prison walls trembled. "Repent, repent," the calm voice from the cloud said again. "The kingdom of heaven is at hand. Do not attempt to harm my servants."

Then the earth shook for a third time and the voice came again saying marvelous words that cannot be spoken by men. After the voice was finished speaking the earth shuddered for a fourth time as if it were about to split itself open. The Lamanites couldn't run away because the cloud of darkness blackened the sky, and they were paralyzed with fear.

Among the Lamanites was a Nephite rebel who had once belonged to the church of God. Through the cloud of darkness this man saw the faces of Nephi and Lehi shining like angels, with their eyes lifted to heaven as if they were talking with some unseen being. The man cried out to the Lamanites, telling them to turn and look.

"What does this mean? With whom are these prisoners conversing?" they asked.

"They talk with the angels of God," cried the man.

"What can we do," the Lamanites asked, "to remove this cloud of darkness that blackens the sky?"

"You must repent and cry out to the voice," the man answered, "until you have faith in Jesus Christ, as was taught to you by Alma, Amulek, and Zeezrom. When you do this, the cloud of darkness will be removed."

Upon hearing this the Lamanites all began to cry out to the voice that had caused the earth to shake. When they did as they were told the cloud of darkness vanished. Afterwards they looked about and found themselves each encircled within a pillar of fire, as Nephi and Lehi had been before. The flames burned intensely but did them no harm, and they were filled with an unspeakable joy and glory. The Holy Spirit of God came down from heaven and entered their hearts as if they were filled with fire.

The pleasant, calm voice came to them again, saying, "Peace be with you because of your faith in my Beloved Son whose presence was prepared from the earth's beginning."

When the people looked up to see where the voice was coming from they saw the heavens open and angels pouring out to minister to them. Three hundred people witnessed these things. These witnesses told to go out into the world without doubts, minister to the people, and declare what they had seen and heard. Most of the Lamanites who heard these testimonies became convinced of their truth, laid down their weapons, gave up their hatred of the Nephites, abandoned the traditions of their ancestors, and returned the Nephites' occupied lands to them. [30 BC]

Chapter 6, 1981 Version

As the 62nd year of elected judges, ended most of the Lamanites had converted, and were actually more righteous and strong in their faith than the Nephites. Many Nephites had become hard, unrepentant, and sinful. They had rejected the word of God, the preaching of the church leaders, and the holy prophecies. In the face of this apostasy among the Nephites the people of the church of God were overjoyed at the Lamanite conversions. [30 BC]

Many of these converted Lamanites came to Zarahemla as missionaries. They announced the nature of their conversion and urged the Nephites to repent. These Lamanite converts spoke with such power and authority that they induced humility in many to whom they spoke.

Many stray Nephites became humble followers of God and Jesus Christ once again. In the 63rd year of elected judges, Nephi and Lehi continued their missionary work to the north, and the converted Lamanites spread out across the land, including into the lands of the Nephites. [29 BC]

It was a time of great peace and prosperity for both the Nephites and the Lamanites alike. Gold, silver, and finely crafted riches were abundant. The harvests were plentiful and the livestock thrived. The women spun threads and made many kinds of wonderful cloth.

In the 66th year of elected judges, the chief judge Cezoram was secretly murdered by an unknown culprit. When his son succeeded him as chief judge, he was also murdered. [26BC]

In the 67th year the people began to lapse back into sinfulness. God had blessed them with wealth and prosperity for so long that they began competing with one another to see who could become the richest. They murdered, stole, and plotted for material gain. Among these plunderers was the band formed by Gadianton who had infiltrated both the Nephites and the unconverted Lamanites. This group, known as the Gadianton Robbers, were the ones responsible for killing the chief judge, and his son who had succeeded him.

The Lamanites and the righteous Nephites were both unhappy to have the robbers operating amongst them, and used all possible means to expose and destroy them. At this time more Nephites than not were under the under the influence of Satan. These people made alliances and covenants with the robbers, using secret signs and secret words so that they could distinguish other conspirators. They helped one another evade injury from these crimes, and also helped them evade government prosecution for the crimes they committed. Under this diabolical conspiracy they murdered, stole, fornicated, and committed all sorts of wickedness that was contrary to the laws of their country and contrary to the laws of God. Betrayals within the conspiracy were punished harshly by the wicked justice of Gadianton.

These were the secret conspiracies, oaths, and covenants that Alma had warned his son about, that would destroy the people if they were ever known and used. Gadianton had not acquired this secret and diabolical knowledge through the records that Helaman had kept. Instead, they had been delivered straight to his heart from the same devil who enticed Adam and Eve to taste the forbidden fruit, from the same being who conspired with Cain to kill his brother Abel and who had been leading men astray ever since. These secrets came from the same devil who had provoked the people to build a great tower so high that they could climb to heaven, and who had conspired with the descendants of the great tower builders to spread the works of darkness and abominations in this new land until he dragged them down to destruction and everlasting hell. This same devil had now provoked Gadianton to carry on his works of darkness and secret murders as he had since the beginning of time. This same devil is author of all sin.

The devil had taken hold of the hearts of many Nephites who had become incredibly wicked. Most of them turned away from righteousness, defied the commandments of God, and worshipped the idols of gold and silver. It all happened very quickly.

In the 68th year of elected judges, the Nephites had become an overwhelmingly unrighteous people and grew even more so. While the Nephites' belief in God had declined the Lamanites' belief had grown. It was the Lamanites who now kept the commandments of God, and walked in righteousness and truth before God. As the Spirit of God withdrew from the Nephites God showered the Lamanites with his blessings because of their willingness to believe in his words.

The Lamanites hunted out the corrupt band of Gadianton Robbers amongst themselves and preached to the wicked in their midst. Because of this, the robbers were utterly destroyed within the Lamanite community.

On the other hand, the Nephites strengthened and supported the Gadianton Robbers until they spread their evil influence throughout the entire land of the Nephites. They seduced the righteous with a generous share of the spoils, and ensnared them in their secret conspiracy. They systematically took control of the government, overturned the laws, and turned their backs on the poor, the meek, and the humble followers of God. The Nephite people were now ripe for total destruction. [34 BC]

Chapter 3, 1830 Version

Chapter 7, 1981 Version

In the 69th year of elected judges, Nephi returned to Zarahemla from his mission in the north, where the people had rejected his words. [23 BC]

Upon his return he was shocked by the state of affairs at home. Gadianton Robbers were seated as judges and had hijacked the power and authority of the land. Wickedness prevailed. The commandments of God were not being observed anymore. There was no longer any justice. The righteous were condemned for their righteousness, while the guilty and wicked had plenty of money, went unpunished, and now ran the government for their own personal profit. The leaders used their offices to more easily fornicate, steal, and kill as they pleased. The change had happened so quickly that Nephi was struck with sorrow and agony of the soul.

"How I wish I could have lived when Nephi[1] first came out of Jerusalem," he exclaimed. "When he first arrived in this promised land, his people could be persuaded to keep the commandments of God. They were slow to sin and quick to listen to God. If I had lived then, I could have known joy at the righteousness of my people. But I must accept that these are my days, and accept the sorrow that comes from these sinful people."

Nephi stood on a tower in his garden along the highway to the market in the city of Zarahemla, and bowed down. Men passing by saw him pour out his grief from the top of the tower, and ran to tell other people what they'd seen. Soon a multitude gathered, wondering what caused such mourning. When Nephi arose he saw the people gathered before him.

"Why have you gathered?" he asked. "So that I can tell you about your sinfulness? I stand on this tower so that I can pour my soul out to God and lament the sinfulness I have found here. You marvel at my mourning when you should be marveling at how easily the devil has captured your hearts. How could you have yielded to the enticements of the devil who is only trying to consign your souls to everlasting misery? Repent and turn towards the Lord God. Why has he forsaken you? This has happened because you have hardened your hearts and not listened to the good shepherd. You have provoked him to anger against you. Unless you repent you will be scattered as meat for dogs and wild beasts, instead of being gathered up."

"How could you have forgotten your God who has delivered you? You do this to receive the empty praise of your fellow men, and to receive gold and silver. You've set your hearts on accumulating wealth and inflating your vanity. For these things you murder, plunder, steal, and bring false witness against your neighbor. Unless you repent, you are going to suffer. Unless you repent, this great city and all the great cities of our land will be taken away, and you will have no place in them. Unless you repent, God will withdraw his strength that protects you from your enemies."

"God has said," continued Nephi, " 'I will not give my strength to help the wicked. I will help only those who repent and listen to my words.' "

"Unless you repent, the Lamanites will be better off than you. They are more righteous than you are. They have not betrayed the great knowledge that you've received. Because of this, God will give them longer lives and greater fertility, while those of you who don't repent will be destroyed. Shame on you for letting this great abomination become established among you. You have united yourselves with that secret conspiracy led by Gadianton. You will find that the reward for your pride and pursuit of wealth will only be misery. Your wickedness and abominations will only bring you misery. Unless you repent you will destroyed, and your lands will be taken away from you. I know these things are true because the Lord God has made them known to me. I hereby testify that these prophecies will be fulfilled."

Chapter 8, 1981 Version

When Nephi said this he angered a lot of men, including the judges who belonged to the gang of robbers. "Why don't you seize this man," they asked the people, "and bring him forward to be condemned for his crimes? Didn't you just hear this man accuse our judges, and rebel against our laws?"

In fact, Nephi spoke out about the corruption of their laws, but nothing he said ran contrary to the commandments of God. The judges were angry because he spoke honestly about their secret conspiracies and works of darkness. But they were afraid to personally arrest Nephi because they were worried that the people might oppose them. They asked the people to have him arrested.

"Why do you let this man rebel against us?" they asked. "He also condemns all of you people, and consigns you to destruction. He tells us that our great cities will be taken away from us and that we will have no place in them. We all know this is nonsense. We are powerful, our cities are great, and our enemies are powerless over us."

In this way the judges incited the people's anger against Nephi, and caused conflicts among them. There were some who disagreed with the judges, and said, "Leave this man alone. He is a good man, and unless we repent, what he prophesies will surely come to pass. The judgments about our sinfulness that he's testified to are correct. He knows what will happen to us just as surely as he knows about our sinfulness. If he were not a prophet, he could not have testified as he did."

The men who wanted to arrest and destroy Nephi were afraid to do so. Seeing that he'd won approval for his views from many of the men assembled, Nephi spoke again. "Brothers, you've read about how God gave Moses the power to divide the waters of the Red Sea so that our ancestors escaped from the Egyptian armies. You can remember how the waters closed upon the Egyptians, and drowned them after our people had passed through. If God could give this much power to one man, then why do you argue that he hasn't given me the power to know about the judgments you will receive if you don't repent? Not only do you deny my words, but you also deny the words that have been spoken by our ancestors including this man Moses, who prophesied about the coming of the Messiah. Didn't Moses testify that the Son of God would come? Just as Moses lifted up the brass snake in the wilderness, so too will God lift up the Messiah who will come. Just as those who saw the snake, lived, so too will those who see the Son of God with faith, live eternally.

"It wasn't just Moses who testified to these things," Nephi continued, "but all the holy prophets since the days of Abraham. When Abraham saw the coming of the Messiah he rejoiced and was filled with gladness. Even before Abraham there were many others who were called by God and shown the coming of his Son, thousands of years before his arrival. They saw how the redemption of men would become possible. Since the days of Abraham many prophets have testified about these things including the prophets Zenock*, Ezias*, Isaiah, Jeremiah, and Zenos*, who was even killed for his bold prophecies."

> *Zenock, Ezias, and Zenos are Old World Hebrew prophets for whom all historical references are lost outside The Book of Mormon. Nephi's knowledge of these prophets comes through Laban's brass plates brought from Jerusalem.

"Jeremiah prophesied the destruction of Jerusalem, and we know that Jerusalem was destroyed just as Jeremiah predicted. So how can you disbelieve in the coming of Jesus Christ according to his prophecy? How can you dispute that Jerusalem was destroyed? Do you claim that sons of Zedekiah, except for Mulek, were not killed? Don't you know that the descendants of Zedekiah who are among us were survivors of that destruction?

"Our ancestor Lehi was driven from Jerusalem because he testified about these things. Our ancestor Nephi also testified about this, along with almost all of our ancestors down to this time. They have prophesied the coming of Jesus Christ, and have rejoiced as they looked forward to that day of his coming. Jesus Christ is the God who was with them, who manifested himself to them so that they could be redeemed. They gave their devotion to him because they knew about what would come. You know these things are true, and cannot deny them unless you lie. In your lying about this, you have sinned. You have rejected these things in spite of all the evidence that you've received from heaven and from earth telling you that these things are true. But you've rejected the truth, rebelled against God, and instead of preparing yourselves for heaven where corruption and filth are not allowed, you are preparing yourself for the anger of God on judgment day. Because of your murders, wickedness, and fornication you are ripe for destruction unless you repent, and do it soon.

"Destruction is now at your doorstep," concluded Nephi. "If you go to the chief judge's throne right now, you will find that your chief judge has been murdered and lies in his own blood. He has been murdered by his own brother who now seeks to be the chief judge. Both of these men belong to your secret band of Gadianton. This Gadianton of yours is the evil one who wants to destroy the souls of men."

Chapter 9, 1981 Version

After Nephi had finished speaking five of the men who were assembled ran off to the chief judge's throne. On the way there they said, "Now we will know for sure if this man is a prophet, and whether God has commanded him to prophesy to us. I don't believe that he is a prophet. But if he's right about the chief judge being dead, perhaps the other things he says are true as well."

When they arrived at the throne they found the chief judge lying dead in his own blood. When they saw the truth of Nephi's words they were overcome with fear at the possibility that Nephi's other prophecies might be fulfilled. They fell to the ground unconscious.

After the judge had been murdered by his stealthy brother, his servants raised the cry of murder while the brother had slipped away. As people gathered around the throne they found the five men lying on the ground. Not knowing about the scene in Nephi's garden, they said, "These must be the murderers, and God has struck them down so they couldn't run away."

The five men were immediately arrested and thrown into prison. The next day the people gathered to mourn and pay their respects to the slain judge. Among those present were some who'd been at Nephi's garden on the previous day, and heard his words. "Where are the five men who were sent to verify the truth of Nephi's words?" they asked.

"We don't know about the five men you mention," answered others, "but we have thrown the judge's five murderers into prison."

The judges had the five brought forward, and asked them to explain what had happened. "We ran to the throne and saw everything just as Nephi had described it," they said. "We were so astonished that we fell to the ground. When we recovered, we found ourselves in prison.

We don't know who killed the chief judge. He was already dead when we arrived."

"We know that Nephi is behind this," the judges declared. "He must have conspired with someone to kill the chief judge so that he could trick us into believing in his prophecies, and convert us to his faith. He pretends to be a great man who is chosen by God to be a prophet. But we know better. He will confess his crime and tell us who the real murderer is."

The five men were freed, but they disagreed with the judges accusation of Nephi as a conspirator to murder. The judges had Nephi arrested anyway, and interrogated him. The judges tried to trick Nephi into incriminating himself.

"We know that you are in alliance with the murderer," they said. "Tell us who he is. If you acknowledge your part in this we will give you money and spare your life."

"You fools," Nephi answered, "are blind and stubborn. How long do you think that God will permit your sinfulness? You should be howling and mourning at the great destruction that awaits you if you don't repent. You say that I conspired to kill the chief judge because I knew of his death, just as I knew about the wickedness and abominations amongst you. You are angry and want to kill me because I've shown you a sign. Well let me show you another sign and we'll see if you still want to destroy me.

"Go to the house of the chief judge's brother and ask him if he agrees with my testimony that he has killed his brother. He will say, 'No,' and tell you that he is innocent. Then inspect his cloak and you will find fresh blood on it.

"When you have seen this," Nephi explained, "then ask him, 'Where did this blood come from? Isn't this the blood of your brother?'

"He will then tremble and become pale, as if death were upon him. Then say to him, 'Because of your fear and the paleness of your face we know you are guilty.'

"At this point," Nephi continued, "his fear will become so great that he will confess everything and abandon his claims to innocence. He will tell you that I, Nephi, had nothing to do with the murder except what was shown to me by the power of God. You will know then that I am an honest man, and that I am sent by God."

When the people confronted the judge's brother all of Nephi's predictions were fulfilled. At first the brother denied the crime, but then confessed. Nephi was released.

There were some who believed what Nephi said, and others who recognized the truth from the testimony of the five who'd been imprisoned. There were some who knew that Nephi was a true prophet of God. There were others who said, "He must be a god or else he couldn't have known what he knew. He told us the thoughts in our hearts, and he informed us who the true murderer of the chief judge was."

Chapter 10, 1981 Version

The people parted and went their separate ways leaving Nephi standing alone. He wandered back toward his home and pondered the things God had shown him. He was deeply saddened by the wickedness of the Nephite people, their secret conspiracies, their plundering, and their sinfulness. In this state of thought a voice came to him saying, "You are blessed, Nephi, for everything that you've done. I have seen how steadfastly you've declared the words that I've given to you and my people. You have been fearless in advocating my commandments, without even thinking about your own life. Because of your perseverance I will bless you forever and make you mighty in word, deed, and faith. Since I know that you won't ask for anything contrary to my will, anything that you ask for will be done."

"I am your God, Nephi. I say these things with the angels as witness. You will have power over your people. If the people are wicked, you may afflict them with famine, disease, and destruction. Whoever you bless will be blessed in heaven, and whoever you curse will be cursed in heaven. If you order a temple to be destroyed, it will be done. If you order a mountain leveled, it will be done. If you order me to strike your people, they will be struck."

"Now Nephi, go and tell your people that their God has said, unless they repent, they will be struck down and destroyed."

After God spoke these words Nephi turned around and went back to declare what God had told him to say. Despite the miracle that Nephi had just demonstrated, concerning the murder of the chief judge, the people wouldn't listen to anything he had to say.

"Unless you repent," Nephi told them, "you will be struck down and destroyed."

When they tried to arrest Nephi and throw him in prison for speaking out against them, the Spirit of God picked him up and carried him from one group to the next. At every gathering of people he said what God had commanded him to speak, until eventually he had addressed all of his people with this same message. But still they would not listen to his words.

In the 71st year of elected judges, the people broke into contentious factions and began killing one another with their swords. [21 BC]

Chapter 4, 1830 Version

Chapter 11, 1981 Version

In the 72nd year of elected judges, wars between the different Nephite factions spread across the land. Most of this war and destruction was instigated by the band of Gadianton Robbers. [20 BC]

In the 73rd year Nephi cried out to God saying, "Oh God, do not let my people be destroyed by warfare. Instead, bring them a famine to remind them of their God. Perhaps then they will repent and turn to you." [19 BC]

And so a great famine came across the land for several years, and the widespread warfare ended. In the 75th year the land was dry and barren, and there was no harvest at all. Thousands died in the areas where the most wicked people lived. When the people saw that they were about to die from starvation they remembered God, and the words that Nephi had spoken. They pleaded with their judges and leaders to have Nephi intervene on their behalf. "We know that you are a man of God," they said to him. "Won't you please ask God to end this famine before all of your prophecies are fulfilled?" [17 BC]

When Nephi saw that the people had repented and humbled themselves, he cried out again to God. "Oh God, as you can see, the people have repented. They have swept the Gadianton Robbers away and put an end to the secret conspiracies. Please God, will you turn your anger away from them now because of their humility? Please be satisfied with the

wicked men among them who have already perished. Please listen to my request and make my words manifest. Send us rain so that we can have harvests and food to eat again. You said that if the people repented, you would spare them. You can see now that they have repented due to the famine that you sent. Let them have another chance to show their devotion to you. I ask that you give them your blessing."

In the 76th year of elected judges, God withdrew his anger from the Nephite people, and brought rain to the land. With the rain came abundant harvests once again. The people rejoiced and gave their thanks to God. They now knew that Nephi was a great prophet with profound authority and power given to him by God. [16 BC]

The people prospered and multiplied across the face of the land going to the north and the south, from the sea on the east to the sea on the west. In the peace that prevailed the church membership grew until more Nephite and Lamanite people belonged to it than didn't.

In the 79th year the perennial conflicts between the people arose once again. As the conflicts developed Nephi and his brother Lehi received many revelations every day. Their diligent efforts and preaching successfully brought peace once again. [13 BC]

In the 80th year of elected judges, some Nephite rebels, who had previously united with and become Lamanites, conspired with another faction of Lamanites to start warring again. They hid themselves in the mountains and periodically raided, killed, and plundered, then retreated again to their mountain hideouts. As their successes grew so too did the numbers of people who joined them. When the bandits uncovered the secret plans of the Gadianton Robbers they became the next incarnation of robbing conspirators and were known by the same name. They raided and brought destruction to both the Nephites and the Lamanites. [12 BC]

The people organized an army to end the raiding, and sent this army into the mountains to search out and destroy the robbers. But the robbers had become so strong that they drove the people's army out. In the 81st year the people's army tried destroying the robbers once more. They succeeded in killing many of them, but suffered many losses and were driven from the mountains again. The robbers were so strong, numerous, and deeply rooted in the mountainous terrain that the Nephite army was unable to defeat them. The growing threat spread fear and trepidation across the land. [11 BC]

The robbers grew in numbers, became ever bolder with their successful raids and began stealing women and children, taking them as captives back to the wilderness. Because the people understood that this great evil was a direct consequence of their sinfulness, some became inspired to remember their God.

In the 82nd year of elected judges, the people began turning away from God, and in the 83rd year their apostasy was rampant. [9 BC]

In the 85th year their pride and sinfulness made them ripe for destruction once again. [7 BC]

Chapter 12, 1981 Version

From this story of the Nephites you can see how fickle the hearts of men can be. You can see how God blesses and provides prosperity for those who trust in him. You can also see how men who become prosperous when God gives them bountiful harvests, large flocks of livestock, and all kinds of riches, quickly forget God when things are easy. When God spares their lives and protects them from their enemies they are thankful for a moment, and then violate his good will while basking in their easy lives of wealth and safety. When they forget him, God reminds them of their tenuous hold on life by bringing them terrible wars, famines, and disease.

Men are foolish, vain, quick to sin, and slow to do good. They are quick to listen to the devil and become fixated on material things. They are quick to show their pride and be boastful, while they are slow to remember their God, to listen to his advice, and walk in the path of wisdom. They are often unwilling to let God, their creator, rule over them or guide them.

Men are less than the dust which obeys God's commands. The mountains and hills obey God's words. They tremble, shake, and are broken by the power of God's voice. If he says to the earth, "Move," it moves. If he says to the earth, "Stop, I want the day to be of longer duration," that is what happens. For it is the earth's movement, not the sun's that determines the day's length, all according to God's word. If he ordered the oceans to dry up,

it would be done. If he ordered a mountain to rise up and fall upon a city, it would happen, and the city would be buried. If a man hides his treasure and God orders that it be cursed because of the man's sinfulness, it will be cursed and remain hidden from everyone forever. If he says to a man, "Because of your sinfulness you are cursed forever," the man is forever cursed and cut off from God. Sorry is the man to whom this happens, for he can never be saved. And this is exactly what God will say to those who do not repent.

Blessed are those who listen to the voice of God and do repent. These are the men that will be saved. May God grant all men the opportunity to repent their sins, become reformed to goodness, and be restored to grace according to the acts in their lives. I hope that all men will be saved. But I have read that on the day of judgment many will be cast out from the presence of God. Those who are rejected by God will find themselves in a state of eternal misery. This will be the fulfillment of God's words when he said, "Those who have done good will have life everlasting, and those who done evil will have everlasting damnation." So it will be.

Chapter 5, 1830 Version

Chapter 13, 1981 Version

In the 86th year of elected judges, the Nephites, for the most part, remained in a wretched state of wickedness, while many Lamanites were strict observers of God's commandments as given to Moses. [6 BC]

At this time there was a Lamanite named Samuel who came to Zarahemla to preach to the people. After several days of preaching he was thrown out and decided to return to his home. On his way back the voice of God came to him saying that he should return to Zarahemla and prophesy the words that came to his heart. When he arrived at the city walls he was denied entry. So he climbed up on the wall, stretched out his arms, and loudly cried out the prophecies that God put into his heart.

"I am Samuel the Lamanite," he cried out. "I have come to speak the words that God has put into my heart. God wants you to know that the sword of justice hangs over you people, and that within 400 years this sword of justice will fall upon you. This heavy destruction that awaits you and your descendants is sure to come. Nothing can prevent it except your repentance and faith in Jesus Christ who will surely come into the world, suffer, and be killed for his people."

"An angel of God has told me some great news, and sent me to share it with you, but you wouldn't let me inside your city to receive my words.

"God has sent me to tell you this, 'You Nephites have become a terribly hard hearted people. Unless you repent I will withdraw my Spirit and my protection from you. Unless you repent I will quit putting up with you, and I will turn the hearts of the Lamanites against you. Within 400 years I will afflict your people with wars, famine, and disease. When my fierce anger comes, the fourth generation of your enemies will witness your total destruction. This devastation will surely come unless you repent.'

" 'If you do repent,'" Samuel continued speaking God's words, " 'I will turn my anger away. Blessed are those who do repent and turn to me. And pity to those who don't. Pity to this great city of Zarahemla. It is only because of those who live here in righteousness that this city is saved, because I can see that most people who live here have turned their hearts away from me. I will bless and save those among you who repent. If it weren't for the righteous among you I would send fire down from heaven to destroy this city. But a time will come when you will cast out the righteous among you, and be ripe for destruction. Beware great city, of the wickedness and abominations within you. The same holds true for the city of Gideon and all the other great Nephite cities.'

" 'A curse will come upon the land because of the people's wickedness and abominations. Anyone who tries to hide their treasures from me will find that they are cursed, and that their treasures will disappear, unless they are righteously stored for the purposes of God. When the time of destruction comes, you Nephites will hide your wealth from your enemies before running away. In the end you will lose both your wealth and your lives.'

"You and your wealth will both be cursed," Samuel continued, "because you worship your riches more than you worship God, who has given them to you. You forget to thank God who provides for you, but you always remember the wealth that he provides. Instead of thanking him, you fill your lives with pride, boastfulness, envy, conflict, malice, persecutions, murder, and all sorts of sinfulness. Because of this, God will bring a curse upon your land and upon your riches.

"I pity you because the time has arrived when you now throw your prophets out. You mock them, throw stones at them, kill them, and subject them to all manner of indignities, just as people have done in times past. I've heard you say, 'If we had lived in the times of our ancestors, we would never have killed our prophets, stoned them, or cast them out.'

"I say to you that you are much worse than your ancestors. If a prophet comes among you and points out your sinfulness, you will become angry with him, cast him out, and seek his destruction. You will call him a false prophet, a sinner, and a servant of the devil because he shows you your evil deeds. On the other hand, if a man came among you who filled you with flattery, told you that your sins were nothing to worry about, and advised you to walk proudly while doing anything your heart desired, you would declare him a true prophet. You would look up to such a flatterer, shower him with part of your wealth, and give him the finest clothing to wear. Because he tells you what you want to hear, you would find him faultless in your eyes.

"You are a wicked and perverse generation of stubborn people. How long do you really think that God will put up with you? How long will you allow yourselves to be led by blind and foolish guides? For how long will you choose darkness over light? God is already angry with you, and has cursed the land because of your sinfulness. The time will soon come when he will curse your riches and make them so slippery that you cannot hold onto them. When you find yourselves in poverty crying out vainly to God, you will realize that your desolation is complete, and your destruction is certain.

"Oh how you will howl and weep in lament, saying, 'If only I had repented, if only I hadn't killed the prophets, stoned them, and cast them out, if only I had remembered God for the riches he gave us, then I wouldn't have lost everything I had. But now, my wealth has vanished and nothing can be done. The tools that I have today will be gone tomorrow. The swords that we have for battle will disappear before we need them. Oh how I wish I'd repented back when God's word was given to us. Because we didn't repent, we are surrounded by demons and angels of the devil who seek to destroy our souls. In spite of our past sinfulness, oh God, won't you turn your anger away from us now?'

"These will be your words in those days. Your days of probation are behind you. You will have procrastinated about your salvation until it is too late, and your destruction is certain. You will have sought all your lives for things you couldn't keep. You will have spent your days trying to find happiness through sinful living that is contrary to the nature of righteousness, and contrary to the will of God. Oh people of this land, listen to my words. I pray that you will repent and be saved, and that God's anger will be turned away from you."

Chapter 14, 1981 Version

Samuel the Lamanite prophesied many more things, some of which cannot be written, and some of which can.

"I will give you a sign to watch for," he said, "that will inform you of the time of Jesus Christ's arrival. Five years from now he will come to redeem those who believe in his name. You will see great lights in heaven, and in the night before he comes there will be no darkness. After the night that is as bright as a day has passed, you will know that Jesus Christ has been born. After the second day of light has passed, a new star, such as has never been seen, will rise in the evening sky. This also will be a sign to you that Jesus Christ has come. And this is not all. There will also be many other signs and extraordinary events in the heavens.

"When these things happen," Samuel the Lamanite continued, "you will be so amazed that you will fall to the ground. Whoever believes in Jesus Christ will find eternal life. I have been commanded by God, through his angel, to tell you these prophecies. God has commanded me to say these words for him, 'Cry out to my people', he said, 'tell them to repent and to prepare for the way of God.'

"I can see that you're angry with me because I am a Lamanite who has spoken harsh words to you. But these are words that God has commanded me to say. So now you want to destroy me and cast me out. I've climbed on top of this wall to tell you about the judgments of God that await you if you do not repent for your sinfulness. I wanted to let you know of the coming of Jesus Christ, the Son of God who is the creator of heaven and earth, and of all things since the beginning of time. I wanted to tell you about the coming signs in hopes that you will repent and believe in his name. If you believe in his name and repent all of your sins, you will receive a remission for them through his intervention.

"I will give you another sign so that you will know the time of Christ's death. For in order for salvation to occur, Jesus Christ must first die. It is necessary that he dies in order for the resurrection of the dead to occur, whereby men will be brought into the presence of God. His death will signal the resurrection and redemption of all mankind from the first death, the spiritual death, that we have inherited from the fall of Adam. Until Christ dies, all mankind has been cut off from the presence of God, and are considered dead to everything spiritual and worldly. Christ's resurrection will bring everyone back into God's presence.

"Whoever repents will not be cut down and thrown into the fire. Those who haven't repented will be cut down, thrown into the fire, and die a second death. They will forever be cut off from everything righteous. So repent, unless by having known these things, and not having repented, you condemn yourselves to be brought down by this second death.

"You will know the time of Christ's death by another sign. On the day that he dies, the sun, the moon and the stars will be darkened throughout the span of three days time, from the moment of his death until the time of his resurrection from death. At the moment of his death thunder and lightning will occur for many hours, the earth will shake, and rocks that make up the face of the earth will be broken into pieces. There will be great storms. Mountains will fall down into the valleys, and valleys will be lifted up as mountains. Highways and cities will be broken and made desolate. Graves will be opened, and the dead will be yielded up. Saints will appear to many people.

"The angel has told me that many people will see greater things than these, as

265

demonstrations designed to convince them that there is no reason for disbelief among men. Those who believe will be saved, while those who disbelieve will receive a righteous judgment for they will condemn themselves. I want you to remember that whoever perishes, does so to himself. Whoever sins, does so to himself. This is the freedom that God has given you, to act on your own behalf. You are free to know good from evil, and free to choose life or death. You can be good, and be restored to that which is good. Or you can do evil, and be condemned to evil forever."

Chapter 15, 1981 Version

"Unless you repent your homes will be destroyed," Samuel the Lamanite prophet continued speaking. "Unless you repent your nursing women will have great reasons to mourn because there will be no place of refuge. Pregnant women who are unable to flee, will be trampled and left to die. I pity the Nephites who refuse to repent when they see the signs that I've described. You have been God's chosen people. He has disciplined and criticized you for your sinfulness because he loves you.

"God has hated the Lamanites because of their evil deeds and because of the sinfulness of their ancestors. But now salvation has come to the Lamanites through the Nephite's preaching, and God has prolonged their days. If you look, you'll see that the majority of the Lamanites are now faithful to God, and keep the commandments, statutes, and judgments that God gave to Moses. The majority of the Lamanites are working hard to convert the rest of their brothers to the knowledge of truth. Because of this, there are many conversions every day of Lamanites who have come to recognize the wicked and abominable traditions of their ancestors. They have come to believe in the holy scriptures and the prophecies of the holy prophets that lead them, through faith in God, towards repentance and a change of heart. As you know, these people are firm and resolute in their faith because they have been made free.

"These converted Lamanites have buried their weapons of war, and know that it is a fearful sin to ever use them again. They would rather be oppressed and killed by their enemies than to lift these swords in their own defense.

This is because of their faith in Jesus Christ. They know that God will bless them and extend the days of their descendants because of the strongness of their enlightenment. Even if their descendants' belief falters, God will extend their days until a restoration of the truth occurs. This restoration has been spoken of by our ancestors, and by many prophets including Zenos.*

*Zenos is an Old World Hebrew prophet for whom all historical references are lost outside The Book of Mormon. Nephi's knowledge of Zenos' prophecies comes through Laban's brass plates brought from Jerusalem.

"God has extended his promises to the Lamanite people into the latter days regardless of the sinfulness that they will come to. They will be driven, hunted, oppressed, killed, and scattered without any place of refuge. But God will be merciful to them because according to the prophecy, they will eventually return to the truth. This truth is the knowledge and acceptance of their redeemer Jesus Christ, who is the great and true shepherd. And these distant descendants of the Lamanites will be counted as his sheep.

"Therefore unless you repent, even they will be better off than you are. Because of the wicked traditions of their ancestors, they have not been shown the mighty works of God that have been shown to you. If they had seen what you have been shown, they would never have lost their faith as you have. So God has said, 'I will not utterly destroy the Lamanite peoples. In the day of my wisdom I will cause them to return again to me.'

"Regarding you Nephites, this is what God has said, 'If they don't repent and obey my will, I will utterly destroy them because of their disbelief. I will bring this destruction upon them regardless of the many mighty things I have done for them in the past.'

"As surely as God lives, these things will come to be."

Chapter 16, 1981 Version

Many people heard Samuel the Lamanite's words spoken from atop the city walls of Zarahemla. Those who believed what Samuel had said went out in search of Nephi to confess their sins and be baptized.

But there were many who didn't believe what Samuel had to say, and were angry with him for having said it. As he stood on the wall these people threw stones and shot numerous arrows at him. But because the Spirit of God was with him, Samuel was an impossible target to hit. After seeing this miraculous protection, many more people came to believe in what he'd said, and went to Nephi for baptism. As a result of this, Nephi was busy baptizing, prophesying, preaching, crying out for the repentance of the people, revealing signs, and working miracles among the people so they'd know that Jesus Christ was coming soon. Nephi had prophesied many things to come, so that people would recognize these signs when they happened. He did this with the intent of catalyzing people into belief. So when the people heard Samuel speak many of them chose to repent, confess their sins, and be baptized.

But the majority of them didn't believe what Samuel said. When they saw that they couldn't hit him with stones and arrows they called officers of the law to come and arrest him. "Arrest this man and take him to prison," they said. "He is possessed by the devil, and because of this we are unable to hit with our stones and arrows."

When the officers tried to capture Samuel he jumped down from the city wall and escaped. He returned to his own country where he preached and prophesied among his own people, and was never again heard of by the Nephites.

In the 87th year of elected judges, the majority of the Nephite people held onto their pride and wickedness, and a minority of them maintained their faith in God. [5 BC]

In the 90th year some of the signs that had been predicted were revealed, and the words of the prophets began to be fulfilled. Angels appeared to wise men and declared that the good news that was written in the scriptures was about to be fulfilled. [2 BC]

In spite of the signs and miracles the unbelievers hardened their hearts further. "Some of these events, among so many, were correctly guessed," they conceded, "but we know that all these great events that were predicted will not happen."

These people used their rational thought to declare, "It is not reasonable to believe that someone such as this Jesus Christ will come. If he is truly the Son of God, why won't he show himself to us as well as the people of Jerusalem? We know that this is just a wicked myth that was handed down to us by our ancestors to try and make us believe in something that will supposedly happen in some distant land. Because these prophecies purport to take place in this distant land that we cannot see with our own eyes, how would we know whether or not they are true? These believers are really only cunning practitioners of the devil's mysterious arts who want to keep us down as servants to their words, and servants to them. They want us to be dependent on them to teach us the word and keep us in ignorance for the rest of our lives."

Many more foolish and vain things were said. The people were disturbed because Satan continually provoked them into sinfulness, by spreading rumors and instigating conflicts across the land. Satan hoped to harden the hearts of the people against all that was good, and against all that was about to come. In spite of all the miracles and signs, Satan was successful in holding onto the hearts of many people all across the land.

THE THIRD BOOK OF NEPHI — 1 BC TO AD 35

From Plates Inscribed by Nephi[3], the Son of Nephi[2] then Abridged
and Later Inscribed onto the Book of Mormon plates by Mormon

Jesus Christ is born in Bethlehem and signs of his birth appear to the Nephites. When Jesus Christ
dies earthquakes, floods, fires, and storms destroy the Nephites' cities and kill most of the people.
This destruction is followed by three days of total darkness until Jesus Christ is resurrected. After
his resurrection, Jesus Christ visits and ministers to the Nephites, giving them his true gospel.

THE THIRD BOOK OF NEPHI SUMMARY

Nephi[3] lived in the Western Hemisphere during the time of Jesus Christ's
birth and death in Israel. This book chronicles the events of the Nephite people
during the life of Jesus Christ, and his visitation to the Nephites after his
resurrection from death.

Nephi[3] who authored this book is the grandson of Helaman[2], the son of
Nephi[2], and the nephew of Lehi[2], authors of the Book of Helaman; and is also a
distant descendant of Nephi[1] who was born in Jerusalem six-hundred years
earlier.

The Third Book of Nephi opens with the departure of Nephi[2], who left the
land of Zarahemla and mysteriously disappeared. Before leaving he put the
records in the custody of his son Nephi [3].

When Nephi[3] began his record, miracles and fulfilled prophecies seemed to
signal the immediate arrival of Jesus Christ. When the prophesied time arrived
and the sign of Jesus' coming had not been seen, the people who were hostile to
the church threatened to start killing those who continued to believe. Just before
the scheduled execution of believers the prophesied night happened. When that
night's darkness failed to come everyone knew that something unprecedented
was approaching. A new star appeared in the sky and people who were sitting
on the fence, waiting, chose to believe and converted to the church of God. These
events became a new basis from which the passing years were counted. Great
numbers of people were baptized and peace descended upon the land.

When several more years passed and Jesus Christ still hadn't come to the
Nephites, the people again began to doubt the validity of the prophecies and the
truth of the signs. Then something truly remarkable happened. The converted
Lamanites' skin turned as white as the skin of the Nephites. The converted
Lamanites became Nephites in appearance as well as in name.

Meanwhile, the Gadianton Robbers became increasingly brazen in their
efforts to plunder and overthrow the Nephites. These robbers had far surpassed
the Lamanites as the greatest threat to the civilized Nephite people. When they
demanded that the Nephites surrender or be destroyed, the Nephites gathered

their horses, chariots, livestock, and food supplies in one place to defend themselves. Tens of thousands of people gathered in Zarahemla for the coming battle. Because the Nephites were now solid in their service to God they defeated the robbers, killed their leaders, and restored the peace. Even though he hadn't come to Zarahemla yet, the Nephites knew that Jesus Christ had come into the world.

In the peace that followed the people prospered and again became vain and unequal in their relative wealth. Within thirty years of the events signaling the birth of Jesus Christ the church of God became so badly corroded that only small bands of Lamanite converts remained faithful. Murder, instead of law, became the rule of the land. Within a span of just six years after their great victory over the Gadianton Robbers the people of Zarahemla had gone the distance from being mostly righteous to mostly sinful. After the prophets and chief judge were killed a conspirator named Jacob[3] declared himself king.

Because Nephi remained faithful to his belief in Jesus Christ he became the pillar of the church, and angels appeared to him daily. People either resented him or honored him as he traveled the land calling for repentance. His efforts resulted in numerous baptisms, miracles, and a strengthening of the faith in the year AD 33.

In AD 34, cataclysmic events occurred. First, a great storm arose that was more destructive than any storm ever known. Then the city of Zarahemla burst into flames. The city of Moroni sank into the sea and the people drowned. The city of Moronihah and its people were buried alive beneath a mountain, and general destruction spread its reach southward. To the north, tornadoes and earthquakes broke the land to pieces, killed the people, and destroyed the cities. The result was a wasteland everywhere.

Three hours after it began the environmental violence ended and absolute darkness fell. No fires could be lit or light of any kind could be made. Then came the three days of total darkness that Samuel the Lamanite prophet had foretold. The survivors wept and cried, wishing that they'd repented and kept their faith.

The voice of God fell upon them, affirming that his power had caused this vast destruction as punishment for the people's sinfulness. The survivors, God said, were spared because they were less sinful and deserved an opportunity to repent and receive eternal life. "I am Jesus Christ, the Son of God," the people were told. "I have come to redeem the world and save it from sin. If you come to me, you will be received. For this, I have sacrificed my own life and been raised up again. So repent now, and be saved." After three days of darkness, the light returned and the people looked out across their ruined land.

The people gathered and marveled at all that had happened, and a soft voice came from the sky, heralding the arrival of the Son of God. Jesus Christ descended slowly from the clouds, clothed in blinding whiteness, until he stood before them.

"Behold, I am Jesus Christ, whom the prophets foretold," he said. "I have redeemed the sins of the world and suffered the will of God from the beginning." He invited the people who'd fallen at his feet to come and touch him, and to witness the wounds from his crucifixion.

Jesus Christ asked Nephi to come forward as his first chosen disciple. He also chose eleven other disciples to help serve him. He showed the twelve disciples how people must be baptized in his name in order to be redeemed.

"You must repent and become as little children, believe in me, and be baptized in my name or you cannot receive my blessings or inherit the kingdom of God," said Jesus Christ. "This is my doctrine."

He then preached to the people about repentance, baptism, and the path of righteousness. Just as he had done in the Old World, Jesus Christ delivered his celebrated Sermon on the Mount to the Nephite crowd.

Jesus Christ explained to the Nephites that Gentiles in the future would come to torment, kill and dominate the Nephites' descendants, the Native Americans. He told how these Gentiles would bring the knowledge of the Nephite history to all the world because of their faith in Jesus Christ. He prophesied that those Gentiles who did not hold true to him would be trampled by the Native Americans, who would return to God in the latter days.

Jesus Christ then called the sick, the blind, and the crippled to come forward and be healed. He blessed the people generally, and blessed the children individually, after which the heavens opened and angels came down to instruct the children about God's love.

Jesus Christ then took his twelve disciples aside and asked them to bring him wine and bread. He showed them the sacrament of giving broken bread to eat, and wine to drink, in remembrance of him, so that his spirit would always be with them. He instructed them in prayer, in ministering to the people of the church, and about avoidance of the devil.

Before departing for heaven he gave the disciples one last commandment. "Do not let anyone who is unworthy of the sacrament, partake of it," he said. "Those who do so, will be damned." He also instructed the disciples on how to accept the unworthy, allow them to repent, be baptized, and become worthy of the sacrament. In parting he touched each of the twelve disciples individually and gave them the blessing of the Holy Ghost.

The clouds then descended and enveloped Jesus Christ as he ascended to heaven. That night the word went out that Jesus Christ would appear again the following day. People from across the land traveled all night to witness Jesus Christ for themselves.

The following day, after Nephi was baptized by the disciples and after he then baptized each of them, Jesus Christ came down from heaven in the company of angels. After witnessing their prayer and devotion, Jesus Christ gave thanks to God for their faith in him. He explained the sacrament to the people, and the promises made by God to the family of Israel, of which they were a part. He told of the future in which the Gentiles would come to dominate their descendants.

Jesus Christ told the Nephites that he would give them a sign that their descendants could watch for that would let them know when the day of judgment was near. "When these words about your descendants' ancestry through the family of Israel are made known to the Gentiles," Jesus Christ told the Nephites, "through the power of the Holy Ghost and my Father, the time is near. At that time, these same Gentiles will have conquered and scattered your descendants. Through the wisdom of my Father, this knowledge shall be reestablished in this land where the people are governed in freedom, and your remnant descendants will learn of their ancestry through these Gentiles."

Jesus Christ promised that one of his servants would be the recipient of a great and amazing work. He told how some would not believe it even though his servant would declare it to be the truth. (Presumably, this great work is *The Book of Mormon*, and his servant is Joseph Smith.) "My servant will be tormented because of those who do not believe him," said Jesus Christ. "When this time comes, I will cause my words to come to the Gentiles through this man."

Jesus Christ told of the terrible destruction that would come to those who did not believe and repent. He told how those future people who converted to his church would build the New Jerusalem, and all of Israel's descendants would be gathered together again. "The power of heaven will come down among them and I will be in their midst," he promised.

Jesus Christ quoted the prophecies of Isaiah from the Old Testament and told the Nephites that these prophecies would be fulfilled. He asked to see the Nephite's records, and when he read them pointed out errors and omissions that he directed the disciples to correct. He dictated words from the Old Testament prophet Malachi, and directed the disciples to include these words also in their written records.

For three days, Jesus Christ ministered to, taught, and healed the Nephite people before he ascended to heaven a second time.

Jesus Christ appeared one more time to the disciples and advised them to name their church after him. He told them that church members must repent and be baptized in the name of Jesus Christ. He instructed his disciples to write down what they had seen and heard. He let them know that he was pleased with this generation of Nephites, and that they would be saved. He explained that after four generations had passed their descendants would turn away from him in pursuit of material wealth, and would be lost.

Before he left for the final time Jesus Christ asked his disciples what they wanted of him. Nine of them asked for, and were granted, a place in heaven after their mortal lives had ended. The other three were given immortal life on earth, until the time that Jesus Christ returned on the final day of judgment. They were allowed to remain on earth, unchanged, so that they could stand witness to the unfolding events of the world. All of the disciples then became devoted missionaries, who spread the word of Jesus Christ and made converts among the people for as long as they lived.

THE THIRD BOOK OF NEPHI - TRANSLATION

Chapter 1, 1830 and 1981 Versions

In the 92nd year of elected judges, and the 600th year since Lehi left Jerusalem, Lachoneus served as chief judge and governor of the Nephite people. [1 BC]

Earlier that year Nephi[2] had left Zarahemla and disappeared. Before leaving, he transferred possession of the brass plates, and all the sacred records since the time of Lehi, into the hands of his eldest son, who was also named Nephi.

Prophecies were being fulfilled as the year progressed. People saw signs and miracles. But some said that the prophecies of Samuel the Lamanite prophet were already past due. These people were pleased, and announced to their fellow men, "Look, the time of Samuel's prophecies has come and gone. Your faith in his words has been in vain."

These verdicts of unfulfilled prophecies created an uproar. The people who believed in the prophecies were saddened, and began to fear that the prophesied events might not happen. But in spite of their doubts they continued to look for the predicted day in which there would be no night. The unbelievers held such great power that they were able to pass a sentence of death against all believers, if the prophesied night without darkness didn't occur by a specified day.

When Nephi[3] heard of this wickedness he fell into a deep sorrow. He bowed down to the earth and cried out to God on behalf of his people, who were about to be destroyed for their faith in the prophecies. After crying out to God all day the voice of God came to him, saying, "Pick yourself up and be of good cheer. The night without darkness that has been prophesied will happen tonight. Tomorrow I will be born into the world, and I will begin fulfilling all the prophecies that have been spoken of by the holy prophets. I will fulfill all of those things that have been made known to men since the beginning of the world. I come to fulfill the will of the Father, and of his Son, through my own flesh. The time has come. Tonight the sign will be given."

That night God's words were fulfilled, as spoken. When the sun set there was no darkness and the people were amazed. Many who hadn't believed in the prophecies fell to the ground as if they were dead. Their plans to kill all of the believers was abruptly cancelled when the prophesied night without darkness came upon them. People began to understand that the Son of God would shortly appear. In their astonishment everyone fell to the ground.

Those who didn't believe became afraid because of their sinfulness, and their absence of belief.

Throughout the entire night it was as light as high noon. When the sun rose the next morning the people knew that Jesus Christ had been born by the signs that had been given. Everything happened just as the prophets had predicted, and a new star appeared in the sky.

Satan then spread his lies among the people, and encouraged them to disregard the signs and wonders they'd witnessed. But most of the people did believe and were converted to God. Nephi and his priests baptized many people and accepted their repentance. Peace spread across the land as the people reformed themselves. Disagreements subsided, except for some cases in which individuals went out and preached, in error, that it was no longer necessary to observe the law of Moses. But those people who misunderstood the scriptures were soon converted and convinced of their mistakenness.

In the 93rd year of elected judges, there was peace across the land except for occasional incidents committed by the Gadianton Robbers who still infested the mountains, and hid in their secret strongholds. [AD 1]

In the 94th year these incidents increased in frequency and severity as the Nephites, who didn't convert, fled to join them. In addition, many rebellious, adolescent Lamanites were enticed by lies and flattery to also join the Gadianton Robbers. The defections of this younger generation weakened the faith and righteousness of those Lamanite parents whose children deserted them. [AD 2]

Chapter 2, 1981 Version

In the 95th year of elected judges, the people began to forget the signs and wonders that they'd seen and heard, and became dismissive of more signs as they closed their hearts and minds. Some people even suggested that the devil had been responsible for the amazing events. By blinding the people to the truth Satan led many to believe that the doctrine of Jesus Christ was a vain and foolish thing. As the years passed the people's wickedness and abominations grew ever stronger. With Satan leading their hearts these people disbelieved that any further signs would come, and general sinfulness spread across the land. [AD 3]

In the 100th year of elected judges, and the 609th year since Lehi had left Jerusalem, 9 years had passed since the night without darkness when Jesus Christ had been born into the world. At this time the Nephite people began to count their years since the birth of Jesus Christ instead of since the time when judges were first elected. [AD 9]

[From this point forward the referenced years in The Book of Mormon match today's dating convention. For example, the Nephites "13th year after the birth of Jesus Christ" is chronologically the same as our AD 13.]

Nephi's father Nephi[2] was still missing, and no one knew where he was. In spite of all the preaching and prophesying, most of the people had lapsed back into wickedness.

In the 13th year after the birth of Jesus Christ, wars and conflicts became widespread. The Gadianton Robbers became so numerous, and their predatory attacks resulted in the deaths of so many people that the Nephites and the Lamanites had to do something. The Lamanites who had converted to Jesus Christ united with the Nephites to arm themselves and defend their lands, rights, church, freedoms, and families against the robbers. If they didn't, they were faced with complete destruction.

When these converted Lamanites united with the Nephites to jointly defend themselves, an amazing miracle happened. The curse of dark skin was lifted from the Lamanites, and their skin color became as white as the skin of the Nephites. The children of the Lamanites also became fair skinned. These transformed Lamanites were all counted as Nephites and were thereafter called Nephites.

In the 14th year the Nephites drove the Gadianton Robbers from their lands, and back into their secret mountain strongholds.

In the 15th year the robbers came out of the mountains to attack the Nephites yet again. This time, because of the wickedness of the Nephite people, the robbers were able to gain and hold ground against the Nephites. Because of their persistent sinfulness, the sword of destruction hung once again over the Nephite people's heads.

Chapter 2, 1830 Version

Chapter 3, 1981 Version

In the 16th year after the birth of Jesus Christ, Governor Lachoneus received a letter from the Gadianton Robbers' leader, Giddianhi. "Noble Governor Lachoneus," it read, "I write to praise you and your people for the firmness with which you maintain your supposed rights and freedoms. You stand as if you were supported by the hand of a god in the defense of your lands and your so-called country. It seems a pity to me, noble Lachoneus, that you should be so foolish and vain as to imagine that you can stand up against the many brave men at my command who only wait for my word to destroy you. I know of my men's indomitable spirit and their enduring hatred of you for the many wrongs that you've done to them. If I say so, you will be utterly destroyed.

"So I write to you," Giddianhi continued, "out of regard for your own welfare. If you surrender your army, your lands, your cities, and your possessions I will spare you from destruction. I invite you to unite with us, embrace our secret conspiracies, and become like us. We want you as partners, not as slaves. If you do as I say, I swear that you will not be destroyed. If you do not do as I say, I will command my armies to come against you until all of your people are extinct.

"I, Giddianhi, am the governor of the secret society of Gadianton. I personally know that our society, which has been handed down to us from ancient times, is good. I write in hopes that you will surrender without the unnecessary shedding of blood. I only want to restore my people to the rights and possessions that you have stolen from them. If you refuse my offer, I will avenge their wrongs."

When Governor Lachoneus read this letter he was amazed at the boldness of Giddianhi. He was demanding possession of the Nephite's lands, and threatening to avenge the supposed wrongs of people who hadn't been wronged at all. These people had only themselves to blame for defecting to the abominable robbers. Since Lachoneus was an honest and courageous man, he couldn't be frightened by the demands and threats of these insidious robbers. He paid no attention to the letter. Instead, he commanded his people to cry out to God for strength against the horde of robbers who now threatened them.

Lachoneus sent out a proclamation among his people to gather their families and their livestock into one place, and then ordered the construction of fortifications to protect them. He placed an army of Nephites, including the former Lamanites who were now Nephites, as guards to watch over them day and night. "Unless you repent of your sinfulness," he said to them, "and cry out to God, you will be destroyed by these Gadianton Robbers."

So powerful were these words and prophecies of Lachoneus that the people became fearful if they didn't comply. So the Nephite people once again turned to God as Lachoneus had commanded them to do.

Lachoneus then organized his people into armies led by captains. The chief captain was a man named Gidgiddoni, who was also a great prophet and chief judge chosen by the people. "Let us go to the mountains," the people said to Gidgiddoni, "and destroy the robbers in their own lands."

"No," replied Gidgiddoni. "If we attack them there, God will permit our defeat. We must prepare ourselves for their attack, and gather our armies together. We will wait until they attack us. If we do this, God will give us victory."

In the 17th year after the birth of Jesus Christ tens of thousands of Nephites gathered together near Zarahemla with their cattle, horses, chariots, and harvests of grain, to defend themselves against their enemies. They gathered to the south of Zarahemla because there was a great curse on the land to the north.

When they all came together as a unified group, they came to fear the words that Lachoneus had spoken. So they repented for all their sins, and prayed to God for deliverance from their enemies when the great battle came. While they waited for their enemies to attack Gidgiddoni had them make weapons, shields, and armor of every kind, according to his instructions.

Chapter 4, 1981 Version

In the 18th year after the birth of Jesus Christ the army of robbers were ready to do battle and came down from the mountains to fight. They easily took possession of the undefended land and cities that had been abandoned by the Nephites. But there was no wild game or food for the robbers in the abandoned areas because the Nephites had left it desolate. They had taken all of their harvests and livestock with them when they left. Without wild game to hunt, or Nephite farms to plunder, the robbers found subsistence outside their wilderness lands impossible. Their only option was to attack and overcome the Nephites at their stronghold. The Nephites had stripped the land of all subsistence and had gathered together enough horses, cattle, and provisions to endure a siege of seven years duration.

In the 19th year Giddianhi resolved that it was necessary to attack the Nephites. His robbers had no interest in becoming farmers themselves, or growing crops on the abandoned Nephite lands. If they did, he reasoned, the Nephites would merely attack their scattered farms as his robbers had previously done to them. Their only chance of success lay in robbing and plundering the Nephites.

When the time of the great battle arrived the robbers came dressed in lambskin loincloths dyed in blood. Their heads were shaved and protected by helmets, and their bodies were protected by fearsome looking armor. When the Nephites saw the terrifying appearance of the robbers' army they fell to the ground and cried out to God to deliver them from this horrible enemy. Seeing this, the robbers roared with joy because they supposed that the Nephites had fallen from fear and terror of their army. But they were mistaken. The Nephites were not afraid of anything but their God to whom they prayed for protection. When the robbers rushed forward to attack, the Nephites were prepared to meet them with the strength of God on their side.

The great battle was terrible. It was the biggest slaughter of Lehi's descendants since their ancestors had left Jerusalem hundreds of years ago. In spite of Giddianhi's boasting, threats and oaths, the Nephites prevailed and drove the robbers' army back. Gidgiddoni ordered the Nephite army to pursue the robbers to the edge of the wilderness border, and not to spare any of the robbers that fell into their hands. In the course of this bloody retreat the robbers' leader, Giddianhi, fought hard but was overtaken and killed.

The robbers' army was pushed back to the edge of the wilderness, and the Nephites returned to their own stronghold and waited. For the next two years all was quiet. In the 21st year after the birth of Jesus Christ the robbers came forward again and surrounded the Nephites' stronghold, thinking that they could cut them off from their lands and force them to surrender. By this time the robbers had a new leader named Zemnarihah who led the siege against the Nephites.

While the Nephites were well supplied and prepared for a long siege, the robbers lacked any provisions of their own. The lands around Zarahemla were void of the wild game that the robbers normally depended upon to feed themselves. Their only source of food came from their hunters, who brought it to them from the wilderness. This resulted in further depletion and scarcity of wild game along the wilderness boundaries. The invaders were starving while they laid siege to the Nephites. Partly because of the robbers' persistent hunger the Nephites were able to fight successfully every day, and killed tens of thousands of the invaders. As a result of the cumulative destruction of their forces the robbers lost their motivation, and wanted to withdraw. So Zemnarihah ordered his army to retreat to the lands far north of Zarahemla.

Gidgiddoni knew of their plans, of their weakness from starvation, and of the massive depletion of their army's numbers. So that night he sent out his own army to cut off their path of retreat. When the weakened robber army awoke the next morning they found themselves facing the Nephite army from all sides. Thousands of robbers surrendered to the Nephites, and the rest were killed.

Zemnarihah was captured and hung from a tree until he was dead. Afterwards the Nephites felled the tree and cried out to God. "May God preserve his people in righteousness and holiness of heart," they shouted out, "so that all those who seek to kill them through force and secret conspiracies will fall, just as this man Zemnarihah has been felled. May the God of Abraham, of Isaac, and of Jacob[1] protect this people in righteousness as long as they call on him for their protection."

The entire body of Nephites broke into song together, praised God for the great victory he had given them, and thanked him for deliverance from their enemies. "Hosanna to the God Most High," they cried out. "Blessed is the name of the Lord God Almighty."

Their hearts were filled with joy and their eyes were filled with tears. They knew that it was because of their repentance and their humility that they had been delivered from an everlasting destruction.

Chapter 5, 1981 Version

There were no Nephites now who doubted the words of the holy prophets. They knew Jesus Christ had come because of the signs and the fulfilled prophecies. Because of this they were certain that the remaining prophecies would also be fulfilled. The Nephites repented for their sins, abominations, and fornications. They served God with diligence all day and all night.

The robbers that the Nephites had captured were thrown into prisons where the word of God was preached to them. All those robbers who repented for their sins and promised to never murder again were set free. For every robber who repented, there were just as many who held murder in their hearts. Those who threatened others were condemned, and punished according to the law. This put an end to the murders and secret conspiracies.

Many amazing things transpired at this time that cannot be written into this book. It would be impossible to mention even a hundredth of what happened in the 25 years following the birth of Jesus Christ. While there are records of much of it, a shorter and truthful account was made by Nephi and engraved onto the plates from which I, Mormon, read. From these, I make my own account on plates that I've made with my own hands.

I am named Mormon after the place where Alma established the first church of God. I am a disciple of Jesus Christ, the Son of God. I have been called by him to declare his word among his people, so that they may have life everlasting. It is necessary, according to the will of God, that the prayers of my holy ancestors be fulfilled through the making of this record of what has happened before me. But this is only a small record of the many things that have taken place since the time that Lehi left Jerusalem until the present time. I make this record from the accounts given by

those who witnessed these things, as well as what I've have seen with my own eyes. I know that my record will be an honest and truthful account, even though there is much that I need to leave out.

I am a pure descendant of Lehi. I am thankful to God, and my Savior Jesus Christ, for having brought my ancestors out of Jerusalem, and I am thankful for the knowledge about the salvation of our souls that has been given to my people. God has blessed the family of Jacob[1] and has been merciful to the descendants of his son Joseph[1]. To the degree that the descendants of Lehi have kept his commandments, God has blessed them and given them prosperity according to his word.

I am certain that God will again bring the descendants of Joseph to the knowledge of the Lord, their God. God has promised to restore the family of Jacob to the knowledge of the covenants that he has made with them. When this happens they will know of their Redeemer, Jesus Christ, the Son of God. The remnants of Jacob's descendants will be gathered up from all corners of the earth to be restored to their own lands from which they have been scattered. So it will be.

Chapter 3, 1830 Version

Chapter 6, 1981 Version

In the 26th year after the birth of Jesus Christ all of the Nephite people returned to their own lands, along with their flocks, herds, horses, cattle, possessions, gold, silver, and remaining food provisions. Some moved southward, while others moved northward. They gave the reformed robbers who wanted to remain among them, in peace, enough land for subsistence. In so doing, they established a state of peacefulness across the land. The Nephite people became prosperous again. They passed laws to establish equity and justice among everyone. The only thing that could prevent them from perpetual prosperity, was a relapse of their sinfulness.

Under the leadership of Gidgiddoni and the chief judge Lachoneus many new cities were built and many old cities were repaired. Highways and roads were constructed to connect the cities and the lands. Peace persisted through the 28th year.

In the 29th year after the birth of Jesus Christ the people's prosperity turned inexorably towards vanity and boastfulness. Class divisions arose according to the people's possession of wealth. The wealthy became well educated while the poor were left in ignorance. The rich persecuted the poor, while the poor were humble and penitent before God. The inequality became so great that the church began to fracture.

In the 30th year the church fell apart except among a few of the converted Lamanites. These people were immovable in their faith and unshakable in their adherence to the laws of God.

It was Satan who caused the fall of the Nephite people into sinfulness. Through his great power he stirred the people up and caused them to act wrongly. He filled them with pride and vanity. He tempted them with power, authority, and wealth. Because of Satan's intervention the period of peace was just a few, brief years. Through his temptations the devil incited the people to do whatever wickedness he desired. The people were in open and defiant rebellion against God, not out of ignorance, but out of willfulness.

In the midst of all this sinfulness inspired men stepped forward to preach and testify boldly about the awful state of the people. They reminded the people of the redemption that God would give them through the resurrection of Jesus Christ after his death and suffering. There were many renegade lawyers, priests, and judges who were angry with these inspired preachers for stirring the people up. Even though no one could be legally executed without signed orders from the governor, many of these inspired preachers were secretly condemned and killed by the renegade judges without the governor's knowledge.

Complaints were eventually lodged against the renegade judges who violated the laws and put prophets of God to death. When they came before the governor to be judged, their friends, relatives, lawyers, and priests stood with them in dishonest denial of their violations. These people entered into an unholy conspiracy with the devil against all righteousness. They conspired to destroy people of God, and to deliver themselves from the clutches of justice. They sought to overthrow the laws and rights of their country, end freedom, destroy the governor, and replace him with a king to whom all the people would be subjects.

Chapter 7, 1981 Version

In the 30th year after the birth of Jesus Christ the renegade judges murdered Governor Lachoneus, but were unsuccessful at enthroning a king. The governor's murder incited conflict among the people and destroyed the government. The people were divided against each other into tribes of family, friends, and secret alliances. Each tribe had its own leader, but there was no leader of the land because there were so many tribes with so many different leaders.

The people let themselves be led by the power of Satan. The secret conspiracies of tribes, who'd murdered the prophets, now destroyed law and order. Except for a few righteous men the people had almost entirely lapsed into sinfulness. Only six years after their great victory over the robbers, the people had turned away from righteousness, like a dog eating his own vomit, or a pig wallowing in the mire.

The main conspirators gathered together and followed a leader named Jacob[3], who they called their king. This man Jacob had been one of the people most vocal in his opposition to the prophets of Jesus Christ.

Though the majority of the people lapsed into unrighteousness themselves, they were united in their hatred of these conspirators who had toppled the government. When Jacob saw a growing threat to his power he fled into the north, where he established a kingdom of dissenting renegade Nephites.

In the 31st year after the birth of Jesus Christ the divided tribes of people were too disorganized and fractured to form a central government, but they did agree not to fight with each other. They managed to arrange a fragile peace by establishing defined territorial boundaries with each other. But meanwhile, the prophets of God were stoned and cast out.

Nephi grieved for his people. He'd been visited by angels, heard the voice of God, and seen the power of Jesus Christ's ministry. He'd watched helplessly as his people had fallen from righteousness into wickedness and abomination. He went out and spoke strongly about repentance and the remission of sins through faith in Jesus Christ. Nephi ministered to his people with such power and authority that it was impossible to disbelieve in what he said. His faith in God was so great that angels spoke to him every day. In the name of Jesus Christ he cast out devils and unclean spirits. When his brother was stoned to death for speaking out against sinfulness, Nephi raised him from the dead.

When the people saw the power of the miracles that he performed in the name of Jesus Christ, many of them grew angry with him. Very few of those who witnessed these miracles were restored to God. But those who did became convinced of the power of God, and were supported in their belief in Jesus Christ. Those who were healed by the Spirit of God were then able to perform miracles themselves. All of those who repented were baptized with water by Nephi ,or his ordained ministers, and received remission from their sins.

In the 33rd year after the birth of Jesus Christ many people repented and were baptized.

Chapter 4, 1830 Version

Chapter 8, 1981 Version

We know that the following record is true, wrote Mormon, because it was kept by a very honest man. We know of his honesty because of the many miracles he performed in the name of Jesus Christ, and the certainty that no man can do miracles in the name of Jesus Christ except a man who has cleansed himself of every speck of sinfulness.

With the passing of the 33rd year after the birth of Jesus Christ the Nephite people began to look earnestly for the three days of unbroken darkness that Samuel the Lamanite prophet had foretold. In spite of the many signs that had already been fulfilled there was great doubt and debate among the Nephites concerning this prophesied event.

In the 34th year after the birth of Jesus Christ a great storm arose that was more terrible than any storm ever known. The thunder from this storm was so powerful that it shook the whole earth as if to tear it apart. The city of Zarahemla burst into flames. The city of Moroni sunk into the sea and the

inhabitants drowned. The earth rose up and buried the city of Moronihah such that the place where the city had been, became a huge mountain. In the lands to the south the destruction was catastrophic. To the north the destruction was even greater.

The storms, whirlwinds, and earthquakes totally changed the face of the land. Highways and roads were broken up and ruined. Smooth places became rough. The great Nephite cities were sunk, burned, and shaken to pieces. The inhabitants were killed. Buildings fell to the ground and the cities were left desolate. Some cities were left standing but were greatly damaged. Most of the people were killed, and some were swept away by the whirlwinds, never to be seen again.

After three hours of these sustained storms and earthquakes everything became still, and the earth fell into total darkness. There was no light whatsoever. No candles, torches, or fires could even be lit. There was no sun, no moon, and no stars. There was only total darkness across the face of the land. For three days no light of any sort was seen. The survivors mourned, howled, and wept continuously because of the destruction that preceded the darkness and also because of the terrifying darkness itself.

"If only we had repented before this terrible day," some were heard to say, "then our people would have been spared, and the great city of Zarahemla would not have burned."

In another place the people cried out, "If only we had repented before this terrible day, and not killed the prophets, if only we hadn't stoned them and cast them out, then our mothers, daughters, and children would have been spared. If only we'd done differently then the great city of Moronihah would not have been buried beneath a mountain."

These are just samples of the great and terrible howlings of the surviving people.

Chapter 9, 1981 Version

A great voice was then heard by all the scattered survivors cross the land. "Woe unto this people," the voice said. "and woe unto all the people of the earth unless they repent. The devil and his angels laugh and rejoice today because of the deaths of my people. It is because of their sinfulness that they have died. I burned the great city of Zarahemla and all of its inhabitants. I have sunk the great city of Moroni into the sea and drowned its inhabitants. I have buried the great city of Moronihah and all its inhabitants to hide their sins and abominations from my sight. I have done this so that the blood of the prophets and saints will be avenged.

"I have caused the city of Gilgal to sink into the earth and entomb its inhabitants. I have drowned the cities and inhabitants of Onihah, Mocum, and Jerusalem beneath the waters to hide their sins and abominations from my sight. I have done this so that the blood of the prophets and saints will be avenged. I have buried the cities and inhabitants of Gadiandi, Gadiomnah, Jacob, and Gimgimno beneath valleys and hills to hide their sins and abominations from my sight. I have done this so that the blood of the prophets and saints will be avenged.

"In particular I have burned the great city Jacobugath and its inhabitants. I have done this because this city was occupied by the people of King Jacob, and was the most wicked city on earth. It was these people who practiced secret murders and conspiracies, destroyed the peace of my people, and destroyed the government. I have done this so that the blood of the prophets and saints will be avenged.

"I have also burned the cities and inhabitants of Josh, Gad, and Kishkumen because they stoned and cast out the prophets that I sent to advise them of their sins and abominations. I did this to hide their sins and abominations from my sight. I have done this so that the blood of the prophets and saints will be avenged. I have purged the land far and wide with great destruction to cleanse it of sinfulness and abominations.

"You that were spared were more righteous than those who perished. I ask that you return to me, repent your sins, and become converted so that I can heal you. If you come to me, you may have eternal life. I open my arms to receive you. Whoever comes will be received and blessed. I am Jesus Christ the Son of God. I have created the heavens and earth, and all things in them. I was with God the Father in the beginning. I am in God the Father, and God the Father is in me. Through me the name of God the Father is glorified.

"I came to my people in Old Jerusalem to fulfill the prophecies in the scriptures, but I was not received by them. Those who did receive me have become the sons of God as will those who believe in my name. Through me the law of Moses is fulfilled. I am the light and life of the world. I am Alpha and Omega, the beginning and the end.

"I ask for no more blood sacrifices from you. I will no longer accept your burnt offerings or sacrifices. Instead, I want you to offer me the sacrifice of your broken heart and contrition so that I may baptize you with fire and the Holy Ghost. At the moment of their conversion the Lamanites were unknowingly baptized with fire and the Holy Ghost. I have come to bring redemption to the world and save earth's people from sin. Whoever comes to me as a little child will be received and will enter the kingdom of God. For this I have laid down my life, and then taken it up again. Repent people, come to me and be saved."

Chapter 10, 1981 Version

All the surviving people everywhere across the land heard the voice in the darkness, and the words that were spoken. The people were so astonished that they stopped their crying, and mourning for their dead relatives. For many hours there was peace and silence.

The voice came again to all the people of the land saying, "You people of these great fallen cities are descendants of Jacob[1] and members of the family of Israel. I have gathered you often as a hen gathers her chicks under her wings. I have nourished you. Many times I have tried to gather up those who have fallen and been refused. Many more times I will gather up those of you who repent and return to me under my protective wings. Those who do not return to me will find their homes desolate until the covenants to your ancestors are fulfilled."

After these words the people began to weep and howl once again at the loss of their relatives and friends. In the morning after the third day of darkness the blackness lifted. The earth stopped shaking and the groaning ended. The people's mourning and wailing gave way to joy and thanksgiving in praise of their redeemer Jesus Christ. The prophets' scriptures were being fulfilled. Those people who had

279

maintained their righteousness, who had listened to the prophets, and who had not harmed the prophets were spared from being buried, drowned, burned, crushed, and carried away by the storms.

Whoever reads these and other scriptures, wrote Mormon, needs to understand that this destruction and death by fire, smoke, storms, and earthquakes is the fulfillment of the prophecies given by many holy prophets. Many prophets foretold these events at the time of Jesus Christ's arrival. Many of them were killed for saying so. These prophets who spoke of these things include Zenos and Zenock.

Our ancestor Jacob also testified about the remnant descendants of his son Joseph[1], Mormon continued. And are we not those remnant descendants of Joseph? These events are described on the brass plates that Lehi brought with him from Jerusalem.

In the 34th year after the birth of Jesus Christ the Nephites, and the former Lamanites who were spared from destruction, were showered with blessings. Soon after Jesus Christ's ascension he appeared in person to the surviving Nephite people, and ministered unto them.

Chapter 5, 1830 Version

Chapter 11, 1981 Version

Great crowds of people gathered together around the temple in Bountiful where they witnessed in wonder the changes to the landscape around them. They talked about Jesus Christ and the fulfillment of signs that attended his death. While they were conversing a voice came to them as if it were from heaven. The voice was soft, but penetrating. Though they couldn't understand it, or see its source, the voice caused their hearts to burn. The voice came a second time but was still beyond their comprehension.

The third time that the voice came to them the people opened their hearts to hear it and raised their eyes to heaven, because that was where the voice was coming from. This time they did understand it.

"Look, this is my beloved Son," said the voice, "who has glorified my name and with whom I am well pleased. Listen to him."

With their eyes raised to heaven they saw a man descending towards them clothed in a white robe. He came down and stood in their midst. Everyone turned their eyes to him in silence, not knowing what it meant. They thought he was an angel who had appeared before them.

He stretched out his hand and spoke. "I am Jesus Christ, whom the prophets have foretold would come into the world. I am the light and the life of the world. I have drunk from the bitter cup which God the Father has given to me. I have glorified God the Father by taking upon myself the sins of the world. I have suffered the will of God the Father in all things since the beginning of the world."

When Jesus Christ spoke these words the whole crowd fell to the ground, because they remembered the prophecies saying that Jesus Christ would show himself to them after his ascension into heaven.

"Rise up and come to me," said Jesus Christ, "so that you can put your hands into the wound on my side and feel the holes of the nails in my hands and feet. You will then know that I am the God of Israel and the God of the whole earth who has been killed for the sins of the world."

The crowd rose and did as Jesus Christ had asked. One by one they put their hands into his side and felt the imprints from the nails, until they had all witnessed this miracle for themselves with their eyes and with their hands. Afterwards they all knew, with certainty, that this was Jesus Christ whom the prophets had said would come.

After the people had witnessed the truth for themselves, they all cried out with one voice saying, "Hosanna! Blessed is the name of God most high." They all fell at the feet of Jesus Christ and worshipped him.

Jesus Christ called out to Nephi and commanded him to come forward. Nephi arose and came to Jesus Christ where he bowed down and kissed his feet.

"Rise up," Jesus Christ said to Nephi. When Nephi had arisen, Jesus Christ said to him, "I give you the power to baptize these people when I ascend again to heaven."

Jesus Christ then called eleven others forward, and conveyed to them the same power that he had given to Nephi. "In the following way you will baptize your people, and there must be no arguments among you in this regard. Whoever repents of his sins and wants to be baptized in my name must go down and stand in the water when you baptize them. These are the words that you must say, 'By the authority given to me by Jesus Christ, I baptize you in the name of the Father, the Son, and the Holy Ghost. Amen.' Then you must immerse them in the water and then bring them back out. Only in this manner may you baptize in my name because the Father, the Son, and the Holy Ghost are one. I am in the Father and the Father is in me. The Father and I are one.

"From this point forward there must be no arguments among you regarding baptism or doctrine, as there have been in the past. He who shows the spirit of conflict is not of me, but of the devil, who is the father of all conflict. It is the devil who stirs up the hearts of men to fight against one another with anger. My doctrine does not include anger and conflict between people. My doctrine calls for the abandonment of such things.

"My doctrine has been given to me by God the Father who commands that all men, everywhere repent their sins and believe in me. Whoever believes in me and is baptized will be saved, and will inherit the kingdom of God. Whoever doesn't believe in me and isn't baptized will be damned. This is my doctrine as has been given by God the Father. Whoever believes in me also believes in God the Father, and in God the Holy Ghost, for God the Father, the Holy Ghost, and I are one.

"This is my doctrine. Whoever builds on this, builds on my rock, and the gates of hell will have no power over them. Anyone who declares more or less than this, and claims it as my doctrine is an agent of evil. Such a person does not build on my rock, but on sand. For them the gates of hell stand wide open to receive them when the floods come and the winds beat down upon them. Go out then among the people and declare the words that I have spoken across the broad extent of the earth."

Chapter 12, 1981 Version

[Chapters 12, 13, and 14 in the Third Book of Nephi embody mostly the same text as found in Chapters 5, 6, and 7 of Matthew from the New Testament. These three chapters comprise what is known in the Bible as Jesus

Christ's Sermon on the Mount. Most of the text in Chapters 12, 13, and 14 is identical, word for word, with the corresponding chapters of Matthew. What differences there are, are mostly minor word substitutions, slight rephrasings, and added introductory phrases. The message that is conveyed in these chapters of the Third Book of Nephi is not significantly different than the Sermon on the Mount found in the Bible.

Chapter 12, The Third Book of Nephi, is 78% identical, word for word, to Matthew, Chapter 5.

Chapter 13, The Third Book of Nephi, is 92% identical, word for word, to Matthew, Chapter 6.

Chapter 14, The Third Book of Nephi, is 95% identical, word for word, to Matthew, Chapter 7.

Because the Sermon on the Mount is such a pivotal part of both the New Testament and The Book of Mormon, text found in The Book of Mormon that is not present in the New Testament is italicized.]

After Jesus Christ had spoken to Nephi and the other eleven men whom he had chosen to receive his power and authority, he stretched out his hand to the Nephite crowd.

"You will be blessed if you listen to the words of these twelve men whom I have chosen from among you," said Jesus Christ to the crowd. "They will be your servants. I have authorized them to minister to you, and I have given them the power to baptize you with water. After you are baptized with water, I will baptize you with fire and with the Holy Ghost. Those of you who believe in me, and are baptized, are blessed. After that you will have seen me and know that I am. But even more blessed will be those who believe your words after you testify to them that you have seen and known me. Those who believe your words and become baptized in humility will also be visited by fire and blessed by the Holy Ghost. They too will receive a remission of their sins.

"Blessed are the poor in spirit who come to me, for theirs is the kingdom of heaven. Blessed are all of those who mourn, for they will be comforted. Blessed are the meek, for they will inherit the earth. Blessed are all of those who hunger and thirst after righteousness, for they will be filled with the Holy Ghost. Blessed are the merciful, for they will obtain mercy. Blessed are all the pure in heart, for they will see God. Blessed are all the peacemakers, for they will be called the children of God. Blessed are all of those who are persecuted in my name, for theirs is the kingdom of heaven. Blessed are all of those who men revile and persecute, and about whom all manner of evil things are falsely said because of me. Be joyful and glad, for your reward in heaven will be great. Remember that the prophets who came before you were persecuted also.

"You people are the salt of the earth, but if you lose your savor how can the earth be salted? The salt will become good for nothing, except to be cast out and be trampled underfoot. You are the light of your people, like a city that is built on a hill and cannot be hidden. Do men light a candle and hide it under a basket? No, they put it on a candlestick so that it shines light throughout the house. So let your light shine for all people, so that they may see your good works and glorify your Father in heaven.

"I have not come to destroy the law or the prophecies. I have come to fulfill them. Not one bit of the law has been rescinded, but through me these laws and prophecies are fulfilled. *I have given you the law and the commandments of my Father. You must believe in me, repent your sins, and come to me with a broken heart and a repentant spirit. You have the commandments before you and can see that the law is fulfilled. Come unto me and be saved. Unless you keep my commandments you may not enter the kingdom of heaven.*

"You have heard it said, and seen it written since ancient times, that you should not kill, and that whoever did kill would be in danger of the judgment of God. But I say to you that whoever is angry with his brother will be in danger of God's judgment. And whoever speaks to his brother with contempt will be in danger of judgment. Whoever says, 'You fool,' will be in danger of hell fire. If you come to me, or want to come to me, and remember that your brother stands against you, seek him out first and reconcile yourself with him. Then come to me with a clean heart, and I will receive you. If you have adversarial relations with others, get them out of the way before you find yourself imprisoned. If you owe money to others, pay them back. If you are imprisoned for your debts how can you repay them?

"It has been written since ancient times that you must not commit adultery. But I say to you, that whoever looks on a woman with lust has already committed adultery in his heart. *It is my commandment that you let none of these things enter into your heart. It is better that you should deny these things to yourselves than to be cast into hell for them.*

"It has been written that whoever wants to dismiss his wife should give her written papers of divorce. But I say to you that whoever dismisses his wife, except for the reason of adultery, causes her to be an adulterer. Furthermore, whoever marries a divorced woman is also an adulterer.

"It is written that you should not swear, but also that you should honor your oaths to God. I say that you should not swear at all, not by heaven, because it is God's throne, or by the earth, because it is his footstool. You shouldn't swear by your own head because you cannot change the color of any of your hairs. Let your promises be simple. Say yes, or say no. To swear beyond your promised word is evil.

"It has been written that revenge should take the form of an eye for an eye, and a tooth for a tooth. I say to you that you should not resist evil. If someone strikes you on the right cheek, turn the other cheek to him also. If someone takes you to court for your coat, give him your shirt as well. If he compels you to go a mile, go two miles with him. Give people what they ask for, and don't turn away from those who wish to borrow.

"It is written that you should love your neighbor and hate your enemy. But I say to you that you should also love your enemies. Bless those who curse you, do good to those that hate you, and pray for those who treat you badly or persecute you. By doing this you become the children of my Father in heaven, for he makes the sun rise on evil and on good.

"*Those things which have been the law since ancient times are in me fulfilled. Old ways have passed and new ways have arrived. I want you to be as perfect as I am, and as perfect as your Father in heaven is.*"

Chapter 13, 1981 Version

[Chapter 13 in the Third Book of Nephi embodies mostly the same text as found in Chapter 6 of Matthew

from the New Testament. Of the text in Chapter 13, 92% is identical, word for word, with the corresponding chapter of Matthew. The differences are mostly minor word substitutions, slight rephrasings, and added introductory phrases.

Because the Sermon on the Mount is such a pivotal part of both the New Testament and The Book of Mormon, text found in The Book of Mormon that is not present in the New Testament is italicized.]

"You should give to the poor," Jesus Christ says, in his sermon to the Nephites, "but you should be careful to avoid being seen by others in doing so. If you give publicly to impress others, you will find no reward from your Father in heaven. When you do give alms, do so privately and without fanfare. Only hypocrites do this so that they will be admired by other men. This is all the reward that they will receive. When alms are given secretly so that only your Father in heaven can see, he will reward you openly.

"When you pray, don't make vain repetitions as the heathens do when they imagine that their public speaking is being heard. Be private in your prayer because your Father knows what you need before you even ask him.

"I prescribe this prayer: 'Our Father who art in heaven, hallowed be thy name. Thy will be done on earth as it is in heaven. And forgive us our debts, as we forgive our debtors. And lead us not into temptation, but deliver us from evil. For thine is the kingdom, and the power, and the glory, forever. Amen.'

"If you forgive men for their trespasses, your heavenly Father will also forgive you. If you fail to forgive men for their trespasses, your Father will not forgive you for your trespasses.

"When you fast, don't show off about it, the way hypocrites do. The only reward that they will receive is the appearance of fasting that they present. When you fast, anoint your head and clean your face. Fast secretly so that only your Father in heaven will know, so that he can reward you openly.

"Don't horde earthly treasures where moths and rust can ruin them, or where thieves can steal them. Store up treasures for yourself in heaven where moths, rust, and thieves cannot touch them. Wherever your treasures are is also where your heart will be.

"Your eyes are the light of your body. If your eyes are pure, your body will be filled with light. If your eyes are evil, your body will be filled with darkness. Without light, the darkness is overpowering.

"No man can serve two masters. Either he will hate one and love the other, or else he will hold to one and despise the other. You cannot serve both God and idols."

Chapter 6, 1830 Version

When Jesus Christ spoke these words he looked upon the twelve that he'd chosen and said to them, "You must remember the words that I have spoken because you are the ones that I have chosen to minister to my people.

"Quit worrying so much about your life, your food, your drink, and your clothing. There is more to life than food, and more to your body than its appearance. Think about the birds that fly. They don't plant seeds, harvest crops, or gather in buildings, but your heavenly Father feeds them. Are you any better off than they are? Do your worries add anything to your stature?

"Why do you worry so about your clothing? Think about the lilies in the field and how they grow. They don't work and they don't spin thread. And yet even King Solomon in all his glory was not as good looking as one of these lilies. If God clothes the fields in grass that is here today and gone tomorrow, won't he also clothe you if you have faith?

"Quit worrying about what you're going to eat, what you're going to drink, and how you will be clothed. Your heavenly Father knows you need these things, but look first to the kingdom of God and his righteousness, and all these things will be provided for you. Don't think about tomorrow because tomorrow will take care of itself. Take care and do good today."

Chapter 14, 1981 Version

[Chapter 14 in the Third Book of Nephi embodies mostly the same text as found in Chapter 7 of Matthew from the New Testament. Of the text in Chapter 14, 95% is identical, word for word, with the corresponding chapter of Matthew. What differences there are, are

mostly minor word substitutions, slight rephrasings, and added introductory phrases.

Because the Sermon on the Mount is such a pivotal part of both the New Testament and The Book of Mormon, text found in The Book of Mormon that is not present in the New Testament is italicized.]

When Jesus Christ had spoken these words he turned again to address the Nephite crowd.

"Don't judge others unless you want to be judged yourself. Others will treat you as you treat them. Why are you so eager to find fault in your brother when your own faults are often even greater? You are always so willing to correct your brother's faults, but unwilling to correct your own, even when they are larger than his. You are hypocrites. You must correct your own faults first before you can even clearly see the faults of your brother.

"Don't give holy things to dogs, or pearls to pigs, unless you want them to trample on them and then assault you. Ask, and it will be given to you. Seek, and you will find. Knock, and the door will be opened for you. What man is there, who, if his son asks for bread, gives him a stone? Or if he asks for a fish, gives him a snake? If you sinful people know how to give good gifts to your children, imagine how much more your Father in heaven will give good things to those who ask him.

"Do unto others as you would like them to do for you. This is the law and the teaching of the prophets. The gate is wide and the path is broad that leads to destruction. There will always be many who go that way. Because the path to heaven and the gate that leads there are narrow, fewer will find it.

"Beware of false prophets who come to you in sheep's clothing. Inwardly they are ravening wolves. You will know them by their fruits. Do men gather grapes of thorns, or figs of thistles? Good trees bring good fruit; but a corrupt tree brings evil fruit. Trees that don't bring good fruit are cut down and cast into the fire, and by their fruits you will know them.

"Not every one who says to me, 'Lord, Lord,' will enter into the kingdom of heaven. But those who do the will of my Father in heaven, will enter. Many will say to me on that day, 'Lord, Lord, have we not prophesied in your name? In your name we have cast out devils, and in your name we have done many

wonderful works.' And then will I say to them, 'I never knew you. Depart from me, you who have worked in sinfulness. Whoever hears these words of mine and follows them, I will think of as a wise man, who built his house upon a rock. When the rains descend, the floods come, and the winds blow and beat upon that house, it will not fall because it was built upon a rock. Everyone that hears these words of mine and does not follow them will be likened to a foolish man who built his house upon the sand. When the rains descend, the floods come, and the winds blow and beat upon that house, it will fall."

Chapter 7, 1830 Version

Chapter 15, 1981 Version

Jesus Christ looked out at the Nephite crowd and said, "You have now heard the things that I taught in the Old World before I ascended to my Father in heaven. Whoever remembers these words of mine and acts in accordance with them will be raised up by me on judgment day."

Having said this Jesus Christ became aware that there were people who were confused about the application of the laws of Moses. They didn't understand that the old ways had passed and that new ways had arrived.

"Don't confuse yourselves with my words concerning the passing of the old ways and the arrival of the new ways. The laws that were given to Moses are fulfilled. It was me who gave those laws to Moses. It was me who made the covenants with my people of Israel. In me, the laws are fulfilled. Because my coming fulfills the old laws, these old laws have come to an end in me. I do not negate the prophets. All their prophecies that are unfulfilled in me, will yet be fulfilled. Just because I have said that the old ways have passed doesn't mean that I have denied the prophecies yet to come. The covenant that I made with my people is not yet complete, but the laws that were given to Moses have ended in me. I am now the law and I am the light unto my people. Look to me and endure to the end, and you will find eternal life. I have given you new commandments. Obey them. This is the new law that the prophets have foretold through me."

After saying this Jesus Christ turned to his chosen twelve. "You are my disciples, and you are the light to your people who are descended from Joseph of Egypt. This land is your inheritance, given to you by my Father in heaven. My Father didn't want me to tell your relatives in Jerusalem about you or about the other tribes of Israel that he has led away. Only this much was I instructed to say to them, 'There are other sheep who are not part of this flock who will also be brought to me. They too will hear my voice and know there is really just one flock and one shepherd.'"

"Because of their stubbornness and skepticism the people of Jerusalem didn't understand my words, and I wasn't instructed to say any more. My Father in heaven has instructed me to tell you that your people have been separated from them. It is because of their sinfulness that they know nothing of you or the other separated tribes. When I spoke about my other sheep who were not part of their flock, it was you that I referred to. Mistakenly, they presumed that I was speaking of the Gentiles who should be converted through their preaching. I clearly said that these other sheep of mine would hear my voice, but I have never spoken to the Gentiles except as the Holy Ghost. But you have seen me and heard my voice. You are my sheep. You are counted among those whom my Father has given to me."

Chapter 16, 1981 Version

"I have other sheep apart from you people in this land, and apart from the people around Jerusalem," Jesus Christ continued. "These sheep of whom I speak have not yet heard my voice or seen me. But my Father in heaven has instructed me to visit them also, so that I may be seen and heard by them. Although there are many sheep in many lands, there is only one flock and one shepherd. I must go to them now.

"It is my command to you that you must write my words down after I am gone. If the people of Jerusalem do not learn of you and the other lost tribes through the Holy Ghost, then your written history will be made known to their descendants through future Gentiles. These Gentiles who believe will bring knowledge of me, their Redeemer, to the scattered descendants of those who do not believe. I will gather my people together from the four corners of the earth to fulfill the promises that my Father in heaven has made with the entire family of Israel. The Gentiles will be blessed because of their belief in me, and in the Holy Ghost who bears witness of me and my Father.

" 'Because of the Gentile's belief in me,' says my Father, 'and because of Israel's disbelief of you, the fullness of truth in the latter days will be made known to the Gentiles. But curses will fall on those unbelieving Gentiles who come to this land and conquer the scattered outcast descendants of Israel.' Because of my Father's great mercy to the Gentiles and because of his judgments against the family of Israel, he will allow his people to be tormented, conquered, afflicted, and killed.

"My Father has instructed me to tell you this, 'When the day comes that the Gentiles sin against my gospel, reject its truth, inflate themselves with pride, put themselves and their nation above all the other people on earth, lie, deceive, murder, fornicate, perform priestcrafts, and secret abominations, I will withdraw the fullness of my gospel from among them. At that time I will remember the promises I have made to the family of Israel and I will bring my gospel to them. The Gentiles will lose their power over them and the descendants of Israel will know the fullness of my gospel. But if the Gentiles repent and return to me they will be counted among my people, the family of Israel, and I will protect them from being trampled.'

"Those who do not return to me and listen to my voice will be destroyed by my people. Those unrepentant Gentiles will be like salt that has lost its savor and is good for nothing except casting out and being trampled underfoot.

"My father has instructed me to give this land to this people as their inheritance. When this happens, these words of the prophet Isaiah will be fulfilled, 'The watchmen will lift up their voices together in song because they will see eye to eye when God again brings Zion. Rejoice and sing together you wasted places of Jerusalem. God has comforted his people and redeemed Jerusalem. God has shown his holy arm to the eye of all nations, and all the ends of the earth will see the salvation of God.'"

Chapter 8, 1830 Version

Chapter 17, 1981 Version

"My time is at hand," said Jesus Christ to the Nephite crowd. "I can see that you are tired, and are having a hard time understanding everything that my Father has instructed me to tell you. So go back to your homes and think about what I've said. In my name, pray to my Father in heaven for understanding, and prepare your minds for my return tomorrow. I must go to my Father now. I must also go personally visit with the lost tribes of Israel. These tribes are not lost to my Father because he knows where he has taken them."

When Jesus Christ looked around at the assembled Nephites he saw that they were in tears. They wanted him to stay longer with them.

"I am filled with compassion for you," he declared. "If there are sick among you, bring them forward. If any of you are crippled, blind, diseased, maimed, leprous, withered, deaf, or ailing in any way come forward and I will heal you. I sense that you'd like me to show you what I have done with your relations in Jerusalem, and your faith is sufficient enough for me to heal you."

The sick, ailing, crippled, blind, dumb, and injured Nephites were brought forward, and Jesus Christ healed every one who was brought before him. Everyone who was whole and everyone who was healed then bowed down at his feet and worshipped him. They kissed his feet and bathed them in their tears.

Jesus Christ then asked that all the little children should be brought forward. So the people brought their children and set them on the ground around him. When all the children were gathered around him Jesus Christ asked that everyone kneel down on the ground.

"My father," he said, "I am troubled with the sinfulness of the people of Israel."

Jesus Christ then kneeled down and prayed to his Father in heaven. The things that he said cannot be written, but those who were present made record that no eyes had ever seen, and no ears had never heard such great things as those that he spoke to his Father. What he said was so amazing that no tongue could speak it, no heart could conceive of it, and no one could ever even imagine the joy which filled

their souls while he prayed to his Father. When he was finished, he arose, and the Nephite crowd was overcome. He asked them to rise up also.

"You are blessed because of your faith," he said while crying tearfully, "and I am filled with joy."

Jesus Christ took the children one by one, blessed them, and prayed to his Father for each of them. When he was finished, he wept again.

"Look at your children now," he said.

The Nephites watched as the heavens opened and angels engulfed in fire descended towards them. The angels came down and encircled the children with their fire, and ministered to them individually. We know that this is true because all of the 2,500 people who saw and heard this amazing event made record of it.

Chapter 18, 1981 Version

Jesus Christ asked his disciples to bring him some bread and wine. Then he asked the Nephites to sit on the ground. When the disciples returned he took the bread, broke it with his hands, and blessed it. He gave some of the broken bread to each of his disciples and asked them to eat it. He then asked the disciples to go out among the crowd and give each of them some bread also.

After everyone had received and eaten their bread he said to his disciples, "I will ordain one of you with the power to break the bread, bless it, and give if to the people of my church who are baptized in my name. I want you to break the bread, bless it, and give it out just as you have seen me do. Do this in remembrance of my body that I have shown to you. This is meant as a testimony to my Father that you always remember me. As long as you remember me you will have my Spirit with you."

Jesus Christ then asked his disciples to drink the wine that they had brought to him in a cup. He asked that they also give wine to the crowd to drink in the same way.

After the disciples and the crowd had all tasted the wine he said to his disciples, "You are blessed because of your actions. By fulfilling my commandments you bear witness to my Father that you are willing to abide by my instructions. Give wine in this way to those who repent and are baptized in my name, in remembrance of my blood that I have shed for you. When you do this you bear witness to my Father, that you always remember me. As long as you remember me you will have my Spirit with you.

"I give you this commandment to do these things. If you do as I have commanded, you will be blessed, because in doing so you demonstrate that you are built upon my rock. Any of you who do more or less than this are not built upon my rock, but are built upon a sandy foundation that will fall down when the rain arrives, when the floods come, and when the winds blow. When you fall, the gates of hell are open to receive you.

"You will be blessed only if you keep the commandments that my Father has told me to give you. You must always watch out and pray or else the devil's temptations will take you captive. Just as I have prayed amongst you, I ask that you pray in my church among my people who repent and are baptized in my name. I am the light and this is my example to you."

After saying these words to his disciples, Jesus Christ turned to the crowd and said, "You must always watch out and pray because Satan wants to have you. He wants to harvest your souls like so much wheat. You must always pray to my Father in my name. If you want something from my Father, ask for it in my name. If it is right, and if you believe that you will receive it, it will be given to you. Pray for your families in my name, and your wives and children will be blessed.

"I want you to meet together often and not prevent any man from joining you in your meetings. Invite everyone, pray for them, and do not cast them out. If they come, pray for them in my name and in the name of my Father. Hold up your light so that it may shine for the world to see. I am the light that you will hold up. Do as you have seen me do, and pray to my Father. You have seen that I have asked all of you to come to me, to feel me, and to see me. This is what I want you to do in the world. Whoever breaks this commandment will surely be led into temptation."

Jesus Christ turned once again to his disciples, and said, "I will give you one more commandment and then I must go to my Father to fulfill other commandments he has given to me. Do not allow anyone to knowingly take the bread and wine that represent my body and blood if they are unworthy. Those who eat and drink my flesh and blood, and aren't worthy of it, will eat and drink damnation of their soul. If you know a man is unworthy to eat and drink my flesh and blood you must forbid it. Even so, you must not cast him out from among you. You must pray to my Father for him, and if he repents and is baptized in my name, then you should give him my flesh and blood. If he doesn't repent, he will not be counted among my people because he might destroy them. I know all of my sheep, and all of them are counted. Do not cast him out of your churches or your places of worship, or stop ministering to him. They may yet repent and come to me with clean hearts. If they do, I will heal them and you will be the means of bringing salvation to them.

"Keep these commandments so that you will not be condemned, because pity to the man who my Father condemns. I give you these commandments because of the conflicts that have arisen among your people in the past, but if there are no conflicts among you, you will be blessed. Now I must go to my Father."

When Jesus Christ finished speaking he touched each of his chosen disciples with his hand, one by one, and spoke something to each of them. The crowds didn't hear what he said, but the disciples testified that he gave them the power to give the Holy Ghost. Later, I will show you that this is true.

After Jesus Christ touched each of the disciples, a great cloud came and overshadowed the crowd so they couldn't see him. While he was hidden from sight he ascended back into heaven.

Chapter 9, 1830 Version

Chapter 19, 1981 Version

After Jesus Christ ascended into heaven the crowd dispersed. Every man took his wife and children and returned home. Before darkness fell word spread across the land that Jesus Christ had personally come and ministered to the Nephite people, and that he would return the following day. Throughout the night the word spread further, and many people traveled all night long to be present when Jesus Christ arrived again.

The next morning the crowd gathered around Nephi and the other eleven disciples before breaking into twelve groups. Each of the twelve disciples taught one of the twelve groups. The disciples had them kneel on the ground and pray to the Father in heaven in the name of Jesus Christ. After that the disciples arose and ministered to the people, saying exactly the same words that Jesus Christ had told them to use, the day before. They prayed for what they most desired, that they would receive the Holy Ghost. After prayer the disciples went to the water with the crowd behind them. Nephi was the first to immerse himself in the water to be baptized. Then he baptized all the other disciples.

When the twelve disciples had been baptized the Holy Ghost fell upon them, filling them with his spirit and with his fire. A fire came down from heaven and encircled them, followed by a host of angels who came down and ministered to them. The whole crowd witnessed this spectacle and bore witness of its occurrence. While the angels were ministering to the disciples Jesus Christ himself arrived. He stood amidst the group of disciples and also ministered to them.

Jesus Christ then spoke to the crowd and commanded them to kneel down on the ground again. When everyone was kneeling he commanded his disciples to pray. They prayed to Jesus Christ, calling him their Lord and God.

Jesus then walked a short distance away from his disciples. He bowed down and said, "Thank you Father for giving the Holy Ghost to these disciples that I have chosen. They have been chosen in particular among all the people of the world because of their belief in me. I pray that you will give the Holy Ghost to everyone who believes in their words. You can see that they believe in me and that they pray to me because I am with them. Now I pray on their behalf, in hopes that those who will believe in what they say, will also believe in me. I pray that I may be in them as you, my Father, are in me. I pray that we may be one."

After Jesus Christ finished praying to his Father he returned to his disciples and found them still praying to him, unceasingly, just as he had told them to do. He blessed and smiled on them as they prayed, and the brilliant light of his appearance shone upon them. In so doing they became as white as the brilliant white of Jesus Christ's clothing, a whiteness that was brighter than anything on earth.

"Pray on," Jesus Christ said to them. And they continued praying.

Again Jesus Christ walked a short distance away and separated himself from them. He bowed down again and said, "Thank you Father for purifying those whom I have chosen. I pray for them and also for those who believe their words. I pray that those who have faith in my disciples words may be purified in me just as my disciples have been. I pray for those people of this world that you have given to me. I pray that they may be purified in me, that I may be in them, as you, my Father, are in me. I pray that we may be one, and that I may be glorified in them."

Having said this Jesus Christ returned to his disciples and still found them praying ceaselessly to him. Jesus Christ smiled on them again, and they were as brilliantly white as he was. He stepped away again and prayed to his Father. He prayed this time in words that cannot be spoken or written. Even so the crowd witnessed this and understood the meaning of these unspeakable words in their hearts.

When he finished praying he again came back to his disciples and said to them, "I have never seen such great faith among all the Jews. I couldn't show them miracles like these because of their failure to believe. None of them have seen or heard anything as great as what I have shown to you."

Chapter 20, 1981 Version

Jesus Christ told the crowd to rise up and stop praying aloud, but to continue praying silently. He broke some bread and gave it to his disciples to eat, then told them to do likewise with the crowd. After this was done he gave them wine to drink, and then told them to do this also with the crowd.

"Anyone who eats this bread, eats my body in his soul," said Jesus Christ to the crowd. "Anyone who drinks this wine, drinks my blood in his soul. Those who do so will never be hungry or thirsty. They will be filled."

When the crowd had eaten and drunk the bread and wine that were given, they were filled with the Spirit. They cried out in a single voice giving glory to Jesus Christ.

"My Father in heaven has commanded me to explain the commandment that he has given to you as a remnant of the family of Israel. I have said that the words of Isaiah would be fulfilled. When they are, this will be the completion of the promises made by my Father with his people, the family of Israel. The broadly scattered remnants of Israel's family will be gathered together and brought to the knowledge of their God who has redeemed them. My Father has commanded me to give you this land as your inheritance. If the Gentiles who scatter my people do not repent after receiving my blessing, then your descendants will go among them as lions go among the animals of the forest, or as a young lion does among amongst a flock of sheep. Even though your descendants will be outnumbered, they will track the unrepentant Gentiles down and tear them to pieces. There will be no rescue for them.

"I will gather up my people like a farmer gathers his wheat after threshing the cut stalks. I will make my people as strong as iron or brass so that they can beat their enemies into pieces. The Gentile's former wealth will be dedicated to God. It is I, Jesus Christ, who will do this. 'The sword of justice will hang over the Gentiles on that day, and unless they repent, it will fall upon them and all other Gentile nations,' says my Father. Afterwards I will reestablish my people.

"I will establish your people in this land to fulfill the promises that I made with your ancestor Jacob[1], who is known as Israel. This will be the New Jerusalem. The powers of heaven will be with you, and I will be with you. I am the one whom Moses spoke of when he said, 'God will raise up a prophet like me among you. You must listen to whatever he says to you. Those who don't listen to him will be cut off.'"

"Samuel and all the prophets have spoken of and testified about me. You are the children of the prophets, and the children of Israel. When my Father said to Abraham, 'Through your descendants all the people of the world will be blessed,' it was your family he was talking about. After raising me up, my Father has sent me first to you. I have come to bless you and divert you from sinfulness because you are the children of his promises.

"The Gentiles will be blessed by the Holy Ghost and become the strongest people on earth. They will scatter my people and become tormenters to your descendants in this land. 'If, after receiving my full gospel, they turn their hearts against me,' says my Father, 'then I will turn their sins against them. I will then remember the promises that I've made with my people to gather them together and give them back the land of their inheritance, the promised land of Jerusalem.' This time will come when my full gospel is given to them and they come to believe that I am Jesus Christ, the Son of God, and they pray to my Father in my name.

"When this time comes, the watchmen will raise their voices and sing together. Everyone will see eye to eye. Their lands of inheritance will be given back to them. There will be an outbreak of joy when my Father comforts his people and redeems Jerusalem.

"My Father will reveal his holy power to the eyes of all nations and all the earth will see the salvation of my Father. They will see that my Father and I are one. This will be the fulfillment of the ancient prophecies of Isaiah that say, 'Awaken again you holy city of Jerusalem, and put on your best clothing. From this time forward no one will come to you uncircumcised or dirty. Shake off your dust, Jerusalem, and arise. Loosen the ropes around your neck that hold you captive. You have sold yourselves cheaply, but will be redeemed without money.'

"When this day comes, all the people will know that it is I, Jesus Christ, who has redeemed them. This is what Isaiah is talking about when he wrote, 'How beautiful are the feet of he that brings us this good news, who brings us peace, and says to Zion, that God reigns. Get out of the dirty cities. Become clean vessels of God. Don't run away in fear because God goes before you, and the God of Israel will guard you from behind. My servant will prosper and be exalted in spite of his appearance of abuse. Kings and nations will shut their mouths and listen to his words.'

"All of this will surely come. The promises of my Father will be fulfilled, and Jerusalem will again be occupied with my people. It will be the land of their inheritance."

Chapter 21, 1981 Version

"I will give you a sign," Jesus Christ said to the Nephites, "so that your descendants will know I am about to gather them in from their dispersion and reestablish them in my Zion. When these words about their ancestry through the family of Israel are made known to the Gentiles, through the power of the Holy Ghost and my Father, the time is near. At that time, these same Gentiles will have conquered and scattered your descendants. Through the wisdom of my Father, this knowledge shall be reestablished in this land where the people are governed in freedom, and your remnant descendants will learn of their ancestry through these Gentiles.

"When this knowledge is brought to your descendants, they will have dwindled in strength and numbers as a result of their unbelief and sinfulness. It behooves my Father that this knowledge will come from the Gentiles so that he may show his power to them, in hopes that they too will soften their hearts, repent their sins, come to me, and be baptized in my name. I want them to know the truth of my doctrine so that they may be counted among my people also. When these things happen it will be a sign to your descendants that the work of my Father in fulfilling his promises to his people of Israel has already begun. When that day comes, kings will be silent because they will see and hear things that they hadn't imagined possible. When that day comes, my Father will perform a great and amazing work among the people. There will be some who do not believe it, even though my servant will declare it to them.

"My servant will be tormented because of those who do not believe him, but they will not hurt him because his life will be in my hands. I will heal him and show those who oppose him that my wisdom is greater than the cunning of the devil. When this time comes, I will cause my words to come to the Gentiles through this man. Those who do not believe these words will be cut off from among my chosen people. My remnant people among the Gentiles who are descended from Israel will become like lions among their prey. These people will track down and tear unbelievers to pieces. Rescue for them will be impossible.

"My people's hand will be lifted up against their enemies who have been cut off. It will be a terrible pity except to those Gentiles who repent. 'I will destroy their horses and chariots,' my Father has said. 'I will destroy their cities and fortresses. I will end all witchcrafts in the land, and banish soothsayers. I will smash their idols. Lies, deceptions, enviousness, conflict, priestcraft, and fornication will come to an end. On that day, whoever doesn't repent and come to my beloved Son, will be destroyed. I will cut them off from the family of Israel. I will exercise such vengeance and fury on them as they have never imagined possible.' "

Chapter 10, 1830 Version

" 'But if they repent, listen to my words, and soften their hearts,' " Jesus Christ continued quoting his Father, " 'I will establish a church among them that allows them to enter into my covenant and be counted among the family of Israel to whom I have given this land as an inheritance.'

"These Gentiles who convert," continued Jesus Christ, "will assist my people who are descended from Israel in building a city that will be called New Jerusalem. They will help my people to gather up their scattered remnants from across the land, and bring them all to New Jerusalem. The power of heaven will come down among them and I will be in their midst. The work of my Father will begin on that day. His gospel will be preached among the remnants of his people, including the lost tribes. The work will begin to prepare the way so that they may come to me, call on the Father in my name, and be gathered to the land of their inheritance.

" 'I will lead them from the front,' says my Father, 'and I will also protect them from behind.' "

Chapter 22, 1981 Version

"When this day comes," said Jesus Christ, " these prophecies of Isaiah will be fulfilled."

[The text that Jesus Christ quotes in Chapter 22 of the Third Book of Nephi is virtually indistinguishable, word for word, from Chapter 54 of Isaiah from the Old Testament.]

Sing out, Jerusalem, it is time to rejoice. It is time to return to the lands from which you've been driven, and to govern the lands that once conquered you. The sorrow of your past is behind you, and is now forgotten. God the Redeemer has returned to you from his abandonment, and will take you back. In his anger he turned his back on you, but in his everlasting love he has shown his mercy.

"Just as I swore to Noah to never again flood the earth," says God, "so too will I never flood you with my anger. I promise you peace unbroken. I will rebuild your homes, give you prosperity, insure fair government, and keep your enemies away. When the promised day comes, no weapon will defeat you. This is my blessing."

Chapter 23, 1981 Version

"The words and prophecies of Isaiah are great," said Jesus Christ. "I command you to read them carefully and study them. Isaiah spoke truthfully for the people of Israel and also for the Gentiles. Likewise pay attention to my commandments to you, and write the things that I have told you so that they will be known and spread by future Gentiles, according to the will of my Father. Whoever listens to my words, repents, and is baptized will be saved.

"If you review what the prophets have said, you will find many of them that verify this. There are other scriptures that you do not have, that I want you to write down. Bring me the records that you have kept."

Nephi brought the records to Jesus Christ, who looked through them and said, "I commanded my servant, Samuel the Lamanite, to tell you certain things that aren't mentioned here. Didn't he say that on the day my Father glorified his name in me, that many saints would arise from death, appear to you, and minister to you? Didn't this happen?"

"Yes Lord," the disciples said, "Samuel did prophesy that, and it was fulfilled."

"Then why is it not written that these saints arose and ministered to you?" asked Jesus Christ. He commanded that this be included in the record.

Chapter 11, 1830 Version

Jesus Christ then gave the disciples additional scriptures to record and commanded them to teach them to the people.

Chapter 24, 1981 Version

Jesus Christ commanded that the disciples write down these dictated words that his Father had given to the Old Testament prophet Malachi.

[The text that Jesus Christ dictates in Chapter 24 of the Third Book of Nephi is virtually indistinguishable, word for word, from Chapter 3 of Malachi from the Old Testament.]

"I will send a messenger before me to prepare the way," said God to Malachi. "The God whom you await will come suddenly to the temple. I will come like a fire that purifies gold or silver to purify my people. I will come to you in judgment with swift punishments for sorcerers, adulterers, liars, oppressors, and those who turn strangers away."

"I am God unchanging. You have disobeyed my laws and yet I still allow you to return to me. You have robbed me by denying me tithes and offerings. For this you have received my curses. Why don't you try bringing your offerings to me and receive my blessings instead? Your words against me are filled with arrogance as if I weren't paying attention. But I have kept a book of remembrance of those who feared and loved me. They will be mine. They will be spared. Then you will see the difference between how I treat the righteous and the wicked among you, and the difference between those who serve God and those who don't."

Chapter 25, 1981 Version

[The text that Jesus Christ dictates in Chapter 25 of the Third Book of Nephi is virtually indistinguishable, word for word, from Chapter 4 of Malachi from the Old Testament.]

"The day of judgment is coming," said God to Malachi, "and the proud and wicked will be burned up like straw in the oven. But for those who fear my name, the Son of Righteousness will rise up with healing wings like calves let loose in the pasture. The wicked will be trampled like ashes underfoot. Remember to abide by the laws that I gave my servant Moses. I will send you Elijah the prophet before the great and terrible day of judgment. He will turn the hearts of fathers to children, and children to fathers, or I will destroy the earth with my curse."

Chapter 26, 1981 Version

Jesus Christ explained many things, both great and small, to the Nephite crowd.

"My Father has commanded me to give you these scriptures that you didn't have," he said, "so that they would be available for future generations."

He told them of things from the beginning of time through the time of earth's end. He explained the day of judgment to them, the day when all the people from the whole earth would be judged according to their lives, whether they were good or evil. Those who were good would be rewarded with life everlasting. Those who were evil would be eternally damned, all according to the mercy, justice, and holiness of Jesus Christ.

Chapter 12, 1830 Version

"While the plates of Nephi contain more than what it is written here," wrote Mormon, "it is not possible to write even a hundredth part of what Jesus Christ taught to the Nephite people. The words that I have included are those things that need to be known and brought to our descendants through the future Gentiles, according to the spoken words of Jesus Christ. If those who receive these words believe in them, greater things yet will be shown to them. For those who don't believe these words, these greater things will be withheld, and lead to their condemnation. Even though I want to write down all of Nephi's words, God has forbidden me to do so."

For three days Jesus Christ taught the Nephite people. He appeared to them often, breaking bread, blessing it, and giving it to them. He taught and ministered to the children showing them even greater things than were shown to the adults, so that the fathers learned these things from their children.

By the time Jesus Christ ascended into heaven for the second time, all of the sick and crippled people were healed, the blind could see, and the deaf could hear. He even raised a man from death. The day after his ascension the crowds gathered together. They saw and heard their children, even the babies, saying the most amazing things that were forbidden to be written down. The disciples whom Jesus Christ had chosen baptized and taught all those who came to them. All of these people were afterwards filled with the Holy Ghost. Many of the people saw and heard unspeakable things that they were forbidden to write down. They taught and ministered to each other, and everyone dealt fairly with one another. All those who were baptized in the name of Jesus Christ became members in the Church of Christ.

Chapter 27, 1981 Version

The disciples became missionaries who traveled and taught the things that they had seen and heard, and baptized people in the name of Jesus Christ. One day they were gathered together in prayer and fasting when Jesus Christ appeared to them because of their prayers to the Father in his name.

"What can I give to you?" he asked as he stood before them.

"What should we call our church?" the disciples asked. "People are already arguing about its name."

"Why should anyone argue about such a thing?" asked Jesus Christ. "Haven't they read the scriptures that say you must take my name of Jesus Christ? You should be known by this name until the last day. Whoever takes on my name and keeps it until the end will be saved on the last day. Whatever you do, you must do it in my name. Therefore you must name the church after me also.

"You must call upon my Father in my name so that he will bless the church for my sake. How can it be my church if it isn't named after me? If a church is named after Moses, then it will be Moses' church. If a church is named after some man, then it is the church of that man. But if it is named after me then it is my church, if you also teach my gospel. So build your church based on my gospel, do everything in my name, and call upon my Father in my name, because if you do so my Father will hear you.

"If a church is built on the works of men, or on the works of the devil, instead of on my gospel, they may have a season joy, but in the end its members will be cut down and cast into the fire of no return. Men cannot escape the acts of their lives. It is for these acts that many are cut down, so remember my words carefully.

"I have given you my gospel. This is why I came into the world. It was the will of my Father, and the reason that my Father sent me. I was sent so that I would be lifted up on the cross and draw all men to me. Just as I have been lifted up by men, so too should men be lifted up by my Father to stand before me and be judged by their lives to determine whether they are good or evil. Whoever repents and is baptized in my name will be filled. If he stays with me to the end I will hold him guiltless before my Father on judgment day.

"Anyone who doesn't stay with me to the end will be cut down and cast into the fire of no return because of my Father's justice. This is the word that he has always given to men, and he always fulfills his word. Nothing dirty can enter into his kingdom of heaven. Only those who have washed their clothing in my blood, through their faith and repentance of all sins, may enter. This is my commandment to you. Repent and be baptized in my name so that you may be sanctified by the Holy Ghost, and stand spotless before me on judgment day.

"This is my gospel. You know what you must do in my church. You must do as you have seen me do. If you do these things you will be blessed and lifted up on judgment day."

Chapter 13, 1830 Version

"Write down everything that you've seen and heard except for those things that you've been forbidden to write down," Jesus Christ continued saying. "Write the story of this people so that others will know of your history. From the books that have been written, and will be written, this people will be judged. Through these books, your lives will be known to men. Likewise, all things are written down by my Father. Through his books, the world will be judged. You will be the judges of your people according to the judgment that I will give to you. What kind of men should you be? Be like me.

"Now I must return again to my Father. I remind you that whatever you ask of my Father, ask for it in my name and it will be given to you. Ask, and you will receive. Knock, and the door will be opened. My joy is great because of you and this generation. Even my Father and the holy angels rejoice because of this generation. None of you who are now alive will be lost.

"But I am greatly saddened because the fourth generation after you will be led away captive into hell. They will sell me for silver and gold and other treasures that are subject to rot and theft. When this happens I will visit them and turn their earthly treasures onto their heads.

"Enter through the straight and narrow gate that leads to life. Few will find it because the gate that leads to death is broad and easily traveled, and many people will walk that way to their own destruction."

Chapter 28, 1981 Version

"What would you want from me after I've gone to my Father?" Jesus Christ asked each of his disciples, one by one.

Nine of them said, "We'd like to come quickly to heaven after we've finished our lives and completed our ministry."

"You are blessed," said Jesus Christ, "for having desired this thing from me. After you are 72 years old you may come to my kingdom and find rest."

"And what do you want after I'm gone?" he asked of the other three disciples.

The three hesitated, afraid to ask him for what they really wanted.

"I know your thoughts," Jesus Christ stated. "You want the same thing that my beloved friend John, who helped me with my ministry among the Jews, also wanted. You are even more blessed. You will never die, but will live to see all the works of my Father that will be performed among men, from now until judgment day, when I will come again in glory with all the powers of heaven. Between now and then you shall live as immortals. But when I do come again, you will be transformed in an instant from mortal to immortal. Then you will be blessed and received in the kingdom of my Father.

"From now until judgment day you will know no pain or sorrow except for the sins of the world. I will do this for you because you have wanted it from me, and because you want to bring me the souls of men while the world still stands. In the end you will sit down in the kingdom of my Father and be filled with joy. You will be with me just as I am with my Father, with whom I am one. The Holy Ghost witnesses the relationship of my Father and me, and my Father gives the Holy Ghost to men because of me."

When Jesus Christ finished speaking he touched the first nine of his disciples with his finger and then he departed. The sky opened and the disciples were lifted up into heaven where they saw and heard things that they were forbidden to reveal. They were transformed in spirit in order to behold the presence of God.

I do not know whether they were mortal or immortal thereafter but I do know that they returned to the earth and ministered to all the people. They brought all who would believe their preaching into the church. Many were baptized and all of these people received the Holy Ghost.

When they were thrown into prison by those who didn't believe, the prisons couldn't hold them, and were broken apart. When they were thrown into pits in the earth they were delivered from their depths with the word of God. When they were thrown into furnaces they were not burned. When they were thrown into dens of vicious beasts they played with the beasts like children with lambs.

They went forth among the Nephites and preached the gospel of Jesus Christ to people all across the land. Many were converted to God and united into the Church of Christ. The people of that generation were blessed, just as Jesus Christ had said they would be.

I, Mormon, am nearly finished speaking of these things. I was prepared to write the names of the three who lived immortally among men, but God forbade me to do so. They are to remain hidden among other men. But I have seen them, and they have ministered to me. They will be among the Gentiles in the future, but the Gentiles will not know who they are.

The time will come when God will have them minister to all the scattered tribes of Israel, all of the nations, and all of the people of the earth. They will bring many souls to Jesus Christ because of the strong persuasive power of God that is in them. They are like angels of God who can appear instantly to anyone they want to visit with. Amazing things will be performed by them before judgment day, when all people will stand before Jesus Christ to be judged.

If you read the scriptures you will surely know that the amazing works of Jesus Christ will surely come to pass. Pity on those who do not listen to the words of Jesus Christ or to those he has sent out among the people to speak on his behalf. Whoever rejects the words of Jesus Christ will not receive his mercy on judgment day. It would be better for them if they had never been born. Do you imagine that you could ever free yourself from the justice of an offended God, and find salvation after trampling him beneath your feet?

I have asked God about the three immortals to learn more of their physical nature. He told me that their bodies have been changed to keep them free from death, from pain, and from sorrow, except the sorrow they know from the sins of the world. This change is different from the change that will take place on judgment day, but they have been changed in such a way that Satan cannot tempt them. They were sanctified in the flesh so that they are free from the powers of the world. They will remain this way until judgment day, when they will receive an even greater change and be received into the kingdom of God, to live eternally in heaven.

Chapter 29, 1981 Version

God, in his wisdom will see that these words come to the future Gentiles in accordance with his promises made to the family of Israel. When the Gentiles receive these words your descendants will know that the restoration of their lands of inheritance has already begun. The words of God, as spoken by his holy prophets, will all be fulfilled. God will remember and keep all of his promises to the family of Israel.

These are not idle promises. When these words come forth, God's justice will soon be at hand. Pity to those who reject the work of God and deny Jesus Christ. Pity to those who deny the revelations of God. Pity to those who say that God no longer works through revelations, prophecy, the gift of tongues, healings, or by the power of the Holy Ghost. Pity to those who seek gain by saying that Jesus Christ cannot perform miracles, because those who do so will become like the sons of hell, and receive no mercy. Pity to those who reject the Jews or any faction of the family of Israel because God remembers his promises to them. Do not imagine that you can turn God's right hand into his left hand, or that he will fail to fulfill his promises to the family of Israel.

Chapter 14, 1830 Version

Chapter 30, 1981 Version

Listen, you Gentiles, and hear these words of Jesus Christ, the Son of God, that I have been commanded to say to you, "Stop behaving wickedly and repent for your evil acts, your lies, deceptions, adultery, secret abominations, idol worship, murder, priestcraft, envy, conflicts, and all other forms of sinfulness. Come to me and be baptized in my name so that you may receive a remission from you sins, be filled with the Holy Ghost, and be counted among my people, the family of Israel."

THE FOURTH BOOK OF NEPHI — AD 34 TO 320

From Plates Inscribed by Nephi[3] a Disciple of Jesus Christ, by Nephi[4], the Son of Nephi[3], by Amos[1], Son of Nephi[4], and by Amos[2] and Ammaron, the Sons of Amos[1], then Abridged and Later Inscribed onto the Book of Mormon Plates by Mormon

Not a single Lamanite is left in the Western Hemisphere after all of them convert to the Church of Christ and become Nephites. It is a time of miracles. The people who personally saw Jesus Christ die and pass on. As the people again become wicked, Nephites are again converted to Lamanites.

THE FOURTH BOOK OF NEPHI SUMMARY

The Fourth Book of Nephi quickly covers the 286 years of Nephite history following the New World visitation of Jesus Christ after his resurrection in Jerusalem. The keeping of the Nephite records was passed from Nephi[3], to his son Nephi[4], to his son, Amos[1], to his son, Amos[2], and then finally to his brother, Ammaron.

After Jesus Christ left the Nephites and returned to heaven his disciples established the Church of Christ throughout the land. By the year AD 36 they had converted and baptized all the Nephites and Lamanites in the land. These conversions transformed all the Lamanites into Nephites, and there were no criminals, sinners, or Lamanites left. It was a time of peace and justice, a time without poverty or wealth. The disciples of Jesus Christ performed healings, brought the dead back to life, and performed miracles in his name. The Nephite's destroyed cities were rebuilt.

By AD 110, nine of the disciples had died and gone to heaven, and new disciples were ordained to replace them. Except for the three immortal disciples, the generation that had witnessed Jesus Christ also died away. The long peace began to fracture when a small band of people revolted against the Church of Christ and called themselves Lamanites, the first of their kind in 74 years.

Two centuries passed and the Nephites became populous and wealthy again with divisions of class, and in degree of devotion to God. In time new churches arose, purporting to follow Jesus Christ, but failed to follow his precepts and teachings. False churches began to persecute the true followers and disciples of Jesus Christ. Attempts to imprison and kill the followers of Jesus Christ failed, and the Nephite people declined into sin and corruption.

By AD 100 the people again divided into two groups. The Nephites believed in and followed the teachings of Jesus Christ. The Lamanites opposed the gospel of Jesus Christ and taught their children to hate the Nephites. As time passed, the Lamanites grew strong at the expense of the Nephites.

By AD 244, the Lamanites far outnumbered the Nephites, and the faith of the Nephites dwindled as they sought wealth and vanity more than the word of Jesus Christ.

By AD 300. the Nephites were so wicked that it became difficult to distinguish them from the Lamanites. The faithful followers of Jesus Christ were reduced to the disciples themselves and a small group of true believers.

In AD 320, God instructed Ammaron to hide the sacred records away so that they could be preserved for future generations.

The Fourth Book of Nephi - Translation

In the 34th year after Christ's arrival, his disciples established the Church of Christ throughout the Nephite lands. All those who came to them and repented their sins were baptized in the name of Jesus Christ, and received the Holy Ghost.

In the 36th year after Christ's arrival all the Nephite and Lamanite people had been converted. There was no conflict among them, and everyone treated each other honestly. No one was either rich or poor and everyone was free. The disciples healed the sick and crippled, raised the dead, gave sight to the blind and hearing to the deaf. They performed all sorts of miracles in the name of Jesus Christ.

In the years that followed the people prospered and the cities were rebuilt. The people were blessed with many children and the population grew. These people lived by the new commandments of Jesus Christ rather than by the old laws of Moses. They fasted and prayed, and met regularly to hear the word of God.

In the 100th year after Christ's arrival the nine mortal disciples had all gone to God's

paradise, and other disciples were ordained in their place. The generation that had seen and heard Jesus Christ in person had lived their time on earth, and had passed on. It was a time of peace and love. God lived in the hearts of all the people. There was no envy, conflict, fornication, dishonesty, murder, or any manner of sinfulness. The Nephites were happier than any people who had ever been created by God. There were no robbers, murderers, or Lamanites. All the people were one. They were the children of Jesus Christ and heirs to the kingdom of God.

In the 110th year after Christ's arrival Nephi^3's son, Nephi^4 died, and his son Amos^1 continued the record for the next 84 years. During the time of Amos the peace of Jesus Christ continued, except for a small band of people who revolted against the church and assumed the Lamanite name. For the first time since the visitation of Jesus Christ, Lamanites again inhabited the land.

In the 194th year after Christ's arrival Amos died, and his son Amos^2 assumed custody of the records. By this time most of the second generation of Nephites since the time of Jesus Christ had lived their turn on earth and passed on. The Nephite population had grown so large that they spread far and wide across the land. Because of the prosperity that Jesus Christ's blessings had brought to them they were very rich.

In the 201st year after Christ's arrival people were flaunting their wealth and self-importance. They wore expensive clothing, fine pearls, and other ostentatious luxuries. From that time forward there were great disparities of wealth between the different classes of people. The wealthy people built churches for themselves for the purpose of getting richer, and started to renounce the true Church of Christ.

In the 210th year after Christ's arrival there were many churches in the land. Most of these churches professed themselves to be the Church of Christ, but failed to observe most of the gospel that he had given to the Nephite people. They accepted and tolerated all sorts of sinfulness. They knowingly administered the sacrament to people who were unworthy of it. In this way, the churches grew in their sinfulness because Satan had gotten hold of their hearts.

One of these churches rejected Jesus Christ and persecuted the true Church of Christ because of the humility of its members and their belief in Jesus Christ. They despised the faithful because of the miracles that they were able to perform. When they used their power and authority to throw the true believers into prison God broke the prisons open. In spite of the miracles that the faithful performed the unfaithful hated them. They tried to kill them just as the Jews in Jerusalem had tried to kill Jesus Christ. When they threw them into the fire the true believers came out unharmed. No matter how hard the unbelievers tried to hurt the people of Jesus Christ, the faithful did nothing to the wicked in return. But from one year to the next, the number of believers in Jesus Christ grew smaller and smaller.

In the 231st year after Christ's arrival there was a great division among the people. On one side were the Nephites, who were true believers in Jesus Christ. On the other side were the Lamanites, who rejected the gospel of Jesus Christ and taught their children to hate the Nephites.

In the 244th year after Christ's arrival the Lamanites far surpassed the Nephites in numbers and continued building expensive churches in honor of themselves.

In the 260th year after Christ's arrival wicked people reestablished the secret oaths and conspiracies of Gadianton. By this time the Nephites were as vain and sinful as the Lamanites, and the faithful disciples sunk into despair over the sins of the world.

By the 300th year after Christ's arrival the Nephites were so wicked that it was hard to tell them from the Lamanites. The reestablished Gadianton Robbers spread like a plague across the land, building up their treasure of gold and silver.

In the 305th year after Christ's arrival Amos[2] died, and his brother Ammaron took over custody of the records.

In the 320th year after Christ's arrival the Holy Ghost instructed Ammaron to hide the sacred records that had been passed down from generation to generation since Lehi left Jerusalem. Ammaron did as he was told, and the records were hidden so that the prophecies and promises of God to the family of Israel could be fulfilled at a future time.

THE BOOK OF MORMON — AD 321 TO 400

Inscribed and Written onto the Book of Mormon Plates by
Mormon, and his Son, Moroni[2], who are Distant Descendants of
Nephi

At the age of 10, Mormon is given custody of the Nephite records. At the age of 16, Mormon is drafted as the Nephites' military leader. Throughout his life, Mormon leads the Nephites in battle and writes The Book of Mormon upon golden plates.

THE BOOK OF MORMON SUMMARY

The Book of Mormon section within the larger *Book of Mormon*, is authored by Mormon, for whom the entire book is named. Mormon led a diverse life as a military leader, spiritual leader, and as tireless writer, who edited and abridged a thousand years of Nephite records since the time of Lehi's exodus from Jerusalem. He inscribed this abridgement onto a set of golden plates that are formally known as The Book of Mormon. When Mormon was killed by the Lamanites, his son Moroni[2] continued Mormon's book.

The Nephites' years during this period were counted from the time of Jesus Christ's birth and the occurrence of the night without darkness, described in the Third Book of Nephi. For example, the 320th year after Christ's arrival is the same year that we identify as AD 320.

In the year AD 320, the Nephite record custodian, Ammaron, identified the ten year old Mormon as a worthy person to be a future custodian of the records. Ammaron told Mormon that when he reached the age of 24 he should unearth the hidden plates of Nephi, and begin his own account of the Nephites based on what he had seen and heard.

When Mormon was 11, he and his father moved to Zarahemla during a time of intense warfare between the Lamanites and Nephites in which the huge Nephite army ultimately emerged victorious. But because of the Nephites' sinfulness God had withdrawn his blessings, and his disciples, from among the Nephite people. On his journey south to Zarahemla, Mormon observed buildings spread across the land and people as numerous as grains of sand in the sea.

Mormon received a personal visitation from God and an affirmation of Jesus Christ's goodness at the age of 15.

When Mormon was 16, new Lamanite wars erupted, and he was conscripted to lead the entire Nephite army because of his great size and strength. The Nephites were driven ever northward by the huge Lamanite armies. Year after year the Lamanites attacked and killed the Nephites. Sometimes, each of the two opposing armies prevailed and sometimes, they were defeated. Tens of thousands were killed. Without God's support, the Nephite victories were only temporary. When Mormon begged his people to repent and rebuild the church, they turned away. They wanted him as a military commander, not as a spiritual leader.

In the year AD 350, a treaty was reached in which the Nephites received the North American lands to the north of the Central American isthmus, and the Lamanites received the lands of South America. For 10 years after this treaty there was peace, until the year AD 361, when the Lamanites attacked yet again.

As the wars came and went it became evident to Mormon that the Nephites were doomed because God's judgment ran against them. To the degree that the Nephites turned away from God, Mormon also turned away from them and resigned his command. Mormon went to the hill where Ammaron had buried the records, gathered them up, and took them with him for safekeeping.

After a series of successive defeats in which the Lamanites drove the Nephites ever northward, Mormon relented and again assumed command of the Nephite army in spite of the Nephites' unrepentant sinfulness. By the year AD 384, the Nephites had been chased northward to the hill Cumorah in what is now western New York State. Mormon hid all of the records there, including those that he'd abridged and inscribed himself. He was now in his seventies, weary, and sad. In the ensuing battle, 200,000 Nephites were killed by the Lamanite army by swords, axes, bows, and arrows. Only two dozen men from the once mighty Nephite people, survived the climactic battle. These survivors included both Mormon and his son Moroni

Recognizing the futility of fighting any further Mormon addressed the dead, the living, and the yet to be born. He inscribed his final words on the golden plates lamenting for the past, present, and future Nephites, Lamanites, and Gentiles. If they had lived by God, he knew, this tragedy would never have happened. To the Lamanite descendants he urged repentance, belief in Jesus Christ, and baptism in Jesus Christ's name. He prophesied that these records he'd preserved would be the future salvation of his people's descendants, the Native Americans. "You are," he told them, "descendants of the family of Israel."

After the great battle, Mormon, and all the other survivors except Moroni, were hunted down and killed. Moroni was then left alone to complete his father's records.

Moroni told how the Nephite civilization had been destroyed leaving only Lamanites and robbers behind. Now the Lamanites had no one left to satisfy their blood lust except each other. Their legacy had become one of endless warfare.

The three immortal disciples still lived, somewhere, but were not there to witness the Nephite's final ending. Moroni testified that he and Mormon had personally seen them and been ministered by them.

Moroni testified that whoever found the hidden records, The Book of Mormon, would be blessed by God. "Nothing could prevent their future discovery," he said, "because it is God's will that they be revealed. They will come out at a time when the world is in great trouble, and stand as proof that God's miracles still exist. I will speak to you as if I were speaking from the grave because I know that you will receive my words. Anyone who condemns this record is in grave danger of hell fire."

Moroni explained that the Nephite records had been written in a language called "reformed Egyptian," unknown to any other people but his. "Knowing this," he said, "God has prepared a means by which our record can be interpreted."

In conclusion, Moroni instructed his future readers to repent, to believe in Jesus Christ, to be baptized in his name, to partake of his sacrament, and to believe in God's miracles. "Failure to do so," he said, "would result in their eternal damnation."

THE BOOK OF MORMON ~ TRANSLATION

Chapter 1, 1830 and 1981 Versions

I, Mormon, am a direct descendant of Nephi. This is a record of the things that I've seen and heard.

When I was 10 years old, the Nephite record keeper named Ammaron came to me and said, "I can see that you area serious child who observes everything well. When you are about 24 years old I want you to remember everything that you've observed about our people, and go to a hill called Shim in the land of Antum. I have buried the sacred records of our people there. I want you to take out the plates of Nephi and add your account to the records that you find there." [AD 321]

When I was 11 years old my father took me south, into the land of Zarahemla. On our journey I saw buildings covering the land and people as numerous as grains of sand in the sea. At that time there was a war occurring between the Nephites and the Lamanites along the borders of Zarahemla. The Nephites assembled an army of 30,000 soldiers, and in a succession of battles defeated the Lamanites and killed many of them. When the Lamanites withdrew, there was peace in the land for a period of four years. But because of our people's sinfulness, God removed his disciples and their miracles from among us. God also withdrew his gifts and the presence of the Holy Ghost due to our unworthiness. [AD 322]

When I was 15 years old God visited me, and allowed me to taste and know the goodness of Jesus Christ. I wanted to preach to my people but my mouth was closed, and I was forbidden to do so because my people had willfully rebelled against God. The land was cursed because of the stubbornness of the people, but I stayed there anyway, and observed. The Gadianton Robbers infested the lands and aligned themselves with the Lamanites. When they tried to hide their treasures in the earth, they found that the curses on the land made their treasures so slippery that they couldn't pick them up or hold onto them. There was sorcery, witchcraft, and magic everywhere. The devil's power was set loose among us, and the prophecies of

Abinadi and Samuel the Lamanite were fulfilled. [AD 326]

Chapter 2, 1981 Version

That same year a great war began between the Lamanites and my people. Because I was very big for my age I was made a leader in the Nephite army. By the time I was 16 years old I led the army into battle. [AD 326]

In the 327th year after Christ's arrival the Lamanites came at us with such power that my army was frightened, would not fight, and retreated to the north. We fortified ourselves within the city of Angola and tried to defend it, but in spite of our best efforts the Lamanites drove us out. We were then driven from the land of David.

We retreated to the land of Joshua near the western coastline, and gathered up as many of our people as possible and organized ourselves into a single group. The land was filled with robbers and Lamanites. In spite of the imminent threat of destruction my people made no repentance of their evil ways. Because of this there was a huge loss of life and blood on both sides. There was revolution going on everywhere.

The Lamanite army of 40,000 soldiers was led by their King Aaron. In the 330th year after Christ's arrival I led an army of 42,000 Nephite soldiers against them, beat them, and drove them back.

Over the next 14 years the Nephites cried out and repented for their sinfulness, just as Samuel the Lamanite had prophesied hundreds of years earlier. Because of the rampant thieves, murderers, magic, and witchcraft, no one could hold onto their possessions. Oh, how the Nephites mourned and wailed.

When I saw their regret and sorrow before God, my heart rejoiced. I knew that God had been waiting long and patiently for their repentance, and that if they returned to righteousness, he would show them his mercy. But my joy was short lived. Their sorrow was not about repentance, but instead was the sorrow of the damned. God would not allow them to find happiness in sin. They were not coming to Jesus Christ with contrition in their spirit or broken hearts, but with curses for God instead. Many of them wanted to die, but in spite of this they struggled to save their lives

with their swords. I fell into sorrow again because I saw that their moment of earthly and spiritual grace had come and gone unclaimed. During this time I saw thousands of them cut down in rebellion against God, with their dead bodies heaped up like manure across the land.

In the 345th year after Christ's arrival, the Lamanites pushed us backwards until we reached the land of Jashon. This was the area where Ammaron had hidden the records of our people so that they wouldn't be destroyed. In accordance with his instructions I went and made a complete record of the wickedness and abominations that I'd seen since I was a child. I know that on judgment day I will be lifted up, but my heart is filled with sorrow for the wickedness of my Nephite people that I've witnessed throughout my life.

The Lamanites continued to hunt and drive the Nephites northward to the land of Shem. We gathered together there in the 346th year and fortified the city for defense. I spoke to my people and strenuously urged them to fight for their wives, their children, and their homes. My words had some effect because they didn't flee when the Lamanite army of 30,000 soldiers attacked. In fact, we fought so hard that the Lamanites fled from us. We chased them down and defeated them, even without the strength of God on our side. This was a turning point. Shortly thereafter our army reclaimed all the lands of our inheritance from the Gadianton Robbers and the Lamanites.

In the 350th year after Christ's arrival, we made a treaty with the Lamanites and the Gadianton Robbers in which we divided up the lands. The Nephites received lands north of the narrow passage of land that led to the southern lands, and the Lamanites received the lands to the south.

Chapter 3, 1981 Version

For 10 years after the treaty there was no fighting between the Lamanites and Nephites. But during this period I had my people prepare their defenses, and make weapons in preparation for more war.

"Tell your people to repent," God said to me. "If they come to me, get baptized, and rebuild the church, they will be spared."

I did as God asked, but it was in vain. The people didn't realize that it was God who had spared them, and had given them another chance for repentance. Instead of repenting, they turned their hearts against God.

In the 360th year after Christ's arrival the Lamanites sent a message to advise me that they were coming to battle again. I gathered my people together in the land of Desolation near the narrow pass to the south. We placed all of our army at this choke-point to stop the Lamanite army from entering our northern lands.

In the 361st year the Lamanites attacked and were beaten back. They attacked again in the 362nd year and were beaten back again. Great numbers of them were killed and their bodies were cast into the sea. Because of their victories the Nephites began boasting about their greatness. They swore that they would avenge the blood of their friends and relatives who'd been killed in battle by the Lamanites. They swore by heaven and by the throne of God that they'd destroy their enemies and remove them from the land.

My people had become so sinful and abominable that I quit my position of command and leadership with them. I had led them to battle in spite of their wickedness. I had loved them with my heart and soul just as God loved me. I had prayed to God for them, but it was pointless. In the end, they were too stubborn and faithless. Three times I had saved them from their enemies, and they never once repented for their sins.

When they finally swore to avenge themselves, in violation of the words of Jesus Christ, the voice of God came to me. "Vengeance will be mine," said God. "Because your people have not repented after my deliverance of them, it is they who will be removed from the earth."

I refused to fight against my enemies any longer. I did as God asked, and observed the things I saw and heard. So now I write to you, future Gentiles and the family of Israel, in the time when God begins to return you to the lands of your inheritance. I write to all of the earth, and to the twelve tribes of Israel whose lives will be judged by Jesus Christ's twelve disciples of Jerusalem. I write to the descendants of Lehi whose lives will be judged by Jesus Christ's twelve disciples in this land, who will in turn be judged by the twelve disciples of Jerusalem.

This is what the Spirit of God has shown me. Everyone who is descended from Adam must stand in judgment before Jesus Christ. He will decide whether they are good or evil.

I also write to help you believe in the gospel of Jesus Christ, to know that the man seen, heard and killed by the Jews was Jesus Christ, the Son of God. I write to persuade everyone on earth to repent and be prepared to stand in judgment before Jesus Christ.

Chapter 2, 1830 Version

Chapter 4, 1981 Version

In the 363rd year after Christ's arrival, the Nephite army left their defensive positions in the land of Desolation to go fight the Lamanites. When they were defeated and driven back, exhausted, a fresh Lamanite army attacked them. After the Lamanites took the city of Desolation, they killed and imprisoned large numbers of Nephite soldiers. Those who survived fled to the nearby coastal city of Teancum

The Nephites lost the battle for Desolation because they had been the aggressors. You can see how the judgments of God subdue the wicked. When people incite violence and warfare, it is the wicked who punish the wicked.

In the 364th year, the Lamanites prepared to conquer the city of Teancum, but were driven back by the Nephites. After this victory the Nephites became boastful of their strength again and recaptured the city of Desolation. During this campaign thousands of soldiers on both sides were killed.

In the 366th year after Christ's arrival, the Lamanites attacked again. An orgy of blood and killing ensued. The unrepentant Nephites took delight in their wickedness, and both sides rejoiced in the horrible carnage. It was so ugly that it is impossible to adequately write about or describe. This was the worst violence and wickedness that had ever happened among the descendants of Lehi since they left Jerusalem 960 years earlier. In the end, superior numbers of soldiers allowed the Lamanites to reconquer the city of Desolation. After taking Desolation the Lamanites then drove the Nephites out of Teancum and took great numbers of women and children prisoners. These prisoners were then sacrificed to their idol gods.

In the 367th year, the Nephites were driven by rage at the foul murder of their women and children. Again, the Nephites beat the Lamanites back, and drove them from their lands. For eight years after that, the Lamanites left the Nephites alone.

In the 375th year, the Lamanites attacked once again. This time their army was so large that no one even knew how many warriors there were. From this point onward, the Nephites lost all advantage, and the Lamanites swept them from the land like dew on a hot, sunny day. First, the Lamanites conquered Desolation again. When the Nephites retreated to the city of Boaz they were defeated there on the second battle. The Nephites soldiers were driven and slaughtered, and their women and children were sacrificed to the Lamanite idols. The survivors fled again, gathering up all the Nephites from towns and villages in their path of retreat.

When I saw that the Lamanites were about to conquer the whole land, I went to the hill named Shim, and took with me all of the records that Ammaron had hidden there, at the request of God.

Chapter 5, 1981 Version

In spite of the Nephites' wickedness I reversed my decision to withdraw my support. They gave me command of the army again and looked upon me for deliverance from the Lamanites. But I was without hope because I knew the judgments of God would come upon them unless they repented and called out for help from the being who had created them.

When we fled to the city of Jordan and made our stand we successfully drove the Lamanites back. When they came at us again, in Jordan and in other cities, we held them off and protected the Nephite lands beyond us. Nephite communities that weren't gathered into our group were destroyed by fire, and the people were killed.

In the 380th year after Christ's arrival, the Lamanite army attacked us again. In spite of our brave defense, we were defeated by their overwhelming numerical advantage. When we fled, those who retreated faster than the Lamanite advance, escaped. Those who were slower were run down and destroyed.

I don't wish to upset my readers with graphic descriptions of the blood and carnage, but these things must be known. This knowledge must reach our people's descendants and also the Gentiles who God says will scatter and conquer the remnants of our people. So I will write a brief abridgement. I dare not go into too great a detail because I don't wish to inflict great a sorrow on you as a consequence of the wickedness of my people.

I write to our descendants and to the Gentiles who care about the family of Israel in full knowledge that they will ask sorrowfully why our people didn't repent and allow themselves to be held in the arms of Jesus Christ.

These things are written to our descendants, and then hidden away, to be revealed to them through God's wisdom in God's own time. These words will go forth to the Jews who disbelieve, and show them that Jesus Christ is the Son of God. This will happen so that God the Father may bring about his eternal purpose of restoring the Jews and the family of Israel to their land of inheritance that God has given to them.

These words will come to the descendants of our people through the Gentiles so that they may more fully believe the gospel of Jesus Christ. Our people will become dark, filthy, and loathsome beyond anything yet seen. They will be scattered and defeated. All of this will happen because of their unbelief and idolatry. The Spirit of God has stopped trying to connect with the present generation who have turned their backs on Jesus Christ. This generation of my people will be driven like chaff in the wind. My Nephites were once a delightful people who had Jesus Christ for their shepherd and were led by God the Father. They are now led by Satan, like boats tossed on the ocean waves without sail, anchor, or any way to steer. God has reserved the blessings our people might have received, and will give these blessings to the Gentiles who will come and possess this land.

The descendants of our people will be driven and scattered by these Gentiles. Only after this will God remember the promises he made with Abraham and the family of Israel.

God will also remember the prayers of the righteous that have been offered up for them.

So how can you Gentiles stand before the power of God unless you repent and put an end to your evil ways? Don't you know that you are in the hands of God too? Don't you know that he has the power to roll up the whole earth like a scroll between his fingers? So repent, then, and humble yourselves before him or else he will rule in judgment against you. If you don't repent, the remnant descendants of our people will tear you to pieces like a lion, until there is nothing left to deliver.

Chapter 3, 1830 Version

Chapter 6, 1981 Version

Now I need to finish my record about the destruction of my people, the Nephites.

In the 384th year after Christ's arrival I wrote a message to the Lamanite king asking him to let all our people gather around a hill named Cumorah, in the land of Cumorah, for a final conclusive battle. When this request was granted all of the remaining Nephites came to this one place and pitched their tents around the hill, in a land of many lakes and rivers. By coming together as one group I hoped to gain an advantage over the Lamanites and come out victorious. But I'd grown old, and I knew that this was likely to be the last battle of my people. God had commanded me to not let the sacred Nephite records fall into the Lamanites' hands because they would be destroyed. From the plates of Nephi I made this abridged record, and then hid all of the records, except for these few plates that I've given to my son Moroni, on the hill Cumorah.

Our people gathered at Cumorah and watched in fear and terror as the innumerable Lamanite armies marched towards us. They fell upon us with swords, axes, bows and arrows, and mowed us down. When I fell down wounded amidst the 10,000 men who fought with me, the Lamanite warriors passed by, thinking I was dead. My son Moroni also led 10,000 men who fell, as did Gidgiddonah, Lamah, Gilgal, Limhah, Jeneum, Cumenihah, Moronihah, Antionum, Shiblom, Shem, Josh, and 10 others. In the end, 230,000 Nephite soldiers lay dead. The next morning when the Lamanite armies returned to their camps we found that 24 of us, including my son Moroni, had survived the slaughter. From the top of the hill Cumorah we surveyed the carnage. Except for our small band, a few others who had escaped, and the few who had defected to the Lamanites, our entire Nephite people were gone. Flesh, bones, and blood were strewn across the hillside and left on the land, to crumble, rot, and return to mother earth.

My heart was ripped apart in anguish. "My fair people," I cried out, "how could you have departed from the ways of God? How could you have rejected Jesus Christ who stood with open arms to receive you? If you hadn't rejected Jesus Christ, you wouldn't have fallen. But you have fallen, and now I mourn your loss. Unfortunately my sorrows cannot bring you back. The day will soon come when your mortality will turn to immortality and you will stand in judgment before Jesus Christ. You will be judged according to your lives. If you were righteous, you will be blessed along with your righteous ancestors. Oh how I wish you had repented before this great destruction had come over you. But now you are gone, and only God the Father in heaven knows your state. In the end you will be dealt with in accordance with his justice and his mercy."

Chapter 7, 1981 Version

Now I write to the remnant descendants of my people who are spared, in hopes that God will provide them with my words so that they will know something of their ancestors.

You are descended from the family of Israel.

Unless you repent you cannot be saved.

You must lay down your weapons, unless God commands otherwise, and stop finding pleasure in killing.

You must gain knowledge of your ancestors, repent for all of your sins, and believe in Jesus Christ, the Son of God, who was killed by the Jews and arose from death by the power of God. In so doing he has claimed victory over death for himself and for mankind. He will bring about the resurrection of the dead, who afterward will stand before him in judgment. In this judgment he will bring the redemption of the world to those who are found guiltless on judgment day. Those people who are chosen will live eternally in God's kingdom, in his presence, singing endless praises with the choir above, to the Father, the Son, and the Holy Ghost. They will reside in a state of happiness without end.

So repent and be baptized in the name of Jesus Christ. Take hold of the gospel of Jesus Christ that will be set down before you both in this record, and in the record that will come to you through the Gentiles from the Jews. I write with the intent that you should believe the words that the Gentiles will bring to you. If you believe those words, then you should also believe these words. Believe what I tell you about your ancestors and believe the amazing things that have been created by the power of God among them.

You are remnant descendants of the family of Israel. You are counted among the people of God's first promises. If you believe in Jesus Christ, are baptized in his name, first with water, and then with fire of the Holy Ghost, all will be well with you on judgment day. So follow the example of Jesus Christ, and do as he has commanded us to do.

Chapter 4, 1830 Version

Chapter 8, 1981 Version

I, Moroni, will now finish my father's record.

The Nephites who escaped to the south after the great battle of Cumorah were all hunted down by the Lamanites and killed. My father, Mormon, was also killed, and I am now left alone to complete the sad story of my people's destruction. Whether or not I will also be found and killed I cannot know. So I will finish this account and return it to the hidden place with the rest of the buried records.

Four-hundred years have now passed since the birth of Jesus Christ. The Lamanites have hunted my people down from city to city, and place to place, until they are all gone except for me. This great fall was done by the hand of God. Now I see that the Lamanites are at war with one another, and the land bears witness to continual murder and bloodshed. No one sees an end to this warfare. Only Lamanites and robbers still exist in the land.

There are none now left who know the true God except for perhaps the three immortal disciples of Jesus Christ. The wickedness that is now left is so great that I'm not even sure God would want them to remain. My father and I saw them once, and they ministered to us. Whether or not they're still around, no one knows.

I ask that whoever receives this record does not condemn it for its imperfections, especially in relation to things they know that are greater than these words. If it were possible, I would make everything known to you. Like my father, Mormon, I am a descendant of Nephi.

I am the person who has hidden this record on behalf of God. The plates themselves are of no value because God has commanded that no one may have them for material gain. But the record is of immense value, and whoever brings it to light will be blessed by God. No one can bring it to light except by the power given to him by God, and God will only allow this to happen in tribute to his glory and the welfare of the dispersed descendants of the people with whom he's made his promises. According to the word and power of God, these records will be brought out of the darkness of earth and into the light to shine forth as a history of our people. If there are faults in these records, they are the faults of men. I know of no faults, but only God knows everything. Accordingly, anyone who condemns this record is in grave danger of hell fire.

Should anyone say, "Show me the truth of these records or you will be struck down," they should be aware that this is forbidden by God. Whoever judges these records harshly will be harshly judged by God. Remember what God says in the scriptures, "Men may not strike others down or judge, because judgment is mine. Vengeance is mine too, and I will repay."

Those who speak out angrily and act against the work of God, and against the promises he's made with the family of Israel, will pay the price. You cannot destroy the work of God or disregard his commands without danger of being cut down and thrown into the fire. The eternal purposes of God will prevail and his promises will be fulfilled.

Look at the prophecies of Isaiah and the saints who have come before me in this land. They cry out from the dust and they cry out to God, that as long as God lives, his promises will be kept. God will remember the prayers that were made on behalf of their descendants. God remembers the strength of their faith because in his name, they could move mountains, make the earth shake, and cause prisons to fall down. They couldn't be harmed by fires, wild beasts, or poisonous snakes, all because of the power of God's word. They prayed for the man who would bring these records into the world.

Nothing can stop these prophecies from being fulfilled. They will happen because God has said that they will happen. These things will happen at a time in the future when people believe that miracles no longer occur. Our words will be heard as if we were speaking out from death. These things will happen at a time when the blood of saints cries out to God because of secret conspiracies and works of darkness. They will happen at a time when the power of God is denied, when the churches are corrupted by pride, and when church leaders turn against their own members. They will happen at a time of fires, storms, wars, threats of wars, and earthquakes around the world. There will be pollution, murder, stealing, lying, deceptions, prostitution, and all kinds of abominations.

Many people will say, "Do this or do that, it doesn't matter. God will be merciful on the last day." But those who say things like this will be cursed for their sinfulness.

Our words will be heard when churches say, "Give me your money and your sins will be forgiven." But churches should never be organized for financial gain. They will disfigure the holy word of God and bring damnation on their souls. When this day comes, it will be time for these words to be fulfilled.

God has shown me the great things that will happen when these words are revealed. So I speak to you as if you were now present, even though you are not. Jesus Christ has shown you to me, and I know what you are doing. Except for a few, I know that you are all full of pride, wear fine clothing, envy and fight with each other, are filled with malice, involved in persecutions and sinfulness, and that every one of your churches has become polluted with pride. I can see that you love your money, material wealth, and expensive church decorations more than you love the poor, the needy, and the sick.

Oh you polluters, you hypocrites, and teachers who sell yourselves cheaply, why have you polluted the holy church of God? Why are you ashamed to assume the name of Jesus Christ? Don't you think there is greater worth in eternal happiness than in the endless misery that comes from your fascination with the material world? Why do you wear expensive clothing that has no life in it, while others go naked? Why do you allow hunger and sickness to pass you by without notice? Why do you build up your secret conspiracies for financial gain that cause widows and orphans to mourn for the death of their husbands and fathers? Their blood cries out for vengeance upon your heads, and the sword of vengeance hangs over you. The time will soon come when God will avenge the blood of his saints rather than listen to their cries any longer.

Chapter 9, 1981 Version

Now I speak to those who don't believe in Jesus Christ. Will you believe on judgment day when God comes and rolls the earth up like a scroll in his fingers? When the earth melts and you are brought to stand before Jesus Christ will you still say there is no God? Will you deny Jesus Christ when you stand in front of him? Do you think you can stand there then with a guilty conscience? Do you imagine that you can happily live with God when your soul is racked with guilt for having abused his laws?

No, you would be even more miserable living with a holy and just God under the shadow of your guilt and filth, than you would be to live with the other damned souls in hell. When you are brought to stand naked before the holy glory of God and Jesus Christ, an unstoppable fire will burn your body. So instead, turn to God you unbelievers, and cry out to him in the name of Jesus Christ so that you might be found spotless, pure, fair, and white after being cleansed by the blood of Jesus Christ on that last great day of judgment.

I speak now to those of you who deny the revelations of God, who say such things have passed, who say that there are no more revelations, prophecies, miracles, healings, speaking in tongues, or interpretation of ancient languages. I say that if you deny these things, you don't know and understand the scriptures or the gospel of Jesus Christ. Don't the scriptures say that God is the same yesterday, today, and forever without change? If you imagine that God is a changing being, you have imagined a God that is not a God of miracles.

Let me show you a God of miracles. The God of Abraham, of Isaac, and of Israel is the same God who created heaven and earth and all things within them. He created Adam, and through Adam came the fall of mankind. Because of that fall of mankind Jesus Christ has come to redeem us. Because of this redemption of mankind through Jesus Christ men are brought back into the presence of God. Because of Jesus Christ's death and resurrection men are redeemed from an endless sleep and awakened by the power of God.

When the trumpet sounds everyone will come forward. The great and the humble alike will stand before God's judgment and be released from death. Those who have lived their lives in filthiness, righteousness, happiness or unhappiness will live forever, respectively, in filthiness, righteousness, happiness and unhappiness.

If you imagine a God without miracles, I ask you to think about whether or not these things I've spoken of have happened yet? Has judgment day come yet? No. But look around you and notice that God has not quit being a God of miracles. Aren't God's creations amazing things to see? How can we even comprehend the enormity of God's creations? Who can possibly say that a miracle hasn't happened in the creation of heaven and earth, or by the creation of mankind from dust, just by the word of God? Who can say that Jesus Christ didn't perform many mighty miracles, or that miracles didn't come through the hands of his disciples? If miracles were performed then, how can God quit being a God of miracles and also remain as an unchangeable being? I say that God hasn't changed. If he changed, he would no longer be God. I say that he is a God of miracles.

Miracles are not happening among men now because men's belief in God has faded, because they've lost their way, and don't remember to trust in God. Whoever believes in Jesus Christ without doubt, and asks for anything from God in his name, will find that it is granted to him. This is his promise to everyone until the end of the earth.

This is what Jesus Christ said to his disciples in front of all the Nephites, "Go out into the world and preach my gospel to every living creature. Those who believe and are baptized will be saved. Those who don't believe will be damned. If you truly believe in me you can cast out devils in my name, speak in new languages, handle deadly snakes, drink poison without harm, and heal the sick by the laying on of your hands. Whoever believes in my name and doubts nothing will find my words confirmed until the end of the earth."

I ask, who can stand up against the works of God? Who can deny what he says? Who will oppose the almighty power of God? Who will condemn his works? Who will hate the children of Jesus Christ? I say that any of you who condemn, doubt, or oppose God will perish. So don't condemn or doubt God, but listen to what he says. When you are in need of things, ask God for them in the name of Jesus Christ. Believe in God with all your heart and work out your own salvation in fear, before him. Be wise. Strip away your filthiness, and don't give in to lust. If you don't yield to temptation you will be serving the true and living God. Don't be baptized or take the sacrament if you are unworthy of it. Be worthy of these things, and do them in the name of Jesus Christ, the Son of the living God. If you do this until the end of your life you will not be cast out.

I speak to you now as if I were speaking from the grave because I know that you will receive my words. Don't criticize the imperfections of my father or me, but give thanks to God that he has shown you our imperfections so that you will be more wise than we have been.

We have written this record in the language that we know of as "reformed Egyptian," handed down to us and altered in accordance with our spoken tongue. If our plates had been large enough we might have written this record in our altered form of the Hebrew language instead. If we had been able to do that, there would have been no imperfections in our record. But God knows what we've written and also that no one except us knows our language. So he has prepared for you a means by which our record can be interpreted.

We have written all of this down to cleanse ourselves from the blood of our people who have faltered in their belief. We write these things so that the descendants of our people will receive a restoration of our knowledge of Jesus Christ, and in answer to the prayers from all of the saints who have lived before us in this land. May Jesus Christ grant that their prayers are answered according to the saints' faith. May God the Father remember the promises he has made with the family of Israel and bless them forever.

THE BOOK OF MORONI — AD 401 TO 421

Inscribed and Written onto the Book of Mormon Plates by Mormon's Son, Moroni[2]

All the Nephites except for Moroni[2] are killed by the Lamanites. Moroni describes how to confer the power of the Holy Ghost, ordain priests, and administer the sacrament. Baptism of young children is revealed as an evil practice. Moroni seals and hides the records for a future time when they will be found, translated, and made known to the world.

THE BOOK OF MORONI SUMMARY

The Book of Moroni is authored by Mormon's son Moroni[2]. This is the same Moroni, in flesh and blood, who appeared as an angel in Joseph's Smith's bedroom on the night of September 21st, 1823, and told him about *The Book of Mormon* buried on Cumorah Hill outside Palmyra, New York. The Book of Moroni reads like a combined appendix, epilogue, and conclusion to the stories and doctrine presented in *The Book of Mormon*.

Moroni hid from the Lamanite war parties after surviving the great battle on the hill Cumorah. He wrote an abridgement of the history of the Jaredite people from the plates left by the prophet Ether, a thousand years earlier. The Book of Ether is located sequentially just before the Book of Moroni in the published *Book of Mormon*. In this translation the Book of Ether is placed at the beginning of the story because chronologically it records the earliest events described in *The Book of Mormon*.

Moroni hid from the Lamanite war parties and watched as they hunted down and killed all Nephites who would not renounce Jesus Christ, and then continued their warfare against each other.

Knowing that he wrote for the benefit of future generations of Lamanites and Gentiles, Moroni inscribed further instructions that Jesus Christ had given to his disciples. He knew that it was important that these details should not be lost. He carefully described how the power of the Holy Ghost could be conferred by the laying on of hands, how priests were to be ordained in the name of Jesus Christ, and how priests should administer the sacrament of bread and wine.

Moroni described how the truly repentant should be baptized and cleansed of their sins to become members of the Church of Christ. After having been baptized he wrote of the importance of meeting often to fast, pray, take sacrament together, and sing praises to God. Moroni also described how church members who persisted in sinful behavior could be expunged from the church's membership roles.

Moroni then recounted his father's words from a sermon in which Mormon had described how to distinguish deeds and actions done on behalf of God from deeds and actions done on behalf of the devil, and of the importance of faith, hope, and charity.

"God has said that you will know good people by the good lives they lead," said Mormon. "He has also said that an evil man can do no good. All good things come from God, and all evil things come from the devil. It is up to you to know and distinguish good from evil, and the way to judge is as simple as knowing daylight from the dark of night. And I will show you the way to judge for yourselves. Anything that brings you closer to Jesus Christ is good, and anything that pulls you away is evil." Mormon pled with his people to judge carefully and to choose the light and goodness of Jesus Christ.

"How do you act in accordance with the good?" asked Mormon. "This is where faith comes in. If you have faith in Jesus Christ you will have the power to embrace the good. God's miracles have never ended, and it is by faith, that God's miracles continue to happen. According to the words of Jesus Christ no man can be saved unless they have faith in his name. If miracles have ended, then faith has also ended, and the state of man would be beyond repair. How can you ever attain faith unless you also have hope? And what is it you should hope for? You should have hope, through Jesus Christ and the power of his resurrection, to be raised into eternal life. Man also needs to have charity, because without it, he is nothing. Charity involves patience in suffering, being kind, not envying others, or inflating yourself with self-importance. Charity means not being easily provoked, absence of evil thoughts, and never taking pleasure in sinful behavior. Charity is the pure love of Jesus Christ. It endures forever. Whoever possesses charity on judgment day will find that all is well."

Moroni's recital of Mormon's sermon is followed by the inclusion of two letters to Moroni from Mormon. The first of these two letters answers questions concerning the baptism of little children. Apparently, the Nephites had argued as to whether or not it was appropriate and necessary to baptize little children. Mormon consulted with God and, in this letter to Moroni, spoke definitively with God's authority on the subject. Mormon told Moroni that it is a mockery of God's laws to baptize little children because they have not yet had the opportunity to sin. Consequently they have no need to repent or be baptized. He goes on to say that the baptism of children is such a great evil that people who persist in holding this belief without repenting of it will be guaranteed a trip straight to hell on judgment day. Little children who die before they have an opportunity to sin are already guaranteed salvation. It is the people who are old enough to sin who need to repent and be baptized.

In the second letter Mormon described earlier battles in the Lamanite war and the deplorable state of the Nephite people. He lamented that no one would repent, or listen any longer to the word of God. He told of Nephite defeats and Lamanite atrocities, that were followed by even greater Nephite atrocities. He mentioned a specific incident in which, after a Nephite city had fallen, the Lamanites had murdered all the men, and then forced the surviving wives and daughters to eat the flesh of their former husbands and fathers. He described another incident in which Nephite soldiers raped Lamanite women, tortured them to death, and then ate their flesh as a token of their bravery. "How could our great civilization ever have come to this," he asks. "How can we expect God not to destroy us when we act like this?"

In this letter Mormon foresaw the destruction of the Nephites, because of their pride, sinfulness, and renunciation of Jesus Christ. When that finally happened the ancient prophecies would be fulfilled and the Nephites' fate would be the same as that of the ancient Jaredite people.

In his conclusion Moroni reminded future readers of God's mercy and goodness to mankind since the time of Adam. He said that readers could know for themselves that these records were true, by asking God. He asked his readers to remember that all good things have come to them as gifts through Jesus Christ.

"On the final day of judgment," Moroni concluded, "God will say to everyone, 'Didn't I declare my words to you, written by this man Moroni, as if he were crying out to you from the grave?' Whoever puts this knowledge aside and dies in their sins cannot be saved in the kingdom of God. At that time, the covenants and prophecies will be fulfilled. So come to Jesus Christ and be perfected. Give up your sinfulness, and love God with all your might, so that your sins will be cleansed."

Moroni then said goodbye to his readers (AD 421), sealed up the records, and hid them away until such time as they were found, translated, and published.

THE BOOK OF MORONI - TRANSLATION

Chapter 1, 1830 and 1981 Versions

Since completing my abridged account of the Jaredite people I, Moroni, didn't think that I'd have anything more to say. But I'm still alive and hiding from the Lamanites who will kill me if I am discovered. With the Nephites all gone the Lamanites now fiercely continue their warfare amongst themselves.

All Nephites who don't repudiate Jesus Christ are put to death. Because I refuse to

310

renounce Jesus Christ I am forced to wander alone for my own safety.

In spite of my previous thoughts to the contrary, I do have a few more things to add that may be of benefit to our descendants in some future day.

Chapter 2, 1830 and 1981 Versions

These are the words that Jesus Christ said privately to each of his twelve disciples as he called them by name and laid his hands upon them at the time of his first appearance.

"In mighty prayer you will call upon my Father in my name. After having done this, you will have his power when you lay your hands on others and give them the Holy Ghost in my name."

After that, the Holy Ghost was received by everyone whom the disciples laid their hands on in this way.

Chapter 3, 1830 and 1981 Versions

This is the way in which the disciples ordained priests and teachers.

After praying to God the Father in the name of Jesus Christ, they laid their hands upon them and said, "In the name of Jesus Christ, I ordain you as a priest (or teacher) to preach repentance and remission of sins through Jesus Christ, through enduring faith in his name. Amen."

In this way the disciples ordained priests and teachers according to their capabilities and callings. They were ordained by the power of the Holy Ghost, which was in the disciples.

Chapter 4, 1830 and 1981 Versions

This is how the elders and priests administered the sacrament of Jesus Christ's flesh and blood within the church. Because this is how Jesus Christ instructed the disciples to perform this ritual, we know that this is the right way to do it.

The elders and priests knelt down with the church members and prayed to God the Father in the name of Jesus Christ, saying, "God the Eternal Father, we ask you in the name of your Son, Jesus Christ, to bless and sanctify this bread to the souls of those who eat it. May they eat it in remembrance of the body of your Son. May they bear witness to you, God the

Eternal Father, that they are willing to assume the name of your Son, and always remember him, keep his commandments that he's given to them, and may they always have his Spirit with them. Amen."

Chapter 5, 1830 and 1981 Versions

To administer the wine the elders and priests took the cup and said, "God the Eternal Father, we ask you in the name of your Son, Jesus Christ, to bless and sanctify this wine to the souls of those who drink it. May they drink it in remembrance of the blood of your Son that was shed for them. May they bear witness to you, God the Eternal Father, that they will always remember him, and may they always have his Spirit with them. Amen."

Chapter 6, 1830 and 1981 Versions

Now I want to talk about baptism. Men were not baptized unless they demonstrated that they were worthy of it. They had to come to the baptism with broken hearts and repentant spirits, testify that they had truly repented of all their sins, assume the name of Jesus Christ, and express a determination to serve him for the rest of their lives.

When they received their baptism they were cleansed by the power of the Holy Ghost, and made the members of the Church of Christ. Their names were recorded so that they could be remembered and nourished by the word of God, to keep them on the right path, to keep them ever mindful of prayer, and in reliance on Jesus Christ, the author and arbiter of their faith. The church members met together frequently to fast and pray, and to speak with each other about the welfare of their souls. They met frequently to receive the sacrament of bread and wine in remembrance of their Lord Jesus Christ.

The church strictly observed the rules against sinfulness. Whoever was found to be sinful before the testimony of three witnesses, and didn't repent, was removed from the membership list and not counted among the people of Jesus Christ. But as often as they repented and truly asked for forgiveness, they were forgiven.

The church meetings were conducted in accordance with the workings of the Spirit, and by the power of the Holy Ghost. For it was the Holy Ghost who led them to preach, to admonish, to pray, to appeal, and to sing.

Chapter 7, 1830 and 1981 Versions

Now I, Moroni, want to write down some of the words my father spoke about faith, hope, and charity. These represent some of the things that he taught the Nephite people in our synagogue, or place of worship:

"I, Mormon, speak to you by the grace and gift of God the Father, and our Lord Jesus Christ. I speak to those of you who are peaceful followers of Jesus Christ and who rightfully hope to enter the kingdom of heaven.

"God has said that you will know good people by the good lives they lead. He has also said that an evil man can do no good. Any good that an evil man does, or prayers that he offers to God, don't account for anything unless he does them with righteous sincerity. When an evil man gives something, he does so begrudgingly, and his gift counts for nothing before God. It is also counted as evil when a man prays without sincerity in his heart. Such prayers count for nothing with God. Evil men can do no good, and will receive no credit with God for their attempts. Just as a bitter fountain cannot give good water, or a good fountain cannot give bad water, a man who serves the devil cannot follow Jesus Christ, and a man who follows Jesus Christ cannot be a servant of the devil.

"All good things come from God, and all evil things come from the devil, because the devil is an enemy to God. He is always fighting against God, inviting and enticing men to sin. Likewise, God is always inviting and enticing men to do good. Everything that brings men to do good, and love God, is inspired by God. So be careful in your judgment not to confuse evil things as coming from God, or good things as coming from the devil. It is up to you to know and distinguish good from evil, and the way to judge is as simple as knowing daylight from the dark of night.

"The Spirit of Jesus Christ is given to every man so that he will know the difference between good and evil, and I will show you the way to judge for yourselves. Anything that invites you to do good and persuades you to believe in Jesus Christ comes as a gift with the power of Jesus Christ. By this power you will know with perfect knowledge that it is from God.

"Anything that persuades you to do evil, disbelieve in, or deny Jesus Christ, comes from the devil. This is how the devil works. By this you will know with perfect knowledge that it is from the devil.

"Now that you know how to judge in the light of Jesus Christ, see to it that you don't make any bad judgments. Because in the end, you will be judged with the same judgment that you have used. If you work diligently under the light of Jesus Christ to distinguish good from evil, and act accordingly, you will be counted as a child of Jesus Christ.

"How do you act in accordance with the good? This is where faith comes in, and I will tell you how to embrace the good. You see, God knows everything and he has sent angels out to minister to men, and tell them about the coming of Jesus Christ through whom all good things come. God also personally spoke through prophets, telling the people that Jesus Christ would come. In many different ways he told good people that the goodness of Jesus Christ was coming, and that without him, they would remain as they had fallen. Through the ministering of angels, and through the word of God, men learned to exercise faith in Jesus Christ. Through this faith they were able to embrace the good. This is how it was until the time when Jesus Christ came.

"After Jesus Christ came, men were still saved by faith in his name. Through faith, they became sons of God. As surely as Jesus Christ lived, he spoke these words to our ancestors, 'Anything that you ask of my Father, in my name, that is good, and with faith that you will receive it, will be given to you.'

"Do you think that miracles have ended just because Jesus Christ has ascended to heaven to sit with God the Father and claim his rights to administer mercy to men? He has addressed the law of God, and has claimed that all of those who have faith in him may embrace good things. He is the advocate for men who lives in heaven. Do you think miracles have ended because of this? No. Nor have angels stopped ministering to men. These angels are subject to him, and minister according to his command. They show themselves to those who have strong faith and strong minds for godliness.

"The purpose of the angels' ministry is to call men to repentance, to fulfill the promises of God the Father, and to prepare the way of God among men. The angels do this by declaring the word of Jesus Christ through their chosen vessels, so that they can bear their testimony of God. In this way God prepares the way for the rest of men to have faith in Jesus Christ and the Holy Ghost within their hearts. This is how God the Father fulfills his promises to men.

"Jesus Christ has said, 'If you have faith in me you will have the power to do whatever is necessary for me. Repent everyone, everywhere, and come to me. Be baptized in my name, and have faith that you will be saved.'

"If these things that I've spoken are true for you, and God shows you that they are true, have miracles really ended? Have angels stopped appearing to men? Has God withheld the power of the Holy Ghost from men? Or will God do so as long as the earth lasts and there is even one man left here to be saved? No. It is by faith that these miracles are performed. It is by faith that angels appear and minister to men. If miracles end, it will only be because people have stopped believing, and any more miracles are in vain.

"According to the words of Jesus Christ no man can be saved unless they have faith in his name. If miracles have ended, then faith has also ended, and the state of man would be beyond repair. It would be as if no redemption had ever been made. But I know better because I know that some of you have faith in Jesus Christ. I can see it in your meekness. If you didn't have faith then you wouldn't be counted as members of his church.

"I also said that I would speak to you about hope. How can you ever attain faith unless you also have hope? And what is it you should hope for? You should have hope, through the atonement of Jesus Christ and the power of his resurrection, to be raised into eternal life. You can hope for this because this is his promise, if you have faith. If a man has faith he also needs to have hope, but without faith, there is no hope. You cannot have both faith and hope unless you are meek and lowly of heart. Without this, hope is in vain, because nothing else acceptable to God.

"If a man is meek, lowly of heart, and confesses by the power of the Holy Ghost that Jesus is the Christ, he also needs to have charity. Without charity, he is nothing. Charity involves patience in suffering, being kind, not envying others, or being inflated with self-importance. Charity means not being easily provoked, absence of evil thoughts, and never taking pleasure in sinful behavior. Charity rejoices in truth, believes all things, hopes for all things, and perseveres through all things.

"Without charity you are nothing. So become charity without failure. This is the greatest thing of all. Charity is the pure love of Jesus Christ. It endures forever. Whoever possesses charity on judgment day will find that all is well.

"Pray to God the Father with all the energy of your heart that you may be filled with the love that he has given to everyone who is a true follower of his Son, Jesus Christ. Pray that you may become sons of God, and that when he appears to us, we will be like him. May we see him as he is. May we have this hope, and become as purified as he is pure."

Chapter 8, 1830 and 1981 Versions

Soon after I was called to the ministry my father, Mormon, wrote me a letter. In it he said:

"My beloved son Moroni, I want you to know how joyful I am that your Lord Jesus Christ has called you to his ministry to do his holy work. I know that you will always be praying to God the Father in the name of his Holy Son, Jesus Christ. Through his infinite goodness and grace, Jesus Christ will help you maintain the endurance of faith in his name for the rest of your life.

"But now I want to speak to you about something that saddens me deeply. I have learned that there are disputes among you about the baptism of little children. I hope that you will work hard to correct this error among yourselves, because this is the real reason that I have written.

"When I heard about these disagreements I asked God about the matter, and this is what he told me through the power of the Holy Ghost. 'Listen to my words. This is Jesus Christ, your Lord and your God, speaking. I came into the world not to call on the righteous, but to bring sinners to repentance.

People who are well do not need a physician, whereas those who are sick, do. Little children are well because they are not capable of committing sins. For this reason, the curse of Adam does not fall upon them, and has no power over them. Even the law of circumcision is removed through me.'

"Because of these words, Moroni, I know that it is a mockery to baptize little children. Baptism and repentance are only applicable to those who are accountable and capable of committing sins. I want you to teach parents that it is they who should repent, be baptized, and humble themselves as if they were the little children. If they do this, they will be saved along with the little children.

"Little children don't need repentance or baptism. If they haven't yet sinned, they don't need remission. Little children have been saved by Jesus Christ since the beginning of the world. Think of how many little children have died without baptism. If baptism were required, they would have all gone to an endless hell.

"Anyone who imagines that little children need baptism is caught up in bitter sinfulness. He has no faith, no hope, and no charity. This kind of thinking has to end, or else those who hold these ideas will go to hell. It is the worst form of sinfulness to imagine that God would save one child because of baptism while all the others who weren't baptized would perish.

"Unless they repent, misery will come to those who pervert the ways of God in this matter. I speak strongly about this because I have authority from God to do so.

"I have no fear of what men can do to me because I possess the perfect love of charity. I know that all little children are also filled with charity, and will receive salvation. God is not a discriminatory God who saves some little children and condemns others. Because little children cannot repent, they are all alive in Jesus Christ's mercy. Whoever says that little children need baptism disputes the mercy of Jesus Christ, and misunderstands the power of his redemption and atonement.

"Anyone who persists in this practice of baptizing little children is in grave danger of eternal death, hell, and endless suffering. This is what God has told me to say. If you don't abide by God's word in this matter, you will be condemned on judgment day. It is a mockery of

God to deny the mercy of Jesus Christ to little children who cannot repent on their own. Repentance and baptism are only for those who have broken God's laws.

"Baptism is the fruit of repentance. It comes with the faith of fulfilling God's commandments. And the fulfilling of God's commandments brings remission of sins. The remission of sins brings meekness, lowliness of heart, and the visitation of the Holy Ghost who fills men up with the hope of perfect love. This love endures through diligence and prayer until the time when all saints are reunited with God.

"I will write to you again soon unless I am killed by the Lamanites.

"It is the pride of the Nephite nation, and their failure to repent, that has caused this destruction. Pray for them, my son. Pray that they will yet repent. I am afraid though, that the Spirit of God has already abandoned them. In this part of the land they try to extinguish all power and authority that comes from God. They are even denying the Holy Ghost. After having rejected such great knowledge they will surely perish soon. This will fulfill the prophecies spoken by the prophets and by the words of Jesus Christ himself.

"Goodbye my son, until I write to you or see you again."

Chapter 9, 1830 and 1981 Versions

My father, Mormon, did survive and wrote again:

"My beloved son Moroni, I write again to let you know that I am still alive. But I also have some very sad things to tell you.

"I have had another great battle with the Lamanites in which we were defeated. Archeantus, Luram, and Emron have fallen along with huge numbers of our best men.

"I am afraid that the Lamanites will destroy our people because our people refuse to repent. Satan works incessantly to create conflicts among us. When I persistently speak the word of God to them, they become angry with me or turn their hearts away. I am afraid that the Spirit of God has even quit trying to reach them. They've become so angry that they've lost their fear of death, lost their love of each other, and are only interested in blood and revenge.

"In spite of all this you and I should continue laboring diligently to do God's work. If we falter, we too may be condemned. Our task is to defeat the enemy of righteousness so that we may rest our souls in the kingdom of God.

"I have received a message from Amoron telling me that the Lamanites have taken many prisoners after the fall of Sherrizah. After the husbands and fathers were killed, the women and children were forced to eat the flesh of their fathers and husbands. They are also deprived of almost all water.

"In Moriantum the Nephites are behaving just as badly, as they rape and violate the Lamanites' daughters that they hold as prisoners. After raping these women, they torture them to death and then eat their flesh like wild beasts. They do this as a token of their bravery.

"How can our own people act like this and still call themselves civilized? It was only a few years ago that we were a good and delightful people. How can civilized people become like this, and take pleasure in such abominations? How can we expect God not to rule in judgment against us?

"My heart cries out with pity for our cursed people. I pray that God will come out in judgment and hide these sins, this wickedness, and these abominations from his eyes.

"When the widows and fatherless daughters of Sherrizah were abandoned by their Lamanite captors, they were left with some provisions with which to survive. But the Nephite army of Zenephi stole these provisions for themselves, leaving the women to wander off and die.

"The army with me is weak, and many of my soldiers have fled to Aaron's army where they have adopted his brutality. I cannot believe the depravity of my people. They are a disorganized mob now, without any mercy. I am alone now in my convictions, and lack the ability as a single man to enforce my commands anymore. My army has embraced perversion and brutality that includes everyone, young and old. I cannot even describe for you the suffering of the women and children across our land.

"I won't dwell any longer on this horrible scene. You already know for yourself about the wickedness of our people. Their lack of principles and feeling have become even worse than the Lamanites'. I cannot even ask God to help them for fear that he would strike me down.

"I can ask God to help you, my son, and I trust in Jesus Christ that you will be saved. I pray that God will spare your life so that you can witness either our people's return to him, or their total destruction. I know that unless they repent and return to him, they will all perish. If they perish, it will be like it was with the Jaredites because of their willful hearts, and their lust for blood and revenge.

"If we perish, I know that many of our people will defect to the Lamanites.

"If you survive and I do not, I want you to write about all of this. I hope to see you soon because I have all of our sacred records that I want to turn over to you.

"Be faithful to Jesus Christ. Don't let the things I've written bring you down in grief. Let Jesus Christ lift you up. May his suffering, his death, his visitation to our ancestors, his mercy, the hope of his glory, and his promise of eternal life, ease your mind forever. May the grace of God the Father in heaven, and our Lord Jesus Christ abide with you forever."

Chapter 10, 1830 and 1981 Versions

It has been more than 420 years since the birth of Jesus Christ. Now I, Moroni, will write some things that I think may be of benefit to the Lamanite people in the future. After I finish doing so I will seal these records and hide them away. [AD 421]

I strongly advise that whoever reads this record recognizes that it is through God's wisdom that you do so. I want you to remember how merciful God has been to men from the creation of Adam through the time that you receive these words. When you do receive my words, I insist that you ask God the Eternal Father, in the name of Jesus Christ, whether or not they are true. If you ask with a sincere heart and faith in Jesus Christ, he will show the truth of it to you through the power of the Holy Ghost. Through the power of the Holy Ghost you may know the truth of everything.

Whatever is good is also fair and true, and anything that denies Jesus Christ is not good. You may know Jesus Christ through the power of the Holy Ghost. So do not deny the power of

God. This power works through the faith of men, just as it does today, tomorrow, and forever. The gifts of God are numerous, but they all come from God, and must not be denied. These gifts are administered differently, but it is always the same God who brings them all.

One may be given the gift to teach the word of wisdom, and another the gift to teach the word of knowledge. One may be given the ability to work mighty miracles, while another is given the gift of prophecy. One might see angels, while another is given the power to interpret ancient and unknown languages. But all these gifts come from the Spirit of Jesus Christ, to individuals, through his will.

I want you to remember that God is the same yesterday, today, and forever, and that these gifts will never be withdrawn as long as the world lasts, unless men quit believing. So you must have faith, and hope, and charity. Without all of these you cannot be saved and enter the kingdom of God. Without hope you will find the despair that comes with sinfulness.

Jesus Christ said to our ancestors, "If you have faith you can do everything that is necessary for me."

Now I speak to the whole earth. If the day comes when the power and gifts of God are withdrawn, it will only be because of man's failure to believe. Pity to man if this is ever the case. If there is even one among you who does good, he will receive the power and gifts of God.

Whoever puts this knowledge aside and dies in their sins cannot be saved in the kingdom of God. These are the words of Jesus Christ. The time will quickly come when you will know that I am not lying to you. You will see for yourself when you stand in judgment before God and he asks, "Didn't I declare my words to you, written by this man Moroni, as if he were crying out to you from the grave?"

I declare these things in writing so that these prophecies can be fulfilled. They have come from the mouth of God, and proceed from generation to generation. God will show you that what I have written is true. So come to Jesus Christ, embrace his good gifts, and turn away from the evil gifts and filthy things.

As the prophet Isaiah said, "Awaken and rise up from the dust, Jerusalem. Put on your beautiful clothing, daughter of Zion. Strengthen yourselves and expand your borders forever. Don't be confused any longer. The promises that God has made with the family of Israel will be fulfilled."

Come to Jesus Christ and be perfected in him. Renounce your ungodliness. If you deny yourself of ungodliness, and love God with all your strength, then his grace will be sufficient for you. Through this grace you can be perfected in Jesus Christ, and unable to deny the power of God. If you are perfected in Jesus Christ, and don't deny his power, then you are sanctified in him through the blood of Jesus Christ. Through him the promises of God the Father will be fulfilled, your sins will be forgiven, and you will become holy.

I say goodbye now. Soon I will go to the paradise of God until my spirit and body reunite and I am brought triumphantly to meet you before the pleasing judgment of the great Jehovah, the Eternal Judge of the living and the dead.

AFTER WORDS

Up until the 20th century, visions were a commonly reported phenomena among ordinary people, and having visions was accepted as completely normal. Yet today, if people report having visions, or talking to God, they are unquestioningly dismissed as delusional.

What has changed? The English author and philosopher Aldous Huxley posed, and answered, this question as partially a matter of improved diet. Huxley argued that visions can be, and were, induced as a side effect of vitamin-C deficiency, or scurvy. In northern Europe, and for Europeans in northern America, this was a common problem until modern times, particularly during long, cold, northern winters without fresh vegetables. It wasn't until 1753 that the Scottish naval surgeon James Lind demonstrated that sailors provided with periodic rations of limes could avoid scurvy. At the time, this was a closely held British military secret; and it wasn't until much later that the implications of this knowledge became fully integrated into dietary health maintenance of the general population.

Were the visions that Joseph reported, in which he says he saw God and Moroni, true visions as he claimed? Or were they the product of an exceptional imagination? Truth is often relative and metaphoric. I have no doubt that for many people Joseph's visions are truthful accounts of actual events. Many respected people throughout history have claimed to have had visions; but few of them insisted that their visions represented the only true religion. If Joseph's visions were literally true, as the Mormon Church maintains, these claims of authenticity would be substantially strengthened if there was archeological, genetic, or linguistic evidence that supported them. But, there isn't. In the absence of such evidence, Joseph's visions must be taken on faith, seen as metaphorical, or rejected.

Researching this book and translating *The Book of Mormon* has propelled me into a parallel examination of my own Christian heritage. Is the Bible true? If we apply the same standards of authenticity to the Bible that are applied to *The Book of Mormon*, it is difficult to put too much literal credibility on many of the events described in it.

Were the earth and the heavens literally created by God, in seven days, some 6,000 years ago?

Was mankind created in God's image? Or are we the product of a 3.8-billion-year evolutionary process, as the fossil record seems to suggest?

Was the earth entirely covered with water during Noah's great flood? If so, where did all of this water come from, and where did it go afterwards?

Was Jesus Christ really the product of a pregnancy without benefit of any male sperm? Did he really rise from the dead and present himself afterwards for others to see?

Like Joseph's visions, these are things that we can never know for sure, unless we accept faith as our only guiding light. The late Joseph Campbell, during his lifetime of studying myths from all cultures, found that myths represented universal allegories more than literal truths.

- All life dies so that all of life can live. Only by sacrificing our living bodies to death, as Jesus Christ did, do we make way for the eternal, ongoing life of others.
- We are biological life eating other biological life. The sacrament of eating the body and blood of God is not unique to Christianity or Mormonism.
- If God created man in his own image, perhaps all of life was also created in his/her image, as biology striving for consciousness, in which we are only the latest innovation in a long legacy of biological innovation and evolution.

The miracle is that the universe exists and that we are alive to acknowledge its existence. By defining God as some being who resembles man, perhaps we limit the potentiality of God. I have come to see the importance of acknowledging the existence of Spirit without putting any limiting definitions on what it is. Spirit resides within all of us and, if we allow it to, can radiate outward. It can also be received. In contrast, most religions impose a concept of God from the outside, and install intermediaries between individuals and Spirit. While this book is specifically about *The Book of Mormon*, perhaps it also holds a key to understanding other religious scriptures as well.

Many Christian sects have successfully transformed their interpretation of the Bible from literal truth to metaphorical myth, and are thriving as a result of it. Progressives incorporate known scientific and historical facts into their beliefs, while fundamentalists reject facts that violate a literal reading of the scriptures. Even the conservative Roman Catholic Church has adopted Charles Darwin's presentation of evolutionary theory and adapted its perception of the Book of Genesis, as myth, to embrace it.

Perhaps the Mormon Church, through thoughtful, individual members, possesses the wisdom to transform the presentation of *The Book of Mormon* from its present status as exclusive, literal truth to metaphorical truth. If this transformation could be accomplished, much of what is good about the Mormon religion might be renewed and sustained. Without such a transformation, the facts that lie beneath its story line eat away at its foundation. Faith in the absence of evidence is one thing, but faith in the presence of invalidating evidence is another altogether.

SUGGESTIONS FOR FURTHER READING

Mormon America: The Power and The Promise, by Richard N. and Joan K. Ostling, Harper, 2000. In 1997 journalist Richard Ostling was working on a TIME Magazine cover story on the Mormon Church's astonishing $30 billion financial power. He realized that there was an even bigger story to be told than the one he was writing. After finishing "Mormons, Inc." for TIME, he and his wife spent several years researching and writing a clear, well-organized, and analytical story of the Mormon Church and Mormon culture's past, present, and future. The book is remarkable in its unbiased clarity and a journalistic approach that is neither pro-Mormon nor anti-Mormon. Mormons and non-Mormons alike will benefit from reading *Mormon America*.

No Man Knows My History, by Fawn Brodie, Vintage Books, 1995 (2nd Edition). When this biography of the prophet Joseph Smith was first published in 1945, it created a firestorm that still burns today. As the niece of Mormon prophet and president David O. McKay, Ms. Brodie was given access to the deepest levels of the Mormon Church archives under the assumption that her work would reflect well on the church's founder. Instead, her research led her to portray a truthful, if uncomplimentary, picture of the church's past. She was promptly excommunicated and vilified. Today, though, this amazing biography remains in print and is probably the most important biography of Joseph Smith that has ever been written. To not know this man's history is to misunderstand the meaning of his life.

Under the Banner of Heaven, Jon Krakauer, Doubleday, 2003. Religious violence, fanatical fundamentalism, and Mormon polygamy are woven into a story that explores the Mormon Church's tumultuous history. Best-selling author Krakauer investigates the dark side of religious belief, and asks religions to consider accepting responsibility for the problems they create as readily as they take credit for the good that comes from them.

An Insider's View of Mormon Origins, by Grant Palmer, Signature Books, 2002. After a lifetime career as a Mormon Church educator, Palmer reveals what the church knows, and doesn't tell, about its past. Palmer's honesty is breathtaking in presenting the real stories side by side with the official versions of the same stories.

Guns, Germs, & Steel: The Fates of Human Societies, by Jared Diamond, Norton & Co., 1999. While not directly addressing *The Book of Mormon,* this Pulitzer Prize-winning book describes the natural history of mankind's exodus from Africa and subsequent population of the world. Since the story of the Lamanites and Nephites in the Western hemisphere is such a dominant theme in *The Book of Mormon,* this scientifically-documented account of human history is an invaluable resource to understand the ancestry and history of Native Americans.

Thou Art That, and *Myths to Live By,* by Joseph Campbell. Joseph Campbell explores and illuminates the relation of myths to religions. *Thou Art That* focuses on the myths at the core of the Judeo-Christian beliefs, which includes Mormonism. *Myths to Live By* delves into the role of myths in all aspects of human life. Together they illuminate the context in which religious myths such as Mormonism emerge, are adopted, and become rigid dogma.

The Book of Mormon, by Joseph Smith. Readers wishing to make comparisons between the translation found in *Having Visions* and *The Book of Mormon*'s text have many options.

- Photo-reproductions of the original 1830 version are kept in print by two different publishing houses. These allow readers to see the original words and book design (Archive Publishers, 2000, and Herald Publishing, 1970).

- An electronic version of the original 1830 text is available, free, over the internet at www.2think.org/hundredsheep/bom1830/bom_main.shtml, and at www.iNephi.com

- The current, official version (The Church of Jesus Christ of Latter Day Saints, 1981) is also readily available in print, or over the Internet at scriptures.lds.org/bm/contents

Joseph Smith's New Translation of the Bible, Herald Publishing, 1970. Without making any reference to a physical text, Joseph Smith restored the "corrupted" version of the Bible through direct revelation from God. This book presents each page as a double column that compares the re-translated sections in one column with the respective *King James Version* sections in the opposite column.

Doctrine and Covenants, by Joseph Smith. This book documents Joseph Smith's revelations and visions received from God. *Doctrine and Covenants*, along with *The Book of Mormon*, *The Pearl of Great Price*, and The Bible ("as correctly translated") are considered to be the foundational scriptures of the Mormon religion. At this time, *Doctrine and Covenants* and *The Pearl of Great Price* are not available as individual volumes, but are both available as parts of what is called "*The Triple Combination*," a single volume published by The Church of Jesus Christ of Latter Day Saints, 1981, that also includes *The Book of Mormon.*

The Pearl of Great Price, by Joseph Smith. *The Pearl of Great Price* contains the restored, lost books of Moses and Abraham that he says were originally included as part of the Old Testament. In addition to The Book of Moses and The Book of Abraham, *The Pearl of Great Price* also contains the autobiographical Writings of Joseph Smith, and The Articles of Faith of the Mormon Church (available as part of "*The Triple Combination*," published by The Church of Jesus Christ of Latter Day Saints, 1981).

Easy-to-Read Doctrine and Covenants and *The Pearl of Great Price*, by John Charles Duffy, Estes Book Inc., 2001. Like *Having Visions*, Duffy's book is an unofficial, modern-language translation of *Doctrine and Covenants* and *The Pearl of Great Price.*

Other than *The Book of Mormon*, books by Joseph Smith are not always readily available from major sources such as Amazon or Barnes & Noble. They can be ordered through most bookstores or by contacting some of the specialty bookstores listed below:

Sam Weller's Zion Bookstore   800-333-7269 – samwellers.com
Latter-day Harvest   800-741-3787 – ldharvest.com
Seagull Book and Tape   800-999-6257 – seagullbook.com
Deseret Book Company   800-741-3787 – deseretbook.com

In addition, the Internet offers thousands of web pages concerning the Mormon faith. By typing in a combination of words along with "Mormon," you can easily find information on that aspect of Mormonism. For example, enter "book of mormon changes" and you will encounter hundreds of sites dealing with the textual changes made to the original 1830 version. Or try "mormon golden plates," "mormon dissidents," "mormon authority," "mormon priesthood," "mormon polygamy," "mormon women," "joseph smith treasure hunter," etc.

Made in United States
Orlando, FL
21 January 2022